INTERNET PROGRAMMING WITH PYTHON

Aaron Watters
Guido van Rossum
James C. Ahlstrom

M&T BOOKS

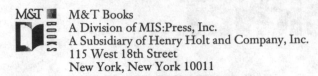 M&T Books
A Division of MIS:Press, Inc.
A Subsidiary of Henry Holt and Company, Inc.
115 West 18th Street
New York, New York 10011

Associate Publisher: Paul Farrell
Executive Editor: Cary Sullivan
Editor: Laura Lewin
Copy Edit Manager: Shari Chappell
Copy Editor: Suzanne Ingrao
Production Editor: Joe McPartland

Dedication

To Aaron's wife Nancy and children Kendall and Jaclyn.

To Jim's wife Susan and children Jennifer and Michael.

To Guido's cat Tom, who has learned when not to catch a mouse.

Acknowledgments

We wish to thank AT&T, CNRI, and Interet for allowing us the flexibility to write this book. We also wish to acknowledge all the contributers to Python over the years, as well as the contributers to the comp.lang.python newsgroup, whose comments, questions, and answers have inspired much of the content of this book. Special thanks is due to CWI in the Netherlands, CNRI, and the membership of the Python Software Association for supporting the development of Python over the years. Aaron would like to particularly thank Neal Clark for supporting this effort and his wife Nancy for picking up the slack at home.

CONTENTS

Chapter Three: Playing 41

Chapter Four: Intrinsic Operations for Common Types 95

Chapter Five: Syntax and Control...... 151

Chapter Six: More Goodies 197

Chapter Seven: Generating HTML: A Case Study in Dynamic Objects 213

Chapter Nine: Protocols...................... 331

Chapter Ten: GUI Programming with Python 355

Chapter Twelve: Embedding Python .. 425

Appendix A: Python versus..... 447

Appendix B: A Brief Guide to the Standard Libraries..................... 451

Appendix C: Regular Expressions...... 455

Appendix D: How to Get Python 467

Index... 469

Chapter One

Introduction

This book discusses methods of Programming in Python, with particular emphasis on Internet-related applications. Python has grown with the Internet, and programmers across the planet use Python for all sorts of Internet applications, from the simplest CGI scripts, to complex server programs, to extensions of the Python-based Grail browser.

This book will also be of interest to people who want to learn Python, but who aren't especially interested in developing Internet applications. Much of the book covers aspects of Python programming of general interest, useful in all application domains, and even the Internet-specific portions of this book provide compelling and accessible examples of techniques that can be used in many different applications. For example, the object-oriented techniques described in the chapters on graphical interfaces and generating HTML are useful for many complex programming tasks, and programmers with no particular interest in graphical interfaces or HTML generation may nevertheless find these discussions useful.

Python, of course, is not only for Internet applications—companies large and small, hobbyists, and highly skilled professional programmers all around the world use Python in all sorts of domains: to control complex hardware, as a steering language for supercomputer computations, as a graphical user interface application builder, and as a code generation language, and just for fun, among other things.

Python Gets the Job Done

Python is a general purpose programming language. Python may also serve as a glue language connecting many separate software components in a simple and flexible manner, or as a steering language where high-level Python control modules guide low-level operations implemented by subroutine libraries effectedin other languages. Python is also easy to learn and use, so it could also serve as an interface for naive users of advanced applications, or as a first programming language.

Behold some qualitative properties of Python:

- **Easy**: Python's simple syntax and elegant and clean semantics is easy for programmers and non-programmers to learn, read, and use. Experienced Programmers will be productive in Python in a day. Novices might be productive in Python in a day and a half. Python's basic syntax looks like a radical simplification of the algol/C/Pascal programming languages and as such is easily learned by people who have some experience with common mathematical notations and/or other common programming languages.

- **Powerful**: Almost any computational concept can be expressed briefly and directly in Python. Despite its "easiness" mentioned above, Python is not a toy language for novices only. Python includes powerful features such as:

  - First-class functions and first-class everything else. Functions, methods, modules, classes, and other components of Python programs may be passed to functions or stored in data structures.

  - Object orientation with multiple inheritance and late binding. Python allows creation of object-oriented class hierarchies, and the object referred to by `name.attribute` is determined at run time via a dynamic name search. For example, as demonstrated in the chapter on generating HTML, these features allow straightforward expression of complex computational concepts, and a high degree of code-reuse.

  - Object-oriented and named exception handling. Errors or other exceptional conditions in Python programs can be trapped using `try..except` statements, and finalization actions can be specified using `try..finally`. This greatly simplifies code that may encounter exceptional conditions that interrupt the normal flow of control of the program. Exceptions may also be organized into inheritance structures.

- Dynamic calling sequences. Python callable objects can accept optional arguments, keyword arguments, or unlimited numbers of arguments. These features allow very generic and highly configurable operations to be implemented in terse Python declarations.

  Highly skilled programmers will find that even the most subtle idea usually translates to a short and clear segment of Python code using the expressive power available. Large complex programs may be implemented in Python, and the end result may be working much sooner than expected, in a smaller and less complex form than anticipated.

- **Extensible and Flexible**: Python can be extended easily to interface with other software systems, and Python can also be easily incorporated into other programs as a component. Furthermore, Python allows extreme flexibility in the treatment of language components. For example, a Python module that is meant to interact with an external system can be tested using a briefly specified "imitation" of the external system written in Python.

Here are some notable technical characteristics of the Python language that justify some of the qualitative claims given above.

- **Interpreted**: Python is dynamically interpreted language that supports byte compilation. Python programs may be developed and tested with the help of the interactive mode of the Python interpreter which allows program components to be debugged, traced, profiled, and tested interactively. Python byte code is also machine independent and may be executed on different hardware and software platforms without recompilation. For example, advanced network applications could load python byte code from a remote machine and execute the code dynamically.

- **Object Oriented**: Python supports object-oriented class structures with multiple inheritance and late binding. Python is also truly object oriented to the core: Everything in Python is an object organized in a flexible and general internal object framework that is beautiful to behold. Experienced C programmers who delve into the source code of the Python distribution will find the core implementation a delightful read. Should the need arise, programmers can create alternate implementations for any basic component of the Python language (such as numbers or even object classes) either in Python code implementations or via compiled language extensions. For example, the numerical Python extensions add general arbitrary dimensional matrices as a "number type," the MESS extensions define an alternate object model for Python, and the `ni.py` module defines hierarchical module structures—all of these optional modules define alternative interpretations for basic operations of the Python core.

- **Dynamic**: Python uses dynamic typing and dynamic resolution of names. For example, an expression `output.write(data)` may write a `data` string to a file object `output`, or it may archive an arbitrary `data` object in an `output` object implemented in Python and stored in main memory, or it may do both at different times depending on the current binding of `data` and `output`. Thus a Python function which reads from `input`, `transforming` the read `data` and writing the result to `output`

```
def send_transformed(input, transform, output):
    while 1:
        data = input.read()
        if not data: return
        output.write( transform(data) )
```

need not know whether the `input` or `output` objects are files or other structures and what the `read`, `write`, or `transform` operations do. This flexibility allows expression of generic operations such as `send_transformed` that may be easily used in many different contexts.

Dynamic typing and dynamic name resolution when properly used, can greatly reduce the size of programs and greatly simplify testing and debugging, especially for programs that interact with complex external systems, some of which may not have been implemented yet.

- **Orthogonally structured**: Python is constructed from a small number of powerful constructs. The simplicity of the language allows different programmers to understand and use each other's code more easily, compared to more complex languages. Python's simplicity also allows new Python programmers to learn the language and become productive quickly.

At the same time the simplicity of the language does not sacrifice expressive power—we claim that there are few features of other programming languages that cannot be emulated directly and easily using Python.

- **Extendible**: Python can be easily extended with interfaces to external programming libraries or new data types via compiled extension modules. Adding new compiled components to Python is easy—much easier than writing stand-alone compiled programs. On most major platforms new compiled components may also be loaded into the interpreter dynamically, on demand.

- **Embeddable**: To another program the Python interpreter looks like a very simple applications programmer interface (API), and this book will show that the interpreter can be embedded within another application as a general purpose scripting/extension or glue/steering tool in a surprisingly straightforward manner.

- **Stable, tested, and upwardly compatible**: Python always has been upwardly compatible through the years and will continue to be upwardly compatible. New versions of the interpreter will always run programs written for old versions of the interpreter. At this point new versions of the interpreter include precious few bug fixes, because the Python core has been thoroughly tested and debugged in thousands of applications for the last several years. Most bugs found these days are obscure and avoidable.

- **Portable and friendly to external software**: Python is written in standard C using Posix input/output conventions and ports to all major platforms that support a Posix interface without problems. Have you ever heard of the BeBox? If you have, congratulations, you are among the select few. We hadn't heard of it until someone informed us that they had ported Python to the BeBox with few problems, just as Python ports to hundreds of other computing environments with little or no problems. Furthermore, internal aspects of the Python interpreter design—such as its reference counting memory management scheme—make it live peacefully with most other software components without technical difficulties.

- **Freely available with unrestricted redistribution in source form**: The Python copyright essentially protects the authors from legal jeopardy and prevents malicious users from attempting to hijack the copyright. Aside from that, Python programmers and users may use Python in source or binary form just about anyway they please. In particular, programmers may create products that use Python and release the product in binary-only form with all Python modules in byte-compiled-only form, and they may sell or give away the result in any manner they think will make them the wealthiest, or the most famous.

If Python is completely free, how can it be as good as we claim? Well, the real answer to that question is that if Python hadn't been free, it wouldn't have had hundreds of programmers testing it, offering suggestions, proposing bug-fixes and enhancements, and contributing extensions and libraries for several years now—and it might never have gotten as good as it is. You can spend a lot of money to buy software that isn't as stable and generally useful as Python.

What Python Does Not Do Well (by Itself)

Python is not intended to be the perfect language for all purposes. We would suppose that most programs written today could be addressed well using Python, but Python alone (without special purpose extensions) would not be suitable for many applications that are generally better addressed by compiled components.

For example, Python alone might not be appropriate for the following example applications for the following reasons:

Data Compression Algorithms

A data compression algorithm translates a stream of data into a smaller form. Usually this involves examining each byte of the data, collecting statistical information on the bytes and their relative order, and emitting a compressed representation, one byte at a time. For suitably large data sizes, most data compressors implemented directly in Python are likely to be too slow for practical purposes due to the inherent overhead of the Python interpreter. To accomplish data compression or similar byte-by-byte applications for large data sets, either add an interface to a compiled special purpose library to Python or consider using a separate stand-alone compiled application, or some other approach.

Device Drivers

A device driver is essentially a piece of software added into an operating system, an interpreted language such as Python is inappropriate as part of an operating system kernel due to the overhead of the interpreter and its extensive use of dynamic memory allocation.

Applications with Millions of Ad Hoc Floating Point Operations

This case is essentially similar to the data compression example. An application that must perform millions of nonuniform floating point operations will likely be too slow in Python alone compared to using a compiled implementation. Critical calculations that are known to slow down a Python implementation could be implemented as C extensions to Python, to allow the higher level logic to be controlled by Python, if this is useful.

 If the operations are uniform (not ad hoc), then the situation is quite different. In this case consider using the numerical Python matrix extension to perform the calculations as aggregate operations. The result may actually be faster than a brute force compiled implementation, because the Python matrix extensions are highly efficient and convenient—at least that's what physicists at the Lawrence Livermore National Labs tell us.

Mission Critical Database Operations

Many database-style operations may be performed directly and easily using Python programs, but for sufficiently important database transactions it is important to have reliable logging, concurrency control, and failure recovery. Implementation of these standard operations shouldn't be attempted by most programmers directly in any language. Instead, get a good database engine that implements these features, and use it.

To use Python in conjunction with the database engine, add an extension module to Python that includes an API for accessing the database, or possibly use the OLE or CORBA or ILU remote object protocols, if this is appropriate.

Huge Monolithic Single Process Applications

Python can solve complex problems, often in simple ways that are extremely difficult to emulate using other languages. But some types of applications may not be greatly simplified by Python's powerful features, requiring very large amounts of very complex code all running in the same process. One possible problem with using Python alone in an application of this kind is that a poorly tested or poorly designed piece of code may corrupt a data structure that is internal to another object or module, because Python does not include data hiding features at this time. In this case it is worth considering using Python initially to prototype the application, and possibly later use Python as a component of the application once critical components have been implemented using C++ or some other language that directly enforces data hiding and strong type checking at compile time.

There is little direct support for data hiding within Python itself, but extensions and embeddings of Python can provide rock solid interfaces that expose only permitted foreign operations to the Python interpreter. Python's restricted execution mode may also provide some (usually extreme) protection within the interpreter itself.

Highly Specialized Simple Operations

For example, if you want to scan a file for a pattern, it may be more appropriate to use a filter program such as the UNIX `fgrep`, `egrep`, or `awk` filters, rather than write a small Python program to the same end.

Larger applications that must be maintained by multiple programmers might be more easily developed, tested, and modified using a flexible general purpose tool like Python, in place of specialized tools. Problems that seem simple and specialized often grow in complexity as they evolve, and as the complexity of the problem grows, the implementation might benefit from Python's advanced object model and error handling mechanisms—features that are frequently difficult or impossible to emulate using specialized tools.

There are other types of applications that are not suitable for direct Python implementations without any support from compiled extension modules. Many of these applications might benefit from using Python as a component of the application, but others might be simply unsuitable for Python—the experienced software engineer must make the call.

Most programming problems do not fall into any of these categories, they are not extremely simple and they are not hugely complex; they are not part of the operating system and they do not manipulate huge quantities of tiny bits of data. Most programs can be implemented using Python, often much more quickly than with other methods, and with more satisfactory results.

Python and the Internet

The Internet and intranets are probably the most popular applications areas for Python at the moment (although engineering applications are now close behind). Python is particularly well suited for Internet and intranet applications because these applications are often highly dynamic, somewhat complex, and often require interfaces with external systems—Python's dynamism, its advanced features, and its ease of extension address each of these requirements in turn, and this book explains how.

The first six chapters are concerned with explaining the Python language, including basic and advanced features.

Introduction: This chapter introduces the book. You are reading it now.

Birds Eye Python: This chapter introduces some of the primary syntactic and semantic features of Python, and discusses the various modes of execution for the Python interpreter.

Playing: This chapter gently introduces the basic components of a Python program using interactive "play" with the Python interpreter. Much of the chapter discusses character string manipulations in detail, because this provides a very accessible platform for illustrating language features, and because strings are important in many application domains, especially in network programming. Other sections introduce the list type, the dictionary type and the use of Python's object-oriented features.

Intrinsic operations for common types: This chapter summarizes most semantic features of the Python language in a single place, by discussing the intrinsic operations of basic object types. Some readers may prefer to scan this chapter initially, rather than read it in detail—referring back to appropriate sections of the chapter as the need arises.

Syntax and control: This chapter covers detailed issues of syntax and the semantics of Python control constructs. Many of these concepts are illustrated by example in the previous two chapters. The contents of this chapter, like those of the previous one, need not be understood in entirety before using the Python language, but the detailed information in this chapter may be useful later.

More goodies: A number of issues of Python programming that don't fit into the other categories (such as byte compilation, and documentation strings) fall into this chapter. Some discussions of this chapter are fairly advanced. Readers should read this chapter lightly at first, and they should not be too concerned if some of the content seems difficult at first, because they may never need to use the aspect they find difficult.

The following three chapters discuss Internet-specific programming using Python.

Formatting HTML, a case study in dynamic objects: This chapter describes techniques for formatting data into HTML representations for presentation on the Web, with particular emphasis on formatting the complex TABLE construct. This chapter intentionally makes use of Python's advanced dynamic features in order to simplify the implementation and to illustrate those features at the same time.

CGI programming: This chapter describes the CGI Mechanism used by the standard "Web" protocol HTTP to allow clients to submit form data (or other data) to Web site server machines, and to receive responses from the servers. The chapter also describes methods for implementing CGI programs using Python.

Protocols: This chapter discusses general issues of implementing protocols using Python, both via direct interactions with network socket structures and via the Python support libraries.

The remaining three chapters of the book describe other aspects of Python programming that are useful both in Internet programming and in other domains.

Extending Python: This chapter describes how to add new compiled components to the Python interpreter, either statically or via dynamically loaded libraries. The detailed example in this chapter describes how to add a new type to Python, and various ways the new module may be built and connected to the interpreter.

Embedding Python: This chapter describes how Python may be added as a component of another program. The detailed example in this chapter embeds Python under a Netscape Server program using the standard NSAPI applications programmer interface. The resulting embedding allows Python to act as a generic scripting and glue language for the Server program.

GUI Programming with Python: This chapter introduces the use of Python as a Graphical User Interface (GUI) language. This topic is quite deep and could fill another book because graphics libraries are complex even when interfaced to Python. This chapter describes the general properties of most GUI programs and gives a detailed description of the use of one of Python's more popular GUI interfaces, the Wpy package, which is portable between Microsoft and Unix platforms.

Background

Guido van Rossum, one of the present authors, wrote almost all of the core implementation of Python, and he continues to be the ultimate arbiter of the core language and its standard implementation. Python also includes numerous libraries and extension modules contributed by many programmers around the world, and many other extensions and contributed libraries are available from the http://www.python.org Python Software Activity (PSA) Web site. The PSA Web is also the standard location for the latest version of the Python interpreter source code, often with binary releases for many platforms available too.

Python was initially written as a component of the Amoeba operating system at CWI in the Netherlands beginning in 1989. Guido specifically designed the Python core architecture to allow uniform interfaces to external software in order to allow convenient high level control of arbitrarily many and arbitrarily complex components, and these features were immediately recognized and appreciated by hundreds of programmers on the Internet when Guido released

Python for free distribution in 1991. Since then the community of Python users and programmers has ballooned, but its exact size is unknowable because it has passed from one machine to another silently over the years. Because many popular Internet services use Python (some of them very extensively, such as http://www.infoseek.com which boasts of billions of "hits") it is reasonable to suppose that hundreds of thousands of people have used Python programs in one way or another. Python is also used heavily in various noninternet applications at places such as NASA Mission Control, Lawrence Livermore National Labs, and the National Bureau of Standards.

Guido currently works at the Corporation for National Research Initiatives (CNRI), a nonprofit research institute that hosts the Python Software Activity (PSA)—a clearing house for Python software and related information. Please see the PSA Web site for extensive further information on the Python universe.

Fasten Your Seatbelt, and Have Fun

We almost forgot to mention that programming using Python is a joy. New programmers will find using Python a blast, and experienced programmers will find Python refreshing and fun.

Once the Python interpreter is installed on your system, fire it up and play with it often. If the interpreter is named python, a very simple interaction with the interpreter might look like this.

```
% python
Python 1.3 (Dec  7 1995)  [GCC 2.6.3]
Copyright 1991-1995 Stichting Mathematisch Centrum, Amsterdam
>>> print "Hello world"
Hello world
>>> 2+8*3
26
>>> raise SystemExit
%
```

NOTE Using raise SystemExit (without catching the exception) is a generic way to get out of the interpreter, but the end-of-file character (which is control-D on UNIX or control-Z on Microsoft platforms) also terminates the interactive interpreter. Be sure to enjoy yourself, and we hope you have as much fun as we have.

CHAPTER TWO

BIRDS-EYE PYTHON

This chapter describes some basic syntactic and semantic features of the Python programming language, and is a preliminary discussion for the following chapters.

Python is fundamentally a very simple language that is easy to use. In this and the next two chapters, we summarize Python's main features, without shying away from certain obscurities in order to provide a compact summary and point of reference. If readers find parts of this discussion difficult, there is a good chance that it is explained in better detail later, or that they will never need the feature that they find hard to understand.

For now, let it suffice to discuss the look of a Python program and the objects that a program contains.

An Example Python Program

So, you wanna know what a Python program looks like? Let's look at one.

```
#!/usr/local/bin/python
import regex, string
word = regex.compile( "[" + string.letters + "]+" )

def countwords(text, pattern=word):
    dict = {} # dictionary mapping word --> frequency
```

```
    end = 0
    try:
        while 1: # loop until error, getting pattern matches from text
            first = pattern.search(text, end) # find a match
            end = pattern.match(text, first) + first
            word = text[first: end]
            try:
                dict[word] = dict[word] + 1 # old word
            except KeyError:
                dict[word] = 1 # new word
    except regex.error:
        pass # triggers when first index goes to -1, terminates loop.
    items = [] # organize data as list of (frequency, word)
    for word in dict.keys():
        items.append( (dict[word], word) )
    items.sort()     # sort ascending
    items.reverse() # reverse, for descending order
    return items
```

```
# if run as a script, count words in stdin.
if __name__ == "__main__":
    import sys
    x = countwords( sys.stdin.read() )
    s = map(str, x)
    t = string.joinfields(s, "\n")
    print t
```

What does it do? This Python module given in the source file word_freq.py can act as either a utility or as a library module. Run as a script with standard input provided, the module consumes the standard input, counting "word" occurrences, and finally prints a list of words (alphabetic sequences of characters) and their frequency in order of decreasing frequency. For example, run with its own text as input we obtain:

```
Prompt>> Python word_freq.py < word_freq.py
(9, 'word')
(6, 'dict')
(5, 'items')
(5, 'first')
... various lines deleted ...
(1, 'append')
(1, 'a')
(1, 'KeyError')
Prompt>>
```

Thus, in the file `word_freq.py` the word `KeyError` appears exactly once, but the word `dict` appears six times.

We can also use the function `countwords` defined in `word_freq.py` interactively.

```
% python
Python 1.3 (Dec  7 1995)  [GCC 2.6.3]
Copyright 1991-1995 Stichting Mathematisch Centrum, Amsterdam
>>> import regex, word_freq
>>> punct = regex.compile( "[,.();-!\"']" )
>>> text = ' "Hello," said I. "Um, hello," She replied. '
>>> word_freq.countwords(text, punct)
[(4, '"'), (3, ','), (2, '.')]
```

In this example, we counted punctuations instead of words, by overridding the default argument `pattern` in `countwords`.

Alternatively, we could use the countwords module in another module, such as wordstats.py:

```
#!/usr/local/bin/python
from word_freq import countwords
from HTMLfmt import HTML, VerySimpleTable

file = open("HTMLfmt.txt", "r")
stats = countwords(file.read())
file.close()
data = (stats[:3] + [("...", "...")] +
        stats[-3:] +[(len(stats), "total words")])
words = []
nums = []
for (n, w) in data:
    nums.append(n)
    words.append(w)
table = VerySimpleTable("Stats for HTMLfmt.txt", words, nums )
doc = HTML("Chapter Statistics", table)
print doc
```

The output of this program generates an HTML document, which has the appearance under the Grail Web browser shown in Figure 2.1.

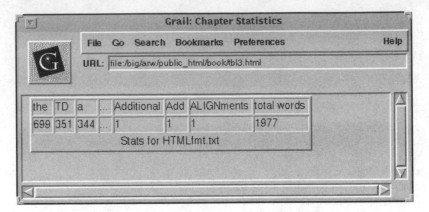

Figure 2.1 Grail presentation of example HTML.

The precise workings of the `word_freq` module are left to the reader to decipher beyond what we have already said because this example is provided exclusively to illustrate some fundamental syntactic features of the Python language before discussing these features in detail.

Execution Modes

There are four primary modes for running the Python interpreter.

The Python Interpreter as Main

This is the most common mode of operation for real Python programs (after they have been developed, debugged, and tested). In this mode, the Python interpreter acts as the main program running a program specified by either an initial Python module source file or by a file which provides the byte compilation of an initial module.

In a line-mode operating system shell interface (for example, from the UNIX or DOS prompt) a Python-main mode program can be started as follows:

```
system-prompt> python module_file arguments...
```

(Here we assume the system shell can find the program named `python`).

On many systems, an initial module file can itself be "made into a stand-alone executable" by associating the module file with the Python interpreter program in some system-dependent manner (for example, using the UNIX "pound bang hack").

Once a module file is associated with the interpreter program, it may be executed from the command line without explicit reference to the Python interpreter:

```
system-prompt> module_file arguments...
```

Frequently the initial module_file of a Python application is a very short program which sets up a number of configuration parameters, checks a few error conditions, imports some other Python modules, and starts a simple function which may be defined in another module. For example, here is an initial module file that starts a simple Web form processor:

```
#!/usr/local/bin/python
# The previous line is the UNIX ``pound bang hack''
# which instructs the system to direct the rest of the content
# of the file to the program /usr/local/bin/python.

print "Content-type: text/html\n\n"  # identify the content-type

import sys            # import the sys module
sys.path.append(".")  # Make sure the other module files can be found.
import feedback       # import the main logic module

Cfg = feedback.Config()  # initialize an object for processing the form
Cfg.GO()                 # Process the form!
```

It is not necessary for the whole program to be written in Python. It is easy to extend Python with additional features written in, e.g., C or Fortran. These "extension modules" become part of Python and can be used to provide additional system calls, access to databases, efficient numeric calculations, or access to other existing programs. Python works well in this role, because it is a very high level language very suitable for use as the main control logic. Large, complex, and efficient programs can be built up from a Python main, additional Python modules, and a small amount of C-language support when required.

The Python Interpreter as Main Under a GUI

Things are a little different when a Python program runs under a Graphical User Interface (GUI) such as Microsoft Windows, because a GUI application has no main program. Instead, it has an *event loop*. When the Python program starts up, it sets up functions to be called for various events such as key presses, mouse events, menu selections, window focus in/out, etc. It then returns control to the OS. Thereafter, Python just waits for the operating system to call these functions. The operating system acts as the main program by catching user and system events and calling the relevant Python function.

Interactive Interpretation Mode

Because Python is an interpreted language, it is possible to type in Python programs and have them executed on the fly. Python starts in interactive mode if no program is specified on the command line. Running Python in interactive mode is extremely useful during the implementation and testing of components of a Python program. Interactive mode is also a great tool for explaining the use of the Python language, and this book will use it extensively. The Python interpreter in interactive mode proceeds by accepting a complete Python statement, executing the statement, and then printing the result if there was a result (and if the result wasn't None, which doesn't echo). This execution strategy is called the "read-eval-print loop" and it is adapted from many other languages, notably the Lisp family of languages. Python usually uses >>> as the initial prompt, indicating that the interpreter expects the beginning of a new statement. The . . . prompt indicates that the interpreter has seen the start of a statement but needs to see more of the statement before the evaluation can proceed. Finally, the value printed in response to the statement (if any) is not prefixed. Thus, in the following example:

```
>>> s = "this"
>>> (s + " ") * 4
'this this this this '
>>> for x in s:
...     print x, ord(x), "|",
...
t 116 | h 104 | i 105 | s 115 |
>>>
```

The first statement s ="this" was an assignment, which had no value. The second statement (s + " ") * 4 evaluated to the string 'this this this this ', which the interpreter printed. The third expression was a for loop, which spanned three lines (with the final empty line signaling the end of the loop body). Although the for loop had no value, the print statements executed during the evaluation of the loop resulted in the printed line following the loop.

Embedded Python

Python can also be embedded in another main program and can be called from the main program in order for the main program to provide services implemented in Python. The extending and embedding Python is covered in detail in the chapters on embedding and extending the interpreter.

Commenting Python Programs

Python allows programs to be annotated by comments, which are ignored by the interpreter. A Python comment starts at a pound character (not inside a string literal) and proceeds to the end of the line. For example:

```
#  Human reader wake up!!!  I'm setting x to 3 here, maybe you should
#    take note, because I'm not sure this is the correct value.
x = 3  # This is another Python comment.
text = " # this is not a Python comment; it's the inside of a string! "
```

A comment notation is a horrible thing to waste; use it.

Another way to add commentary to a Python program is to use documentation strings, as discussed in the next section. Documentation strings have the advantage that they are not ignored, and can be examined at run time.

Indentation Block Structuring

Python uses an indentation convention for grouping blocks of code. For a nonsensical (but syntactically correct) example:

```
def silly_indentation_example():
    for those in "need":
        try:
            solution = "Python"
        # this is the implicit end of the "try block"
        except:
            raise "hell"
        # here is the implicit end of the "except block"
        # and for that matter it ends the entire "try" statement
    # Oh, and by the way, this ends the "for" loop
    if you in spoiled_brats and you.think(life is too_hard):
        try:
            raise "a two year old"
        finally:  # ends the "try" block implicitly, as before
            pull_up(your.pants)
            straighten(your.hat)
            get.a_job(you)  # with apologeze to P.J. O'Rourke
        # this ends the "finally" block and the "try" statement
        print "guess I'm getting to be one of those"
    # here implicitly ends the "if" block
    elif you.dont_like(it):
        you.can_lump(it)
    # here the "elif" block and the if statement end implicitly
# here is the implicit end of the "def" function definition block
```

A Python *code block* is a sequence of statements embedded within the same collection of control statements. The statement sequence is identified by its level of indentation, and the sequence ends when the indentation level returns to the previous indentation level. Thus, Python insists on an indentation discipline which is universal coding practice for good programmers everywhere anyway.

Multiline Statements and Expressions

A consequence of Python's indentation-based syntax is that each simple Python statement must appear (as the parser sees it) on "one line." Once in a while, it is necessary to type a statement of a Python program that must span more than one line (as the human reader sees it) and requires an implicit or explicit line joining. For long expressions, we suggest bracketing the expression in parentheses, because expressions within parentheses always "appear to be on the same line" to Python. A common example of such long expressions are truth valued conditionals and arithmetic computations.

```
while (you.have(hope) and      # to the parser everything from here
       you.breathe() and
       (wallet>10.00 or
        not (credit is bad)))):# to here is the "same line".
   dont_worry(be_happy)
   blessings = ( health +      # similarly, everything from here
                 hope +
                 liberty +
                 cool_technology ) # to here is "one line" also.
```

Another common example of long code fragments bracketed by parentheses are argument sequences to functions, which sometimes get very long.

```
# a function declaration
def latin_conjugation(
     verb_infinitive,
     person=FIRST,
     number=SINGULAR,
     tense=PRESENT):    # everything from "def" to here is one line to Python
   raise RuntimeError, "I don't know Latin!"

# a function call (with explicit keyword argument names)
print latin_conjugation(
            person=THIRD,
            verb_infinitive="ser",
            number=PLURAL,
            tense=SUBJUNCTIVE)
```

Also, long dictionary, list, and tuple displays may be enclosed in curly or square or round brackets, respectively, and broken into multiple lines as needed:

```
   a_list = [ element0,
              element1,
              element2 ] # this is all one assignment
   a_dict = { key1: value1,
              key2: value2,
              key3: value3 } # so is this
   a_tuple = ( element0,
               element1,
               element2 ) # as is this
```

However, there are occasions when a legitimate simple statement (which is not an expression) must be broken over several lines, in this case the intermediate lines may be terminated with a back slash. Just about the only time this is every very useful is in "raise" statements that construct complicated diagnostic messages, or in long assignments:

```
def a_function():
    if ...:
        while ...:
            for ...:
                try:
                    if not (lower_limit <= x <= upper_limit):
                        # Not the explicit line join using a backslash:
                        raise ValueError, \
    "invalid x value %s not in range %s..%s" % (x, lower_limit, upper_limit)
                    else:
                        long_variable_name = \
                            long_function(long_argument1, long_argument2)
```

Identifiers and Keywords

Yawn. This is just like almost every other "algebraic language" in the world (like Algol, Pascal, C, Modula, ABC, C++, java) but we had to talk about it anyway…Tradition.

The lexical portion of the Python parser recognizes indentations, line breaks, punctuations, literal values, keywords, and identifiers. Keywords and identifiers look the same, lexically speaking—they both are given by a sequence of characters starting with an alphabetic or an underscore followed by a series of alphanumerics or underscores.

Since keywords have special importance a keyword cannot be used as an identifier in a program, and if you try to use a keyword as an identifier you will probably get a syntax error, like so:

```
>>> class = "CS134: Fixing all the worlds problems with Python"
  File "", line 1
    class = "CS134: Fixing all the worlds problems with Python"
        ^
SyntaxError: invalid syntax
```

Here class is a reserved Python keyword, and when we tried to use it as an identifier (in interactive mode, as discussed below), Python got very upset with us, and we deserved it. What we should have done is use an identifier, like so:

```
>>> klass = "CS134: Fixing all the worlds problems with Python"
```

Behold the Python keywords (snarfed from the Python reference manual):

```
access    del       from      lambda    return
and       elif      global    not       try
break     else      if        or        while
class     except    import    pass
continue  finally   in        print
def       for       is        raise
```

These are identifiers, not keywords:

```
coffee    x         epsilon     Comfy_Chair
__init__  X         Epsilon     ___too__many___underscores___
raise_    If        Lambda      LAMBDA
_if       IF        LAMBDA3     X11R4
this_identifier_is_probably_too_long_but_long_identifiers_can_be_nice
```

These are neither keywords nor identifiers:

```
$PERL                     # can't start with a dollar sign!
social-security-number    # this is an expression with 3 identifiers.
error message             # this is an invalid sequence of 2 identifiers.
```

A Fearless Tour of Python Data Types

Python is an extremely object oriented dynamic language, and just about every part of Python is an object that can be explicitly manipulated by a running program. This section is a crash course on the most important object types that you are likely to encounter in a Python program.

The *type* of a value determines the valid ways in which that value can be manipulated. The Python core automatically includes a number of basic types, and Python may be extended with additional extension modules that define additional data types as well.

If you want to know the type of a value, use the built-in function type:

```
>>> type("hello world")
<type 'string'>
```

We can list standard names for the usual Python types using the module types and a bit of magic:

```
>>> import types
>>> dir(types)
['BuiltinFunctionType', 'BuiltinMethodType', 'ClassType',
 'CodeType', 'DictType', 'DictionaryType', 'FileType',
 'FloatType', 'FrameType', 'FunctionType', 'InstanceType',
 'IntType', 'LambdaType', 'ListType', 'LongType', 'MethodType',
 'ModuleType', 'NoneType', 'StringType', 'TracebackType',
 'TupleType', 'TypeType', 'UnboundMethodType', 'XRangeType',
 '__builtins__', '__doc__', '__name__']
```

This mystery sequence (slightly reformatted for readability) lists the standard names for the usual Python types (except for the last three strings which each start with a double underscore—these are standard variables that appear in any module, discussed later).

Python objects are grouped into "mutable" and "immutable" types. *Mutable* types cannot be modified, but they as components of data structures which must never change. In particular, dictionary objects require keys to be immutable. An object a is formally *immutable* if whenever a == b then no change to a or b can result in a != b. Everything else is mutable. In particular the following objects are mutables:

- Lists.
- Dictionaries.
- XRange objects.
- Possibly other extension types not covered in this discussion.
- Tuples which contain mutable objects.
- Class instances which have a comparison method __cmp__.) but no hash method __hash__.) [this is a relatively obscure feature].

(XRange objects shouldn't be considered mutable—this is a minor semantic bug in Python 1.3 as of this writing.) All other objects are immutable. In particular, tuples that contain only immutables make highly convenient dictionary keys.

Behold a summary of these types, and how to make or find an example object of each type. Some of this summary may be unclear at first glance, but we feel it's useful to provide a tour of the universe of Python objects up front.

Your Basic Boring Types

Python, of course, has basic boring types like strings and integers. These types are all immutable, because they are very useful as keys to dictionaries and in other structures that require immutable values. All operations on objects of these types (for example, x+1 where x is an integer) leave the old object unchanged.

FloatType

Float objects represent Python floating point numbers. Floating point numbers are always implemented using C language doubles and are subject to the same restrictions (except that Python automatically catches many errors associated with numerical computations). Create one thusly:

```
>>> 1123.5e-7
0.00011235
>>> type(1123.5e-7)
<type 'float'>
```

The preceding computation gives only one of several notations for floats; other notations and related issues are discussed further on.

IntType

Int objects encode integers in Python (except for truly huge integer values, where long objects are useful). Int objects always correspond to C language longs, and are subject to the same limitations, except that Python automatically checks for most numerical errors associated with manipulating integers. Create one thusly:

```
>>> 32767
32767
>>> type(32767)
<type 'int'>
```

There is no way to "change" an integer value: int objects are immutable. Happily, there is no need to ever change an int value, because it always suffices to make a new one (as in x = x+1).

LongType

A Python long object is an arbitrary precision integer. It can be used to represent "whole" numeric values that might normally cause an arithmetic overflow if an int object were used instead. Create one like this:

```
>>> 587657657465476535342    # this won't work as an int
OverflowError: integer literal too large
>>> 587657657465476535342L  # but it's just fine as a long
587657657465476535342L
>>> type(587657657465476535342L)
<type 'long int'>
```

There are performance penalties associated with using long ints when you don't need them—longs are useful for cryptography and certain system level operations involving bit manipulation—most programs need not use them, as int objects are usually big enough.

NoneType

You can't create an object of the NoneType, and you can't do much with an object of this type either. There is only one None object for any given Python instance, named None, a value which conventionally represents no value.

```
>>> None # The value None won't echo below
>>> print None # but it will print.
None
>>> type(None)
<type 'None'>
```

Despite its apparent lack of functionality, None is quite useful—it is often used as a special value marker that can't be confused with an otherwise meaningful value. None is also the value returned by any function which doesn't explicitly return a value using a return statement:

```
>>> def say_hi():
... print "hello world"
...
>>> x = say_hi()
hello world
>>> print x
None
```

We will use None a lot in this book. We hope you find it useful as well.

StringType

A Python string object is an immutable sequence of characters (bytes). Python provides numerous methods for manipulating strings, discuss further on. We've already seen a great number of strings, but for completeness you can create one as follows:

```
>>> "this is a string"
'this is a string'
>>> type("this is a string")
<type 'string'>
```

There are many other ways to create strings, as we will see. There is no such thing as a character type in Python—use strings of length one instead. Note that both single and double quotes may be used to surround a literal string in a Python program.

TypeType

Python types are valid objects also! Just about the only interesting thing you can do with type objects is compare them for equality and print them. That's a lot, however, because it allows programs to be highly polymorphic and adaptable, compared to programs written in languages that do not provide run-time type information.

```
>>> from types import StringType
>>> type("this") == StringType
1
>>> type(StringType)
<type 'type'>
```

Standard Container Types

Python also has a number of standard ways to organize collections of objects into structures.

DictType

Dictionary objects are extremely useful tools that should be used with abandon. A *dictionary* is a mapping of hashable Python objects to arbitrary Python objects. We will discuss dictionaries in great detail, but here we give an example of how to make one:

```
>>> dict =          {"pointer":        "a breed of hunting dog",
...                  "post mortem dump": "a place for dead programmers",
...                  "infinite loop":    "infinite loop"}
>>> type(dict)
<type 'dictionary'>
```

Dictionaries are sometimes referred to as "associative arrays," for reasons we cannot determine.

As mentioned, keys to a dictionary must be hashable, meaning that it is in some sense an "immutable" object. Aside from the restriction that keys must be immutable, there is no restriction on the objects that may serve as keys or values in a dictionary—the same dictionary may contain keys and values of differing types. Always remember that tuples that contain only immutables make fantastically convenient keys.

WARNING

If you define classes with a hash method, be careful that the hash value for an instance never changes so long as the instance serves as a key in a dictionary and that any two instances that compare equal always produce the same hash value. This is a tall order, and if you do it wrong, dictionaries that use these instances as keys may misbehave, so attempt this trickery at your own risk. Do not abuse this obscure feature.

Dictionary Type

A longer name for DictType, maybe this will make your code more readable—who knows?

List Type

You can think of a list object as an array of Python objects, because that's basically what it is. Lists are mutable, which means that their content may be modified, and they can be resized and sorted in place, but they cannot be used directly as keys in a dictionary. Create one thusly:

```
>>> list = ["walla", "walla", "walla", "kalamazoo"]
>>> type(list)
<type 'list'>
```

Lists are *heterogeneous*, meaning that there is no restriction on the types of objects which may be contained in a list—and objects of differing types can reside in the same list. There is much to be said about lists, and we will say more later. Use the notation [ ] to construct an empty list.

Tuple Type

Just about any interesting program should use tuple objects. Tuple objects are "immutable arrays of Python objects." Unlike lists, tuples can never be modified, but they can often be used as keys in dictionaries. Tuples are constructed by the comma operator, and are often enclosed in parentheses.

```
>>> 'this', 1, 'is' , 'a', 'tuple'   # creating a tuple without parens
('this', 1, 'is', 'a', 'tuple')
>>> ('this',1,'is','a','tuple') # another way to get a tuple, with parens
('this', 1, 'is', 'a', 'tuple')
>>> type( ('this',1,'is','a','tuple') ) # the parens are required here!
<type 'tuple'>
```

Like lists, tuples are heterogeneous—arbitrary elements of differing types may reside in the same tuple.

The notations ( ) and (x,) construct the empty tuple and a tuple of length one (containing the value of x), respectively. In the latter notation, the trailing comma is required.

NOTE   With the exception of the `print` statement Python constructs that use comma separators can include a redundant trailing comma. This is useful for editing literal container declarations and also makes programs that automatically generate Python code simpler. For the `print` statement a trailing comma means "no newline."

XRange Type

XRange objects are useful in iterations over linear sequences of integers.

```
>>> for x in xrange(4,100,7):
...     print x,
...
4 11 18 25 32 39 46 53 60 67 74 81 88 95
```

The Python "for loop" always iterates over a sequence object, extracting one object from the sequence at a time.

```
>>> for lyric in ("boogy", "woogy", "bugle", "boy"):
...     print "**", lyric, "**"
...
** boogy **
** woogy **
** bugle **
** boy **
```

In order to provide iterations over sequential sequences of integers (or, more generally, linear sequences of integers), Python provides two standard ways to construct integer sequences—range, and xrange. The range function generates a physical list of integers—which is bad if the range is large because it wastes space, and because a truly huge range might even crash the interpreter. The xrange function, in contrast, produces a "lazy sequence of integers" which only generates an element when it is requested. The objects produced by xrange are of the XRangeType.

```
>>> bigrange = xrange(-10000000, 9000000) # don't try this with range!!!
>>> bigrange[777777] # this generates the member for index 777777
-9222223
>>> type(bigrange)
<type 'xrange'>
```

xrange and range have identical calling sequences:

```
>>> xrange(10)       # from 0 upto (but NOT including) 10
(0, 1, 2, 3, 4, 5, 6, 7, 8, 9)
>>> range(10)        # range is similar, but produces a list object
[0, 1, 2, 3, 4, 5, 6, 7, 8, 9]
>>> xrange(5,15)     # from 5 upto (but NOT including) 15
(5, 6, 7, 8, 9, 10, 11, 12, 13, 14)
>>> xrange(5, 30, 2) # from 5 upto 30, stepping by 2
(5, 7, 9, 11, 13, 15, 17, 19, 21, 23, 25, 27, 29)
>>> range(5, 30, 2)  # range is similar, again.
[5, 7, 9, 11, 13, 15, 17, 19, 21, 23, 25, 27, 29]
```

It's probably a good idea to use xrange for iterations over sequential integers, unless there is a good reason not to.

XRange objects cannot be modified, which makes sense if you think about it. Due to a minor technical problem in Python 1.3, they cannot be used as keys to a dictionary. Whoops. Sorry.

Object-Oriented Objects

Python programs can be organized using object oriented design techniques, simply and directly using the object-oriented features built into the language.

Class Type

This names the type of a Python class object. Class objects are the "entry point" for most of Pythons object oriented features. Classes are used extensively and described in excruciating detail later, but here we show a simple way to make a class object.

```
>>> class example_class:
...     pass # no class variables, no methods... nothing
...
>>> type(example_class)
<type 'class'>
```

Instance Type

Instance objects are "instantiations of a class object." Below `statistic` is a class and `stat` is an instance of that class.

```
>>> class statistic:
...     def __init__(self):
...         self.count = 0
...         self.total = 0.0
...     def add_datum(self, datum):
...         self.count = self.count + 1
...         self.total = self.total + datum
...     def average(self):
...         return self.total/self.count
...
>>> stat = statistic()
>>> for d in (4, 4.5, 3.2, 9):
...     stat.add_datum(d)
...
>>> stat.average()
5.175
>>> stat.add_datum(-5)
>>> stat.average()
3.14
>>> type(stat)
<type 'instance'>
```

Briefly, the statistic class declared above defines a template for instances that keep track of a running sum of data items "sent to it" via the add_datum method, along with a count of the number of items received. The average method of the statistic class computes the average of the currently received items for a given instance.

Classes have a very useful feature called *inheritance*, which allows instances of one class to reuse operations declared for a number of other classes, discussed later. If you want to understand object-oriented programming methods, Python (and this book) is a good place to start.

Standard Callable Objects

Like all good languages, Python allows programs to be organized using procedural abstraction. Thus, instead of writing

```
>>> (9 + 6 + 12 - 7)/4.0
5.0
>>> (8 - 90 + 0.1 - 100 + 8)/5.0
-34.78
>>> (9 + 6 + 12 - 7- 90 + 0.1 - 100 + 8)/8.0
-20.2375
```

and so forth to compute a number of averages, we can abstract the process of computing averages into a function definition.

```
>>> def tot_avg(initial=0.0, *others):
...     sum = initial
...     for other in others:
...         sum = sum + other
...     return (sum, sum/(len(others) + 1.0))
```

Here tot_avg accepts an initial argument and an arbitrary sequence of other arguments that show up in the tuple others. The result of tot_avg(a,b,c, ...) computes the total and the average of the arguments, returned as a pair, as in:

```
>>> tot_avg(9, 6, 12, -7)
(20, 5.0)
>>> tot_avg(8, -90, 0.1, -100, 8)
(-173.9, -34.78)
```

```
>>> tot_avg(9, 6, 12, -7,  -90, 0.1, -100, 8)
(-161.9, -20.2375)
```

Unlike many languages, callable objects of all stripes in Python are first class values which may be passed as arguments to other callable objects, and stored in data structures for later use.

BuiltinFunctionType

A built-in function is a Python function implemented in a compiled part of Python or a Python extension module. The only way to make a new object of this type is to modify the Python C source and recompile/relink Python or build a Python extension module and connect it with Python somehow (i.e., by relinking or by using dynamic linking). Although adding new built-in functions is surprisingly easy, most Python programmers will never need to do it. It is very easy to find built-in functions, however, because they are everywhere:

```
>>> type(type)
<type 'builtin_function_or_method'>
>>> import posix
>>> type(posix.system)
<type 'builtin_function_or_method'>
```

There is no real distinction between a `method` and a `function` in compiled parts of Python.

BuiltinMethodType

This is really just another name for `BuiltinFunctionType`, but it normally refers to a method of a built-in object. For example, Python lists have an associates `sort` method:

```
>>> list = [6,2,9,3,2]
>>> list.sort
<built-in method sort of list object at 7a078>
>>> type(list.sort)
<type 'builtin_function_or_method'>
```

Built-in methods normally either extract some information from an object or perform some operation on the object, for example:

```
>>> list.count(6)
1
>>> list.count(2)
```

```
2
>>> list.sort()
>>> list
[2, 2, 3, 6, 9]
```

Here the `count` method of the `list` object counts the number of occurrences in the list of 6 and 2 respectively, and the `sort` method sorts the list in place.

Function Type

Function objects (which are distinct from built-in function objects) are functions declared either with a `def` construct (which isn't immediately contained in a `class` construct) or with a `lambda` construct. Functions and class methods are the two objects which allow procedural abstraction to be defined in Python. Here is an example function definition, followed by example uses of the function:

```
>>> def change(cents):
...      (dollars, remainder) = divmod(cents, 100)
...      (quarters, remainder) = divmod(remainder, 25)
...      (dimes, remainder) = divmod(remainder, 10)
...      (nickels, remainder) = divmod(remainder, 5)
...      pennies = remainder
...      format = "%s dollars, %s quarters, %s dimes, %s nickels, %s pennies"
...      return format % (dollars, quarters, dimes, nickels, pennies)
...
>>> change(97)
'0 dollars, 3 quarters, 2 dimes, 0 nickels, 2 pennies'
>>> change(391)
'3 dollars, 3 quarters, 1 dimes, 1 nickels, 1 pennies'
>>> type(change)
<type 'function'>
```

Drat. We didn't get the pluralization right. Oh well. Of course, functions are very important and will be discussed in detail later.

Lambda Type

This is another name for `FunctionType`, but it usually refers to anonymous functions created using the `lambda` construct instead of named functions created using the `def` construct. Below is an example use of the lambda construct which many readers will likely find confounding at first sight:

```
>>> def compose(f, g):
...      return lambda x, last=f, first=g: last(first(x))
```

```
...
>>> from math import floor, log
>>> floorlog = compose(floor, log)
>>> floorlog(5551212) # same as floor(log(5551212))
15.0
>>> type(floorlog)
<type 'function'>
```

Python sees no important difference between functions created using `lambda` and functions created using `def`. The compose function could just as well have been defined as follows:

```
>>> def compose(f, g):
...     def result(x, last=f, first=g):
...         return last(first(x))
...     return result
...
>>> floorlog = compose(floor, log)
>>> floorlog(5551212)
15.0
```

MethodType

A method object (distinct from a built-in method object) is an operation associated with an instance of a class. There are two variations of method objects: bound method objects are associated with a particular instance, usually created via the notation `Instance.MethodName`; and unbound methods which are not associated with any instance (yet), usually retrieved from a class object using the notation `Class.MethodName`. The following interaction creates a class Interval, an instance of the Interval class age_range, and a bound method age_range.member assigned to the variable `valid_age`.

```
>>> class Interval:
...     def __init__(self, lowerlimit, upperlimit):
...         self.lower = lowerlimit
...         self.upper = upperlimit
...     def contains(self, other):
...         return self.lower <= other.lower <= other.upper <= self.upper
...     def member(self, value):
...         return self.lower <= value <= self.upper
...     def intersect(self, other):
...         return Interval( max(self.lower, other.lower),
...                          min(self.upper, other.upper) )
```

```
...
>>> age_range = Interval(0,100)
>>> valid_age = age_range.member
>>> type(valid_age)
<type 'instance method'>
```

A bound instance method may be used just like a function, except that the calling sequence used when calling a bound method does not include the first argument declared when declaring the method—because the first declared argument always refers to the instance bound to the method (traditionally named self). The interesting thing about bound methods is that they are associated with an instance and any data the instance "contains." So, for example, changes to age_range.upper are reflected in the behavior of valid_age in the forgoing.

```
>>> valid_age(3) # 3 is valid
1
>>> valid_age(-12) # -12 is not valid
0
>>> valid_age(101)
0
>>> age_range.upper = 130 # let's not be so pessimistic!
>>> valid_age(101)
1
```

Here the integer values 1 and 0 serve as truth values representing true and false, respectively—other truth value conventions as well as other discussions of bound methods are provided later.

NOTE

UnboundMethodType

This type is technically identical to the MethodType, but it is used to refer to unbound methods rather than bound methods.

An unbound method object is a method of a class which is not associated with a particular instance of the class. Unbound methods of a class can be identified by the notation ClassObject.MethodName. Methods are declared by def constructs immediately contained within a class construct. Method declarations require that the first argument (conventionally named self) always represents an instance of the class containing the declaration:

```
>>> class Person:
...     def __init__(self, name):  # the Person.__init__ method declaration
...         self.name = name
...     def greet(self, friend):   # the Person.greet method declaration
...         print "hello", friend
...         print "my name is", self.name
...
>>> Person.greet  # an unbound method of class Person
<unbound method Person.greet>
>>> type(Person.greet)
<type 'instance method'>
```

Unbound methods act much like functions, with one exception: the first argument to the unbound method must be a value for `self` that is an instance of the appropriate class (or one of the subclasses of the class).

```
>>> larry = Person("Larry")
>>> larry.greet("Tom") # this is the ``bound method'' notation
hello Tom
my name is Larry
>>> Person.greet(larry, "Tom") # another way to do it, but unbound
hello Tom
my name is Larry
>>> Person.greet("Larry", "Tom") # but you can't do this!
TypeError: unbound method must be called with class instance 1st argument
```

Unbound methods are particularly useful for calling a method of a specific superclass in a subclass definition. We'll see examples of the need for this later, and you'll probably run into the need for them, eventually.

Other Standard Objects

As we said, just about everything in a Python program is an object that can be manipulated. Here are some other standard types in increasing order of obscurity.

FileType

File objects are the primary interface between Python and the local file system. They generally conform to C stdio file conventions (but recooked in a mild object-oriented flavor). The usual way to make a file is to open one (thus either creating a new file in the filesystem or connected to an existing file in the filesystem).

```
>>> log = open("logfile.log", "w") # open logfile.log for writing.
>>> type(log)
<type 'file'>
>>> log.close()
```

File objects, of course, are a bit complex, and we will discuss them in more detail later.

Module Type

All Python programs consist of a collection of modules. Some modules (like the `posix` module) are compiled parts of Python implemented in some compiled language like C. Other modules are implemented in Python and usually correspond to a single Python source file. For example, if we have the following statements in a file named `mymodule.py`:

```
"This is the doc string for mymodule.py"

def double(x):
    return x + x

magic_constant=29
```

then (if we presume the module is placed in a directory listed in the PYTHONPATH) we can import the module into a Python interactive interpreter session as follows:

```
>>> import mymodule
>>> dir(mymodule)
['__builtins__', '__doc__', '__name__', 'double', 'magic_constant']
>>> type(mymodule)
<type 'module'>
```

Note that the imported module contains the two objects we named in the source file, which we can identify using the `Module.variable` notation:

```
>>> mymodule.magic_constant
29
>>> mymodule.double(6)
12
```

The module also contains three "double underscore" variables we didn't explicitly declare, as discussed further on.

Of special interest is the module __main__, which is always the name of the module which started the Python program.

Traceback Type

A Python traceback object is created when an exception occurs. Tracebacks are an obscure part of Python used by debuggers and other programming tools to figure out what went wrong and where it went wrong after an exception has been raised. After an error has occurred the last traceback is archived in sys.last_traceback in interactive mode.

```
>>> import sys
>>> print 12 + "string"  # This doesn't make sense, so we'll get an error:
Traceback (innermost last):
  File "", line 1, in ?
TypeError: number coercion failed
>>> sys.last_traceback
<traceback object at 12fb68>
>>> type(sys.last_traceback)
<type 'traceback'>
```

Normally, programmers don't need to interact with traceback objects.

WARNING

There is one obscure nuance regarding tracebacks that is worth noting, however. A traceback contains part of the state of the interpreter at the point where the last error occurred, even if the error was caught and handled. Consequently, if you need to be sure that all objects not currently in use by the interpreter are deallocated, you must clear the last traceback so the objects in the traceback may be released. The following boilerplate code will make sure that the traceback has been cleared, whether or not an error has occurred.

```
import sys
try:
    raise "dummy"
except:
    sys.exc_traceback = None
```

The problem of objects "stuck" in tracebacks is usually only a concern for fairly elaborate programs that rely on class instance finalization, but if you suspect that your program is not deallocating objects properly when it needs to do so, try clearing the exc_traceback.

Code Type

This is an obscure piece of Python which should be of interest only to those implementing very fancy applications. A code object is an internal representation for the byte code associated with a function or method created from Python code (i.e., not created via built-in linking). You can get an object of this type by, for example, defining a function and extracting its code object:

```
>>> def add1(x):
...     return x + 1
...
>>> add1.func_code
<code object add1 at 83b08, file "", line 1>
>>> type(add1.func_code)
<type 'code'>
```

`CodeType` objects are also the result of the standard built-in functions `compile` and `eval` as well as the parameter to the `exec` statement.

Frame Type

This is an obscure internal Python type useful for implementing debuggers, profilers, tracers, and other fancy programming tools. We won't discuss frame objects any further in this book.

Other types of objects appear in Python programs, like the "compiled regular expression built-in type" used in the `word_freq` module given above, but the types we have listed here are the standard components of the Python core—other types are provided by extension modules. As mentioned, by adding new compiled components to Python, almost any data structure can be added to Python as a new type, as we will see in the chapters on embedding and extending the interpreter.

N O T E   New in Python 1.4 is the Complex type, which is part of the standard core and is supported by special syntactic conventions. This type is primarily of interest to users of "numerical Python" who require complex numbers as well as the excellent and screamingly fast matrix extensions to Python.

Now that we know what a Python program looks like and now that we have been introduced to the objects animated by a Python program, let's dig deeper and see how a Python program manipulates Python objects.

CHAPTER THREE

PLAYING

This chapter introduces via interactive play with the interpreter. Please fire up an interactive interpreter instance and play along!

A Note On Forward References

It is much easier to learn a language if you already know some of the language. It is also much easier to explain one aspect of a language if you use other aspects of the language in the explanation. In order to explain Python in a natural way, our presentation will sometimes explain one component of Python (for example, strings) using other components of the Python (for example, loops or lists) that have not yet been fully explained. When we "skip ahead" like this we will attempt to explain what is going on, but we also encourage you to try out any "partially explained" concept using the interactive interpreter whenever you find us jumping forward, to bolster your intuition.

Playing with Strings

Python excels at manipulating strings, even though it is not intended as a string manipulation language (and hence provides regular expressions as extension modules rather than as part of the core language).

Strings are sequences of characters which may be created interactively or in programs typing them in as quoted "string literals." In the following discussion, we describe various ways that strings can be manipulated by Python, illustrated with examples entered directly into the Python console-mode interactive interpreter.

In general, real Python programs are run in noninteractive "script mode" or "application mode" where the Python prompt never appears. In this book, however, we will use interactive examples extensively because the reader may follow and imitate our interactive experiments to gain deep insight into the language easily. Except for technical details of error handling and parsing, there is really little difference between the behavior of the interactive interpreter and other interpreter modes, so this approach causes no confusion about the use of the language. So, let's play with some strings!

To "play along" with this discussion, fire up Python in console mode and type in the examples we give (or others you come up with yourself). Always indicate the end of a line to the interpreter by typing a "return."

```
% python
Python 1.3 (Dec  7 1995)  [GCC 2.6.3]
Copyright 1991-1995 Stichting Mathematisch Centrum, Amsterdam
>>> print "Hello world!!!"
Hello world!!!
>>> string10 = "0123456789"
>>> string10
'0123456789'
>>> print string10
0123456789
```

Here (after disposing of the obligatory "Hello world" example) we defined a string "0123456789" which consists of the numeric characters, and assigned the string value to the variable named string10. After assigning the variable, we typed the variable name string10 into the interpreter by itself. Python responded by printing the readable value of the expression (which in this case was trivial). The "readable representation" of a string places the string value in quotes (and may introduce other special markings) to indicate that the value is a string. In this case, without the quotes we could be forgiven for mistaking the value for a number.

The following print statement

```
print string10
```

directs Python to print the contents of the string directly to the interactive session without any special marks.

The Read-Eval-Print Interpreter Loop

This mode of interaction (typing an expression into the interpreter and receiving a value from the interpreter as the value of the expression) is known as the *read-eval-print loop*. Python stole the read-eval-print loop from the Lisp family of languages. Python endeavors to very selectively steal only the best features from other fine languages, as we shall see. One of the beautiful features of Python is that most of the ideas inside are borrowed from somewhere else, but it is all wrapped up in a wonderfully clean, simple, and usable package.

Python's read-eval-print interpreter loop can be used for many purposes. For example, a customer eating at a restaurant with a number of friends might use Python to figure out how much everyone should pay (whipping out her Python-enabled pocket digital assistant).

```
>>> bill = 93.75
>>> tip = bill * 0.15
>>> total = bill + tip
>>> total
107.8125
>>> number_of_people = 5
>>> each_pays = total / number_of_people
>>> each_pays
21.5625
>>> import math
>>> each_pays = math.ceil( each_pays )
>>> each_pays
22.0
```

Each of these expressions is an assignment of form

```
>>> variable_name = expression
```

or a direct expression evaluation (all trivial in these examples) of form

```
>>> expression
value_for_expression
```

Actually, we also used an `import math` statement to make the `ceil` function from the `math` module available (in order to round the amount `each_pays` up to the nearest whole number)—but we will defer discussion of Python modules and related concepts for the moment.

Note that in this restaurant example we are manipulating numeric values, which are distinct from string values. If we try to perform these operations using strings instead, Python will get upset with us.

```
>>> bill = "93.75"
>>> tip = bill * "0.15"
Traceback (innermost last):
  File "<stdin>", line 1, in ?
TypeError: can't multiply sequence with non-int
```

This silly example illustrates that Python doesn't allow you to multiply two string values. Let's talk about what you can do with strings.

String Literals

String literals may be declared to the interpreter using several formats.

```
"Double quotes: you can't put unquoted apostrophies in single quotes."

'Single quotes: "Double quotes inside are okay," she said.'

"""This is a triple double quoted string.  "It can be very long and
   can include both double and single quotes inside (but you
   can't put three double quotes in sequence here)," She said.
   You must use one of the "triple" quote formats to explicitly
   include line-breaks in an interpreted string."""

'''This is a triple apostrophe quoted string.  It works very much
   like a triple double quoted string, except that I can type
   """ without quoting anything but \'\'\' needs to be quoted
   (unless it is intended to mark the end of the string).'''
```

The empty string is a very useful value which may be written as `""`, `''`, or even as `""""""`, if you insist.

As mentioned in the string-internal commentary, triple-quoted strings that span multiple lines will include newline markers as part of the string. For example, we can declare and examine a multiline string as follows:

```
>>> x = """
... this
...
... string
... contains several
... lines"""
>>> x
'\012this\012\012string\012contains several\012lines'
>>> print x

this

string
contains several
lines
```

Note that there are two types of prompts given by the interpreter above. The >>> prompt indicates that the interpreter expects the beginning of an expression or statement, and the ... prompt indicates that the interpreter is reading an incomplete statement and hopes to see the rest of it. In this case, we received the ... prompt while we were in the middle of the triple-quoted string.

Here we assigned a triple-quoted string value to the variable x. Its "readable" representation shows the line breaks as the Python end-of-line marker character ASCII 10 (which is 12 in octal). Internally all strings are represented as sequences of bytes (numbers between 0 and 255), but when a byte is interpreted as a character, it normally shows up as a letter or digit or other typographical mark. However, certain byte values (like 10) have special interpretation for printing. In order to disable the special interpretation for these byte values, Python quotes them when the byte is represented as a string value. However, when a string containing a special character is printed using the print directive, the character is sent without quoting, which in the case of ASCII 10 (newline) results in a new line.

Technically, you can quote any ASCII byte value when inputting an interpreted string. For example:

```
>>> for x in "hello": print oct(ord(x)),
...
0150 0145 0154 0154 0157
>>> print "\150\145\154\154\157"
hello
```

Here the first line iterated through the characters of the string "hello" and printed their octal byte values. The second input line used the values printed in the first response to input the string "hello" in quoted form. Note that when a string is the object of iteration for a `for` loop, the iteration passes over each character of the string as a singleton string. For example, try this:

```
>>> count = 0
>>> for char in "An example":
...     print count, ":", char
...     count = count + 1
...
```

We discuss for loops (and oct and ord) in greater detail further on.

We can use the same quoted notation to declare a "multiline" string on a single line.

```
>>> y = "another\012string\012 with\012multiple lines"
>>> print y
another
string
 with
multiple lines
```

Concatenating Strings, and Reverse Quoting

The `string1 + string2` operation makes a new string that contains the contents of string1 followed by the contents of string2. For example:

```
>>> aboutstring10 = "this is string10:" + string10
>>> print aboutstring10
this is string10:0123456789
```

Here we added the string literal `"this is string10:"` to the front of the value of `string10` to create a new string. We then examined the new value. Unfortunately, because Python did exactly what we asked, there is no space between the "about" message and the value of the string. Let's clean up the formatting a bit:

```
>>> aboutstring10 = "this is string10: " + string10
>>> print aboutstring10
this is string10: 0123456789
```

But this result still doesn't look right, because the included string10 value looks like a number. Let's indicate its value in the aboutstring10 string by using reverse quoting:

```
>>> aboutstring10 = "this is string10: " + `string10`
>>> print aboutstring10
this is string10: '0123456789'
>>> aboutstring10
"this is string10: '0123456789'"
```

Here the reverse quoting on the string10 value instructs Python to convert string10 to its readable representation before concatenating it with the literal.

Because every value in Python may be converted to a string representation, reverse quoting is generally useful for converting any values to strings.

```
>>> quantity = 123
>>> `quantity`
'123'
>>> amount = 45.98
>>> `amount`
'45.98'
>>> ` [ quantity , amount ]`
'[123, 45.98]'
>>> "pay " + `amount` + " for " + `quantity`
'pay 45.98 for 123'
>>> `ord`
'<built-in function ord>'
```

In the last evaluation, we see that even function values (such as ord) can be given a string representation using reverse quoting.

NOTE The default readable representation for a string encloses the string in single quotes, but if a string contains single quotes and no double quotes, Python switches to a double-quote notation. Strings that contain both types of quotes are represented as single-quoted strings, with internal single quotes set off by backslashes. If you want a "printable" instead of a "readable" representation for an object, use the str standard built-in function, which returns strings unchanged (without surrounding quotes) but converts all other values to string representations.

String (and Sequence) Indexing and Length

Strings are an example of a Python sequence object. Any Python sequence object has an integral length which can be retrieved via `len(sequence)` and an ordered collection of items which can be retrieved using indexing notation `sequence[index]` where sequence is an integer between `-len(sequence)` and `len(sequence)-1`. Indices outside of the prescribed range cause Python to raise an IndexError. Because the first entry always has index zero, the length of an index is always one more than the largest valid possible index. The items of a string are the characters of the string represented as strings of length one.

```
>>> len(string10)
10
>>> string10[0]
'0'
>>> string10[9]
'9'
>>> string10[10]
Traceback (innermost last):
  File "<stdin>", line 1, in ?
IndexError: string index out of range
>>> string10[-1]
'9'
```

Positive (or zero) indices into a `sequence` give items of the `sequence` in order relative to the beginning of the `sequence`, where `sequence[0]` is the first item, `sequence[1]` is the second item, and so forth. This may seem strange, since humans normally count starting with 1, but mathematicians and computer people find this convention to be the most convenient. Negative indices also seem strange, but Python programmers find them very convenient too, as we shall see.

Negative indices give items of a `sequence` relative to the end of sequence, where `sequence[-1]` gives the last item and `sequence[-2]` gives the penulimate item and so forth.

```
>>> print string10[0], string10[1], string10[2]
0 1 2
>>> print string10[-1], string10[-2], string10[-3]
9 8 7
```

For fun, try the following, and try to guess how it works:

```
>>> str = "a string"
>>> for index in range(10):
...     try:
...         print index, str[index]
...     except IndexError:
...         print index, "out of range"
...     try:
...         print -index, str[-index]
...     except IndexError:
...         print -index, "out of negative range"
...
```

For Loops over Strings

As we have seen, strings may be used as the object of iteration of a `for` loop. A for loop of form

```
for variable in sequence:
    do_something_with(variable)
```

passes over the items of a `sequence` assigning each item to the `variable` and executing the body of the for loop using the assigned value of "member." If the body of a for loop consists of a single statement, it may be placed on a single line, as follows.

```
>>> for char in string10: print char,
...
0 1 2 3 4 5 6 7 8 9
```

Slicing and Repeating Strings

Strings and other sequence objects have a very useful feature called *slicing*. A slice expression extracts a contiguous subsequence of a string easily. Strings and other sequence objects may also be repeated using the `sequence * integer` operation.

```
>>> string30 = string10 * 3
>>> string30
'012345678901234567890123456789'
```

Here we used the repetition operation `string10 * 3` to create a string containing the contents of `string10` repeated three times. The resulting value (assigned to `string30`) is useful in illustrating the slicing operation.

```
>>> strname = "Thomas Alva Edison"
>>> print string30 + "\n" + strname
012345678901234567890123456789
Thomas Alva Edison
```

The above operation assigned Edison's name to `strname` and used string concatenation to print the name against an "index ruler" that helps indicate which portion of the name resides at which index. In this case, we used `\n` as an abbreviation for `\012` (the linebreak character)—abbreviations like these are discussed further on. By comparing the name against the ruler, we see that the first name inhabits indices 0 through 6 of the string and the middle name inhabits indices 7 through 11 and so forth. We can use this information to extract the components via slicing.

```
>>> strname[0:6]
'Thomas'
>>> strname[:6]
'Thomas'
>>> strname[7:11]
'Alva'
>>> strname[12:18]
'Edison'
>>> strname[18:12]
''
>>> strname[12:9999]
'Edison'
>>> strname[12:]
'Edison'
>>> strname[12:] + ", " + strname[:11]
'Edison, Thomas Alva'
>>> strname[:]
'Thomas Alva Edison'
>>> strname[10:] + strname[:10]
'Thomas Alva Edison'
```

The slice expression of form `sequence[start:last]` evaluates to a subsequence of sequence starting at index `start` and preceding through the index just before the index `last`. The variants of this notation `sequence[:last]` and `sequence[start:]` are abbreviations for `sequence[0: last]` and `sequence[start: len(sequence)]`, respectively. Note that `last` values past the end of the string are permitted and interpreted to mean "the rest of the string." Slice expressions of form `sequence[:]` simply create a copy of the sequence (which is useful for other sequence types, but not for strings).

The value for `start` and `last` may be negative just as in the indexing notations.

```
>>> strname[-6:]
'Edison'
>>> strname[-6:-1]
'Ediso'
>>> strname[-11:-7]
'Alva'
>>> strname[7:-7]
'Alva'
>>> strname[-11:11]
'Alva'
>>> strname[1:-1]
'homas Alva Ediso'
>>> strname[-1:1]
''
>>> strname[-43:]
'Thomas Alva Edison'
>>> strname[:-43]
''
```

Note that negative start values "before" the beginning of the string are permitted and assumed to indicate "the beginning of the string." Slices `sequence[start : end]` where the `start` represents a position after the `end` evaluate to an empty string (or an empty sequence in the more general case).

Slices that run off the beginning or the end of the sequence may seem strange, but they can greatly simplify handling of boundary cases in code that manipulates sequences in sophisticated or even not so sophisticated ways. For example, the following function takes a sequence of arbitrary length and prints out fixed length segments, except for the final segment, which just prints the rest of the sequence.

```
>>> def splitter(str, segment_length):
...     start = 0
...     length = len(str)
```

```
...        while start < length:
...             end = start + segment_length
...             print ` str [ start : end ] `
...             start = end
...
>>> s = \
... "now is the time for all good men to come to the aid of their country"
>>> splitter(s, 10)
'now is the'
' time for '
'all good m'
'en to come'
' to the ai'
'd of their'
' country'
>>> splitter(s, 30)
'now is the time for all good m'
'en to come to the aid of their'
' country'
>>> splitter(s, 55)
'now is the time for all good men to come to the aid of '
'their country'
```

The function `splitter` needs no special case handling for the final segment of the sequence, because the slice operator does exactly what we desire. In our experience, the default behavior of slice is usually what we desire, but your mileage may vary, as they say. Also, the extra spaces in ` str [ start : end ] ` are irrelevant, and we would prefer `str[start:end]`, but we included the spaces to indicate that this expression consists of operators and variables, with no literals.

Of course, the splitter function may be used for lists or tuples as well as strings.

```
>>> eg_list = [3,5,1,5,21,6,2,7,4,78,34,6,2,5]
>>> splitter(eg_list, 4)
[3, 5, 1, 5]
[21, 6, 2, 7]
[4, 78, 34, 6]
[2, 5]
```

Raw Input

The strings we have seen so far have been Python literal strings that would normally be written into program text. Of course most strings input into a Python program will usually be read from a file or a terminal device or a network connection rather than literals in a program. To read such external strings, a Python program must use functions which access an input device, such as a keyboard or a file system or a network socket connection. In the case of programs run in console or interactive mode, Python provides a function called `raw_input` which reads a string directly from the keyboard. The `raw_input` function accepts an optional prompt string that is used to prompt the user for input.

```
>>> raw_input
<built-in function raw_input>
>>> quote = raw_input("TYPE A QUOTE: ")
TYPE A QUOTE: My wife Mary, dearly beloved, can't invent worth a damn!
>>> quote
"My wife Mary, dearly beloved, can't invent worth a damn!"
```

Here the evaluation of `raw_input()` first printed the prompt TYPE A QUOTE: to the terminal and then waited for the user to type in the quote, terminated by a return (end of line). The value returned by the call to `raw_input()` gives the string typed, not including the newline.

To get more than one line into a list of lines, try this:

```
>>> linelist = []
>>> while 1:
...     line = raw_input()
...     if line == ".": break
...     linelist.append(line)
...
this is a line
here's another one.
Well, I think I'll stop now!
.
>>> linelist
['this is a line', "here's another one.", "Well, I think I'll stop now!"]
```

Simple Formatting

Python provides powerful formatting facilities derived and extended from the `printf` conventions of the C programming language. We'll delve into more advanced features of the formatting methods once we know more about data types used by those conventions, but we introduce some simple usages here.

As we've seen, strings may be constructed by backquoting, slicing, and concatenation, but for fancy formatting these tools can be cumbersome. For example, we could put double quotes around the value of the quote variable using concatenation.

```
>>> qquote = '"' + quote + '"'
>>> qquote
'"My wife Mary, dearly beloved, can\'t invent worth a damn!"'
>>> print qquote
"My wife Mary, dearly beloved, can't invent worth a damn!"
```

But this method has the disadvantage that it can be very hard to read, especially for more complicated examples. We could get the same effect by specifying that the quote string should be substituted into a "template string."

```
>>> qquote = '"%s"' % ( quote, )
>>> print qquote
"My wife Mary, dearly beloved, can't invent worth a damn!"
```

Here (quote,) is a tuple (a singleton, in this case) holding the values to substitute into the string and the

```
    string % tuple
```

notation generates the result of substituting the appropriate value from tuple into the string wherever a %s directive occurs in the string (and Python permits other directives as well). Here, because we were substituting a single position, we could have dispensed with the tuple, writing:

```
>>> qquote = '"%s"' % quote
```

But in more interesting cases, tuples of values can be used to substitute strings into an arbitrary number of places in a string. For example:

```
>>> ncomputers = 3
>>> make = "itty bitty machines"
>>> price = 1345.56
>>> template = """
... Today I bought %s computers from %s
... for $%s each for a total expenditure of $%s.
```

```
...    """
>>> print template % (ncomputers, make, price, ncomputers * price)
```

```
Today I bought 3 computers from itty bitty machines
for $1345.56 each for a total expenditure of $4036.68.
```

```
>>> print template % (5, "faulty systems inc.", 678.51, 5*678.51)
```

```
Today I bought 5 computers from faulty systems inc.
for $678.51 each for a total expenditure of $3392.55.
```

Here we declare a number of parameters for insertion into a form template followed by a form template. The statement

```
print template % (ncomputers, make, price, ncomputers * price)
```

first computes a string resulting from substituting the value for ncomputers, make, price, and ncomputers*price into the positions of the first, second, third, and fourth %s directive, respectively, and then prints the string. For fun, we used the template again, this time substituting literal values. Python automatically converted the numeric values to string representations for the substitution.

For another example, consider:

```
>>> format = """
... %s once said:
...     %s
... """
```

Here the value of the format variable gives a format for presenting a quotation, with directives where the name of the quoted and the quotation itself should be inserted. We can construct a formatted quote string from this format by using the

```
>>> formattedquote = format % (strname, qquote)
>>> formattedquote
'\012Thomas Alva Edison once said:\012    "My wife Mary, dearly beloved, ca
n\'t invent worth a damn!"\012'
>>> print formattedquote
```

```
Thomas Alva Edison once said:
    "My wife Mary, dearly beloved, can't invent worth a damn!"
```

With the value for the formatted string captured in the `formattedquote` variable we are now in a position to inscribe the string in a file, or dispatch it to a printer, or hand it to an electronic mail handler, or stuff it across a network connection to a process on a computer halfway across the planet, but we shall not do so now for these operations require techniques which will be revealed later.

Searching a String

Many useful string handling operations are encapsulated in the standard Python `string` module. A Python module consists of a group of related Python objects (which may be constants, functions, classes, or any other Python object). A module has its own name space which names these objects, and to access an object in a module's name space the module must be imported using the `import module` statement or, alternatively, some of the named objects of the module must be imported using the `from module import object1, object2...` statement. In this case we will import the string module itself, which allows us to refer the "find" function of the string module as `string.find`.

```
>>> Python_author = "Guido Van Rossum"
>>> import string
>>> string.find(Python_author, "V")
6
>>> Python_author[6]
'V'
```

Here the value assigned to Python_author contains an error, because Guido's full printed name should use a lowercase V. To find the index of the error, we used

```
string.find(Python_author, "V")
```

which returned the location of the first V starting from the beginning of the Python_author.

It is tempting to try to correct the error in `Python_author` by assigning to the index within the string, using the index assignment operation, which is permitted for mutable sequence types.

```
>>> Python_author[6] = "v"
Traceback (innermost last):
  File "<stdin>", line 1, in ?
TypeError: can't assign to this subscripted object
```

However, Python prevents this assignment, because strings are considered to be "immutable objects" (objects which can never change) by Python. It is necessary to have strings immutable to allow various indexed data structures (in particular standard Python dictionaries) to have simple, efficient, and robust implementations. But whatever the justification, we must correct our error in Python_author by creating a new string. One way to perform the correction is to use slicing.

```
>>> t = Python_author
>>> Python_author = t[:6] + "v" + t[7:]
>>> Python_author
'Guido van Rossum'
>>> t
'Guido Van Rossum'
```

Note the old value of the string (stored to the variable *t*) remains unaltered.

The string.find function allows us to iterate over many occurrences of a substring by permitting an optional third argument that indicates the index at which to start looking for the substring.

```
>>> string.find(Python_author, "o", 0)
4
>>> string.find(Python_author, "o", 4)
4
>>> string.find(Python_author, "o", 5)
11
>>> another_string = "this is a string with \"is\" in it several times"
>>> another_string
'this is a string with "is" in it several times'
>>> string.find(another_string, "is")
2
>>> here = 0
>>> while 1:
...     here = string.find(another_string, "is", here+1)
...     if here == -1: break
...     print another_string[:here]+"*"+another_string[here:]
...
th*is is a string with "is" in it several times
this *is a string with "is" in it several times
this is a string with "*is" in it several times
>>> string.find(another_string, "nope")
-1
```

As we see, if string.find fails to find the substring (after the start position) it returns the value -1.

Formatting Conveniences

The string module provides a host of useful formatting functions. For example, the upper-, lower-, and swapcase functions create new strings with all characters converted to uppercase, lowercase, or with the case swapped, respectively.

```
>>> import string
>>> string.upper(Python_author)
'GUIDO VAN ROSSUM'
>>> string.lower(Python_author)
'guido van rossum'
>>> string.swapcase(Python_author)
'gUIDO VAN rOSSUM'
```

Some of the present authors have never actually found a compelling use for swapcase. Let us know if you do. Anyway, it's there if you want it just in case. The lower and upper functions are invaluable, however.

The ljust, rjust, and center functions embed a string in a fixed with string, left justifying, right justifying, or centering, respectively, with the extra characters filled with blanks. The zfill function performs a similar function for numbers (or for strings that represent numbers), except that the extra space is filled with leading zeros, preserving leading signs appropriately.

```
>>> string.ljust(Python_author, 20)
'Guido van Rossum
>>> string.rjust(Python_author, 20)
'    Guido van Rossum'
>>> string.center(Python_author, 50)
'                 Guido van Rossum
>>> string.zfill("+12",8)
'+0000012'
>>> string.zfill(789, 8)
'00000789'
>>> string.zfill("-6", 8)
'-0000006'
>>> string.zfill(3, 23)
'00000000000000000000003'
>>> string.zfill(3.123, 10)
'000003.123'
```

For any of these functions, if the input is too long for the specified spacing, the output will be too long also.

```
>>> string.zfill(3.12345678901, 5)
'3.12345678901'
```

The `ljust(x,i)` and `rjust(x,i)` functions should be replaced with something like `"%-12s" % x` or `"%12s" % x` when the width of the field is known (in this case with the constant value 12).

As illustrated above, this is a particular concern for floating point numbers. For floating point numbers which may have long fractional parts, it is best to use **zfill** in combination with **printf** style formatting or slicing.

```
>>> "%05.2f" % 3.12345678901
'03.12'
```

The formatting conventions used with string substitutions (which follow the printf conventions from standard C) are described more fully in the summary of intrinsic methods for strings.

It is often a good idea to use the string substitution construct to adjoin more than two strings. That is, it is best to use `"%s%s%s" % (string1, string2, string3)` in place of the computation `string1 + string2 + string3`, if the strings may be large, because the first copies each string exactly once, whereas the second copies the content of one of the strings twice. More generally

`"%s%s%s%s%s%s%s" % (s1,s2,s3,s4,s5,s6,s7)`

copies each substring once whereas

`s1 + s2 + s3 + s4 + s5 + s6 + s7`

does a lot of recopying of data in the process of evaluating each subexpression. It is not uncommon for Python programs to manipulate gargantuan strings, so use the substitution notation to cut down on the amount of copying required. To paste together a collection of strings, when the length of the collection can only be known at run time, look to the `string.joinfields` function discussed as follows. For small catenations `x + y + z` sometimes looks better.

Converting Numbers to Strings and Characters

The standard built-in functions oct, hex, and chr, respectively, convert a number to its octal string representation, its hexadecimal string representation, and its ASCII interpretation, respectively.

```
>>> x = 90
>>> print `x`, oct(x), hex(x), chr(x)
90 0132 0x5a Z
```

 The values of oct(x) and hex(x) are string representations of valid numeric literals.

NOTE

Printable versus Nonprintable Chars

When playing with the chr function, one notices that certain ASCII values don't correspond to a printed character, but rather effect the formatting of the screen, or in the case of chr(7), may cause the terminal to make a noise (try it!).

```
>>> print "this is chr(66) [" + chr(66) +"] that's it!"
this is chr(66) [B] that's it!
>>> print "this is chr(10) [" + chr(10) + "] that's it!"
this is chr(10) [
] that's it!
>>> print "this is chr(10) quoted [" + `chr(10)` +"] that's it!"
this is chr(10) quoted ['\012'] that's it!
```

Here we see that the ASCII value 66 generates the printable character B, but the ASCII value 10 (line-feed) effects the formatting of the printed line by advancing the cursor one line position. Printing nonprintable characters such as line-feed (10), carriage return (13), or bell (7), sends the character to the screen (or more generally the output device, whatever it happens to be) unfiltered, and if the output device has a special interpretation for those characters, the characters will cause the line to advance or the terminal to "beep" or what have you. A reverse quoted string, however, will convert all nonprintable characters presented as quoted ASCII values printing the four characters \012 rather than dispatching a line feed.

Toward Building an ASCII Table

Most programming language books contain a table listing the ASCII representations for characters. Because you can use Python to explore the ASCII conventions, we won't give such a table in this book. But for the next several sections, we will aim our sights at defining a function that will generate an ASCII table in order to demonstrate the manipulation of strings. In particular, we develop a Python function print_ascii_table(N,M), which prints an ASCII table for the integers running from N to M-1, for example:

```
>>> print_ascii_table(40,50)
decimal     octal       hex         ASCII
40          050         0x28        '('
41          051         0x29        ')'
42          052         0x2a        '*'
43          053         0x2b        '+'
44          054         0x2c        ','
45          055         0x2d        '-'
46          056         0x2e        '.'
47          057         0x2f        '/'
48          060         0x30        '0'
49          061         0x31        '1'
```

On the way to developing this function, we will intentionally choose to illustrate various useful features of Python that could have been avoided by a braindead approach that would have been no fun at all.

Creating Our First Function

To really have fun with strings, we need to use some procedural abstraction. To this end, let's define a function which returns a tuple containing various interpretations for a number as a string:

```
>>> def ascii_info(number):
...     return ( `number`, oct(number), hex(number), `chr(number)` )
...
```

This function returns the decimal, octal, hexadecimal, and ASCII representations associated with the number, all packaged as a tuple. We can use this function to examine the various interpretations for numbers we find of interest:

```
>>> print ascii_info(40)
('40', '050', '0x28', "'('")
>>> ascii_info(13)
('13', '015', '0xd', "'\\015'")
>>> (a, b, c, d) = ascii_info(88)
>>> print a
88
>>> print b
0130
>>> print a,b,c,d
88 0130 0x58 'X'
```

Here the final assignment

```
>>> (a, b, c, d) = ascii_info(88)
```

is an example of a Python multiple assignment which unpacks the contents of the tuple produced by `ascii_info(88)` into multiple variables in a single statement.

Now, in order to build an ASCII table, we need to format the output of `ascii_info` over a range of numbers nicely.

The string.join Aggregate Operation

Our ASCII table generator will need ways to paste lots of strings together, and the `string.join` and `string.joinfields` functions exist exactly for this purpose.

The `string.join(sequence)` function joins the members of the sequence (which must all be strings) into a single string containing the values of the component strings each separated from the other by a single space. For example, we can pass the tuple result of `ascii_info(N)` to `string.join` in order to translate the tuple into a single string, like so:

```
>>> string.join(ascii_info(13))
"13 015 0xd '\\015'"
>>> print string.join(ascii_info(13))
13 015 0xd '\015'
```

Although the `string.join` function may seem peculiar at first sight, it is highly useful, particularly to help in processing long sequences of strings (and its cousin `string.joinfields` is even more useful. It is quite easy to reimplement `string.join` directly using Python core operations:

```
>>> def alt_join( list_of_string ):
...     result = list_of_string[0]
...     for substring in list_of_string[1:]:
...         result = result + " " + substring
...     return result
...
>>> alt_join( ascii_info(60) )
"60 074 0x3c '<'"
```

But because the value of the `result` variable may get very large, and because it is recopied once per iteration in the for loop, this version of the join operation can get very slow compared to the `string.join(sequence)` function, which is highly optimized and runs quickly even over very large sequences.

Using string.joinfields

But our ASCII table generator will need something more flexible than `string.join`, because spaces as separators aren't enough.

An even more useful aggregate operation on strings is `string.join-fields(sequence, separator)`, which is similar to string.join(sequence) except that the programmer may specify the string to separate the substrings of the sequence. For example, we can hyphenate the result of `ascii_info(N)` or put each substring on a separate line:

```
>>> string.joinfields( ascii_info(30), " -- ")
"30 -- 036 -- 0x1e -- '\\036'"
>>> string.joinfields( ascii_info(23), "\n" )
"23\012027\0120x17\012'\\027'"
>>> print string.joinfields( ascii_info(23), "\n" )
23
027
0x17
'\027'
```

Recall that in the second "readable" string representation, the \012 entries are quoted newlines, and when the same string is printed using `print`, the newlines break the line.

A useful separator value is the empty string. For example, the following sequence will trim off the first and last 10 lines of a text file stringplay.html writing the result to test.test, and it will do it quickly even if the file contains thousands of lines:

```
>>> f = open("stringplay.html", "r") # open stringplay.html for reading.
>>> lines = f.readlines()  # read in lines from stringplay.html as a list.
>>> f.close()              # close the input file.
>>> trimmedlines = lines[10:-10]  # trim off the first, last 10 lines.
>>> trimmedtext = string.joinfields(trimmedlines, "") # empty separator
>>> out = open("test.test", "w")  # open the output file
>>> out.write(trimmedtext) # write the joined lines, all at once
>>> out.close()            # close the output file
```

Try it, but make sure you don't overwrite anything you need.

But for the present purpose, string.joinfields will be convenient for generating our ASCII table.

Introducing range() and map()

But to create an ASCII table we also need to manipulate sequences of integers and translate those sequences to sequences of strings. These are the domains of the range and map functions, respectively.

```
>>> range(20)
[0, 1, 2, 3, 4, 5, 6, 7, 8, 9, 10, 11, 12, 13, 14, 15, 16, 17, 18, 19]
>>> map( oct, range(10) )
['0', '01', '02', '03', '04', '05', '06', '07', '010', '011']
>>> map( oct, range(20, 30) )
['024', '025', '026', '027', '030', '031', '032', '033', '034', '035']
```

Here the range(m) and range(n,m) function invocations generate the range of integers from zero to m and n to m, respectively, as lists. The map(function, sequence) invocation generates a new lists containing the result of applying function to every element of the sequence in turn. Thus, if sequence is a list of form

```
[ item0, item1, item2, ..., itemn ]
```

You can think of map(f, sequence) as generating the new list:

```
[ f(item0), f(item1), f(item2), ..., f(itemn) ]
```

The range, map, and string.joinfields functions can be combined in powerful ways. Below are some silly illustrations:

```
>>> a = range(60, 70) # get a range of numbers 60 .. 70
>>> a                  # print it's representation
[60, 61, 62, 63, 64, 65, 66, 67, 68, 69]
>>> b = map( chr, a ) # map the numbers to ascii characters
>>> b                  # print its representation
['<', '=', '>', '?', '@', 'A', 'B', 'C', 'D', 'E']
>>> c = string.joinfields( b, " :: ")  # join b into into formatted string
>>> c
'< :: = :: > :: ? :: @ :: A :: B :: C :: D :: E'
```

Of course a range of integers may be used as the object of iteration of a for loop as well, which can be used as an alternative to using the map function. So we could generate a poorly formatted ASCII table as follows:

```
>>> for x in range(20,30):  # iterate x from 20 to 29...
...      print ascii_info(x) # print the ascii info for each x
...
('20', '024', '0x14', "'\\024'")
('21', '025', '0x15', "'\\025'")
  ... other lines excised...
('29', '035', '0x1d', "'\\035'")
```

Or we could use map to generate the list of ASCII information, and use the result as the object of iteration of the for loop, to the same effect.

```
>>> for x in map( ascii_info, range(40,50) ):
...      print x
...
('40', '050', '0x28', "'('")
('41', '051', '0x29', "')'")
  ... other lines excised...
('49', '061', '0x31', "'1'")
```

Now, with string.joinfields, range, map, and other utilities previously described we have all we need to generate our ascii_table (and then some).

Building an ASCII Table Generator

First, define a field-formatting function that places any field string (of length smaller than 10) into a right-justified representation padded with extra spaces if needed.

```
>>> def fieldformat(field):
...     return "%10s" % field
...
>>> fieldformat("hello")
'     hello'
```

Now define a function which takes a sequence of fields and joins them into a string, where each field is right justified to a field length of 10, and all fields are separated by pipe characters.

```
>>> def formatfields(list):
...     fieldsformatted = map( fieldformat, list )  # do justification
...     return string.joinfields(fieldsformatted, " | ") # join using bars
...
>>> formatfields(["a", "list", "of", "words"])
'         a |       list |         of |      words'
>>> formatfields( ascii_info(56) )
"        56 |        070 |       0x38 |        '8'"
```

Now, using `formatfields` above, we may define our ASCII table generator as follows.

```
>>> def print_ascii_table(lower, upper):
...     numbers = range(lower, upper)  # get the range of numbers to display
...     headers = ["decimal", "octal", "hex", "ascii"] # set headers
...     # print the header
...     header = formatfields( headers )
...     print header
...     print "=" * len(header) # print "===..." just long enough.
...     # print the content
...     for number in numbers:
...         print formatfields( ascii_info(number) )
...
```

The function first prints a header for each appropriate result of `ascii_info(number)`, then prints a line containing just enough equal signs to underscore the header properly, then iterates across the range of numbers specified, formatting the `ascii_info` for those numbers.

```
>>> print_ascii_table(50,70)
decimal    octal    hex     ASCII
50         062      0x32    '2'
51         063      0x33    '3'
52         064      0x34    '4'
     ...more lines omitted...
69         0105     0x45    'E'
```

Now, this is only one of probably 10 million ways to generate an ASCII table using Python, and it's certainly not the simplest approach, but it did illustrate some useful Python features, and we think it's cute to boot.

The string.splitfields Function

The `string.splifields(str, separator)` function can be thought of as an "inverse" for the `string.joinfields` function, factoring the string str into components separated by the separator, and returning the resulting sequence of components as a list (excluding the separator).

```
>>> string.splitfields("::double::colon::separated::string::::", "::")
['', 'double', 'colon', 'separated', 'string', '', '']
>>> string.splitfields("::double::colon::separated::string:", "::")
['', 'double', 'colon', 'separated', 'string:']
>>> string.splitfields("eggs, butter, flour, spam", ", ")
['eggs', 'butter', 'flour', 'spam']
```

We may combine `string.joinfields` with `string.splitfields` to define a general purpose global substitution function for strings. The `globalsubstitute` function defined below generates a result from the `input_string`, where all instances of `from_string` have been replaced with `to_string`.

```
>>> def globalsubstitute(input_string, from_string, to_string):
...     splitlist = string.splitfields(input_string, from_string)
...     return string.joinfields(splitlist, to_string)
...
>>> teststr = "this is a test string containing 'this' twice"
>>> globalsubstitute(teststr, "this", "that")
"that is a test string containing 'that' twice"
>>> globalsubstitute(teststr, "wally", "willy")
"this is a test string containing 'this' twice"
>>> globalsubstitute(teststr, "is", "was once")
"thwas once was once a test string containing 'thwas once' twice"
```

Try this function on the contents of a largish file; it works great, and it's fun too!

```
>>> f = open("stringplay.html", "r")
>>> text = f.read()
>>> f.close()
```

```
>>> newtext = globalsubstitute(text, "string", "banana")
>>> out = open("test.test", "w")
>>> out.write(newtext)
>>> out.close()
```

Now the `test.test` file contains the sentence "Python excels at manipulating bananas…"

Whitespace Conveniences: string.strip and string.split

The `string.strip` and `string.split` functions are specialized for manipulating white space in strings. In particular, the `string.strip` function returns a new string striping surrounding whitespace (including newlines, tabs, and form feeds) from the beginning and ending of the input string. The `string.split` function is similar to string.splitfields, but it returns a list consisting of the whitespace separated substrings of the input list, with the whitespace removed.

```
>>> string.strip("    this is a string surrounded by whitespace    ")
'this is a string surrounded by whitespace'
>>> string.split("    this is a    string surrounded by whitespace    ")
['this', 'is', 'a', 'string', 'surrounded', 'by', 'whitespace']
```

Converting Strings to Numbers: string.atoi

The `string.atoi` function has two formats: `string.atoi(s)`, which attempts to translate s into an integer using a decimal interpretation, and `string.atoi(s, base)` which interprets the string s as a number under the base given. A base of zero is interpreted to mean that the string should be interpreted as if it were a Python literal integer—with a leading "0" signaling an octal value and a leading "0x" signaling a hexidecimal value.

```
>>> oct(8)
'010'
>>> string.atoi("010")    # interpret as decimal, ignore leading zero
10
>>> string.atoi("010", 0) # leading zero signals octal, for base=0
```

```
8
>>> string.atoi("010", 2) # interpret as binary, ignore leading zero
2
```

Most programmers may never find a need for anything other than the default decimal interpretation of strings, but the other conversions are there should the need arise. There is more to know about `string.atoi` that we will not discuss here. Please see the standard library reference.

...And a Lot of the Above Applies to Lists and Tuples Too!

Because Python shares many operations (indexing, slicing, map, etcetera) among all three sequence object types, much of the above commentary which is not specific to strings also applies to lists and tuples. In particular, the len(s) function, indexing, slicing, for loops, and repetition all work analogously over all sequence types, even ones we haven't mentioned. Furthermore functions that use only the common features among sequence types will work for any sequence argument. For example, the following function works equally well for lists, tuples, strings, and other sequence types.

```
>>> def rotate_left(sequence):
...     firstpart = sequence[0:1]
...     remainder = sequence[1:]
...     return remainder + firstpart
...
>>> rotate_left("abc")
'bca'
>>> rotate_left([2,3,5,7])
[3, 5, 7, 2]
>>> (x, y, z) = ("this", 1, "is interesting")
>>> [x, y, z] = rotate_left( [x, y, z] )
>>> print x, y, z
1 is interesting this
```

NOTE However the operations from the `string` module and the string substitution operation s % x are string specific and do not work with other sequence types.

Playing with Lists

As we have seen, lists may be constructed by dicing up strings.

```
>>> import string
>>> str = """
... here
...
... is
...
... a multiline
... string"""
>>> str
'\012here\012\012is \012\012a multiline\012string'
>>> list = string.split(str)
>>> list
['here', 'is', 'a', 'multiline', 'string']
>>> len(list)
5
>>> another_list = [2,3,5,7,11,13]
```

As shown in the `another_list` assignment, we can also construct lists directly using the list display notation:

```
[ item0, item1, ..., itemn ]
```

Once a list has been constructed, it can be accessed via indexing and modified using index assignment

```
>>> list[0]
'here'
>>> list[3]
'multiline'
>>> list[2] = "was"
>>> list
['here', 'is', 'was', 'multiline', 'string']
```

NOTE

Lists are mutable sequences, as demonstrated in `list[3]="was"`. This assignment modifies the `list`, but does not affect the string object `"a"`, which is not altered.

Lists can also be sliced and slice assigned, which extracts and modifies many elements of the list at once. Slice assignment may even change the length of a list.

```
>>> list[1:3] = ["was", "a"]
>>> list
['here', 'was', 'a', 'multiline', 'string']
>>> list[2:]
['a', 'multiline', 'string']
>>> list[1:4]
['was', 'a', 'multiline']
>>> list [2:99]
['a', 'multiline', 'string']
>>> list
['here', 'is', 'a', 'multiline', 'string']
>>> list[2:4]
['a', 'multiline']
>>> list[2:4] = ["a", "list", "that", "once", "was", "a"]
>>> list
['here', 'was', 'a', 'list', 'that', 'once', 'was', 'a', 'string']
```

The last slice assignment replaced the slice `list[2:4]` with a larger slice, so the list was resized, with the elements of the list shifted to accommodate the replacement slice.

Lists may be either copied or shared. A copy of a list may be constructed using `list[:]` or `map(None,list)`. Copies will not reflect direct modification to the list they were copied from.

```
>>> listcopy = list[:]
>>> listref = list
>>> list[:4]
['here', 'was', 'a', 'list']
>>> list[4:]
['that', 'once', 'was', 'a', 'string']
>>> list[4:] = []
>>> list
['here', 'was', 'a', 'list']
```

In contrast to list copies, references to the same list reflect all modifications to the list reference they share, and this is also true of shared references to any Python object that allows mutations. Thus, the assignment `listref = list` sets `listref` to refer to the same structure as `list`, and hence subsequent in-place modifications to `list` are reflected by `listref`, and modifications to `listref` will be reflected in `list` also.

```
>>> list[1] = "is"
>>> list
['here', 'is', 'a', 'list']
>>> listcopy
['here', 'was', 'a', 'list', 'that', 'once', 'was', 'a', 'string']
>>> listref
['here', 'is', 'a', 'list']
```

List equality tests the equality of the sequence of elements the list contains. The `L1 is L2` predicate is a stronger test that returns true only if `L1` and `L2` are different names for the same object.

```
>>> listcopy2 = list[:]
>>> listcopy2 == list
1
>>> listcopy2 is list
0
>>> listref is list
1
```

N O T E

Lists may contain other lists or dictionaries or tuples, and the substructures may in turn contain other substructures. For example, the following function orders a file such as

```
this : line : 4
that : line : 7
etcetera: 0
```

whose lines end in `:integer` by the integer values at the end of the line, writing the result to an output file.

```
import string
def reorder(infilename, outfilename):
    f = open(infilename, "r")
    text = f.read()
    f.close()
    lines = string.splitfields(text, "\n") # break on newline
    list = []
    for line in lines:
        split = string.splitfields(line, ":")
        int = string.atoi( string.strip(split[-1]) )
        list.append( (int, line + "\n") ) # put newline back.
```

```
        list.sort()
        f = open(outfilename, "w")
        try:
            for (n, line) in list:
                f.write(line)
        finally:
            f.close()
```

The `list` constructed by `reorder` contains tuples. Other examples may construct lists containing other lists, or modules, or classes, or any other Python object.

Truth Values

Lists may contain arbitrary sequences of elements. For example, we may use a heterogeneous list containing many different types of objects to see which of these objects tests true and which tests false when they are used as an `if` condition:

```
>>> def tester(object):
...     if object:
...         print `object`, "tests true"
...     else:
...         print `object`, "tests false"
...
>>> list_of_objects = [
...     None, 0, 1, [], (), "", [[]], [1], ["this", 1, "too"],
...     tester]
>>> list_of_objects.append("oh, and by the way this too")
>>> for object in list_of_objects:
...     tester(object)
...
None tests false
0 tests false
1 tests true
[] tests false
() tests false
'' tests false
[[]] tests true
[1] tests true
['this', 1, 'too'] tests true
<function tester at 73bd0> tests true
'oh, and by the way this too' tests true
```

It is often convenient to use the list repetition notation $L * i$, where L is a list and i is an integer, to create a list of a specific size whose values will be filled in later.

```
>>> initial_list = [ None ] * 6
>>> initial_list
[None, None, None, None, None, None]
>>> initial_list[3] = "first fill in"
>>> initial_list[5] = "second"
>>> initial_list[2] = "third"
>>> initial_list[0] = "fourth"
>>> initial_list[1] = "fifth"
>>> initial_list[4] = "sixth"
>>> initial_list
['fourth', 'fifth', 'third', 'first fill in', 'sixth', 'second']
```

Often it is more convenient to use list.insert and list.append to construct lists. See the discussion of intrinsic methods for lists in the next chapter.

Using Filter and Other Aggregate Functions

Lists have a number of associated aggregate operations. The filter function selects the elements of a sequence that satisfy a test. If the default value of None is provided in place of the test function, the filter function simply produces the elements that have "true" values according to Python's default interpretation:

```
>>> filter(None, list_of_objects)
[1, [[]], [1], ['this', 1, 'too'], <function tester at 73bd0>,
'oh, and by the way this too']
```

If a test function is provided, then the result of the test function when applied to each element determines whether the element appears in the filter result. For example, using the is_false function below we may filter out the elements that test false.

```
>>> def is_false(x):
...     return not x
...
>>> is_false("")
1
>>> is_false("non-empty string")
0
>>> filter(is_false, list_of_objects)
[None, 0, [], (), '']
```

With a little cleverness, we can do more interesting filtering. For example, there are a number of standard sequence objects, all of which support slicing.

```
>>> (x, y, z) = ("this", (1,2,3), [])
>>> for seq in (x, y, z):
...     print `seq[0:0]`,
...
'' () []
```

Extensions may add additional sequence objects (in fact, we implement an additional one later in this book). All sequence objects support slicing, however, and all nonsequence objects do not support slicing.

```
>>> x = 67
>>> print x[0:0]
Traceback (innermost last):
  File "<stdin>", line 1, in ?
TypeError: only sequences can be sliced
```

Hence by converting an error into a false value, we can create the following function, which tests to see if an object is a sequence.

```
>>> def is_sequence(object):
...     try:
...         test = object[0:0] # raises an error on non-sequence object
...     except:
...         return 0 # it must not be a sequence
...     else:
...         return 1 # no error: it's a sequence
...
>>> is_sequence( 5 )
0
>>> is_sequence( [1] )
1
>>> filter(is_sequence, list_of_objects)
[[], (), '', [[]], [1], ['this', 1, 'too'], 'oh, and by the way this too']
>>> def not_sequence(object):
...     return not is_sequence(object)
...
>>> filter(not_sequence, list_of_objects)
[None, 0, 1, <function tester at 73bd0>]
```

Sorting Lists

One of the most useful things you can do with a list is sort its elements.

```
>>> x = [1, 1, 1, 0, 0, 0, 0, 0, 0, 1, 0]
>>> x.sort()
>>> x
[0, 0, 0, 0, 0, 0, 0, 1, 1, 1, 1]
>>> listcopy
['here', 'was', 'a', 'list', 'that', 'once', 'was', 'a', 'string']
>>> listcopy.sort()
>>> listcopy
['a', 'a', 'here', 'list', 'once', 'string', 'that', 'was', 'was']
>>> lengths = map(len, listcopy)
>>> lengths
[1, 1, 4, 4, 4, 6, 4, 3, 3]
>>> lengths.sort()
>>> lengths
[1, 1, 3, 3, 4, 4, 4, 4, 6]
```

In the last application of sort, we sorted the list of lengths from the list listcopy, but in the process forgot which length corresponds to which string. This is not good, this is not right. Let's fix it.

To sort the strings along with their lists, we may pair the length with each string, as follows (and lets mix up the list using reverse, just for fun too…):

```
>>> def lenpairing(sequence):
...     return ( len(sequence), sequence )
...
>>> listcopy.reverse()
>>> listcopy
['was', 'was', 'that', 'string', 'once', 'list', 'here', 'a', 'a']
>>> lenpairing("this one")
(8, 'this one')
>>> lps = map(lenpairing, listcopy)
>>> lps
[(3, 'was'), (3, 'was'), (4, 'that'), (6, 'string'), (4, 'once'),
 (4, 'list'), (4, 'here'), (1, 'a'), (1, 'a')]
>>> lps.sort()
>>> lps
[(1, 'a'), (1, 'a'), (3, 'was'), (3, 'was'), (4, 'here'),
 (4, 'list'), (4, 'once'), (4, 'that'), (6, 'string')]
```

Now we have the strings sorted in increasing order by their lengths. If we are only interested in the strings themselves, we may dispose of the lengths by mapping a "projection function" item1 over lps:

```
>>> def item1(sequence):
...     return sequence[1]
...
>>> item1( [0,6,7] )
6
>>> item1( (3, 'was') )
'was'
>>> map(item1, lps)
['a', 'a', 'was', 'was', 'here', 'list', 'once', 'that', 'string']
>>>
```

This returns a list of the strings sorted in increasing order by length (with the lengths discarded).

Of course, lists have a number of features we have not described, but at this point we suppose you have a general feel for what they are about, and we proceed to have more fun with dictionaries, which are even more interesting.

Playing with Dictionaries

Python dictionaries are highly efficient data structures—so much so that a retrieval from a dictionary containing tens of thousands of elements is not noticeably slower than retrieval from a dictionary containing just two.

Dictionaries associate constant (immutable) Python objects with arbitrary other Python objects. For example, we may associate name strings to phone numbers (represented as integers) by declaring the following:

```
>>> nametophone = { "aaron":9492726, "jim":6679876, "guido":6623468 }
>>> nametophone
{'guido': 6623468, 'aaron': 9492726, 'jim': 6679876}
```

Here we created a dictionary that maps strings to numbers using the "literal dictionary notation:"

```
{ value1 : key1 , value2 : key2 , value3 : key3 , value4 : key4 }
```

Dictionaries of arbitrary size may be created in Python interactive sessions, or within programs using this notation. After creating the dictionary, we asked the interpreter to print the representation for the object named by the variable nametophone, namely the dictionary we just declared. Note that the printed representation for the dictionary lists the entries in a different order than in the assignment because dictionaries are unordered "sets" of pairs, and the implementation reserves the right to print out the content in any order it pleases (so there!). Although we used the previous literal notation, we could just as well have created the dictionary in a piecemeal fashion by declaring the associations using the indexing assignment notation.

```
>>> nametophone = {}
>>> ntp = nametophone
>>> nametophone[ "aaron" ] = 9492726
>>> ntp[ "jim" ] = 6679876
>>> ntp["guido"] = 6623468
>>> nametophone
{'guido': 6623468, 'aaron': 9492726, 'jim': 6679876}
>>> ntp
{'guido': 6623468, 'aaron': 9492726, 'jim': 6679876}
```

It is not uncommon for Python programs to build dictionaries containing tens of thousands of elements like this, one association at a time.

NOTE   The nametophone variable and the ntp variable created above both share a reference to the same dictionary—so changes to one will show up in the other.

Of course, it would not be of much use to create associations in dictionaries without being able to get them back out again. The simplest way to access data from a dictionary is to retrieve the value associated with a key, using the index expression notation

```
>>> nametophone["jim"]
6679876
```

Here the expression nametophone["jim"] instructs the interpreter to attempt to retrieve the value associated with the string "jim" from the dictionary associated with the variable nametophone. Because there was an entry for jim the interpreter printed the associated value.

Testing for Keys

Python will raise a `KeyError` in an attempt to retrieve a value for a key that is absent from a dictionary.

```
>>> nametophone["mark"]
Traceback (innermost last):
  File "<stdin>", line 1, in ?
KeyError: mark
```

One way to allow for the possibility that a key may be absent is to "catch" the error, using a `try/except` construct.

```
>>> for name in ["aaron", "mark"]:
...     try:
...         p = nametophone[name]
...     except:
...         print name, "not found"
...     else:
...         print name, ":", p
...
aaron : 9492726
mark not found
```

NOTE

This example introduces the `else` clause in a `try ... except ...` statement. Using an `else` clause in a `try` statement allows a program to specify actions that should follow only when an operation does not raise an exception. The following program

```
try:
    dubious()
except:
    error_case()
else:
    no_error_case()
```

prevents the `except` clause from catching exceptions raised in `no_error_case()` whereas in

```
try:
    dubious()
    no_error_case()
```

```
        except:
            error_case()
```

the `except` clause will catch exceptions raised by either `dubious()` or `no_error_case()`.

Another way to allow for missing keys is to test for the existence of the key before the retrieval using the `has_key` dictionary method.

```
>>>
>>> for name in ["mark", "aaron"]:
...     if nametophone.has_key(name):
...         print name, nametophone[name]
...     else:
...         print name, "not found"
...
mark not found
aaron 9492726
>>> nametophone.has_key("guido")
1
>>> nametophone.has_key("susan")
0
```

In general the `dict.has_key(value)` method returns 1 (which tests true) if the key is present in the dictionary and otherwise returns 0 (false) in all other situations. This method only tests for `keys` (left-hand members) in the table, not for `values` (right-hand members).

```
>>> nametophone.has_key(6623468)
0
```

Converting Dictionaries to Lists

The dictionary methods `keys`, `values`, and `items` dump out the left-hand members, right-hand members, or pairs of a dictionary, respectively, into a list representation.

```
>>> nametophone.keys()
['guido', 'aaron', 'jim']
>>> nametophone.values()
[6623468, 9492726, 6679876]
```

```
>>> nametophone.items()
[('guido', 6623468), ('aaron', 9492726), ('jim', 6679876)]
```

The main reason to dump the contents of a dictionary as a list is to iterate through the contents of the dictionary, for example, to print a report.

Printing a Simple Report

The following sequence of statements prints a simple report based on the contents of the dictionary nametophone.

```
>>> names = nametophone.keys()
>>> names.sort()
>>> for name in names:
...     print name, "at phone", nametophone[name]
...
aaron at phone 9492726
guido at phone 6623468
jim at phone 6679876
```

In view of the "unordered" nature of dictionaries, we use the list method sort to sort the keys of the dictionary, thus guaranteeing the names are printed in alphabetical order. Then we used a for loop to iterate through the sorted list of names, utilizing the nametophone[name] item retrieval operation to extract the phone number associated with each name in turn.

Dictionaries in Dictionaries

Dictionaries can be included in other data structures, such as lists or other dictionaries. The following iteration uses the raw_input built-in function to populate a dictionary whose keys are tuples of (firstname, lastname) pairs and whose values are dictionaries. The interaction after the last "..." prompt shows the prompts given by the raw input function (for example, "first name: ") followed by the input typed from the terminal (for example, "aaron").

```
>>> info = {}
>>> while 1:
...     fn = raw_input("first name: ")
...     if fn == ".":
...         break
...     ln = raw_input("last name: ")
```

```
...     ph = raw_input("phone: ")
...     st = raw_input("street: ")
...     ctyst = raw_input("city and state: ")
...     key = ( fn, ln )
...     data = { "fn": fn, "ln": ln, "ph": ph, "st": st, "ctyst": ctyst }
...     info[key] = data
...
first name: aaron
last name: watters
phone: 9492726
street: 123 main str
city and state: Holmdel, NJ
first name: guido
last name: van rossum
phone: 6623468
street: 626 w. 6th str
city and state: corvallis OR
first name: jim
last name: ahlstrom
phone: 6679876
street: 554 central ave
city and state: newark, nj
first name: .
```

The `if` statement in the while loop above

```
...     if fn == ".":
...         break
```

breaks out of the loop when the user enters a single dot in response to the `first name` prompt. The constructions

```
...     key = ( fn, ln )
...     data = { "fn": fn, "ln": ln, "ph": ph, "st": st, "ctyst": ctyst }
```

build a key for entry into the `info` dictionary (a two-tuple containing the first and last name) and a dictionary `data` for use as the value associated with the tuple. Finally

```
...     info[key] = data
```

associates the key with the data in the dictionary `info`.

We now have a moderately interesting data structure to play with —a dictionary mapping `name` tuples to `datum` dictionaries—emulating a simple table of personal information. It's even easier to dump out the information from the structure than it is to populate it.

```
>>> for (x,y) in info.items():
...     print x
...     for (z,w) in y.items():
...         print " ", z, " --> ", w
...
('aaron', 'watters')
   ln  -->  watters
   st  -->  123 main str
   fn  -->  aaron
   ctyst  -->  Holmdel, NJ
   ph  -->  9492726
('guido', 'van rossum')
   ln  -->  van rossum
   st  -->  626 w. 6th str
   fn  -->  guido
   ctyst  -->  corvallis OR
   ph  -->  6623468
('jim', 'ahlstrom')
   ln  -->  ahlstrom
   st  -->  554 central ave
   fn  -->  jim
   ctyst  -->  newark, nj
   ph  -->  6679876
```

Here the first `for` loop associates `x` and `y` with the key/value pairs from the info) dictionary (in arbitrary order). Within that assignment the second "nested" for loop in turn iterates through the data dictionary `y`.

For fun, try this:

```
>>> import string
>>> for ((fn, ln), datum) in info.items():
...     print fn, ln
...     print " " + string.joinfields( map(str, datum.items()), "\n ")
...
```

How does it work?

If we are only interested in the name and phone, we can produce a specialized report containing just this information. While we're at it, let's format the name more nicely by breaking the first and last name out of the tuple that we put them in:

```
>>> info.keys()
[('aaron', 'watters'), ('guido', 'van rossum'), ('jim', 'ahlstrom')]
>>>
>>> for x in info.keys():
...     data = info[x]
...     ( fn, ln ) = x
...     print fn, ln, data["ph"]
...
aaron watters 9492726
guido van rossum 6623468
jim ahlstrom 6679876
```

We can also create an index that maps phone numbers to the data records in place of names, by iterating over the values of the info dictionary to build a phoneindex:

```
>>> phoneindex = {}
>>> for data in info.values():
...     phoneindex[ data["ph"] ] = data
...
>>> phoneindex # output hand edited...
{'6623468': {'ln': 'van rossum',
             'st': '626 w. 6th str',
             'fn': 'guido',
             'ctyst': 'corvallis OR',
             'ph': '6623468'},
 '6679876': {'ln': 'ahlstrom',
             'st': '554 central ave',
             'fn': 'jim',
             'ctyst': 'newark, nj',
             'ph': '6679876'},
 '9492726': {'ln': 'watters',
             'st': '123 main str',
             'fn': 'aaron',
             'ctyst': 'Holmdel, NJ',
             'ph': '9492726'}}
```

NOTE

Dictionaries are mutable types that may be shared, and changes to the structure of a shared dictionary will affect all structures that refer to the dictionary. For example, the values in the dictionary `info` and the values in the dictionary `phoneindex` are the same collection of dictionaries indexed by different key sets. Thus, if we convert all the phone numbers in `info` to integer values in place of string values (using `string.atoi`) the change also shows up in the values for `phoneindex`:

```
>>> import string
>>> for data in info.values():
...     phonestring = data ["ph"]
...     data["ph"] = string.atoi(phonestring)
...
>>> info[ ("aaron", "watters") ] [ "ph" ]
9492726
>>> phoneindex["9492726"]["ph"]
9492726
```

We can use the `is` predicate to demonstrate that the `info` entry for (`"aaron"`, `"watters"`) is the same object as the `phoneindex` entry for `"9492726"`.

```
>>> info[ ("aaron", "watters") ] is phoneindex["9492726"]
1
```

Let's conclude our experimentation with dictionaries by developing a function that allows us to extract the phone numbers from the `info` dictionary nicely. This is our first cut:

```
>>> def phone_number( namestring ):
...     namelist = string.split(namestring)
...     nametuple = tuple(namelist)
...     try:
...         data = info[ nametuple ]
...     except KeyError:
...         return namestring + " not present in database"
...     return data["ph"]
...
>>> phone_number("   aaron   watters   ")
9492726
>>> phone_number("Aaron Watters")
'Aaron Watters not present in database'
```

Note that although this function correctly ignores whitespace (via `string.split`), it does not permit the `namestring` to include any upper-case letters. Let's fix that by adding `string.lower`. It also can't find `guido van rossum`, so let's fix that too.

```
>>> def phone_number( namestring ):
...     namestring = string.lower(namestring)
...     namelist = string.split(namestring)
...     nametuple = (namelist[0], string.join(namelist[1:]))
...     try:
...         data = info[ nametuple ]
...     except KeyError:
...         return namestring + " not present in database"
...     return data["ph"]
...
>>> phone_number("   AAroN WATters   ")
9492726
>>> phone_number("Paul Johnson")
'paul johnson not present in database'
```

An Abstract Data Type: Priority Queues

Strings and lists and dictionaries are all well and good, but the real fun is to be had in the use of Python's object-oriented features. By defining new classes that create instances of different kinds, the programmer can pretend that they have added new basic features to the Python language.

For example, Python has no structure that immediately serves as a classical priority queue—an object that allows arbitrary inserts and retrieves the largest object of those inserted, with the optional ability to delete the largest. Here the largest element presumably represents the element with the highest priority that the program using the priority queue must deal with first.

We may define a very simple, useful, and generic priority queue implementation as follows:

```
class PQ0:
    """Very simple priority queue using an unordered list."""
    def __init__(self, compare = cmp):
```

```
        if compare != cmp:
            raise TypeError, "only standard cmp is supported for PQ0"
        self.data = []

    def empty(self):
        return self.data == []

    def addelt(self, priority, elt):
        self.data.append( (priority, elt) )
        return len(self.data)

    def largestp(self):
        return max( self.data )

    def poplargest(self):
        (priority, elt) = item = self.largestp()
        self.data.remove(item)
        return elt
```

Reading the definition from top to bottom: This priority queue implementation stores the elements of the queue in a list `self.data` for all instances. The queue is empty if the `self.data` list is empty. To add an element to the queue, we place the priority of the element and the element itself on the end of `self.data`, and to find the largest element on the queue we use the built-in `max` function to scan the list for the maximum priority. To retrieve and eliminate the element with the largest priority from the list, we retrieve the element and then remove it from `self.data`.

We may use this object implementation to archive strings prioritized by length as follows:

```
>>> import string
>>> quote = "Alas poor Yorick, I knew him, Horatio"
>>> words = string.split(quote)
>>> Q = PQ0()
>>> for w in words:
...     Q.addelt( len(w), w )
...
>>> while not Q.empty():
...     print Q.poplargest(),
...
Yorick, Horatio poor knew him, Alas I
```

Now for small priority queues with, say, only 200 elements and simple integer priorities, this implementation may be perfectly adequate. Eventually, however, the business of using a linear scan to find the largest priority will become oppressive, and a smarter (and more complex) implementation will be in order. The simple implementation also has one disadvantage you just can't avoid: It's boring.

A Fancier Priority Queue

Let's appeal to classical computer science to come up with a priority queue that will work well no matter how large it grows. Truthfully, of course, we have already implemented the beast, so we can explain how this rather subtle structure works by fiddling with it interactively, we hope. Frankly the current authors had trouble understanding this beautiful data structure the first time we encountered it, so readers should not be discouraged if they find the ensuing difficult.

A classical "heap based" priority queue represents a balanced binary tree where each element is larger than all of its descendants.

```
>>> from pq2 import PQueue
>>> Q = PQueue()
>>> for w in words:
...     Q.addelt(len(w), w)
...
>>> Q.displaytree()
 (7, 'Yorick,') at 1
    (4, 'knew') at 2
       (1, 'I') at 4
       (4, 'Alas') at 5
    (7, 'Horatio') at 3
       (4, 'him,') at 6
       (4, 'poor') at 7
```

Here the `displaytree` method printed out each node of the tree followed by its descendants at deeper levels of indentation, and we see that each member of the tree has a priority larger (or the same) as both children beneath it and because this property is uniform across the entire structure, this implies that each element of the tree has a priority at or greater than all of its descendants. Reformatting the tree graphically we have:

```
               ┌I
        ┌knew─┤
        │      └Alas
Yorick─┤
        │         ┌ him,
        └Horatio─┤
                  └ poor
```

To get and remove the largest element from the tree we must remove the top of the tree and swap one of the lower elements that has no descendants up to the top position. The tree may then no longer have the heap property, because the top element may have a smaller priority than one or both of its children, so to restore the heap property the new top must be swapped down the tree with its highest-priority child until the highest-priority child has a lower priority. Let's see how it works in practice:

```
>>> Q.poplargest()
'Yorick,'
>>> Q.displaytree()
 (7, 'Horatio') at 1
    (4, 'knew') at 2
        (1, 'I') at 4
        (4, 'Alas') at 5
    (4, 'poor') at 3
        (4, 'him,') at 6
```

Here we see the tree after all the exchanges have taken place. In this case the 'poor' element was chosen to serve as the new top element, and it was then exchanged with 'Horatio' before it found a new position where the heap property was restored. All other elements of the heap remained in their existing positions.

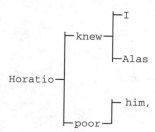

```
                ┌I
         ┌knew─┤
         │      └Alas
Horatio─┤
         │         ┌ him,
         └poor────┤
```

Now, to add a new element to the heap, we insert the element at an available leaf position. At this point, the element may violate the heap property because it may have a higher priority than its parent. No problem! To restore the heap property, exchange the element with its parent until the next parent has a higher priority. Let's look at that operation too:

```
>>> Q.addelt(4, "once")
7
>>> Q.displaytree()
  (7, 'Horatio') at 1
    (4, 'knew') at 2
      (1, 'I') at 4
      (4, 'Alas') at 5
    (4, 'poor') at 3
      (4, 'him,') at 6
      (4, 'once') at 7
```

Whoops! In that case no exchanges were necessary, when once was inserted beneath poor: We try again:

```
>>> Q.addelt(5, "marry")
2
>>> Q.displaytree()
  (7, 'Horatio') at 1
    (5, 'marry') at 2
      (4, 'knew') at 4
        (1, 'I') at 8
      (4, 'Alas') at 5
    (4, 'poor') at 3
      (4, 'him,') at 6
      (4, 'once') at 7
```

In this case, the new element "marry" was inserted beneath "I" and had to be exchanged with "I" and then "knew" before the heap property was restored.

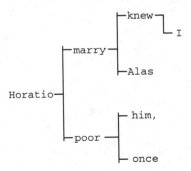

Now, by judiciously picking leaf nodes that keep the tree dense, this structure can insert and delete elements very efficiently, even when it grows very large. For more details, please consult a good book on data structures and algorithms. In order to keep the tree dense, we will use another standard computer science trick that allows us to embed a dense tree in a dense array (or a list, in Python terminology).

```
>>> Q.data
[None, (7, 'Horatio'), (5, 'marry'), (4, 'poor'), (4, 'knew'),
    (4, 'Alas'), (4, 'him,'), (4, 'once'), (1, 'I'),
    None, None, None, None, None, None, None]
```

Here we see the `(priority, item)` pairs embedded in a list where the top of this tree is at index 1 and every node at index i has its parent at index i/2 (using integer division) and its children at indices i*2 and i*2+1, respectively. The index 0 is never used, and some unused indices (filled with None) are left at the end of the list for future inserts.

Alright. Now let's implement this classical priority queue in Python:

```python
class PQueue:

    def __init__(self, comparison = cmp):
        self.cmp = comparison
        self.data = [None] * 8 # presize for 8 elements
        # first element is always empty, first used is 1, no data yet
        self.free = 1

    def empty(self):
        return self.free == 1

    def addelt(self, priority, elt):
        index = self.free
        try:
            self.data[ index ] = (priority, elt)
        except IndexError:
            # self.data is too small, double its size
            length = len( self.data )
            newdata = [ None ] * (2 * length)
            # store the old values
            newdata[:length] = self.data
            self.data = newdata
            # now there ought to be room!
            self.data[ index ] = (priority, elt)
```

```
        self.free = index + 1
        return self._checkposition(index)
```

The PQueue implementation uses a list to hold the elements and their priorities self.data and an index into the end of the list self.free, which always points to the next available index. In the name of generality, the implementation also allows possible alternative comparison functions (so the queue might, for example, sort the priorities from least to largest). The addelt insert operation simply places an element at the end of the array (which might require making the array bigger if there is no more space)—the end of the array is always a leaf position in our embedded tree representation, and the position must be checked for the heap property, and possibly swapped, using the _checkposition method.

Let's look at some more methods in the PQueue implementation.

```
#class PQueue continued...
    def poplargest(self):
        if self.free < 2:
            raise IndexError, "priority queue is empty"
        (priority, largest) = self.data[1]
        self._removeentry(1)
        return largest

    def _removeentry(self, index):
        # restructure the "tree" if other elements remain
        free = self.free
        data = self.data
        last = free - 1
        if last > index:
            data[index] = data[last]
            data[last] = None
            self.free = last
            self._checkposition(index)
        else:
            data[index] = None
            self.free = last

    def largestp(self):
        return self.data[1]
```

The largest entry is always obtained from the heap by simply extracting the entry at self.data[1]. To remove the entry as well, the _removeentry method exchanges the leaf at index `self.free - 1` with the first position and then uses good old `_checkposition` to check the heap property and possibly restore that property via swapping.

Now let's look at the meat of the implementation: the `_checkposition` method and some utility methods it uses.

```
def _parents(self, index):
    if index<2: return ()
    else: return (index/2,)


def _children(self, index):
    a = index * 2
    b = a + 1
    free = self.free
    if a<free:
        if b<free:
            return (a,b)
        else:
            return (a,)
    else:
        return ()


def _checkposition(self, index):
    data = self.data
    comparison = self.cmp
    thisitem = data[index]
    for parent in self._parents(index):
        parentitem = data[parent]
        if comparison(parentitem, thisitem)<=0:
            # parent is smaller: swap, check, return
            (data[parent], data[index]) = (thisitem, parentitem)
            return self._checkposition(parent)
    # find the highest priority child:
    children = self._children(index)
    try:
        thechild = children[0]
    except IndexError:
        pass # no children, nothing to check!
    else:
        # make sure this one has the highest priority
        childitem = data[thechild]
        for child in children[1:]:
            if comparison(data[child], childitem)>0:
                thechild = child
```

```
            childitem = data[thechild]
        # swap, if needed.
        if comparison(childitem, thisitem)>0:
            (data[thechild], data[index]) = (thisitem, childitem)
            return self._checkposition(thechild)
    return index # return the final position
```

Well, okay, perhaps we've been overly clever here, but we did manage with relatively few special cases. The _parents and _children methods return sequences of indices for the parents and children for an index in the embedded tree—in the case of _children it may return one, two, or zero of them. The _checkposition method uses these values to compare the entry at a given position with its parent (if it has one) and its children (if there are any) and swapping the positions in the event that a violation of the heap property is detected.

NOTE   In the naming of _parents and _children, we use a convention sometimes seen in Python programs of using an underscore to indicate that the method is internal to the object implementation. The author of an external module that refers to these methods should understand that they are not part of the external interface for the object instance, and that using these methods directly is probably a mistake. Python does not (yet) enforce information hiding in object implementations, but programmers can indicate which methods are generally available and which methods are only for internal use by adopting naming schemes.

There is only one more method for the PQueue class, the debug dumper that allowed us to examine the state of the queue:

```
#class PQueue continued...
    def displaytree(self, index=1, indentlevel=0):
        print "  "*indentlevel, self.data[index], "at", index
        for child in self._children(index):
            self.displaytree(child, indentlevel+1)
```

Okay. In the file pq2.py, we get even fancier and define some mixins and other fancy stuff that give us some really fancy priority queue implementations. But for this presentation we stop here.

By now you should be bored with watching us play with Python. Go make some toys yourself and have fun!

CHAPTER FOUR

INTRINSIC OPERATIONS FOR COMMON TYPES

The only way to interact with Python objects is via intrinsic operations or functions. There is no way to, for example, get a pointer to an object and poke around or modify in its internal representation, like you can do in C or C++ or most other compiled languages (using one trick or another). Thus, via intrinsic operations a Python object defines the "official" ways that the programmer may interact with the object in a disciplined manner, and prevents the programmer from attempting circumlocutions that experience suggests are usually a very bad mistake.

This section describes the intrinsic operations and functions for interacting with objects of various types that are part of the standard Python "core"— omitting various other methods provided in other modules (such as the indispensable `string` module discussed earlier). These operations are either intrinsic to the object itself (such as `list.append`) or are provided via the standard python built-in names (such as `apply`).

Many of the operations not described in great detail here are discussed in a more discursive manner in the "Playing" chapter, and some of the others are not of great importance within the confines of this book.

Standard built-in intrinsic names are invoked using the "function call" notation, for example:

```
>>> max("sometime", "later", "getting", "the", "words", "wrong",
...     "wasting", "the", "meaning", "losing", "the", "rhyme")
'wrong'
```

Operations that are built into an object may either have an explicit "attribute" representation, such as the sort method of a list object:

```
>>> list = [22, 40, 0, 30, 10, -8, 0]
>>> list.sort()
>>> list
[-8, 0, 0, 10, 22, 30, 40]
```

Or the operation may be implicitly determined via a Python expression construct, such as the "string catenation" operation:

```
>>> fortune_cookie = "You will have exciting business opportunities"
>>> joke_version = fortune_cookie + ", in bed"
>>> joke_version
'You will have exciting business opportunities, in bed'
```

Here the interpretation of the "plus" operator for strings is automagically interpreted by Python to represent string catenation.

In some cases, an operation for an object may be invoked in the evaluation of a Python statement which is not also an expression, for example, in

```
>>> list = range(0, 50, 5)
>>> list
[0, 5, 10, 15, 20, 25, 30, 35, 40, 45]
>>> list[3:6] = []
>>> list
[0, 5, 10, 30, 35, 40, 45]
```

The slice assignment notation list[3:6] = [] automagically invokes the slice assignment operation associated with the list object (in this case, removing items indexed from 3 to 5 from the list).

Generic Intrinsic Operations

There are a number of built-in operations which may be used in conjunction with some or all Python objects.

cmp(X, Y) Standard Order Comparison

Returns the comparison indicator for X and Y, namely zero if the X and Y are equivalent, an integer greater than zero if X is "greater than" Y, or a number smaller than zero if X is "smaller than" Y. The cmp(X,Y) function is used to determine ordinal truth valued comparisons in Python. In other words, Python makes the following interpretations:

Expression	Interpretation
X > Y	cmp(X, Y) is larger than zero.
X >= Y	cmp(X, Y) is not smaller than zero.
X != Y	cmp(X, Y) is not zero.
X <> Y	same as X != Y (but this notation is discouraged).
X == Y	cmp(X, Y) is zero
X < Y	cmp(X, Y) is smaller than zero.
X <= Y	cmp(X, Y) is not greater than zero.

Furthermore the cmp function is used (by default) in the execution of the list.sort() method, as we shall see.

For numeric X and Y, cmp(X,Y) performs the normal "number line" comparison, regardless of the whether X and Y are of different types:

```
>>> cmp(1e20, 1298376235817654123L)
1
>>> cmp(1.6e5, 2675341256431654L)
-1
>>> cmp(123, 123L), cmp(1.23e2, 123), cmp(123L, 1.23e2)
(0, 0, 0)
>>> cmp(123, 124L), cmp(1.23e2, 124), cmp(123L, 1.24e2)
(-1, -1, -1)
```

If X and Y are strings, then `cmp(X,Y)` conforms to the lexographic ordering of the strings.

```
>>> cmp("frogs", "pigs")
-10
>>> cmp("airplane", "aardvark")
8
>>> cmp("hype", "hyperbole")
-1
```

Roughly speaking the default string ordering is the same ordering used in English dictionaries for ordering words represented in lowercase letters.

However, all uppercase letters appear before lowercase letters in the ordering imposed by the ASCII sequence:

```
>>> cmp("Z", "a")
-7
```

So, if you wish to emulate the English dictionary ordering for words with the help of `cmp(X,Y)`, make sure the words X and Y are in the same case first (hint: use the `upper` or `lower` functions from the standard `string` module).

The ordering for lists is analogous to the ordering for strings, except the `cmp` function is called recursively for each member of the list.

```
>>> cmp([1, 2, 3], [1, 2,3 , -5])
-1
>>> cmp([10], [1,2,3])
1
>>> cmp(["hello", 5], ["goodbye", 6])
1
```

Thus, if X and Y are lists, then X is equivalent to Y if X and Y contain equivalent elements (in the same order); otherwise Y is less than X if Y is a prefix of X; otherwise X is greater than Y if, scanning from left to right we have X[i] > Y[i] at the first point where the list elements are not equivalent. Implemented in Python we have:

```
def list_cmp(X, Y):
    if type(X) != ListType or type(Y) != ListType:
        raise "Naughty Naughty!!"
    length = max( len(X), len(Y) )
```

```
for i in range(length):
    try:
        Xi = X[i]
    except IndexError:
        return -1 # X is prefix of Y
    try:
        Yi = Y[i]
    except IndexError:
        return 1  # Y is prefix of X
    cmpXiYi = cmp(Xi, Yi)
    if cmpXiYi != 0:
        return cmpXiYi # first differing pair makes the decision!
else:
    return 0 # if we got to the end without returning, they are same.
```

Comparisons between tuples work the same as comparisons between lists—cmp(X, Y) once again conforms to lexicographic ordering if X and Y are both tuples, and similarly if X and Y are both XRange objects.

hash(X) The Built-In Hash Function

The hash function is defined for any immutable type. It is useful in constructing hash-based data structures; for example, the dictionary type uses the hash function inside the bowels of Python. The primary properties of the hash function is that hash(X) returns an integer, and if X == Y, then hash(X) == hash(Y) (but the converse is not guaranteed).

```
>>> hash("a string")
81670916
>>> hash(78.8)
1717986996
>>> hash(7.88e1)
1717986996
>>> hash( ("turn left, drive", 6, "miles") )
104246182
```

The hash(X) function is only defined for immutable objects X. As we have mentioned, lists, dictionaries, and tuples that contain mutables are considered mutable objects. The hash function will also fail for instances of classes which have a __cmp__ method defined, but no __hash__ method defined.

```
>>> hash([1,5,9])
Traceback (innermost last):
```

```
    File "", line 1, in ?
TypeError: unhashable type
```

As demonstrated above, when the hash function fails it raises a `TypeError`.

You can alter the default behavior of the hash function on an instance of a class by providing a __hash__ magic method.

`X is Y` Identity Test

The truth-valued expression `X is Y` returns true (1) if and only if X and Y are the same object, and return false (0) whenever X and Y are different objects, even if they are equal.

`max( ... ), min( ... )` Maximum and Minimum Functions

The `max()` and `min()` functions return the maximum and minimum of the arguments in their calling sequence, respectively (using the standard ordering defined by the `cmp(X, Y)` function described above).

```
>>> max(1,3,9,2)
9
>>> min(6,7,1,2)
1
>>> max( (5, 8, 9, 73, -90, 69) )
73
>>> list = ["do", "be", "doo", "be", "dowop", "do", "dobee", "dooo"]
>>> min(list), max(list)
('be', 'dowop')
>>> max("dowop")
'w'
>>> min( "do", "be", "doo", "be", "dowop", "do", "dobee", "dooo" )
'be'
```

As seen above there are two calling sequences for max and min: When applied to one argument, the argument must be a sequence (such as a tuple or a list or a string) and the value returned is the minimum or maximum of the elements in the sequence; or alternatively when applied to more than one argument, then the result returned is the maximum or minimum of the arguments.

repr(X), `X`
Standard String Representation

The repr(X) function attempts to convert the value of X to a string representation that Python could read back in and interpret as an equivalent value.

```
>>> repr('string')
"'string'"
>>> repr(1020e9)
'1.02e+12'
>>> repr(range(4))
'[0, 1, 2, 3]'
>>> file = open("junk", "r")
>>> repr(file)
"<open file 'junk', mode 'r' at 11d578>"
```

In the case of files above, there is no reasonable way to print out a file value in such a way that it could be read back in (trust us), so Python "punts" and just returns a string that lists some possibly useful information about the object.

As a convenience, Python also provides a special notation that is equivalent to repr(X), namely `X`.

str(X)
Printing String Representation

The str(X) function is similar to the repr(X) function—both convert X to a string representation—but it doesn't work so hard trying to make a string that can be read back in as an equivalent value.

```
>>> str(34*4.5 - 99.1)
'53.9'
>>> str( "a string" )
'a string'
```

Note that the final value is not bracketed by extra quotes, because `str(X)` returns X if X is a string!

`type(X)`
Retrieve the Type Object of an Object

We have already seen the `type(X)` function. It returns the type object associated with X.

"Hidden" Generic Intrinsic Operations

There are also operations associated with Python objects that the programmer normally cannot access directly.

Truth-Valued Interpretation

Every Python object has a default interpretation as a truth value. Hence, for any value X the if statement

```
if X:
    do_one_thing()
else:
    do_the_other_thing()
```

will either do one thing (if X is interpreted as true) or the other thing (if X is interpreted as false). Other places where truth interpretations are important are in while statements, in elif clauses of if statements and in expressions involving the truth operators and, or, and not.

Most objects are interpreted by Python to mean "true." The exceptions are: None; any sequence with no elements; any numeric value that is equivalent to zero; an empty dictionary; and sometimes class instances that have a __nonzero__ method defined. Thus, the following are all interpreted as false:

```
None  []  ()  {}  xrange(0)  0   0.0   0.0e-12  0L
```

Just about everything else is interpreted as a "true" value. The preferred values for representing true and false directly in Python source code (say, as a flag, or as a returned value to a function) are 0 or None for false and 1 for true, respectively.

Deletion

Once the last reference to an object is destroyed, Python destroys the object. With a few exceptions, this normally means that the space allotted to that object is released for future use, and any references held by the object are destroyed. For example:

```
>>> T = (2,3,5,7,11)
>>> do_something_with(T)
>>> T = None # We're done with T, discard it.
```

In the last statement, the assignment of T to None may destroy the last reference to the tuple we created in the first assignment (unless the intermediate function squirreled away a reference to T someplace). If the assignment destroys the last reference to the object, then the tuple will be destroyed, releasing the space it required, and destroying the internal references to the objects in the tuple (possibly resulting in the destruction of those objects as well).

In a few cases, the destruction of an object can also attempt to do more complex things. For example, the destruction of an open file will cause the file object to be closed. It is generally not good practice to rely on complex object finalization, because it is quite easy to mistake the destruction of a reference to an object with the destruction of the object itself—the object is destroyed only if the destroyed reference is the last reference. In the case of files, for example, it may be possible to run out of operating system resources if you open files without explicitly closing them in the mistaken belief that they are being deleted (and hence closed) behind the scenes.

Of course, in addition to these various generic methods, there are more specific methods that may be applied only to the correct kinds of objects.

Intrinsic Operations for Dictionaries

Dictionaries have two goals in life: to store keys and values and to retrieve them for you.

D[k] Dictionary Indexing

The expression D[k] attempts to retrieve the value in D associated with the key k. If there is no such value, the expression raises a KeyError. Alternatively if k cannot be used as a dictionary key D[k] will raise a TypeError:

```
>>> D = {"Jim": "James", "Bob":"Robert",
...      "Sue":"Oh, Suzanna, don't you cry for me"}
>>> D["Jim"]
'James'
>>> D["Sue"]
"Oh, Suzanna, don't you cry for me"
>>> D["Bill"]
Traceback (innermost last):
  File "", line 1, in ?
KeyError: Bill
```

D[k] = X Dictionary Element Assignment

The assignment D[k] = X attempts to associate the value X with the key k. It will fail with a TypeError if k cannot be used as a key to a dictionary:

```
>>> D["Bill"] = "Billy"
>>> D["Bill"]
'Billy'
>>> D[ ["Bill", "Clinton"] ] = "William the Conquerer"
Traceback (innermost last):
  File "", line 1, in ?
TypeError: unhashable type
```

Here the final assignment failed because a list cannot be used as a dictionary key, but a tuple would have been just fine:

```
>>> D[ ("Bill", "Clinton") ] = "William the Conquerer"
```

del D[k] Dictionary Element Deletion

The statement del D[k] removes the key k and its associated value from the Dictionary. If there is no such key, the operation will trigger a KeyError, or if k is not appropriate as a dictionary key the operation will trigger a TypeError.

```
>>> del D["Jim"]
>>> del D["Sue"]
>>> D
{'Bill': 'Billy', ('Bill', 'Clinton'): 'William the Conquerer',
 'Bob': 'Robert'}
>>> del D["Bob"]
>>> D
{'Bill': 'Billy', ('Bill', 'Clinton'): 'William the Conquerer'}
```

D.has_key(k) Dictionary Key Test

The has_key method of dictionary objects tests to see whether the key k is a valid key currently in the dictionary. It returns 1 (true) if the key is valid, or 0 otherwise. If k is not appropriate as a key to a dictionary, D.has_key(k) will raise a TypeError.

```
>>> D.has_key("Bill")
1
>>> D.has_key("Joe")
0
>>> D.has_key([0])
Traceback (innermost last):
  File "", line 1, in ?
TypeError: unhashable type
```

D.keys() Dictionary Keys Retrieval

The keys method of a dictionary returns a list containing the current keys in the dictionary:

```
>>> D.keys()
[('Bill', 'Clinton'), 'Bill']
```

D.values() Dictionary Values Retrieval

The values method of a dictionary returns a list containing the current values of the dictionary.

```
>>> D.values()
['William the Conquerer', 'Billy']
```

`D.items()`
Dictionary Key-Value Pairs Retrieval

The items method of a dictionary returns both the keys and values of the dictionary, within a list containing tuples of (`key`, `value`) pairs:

```
>>> D.items()
[(('Bill', 'Clinton'), 'William the Conquerer'), ('Bill', 'Billy')]
```

`len(D)` Dictionary Length

Finally the `len(D)` function gives the number of key/value pairs within the dictionary.

```
>>> len(D)
2
```

Dictionary assignment, indexing, `has_key` test, and deletion are all very fast operations regardless of how large the dictionary grows, making dictionaries extremely useful objects, as shown in the "Playing" chapter, and as we shall see. Use them.

Intrinsic Operations for Numeric Types

Many of the intrinsic operations for numeric types define standard arithmetic operations. These methods are valid for int, long, and float objects. Many operations applied to int objects may sometimes trigger an OverFlowError if the result is too large or too negative to fit within the underlying machine representation for ints. Floating point exceptions, however, are sometimes not caught largely because floating point exceptions errors have not been standardized across computing platforms.

`coerce(X, Y)` Arithmetic Conversion

The `coerce` function is invoked by many of the operations discussed below and is also made directly available to the programmer. Before two arguments of different types may be combined using an operation such as addition, the arguments must be converted to compatible types, and this conversion is effected by the `coerce` function:

```
>>> coerce(667, 7.98e5)
(667.0, 798000.0)
>>> (x, y) = coerce(7896, 667654L)
>>> print x, y
7896L 667654L
```

The `coerce` function converts numeric values to the more general of the two argument types, where longs are more general than simple integers, and floats are more general than longs or simple integers.

m + n, m - n, m * n
Addition, Subtraction, and Multiplication

These are the addition, subtraction, and multiplication operations for numeric values respectively. Integer addition is defined by the Peano axioms as follows...(Just kidding!)

m / n Division

This is the division operation. In the case where m and n are both integers or longs, the result is the integer division of m and n to the nearest integer, discarding any remainder. For example, $5/3 == 1$, $(-5)/3 == -2$, $5/(-3) == -2$, and $(-5)/(-3) == 1$.

m % n Modulus

This is the modulus operation, generalized to work with floats and longs as well as with integers. When m and n are both integers, you can think of m % n as the remainder left by the integer division of m by n. In general you can think of this operation as defined by the following function

```
import math
def modulus(m, n):
    x = m - n * math.floor(m/n)
    return x
```

The floor function used above gives the smallest integer larger than m/n. If you don't understand this operation, you probably don't need it right now. Keep this operation in mind and check back later.

- m, + m, abs(m) Unary Minus, Unary Plus, and Absolute Value

These are the unary minus, plus, and absolute value operations, respectively. The absolute value function returns m if m is equal or greater than zero, or otherwise returns –m. We trust you are familiar with the other two. Note that +x will fail if x is not a number.

divmod(n, m) Whole Division and Modulus

An operation which computes the whole number division and the modulus of the division for m and n, returning both as a tuple. For integers and longs, this operation is equivalent to

```
( (m / n), m % n )
```

float(m) Convert to Float

Return the nearest floating point value to m possible within the float representation.

int(m) Convert to int

Return the integer part of m. For example, int(-0.5) == 0 and int 10.4 == 10. If m is too large to fit in a standard integer, this operation raises an OverflowError.

long(m) Convert to Long

Same as int(m) but this operation returns a long integer representation for example:

```
>>> long(1e66)
999999999999999994532233386824744512570964657002124792466584161
4848L
```

This example demonstrates that `1e66` is close, but not exactly `pow(10L, 66)` due to the imprecision of the float representation.

pow(m, n) **Exponentiation**

This returns m raised to the power n. There is another variant of this function, useful for certain peculiar but very important data encryption algorithms. The pow(m, n, k) operation is equivalent to pow(m, n) % k, but has been optimized. Python 1.4 includes the new notation m ** n which is equivalent to `pow(m, n)`, by popular demand.

round(m) **Round to Nearest Whole Number**

This function rounds the numeric value m up or down to the nearest integral floating point value.

Intrinsic Operations for Int Objects and Long Int Objects

There are a number of "bit operations" that may be performed on integers or longs, but don't make sense on floats. These operations manipulate the binary representation of their arguments, and we will not cover them in detail. They are analogous to the C language operations of the same notation (except that they will work with arbitrary precision longs).

These are all obscure Python operations, which are not frequently used.

~ m	Bitwise inversion
m >> n	Bit shift right
m << n	Bit shift left
m & n	Bitwise conjunction
m ^ n	Bitwise exclusive or

m | n   Bitwise disjunction

We will not have occasion to use these much, so please consult the documentation of the standard distribution for more details on these operations.

In addition, There are a number of facilities for converting integers to strings, aside from the standard repr() and str() conversion methods.

chr(m)   Convert to character: Return the character with ASCII value m. (This is the inverse of ord(c)).

hex(m)   Convert to hexadecimal string: Return a string containing the hexidecimal representation for m.

oct(m)   Convert to octal string: Return a string containing the octal representation for m.

Intrinsic Operations for Floats

Although we have covered the "official" standard built-in operations for floats, we must mention here that a lot of very important functions are also available from the standard math module. We list them here without comment, except to say that they are based directly on the underlying standard C language functions of the same name and with similar calling sequences.

```
acos(x), asin(x), atan(x), atan2(x,y), ceil(x), cos(x), cosh(x),
exp(x), fabs(x), floor(x), fmod(x,y), frexp(x), hypot(x,y),
ldexp(x,y), log(x), log10(x), modf(x), pow(x,y), sin(x), sinh(x),
sqrt(x), tan(x), tanh(x).
```

The one exception to the rule is the hypot(x, y) function which is not defined in libc. The value of hypot(x, y) produces sqrt(x*x + y*y) except that the latter will overflow more often, so hypot should be preferred.

The math module also defines the constants pi and e. Look them up in a good math book if you aren't familiar with these constants.

An example usage of the math module might be

```
>>> import math
>>> math.sin(math.pi/2)
1.0
```

```
>>> math.e
2.71828182846
>>> math.log(math.e)
1.0
>>> math.log10(1000000000000000L)
15.0
```

Of course, the math module automatically converts ints and longs to floats before applying these mathematical operations to an argument.

Intrinsic Operations for Sequences (Lists, Tuples, Strings, and Sometimes XRanges)

Sequence objects represent ordered sequences of objects. Python provides a number of basic sequence objects. String objects are immutable sequence objects optimized for containing characters. Tuples are sequences of arbitrary Python objects which cannot be modified (although mutable objects they contain may be modified). Lists are the most general sequence type: They contain arbitrary Python objects and may be modified and resized in place. XRange objects are "lazy" linear sequences of integers (that may repeat, as we will see below).

All of these sequence operations share a number of common operations.

s[i] List Indexing

The indexing notation s[i] is shared with dictionary objects. It returns the object at index i in the sequence s. There is an important and useful convention that Python supports for sequence objects: In addition to positive indices (which index relative to the left side of the sequence), python supports negative indices:

```
>>> Name = "Fred"
>>> print Name[0], Name[1], Name[2], Name[3]
F r e d
>>> print Name[-1], Name[-2], Name[-3], Name[-4]
d e r F
>>> Primes = (2, 3, 5, 7)
>>> print Primes[0], Primes[1], Primes[2], Primes[3]
```

```
2 3 5 7
>>> print Primes[-1], Primes[-2], Primes[-3], Primes[-4]
7 5 3 2
```

As demonstrated above, positive indices start at zero and proceed to one less than the length of the sequence, indexing the sequence from left to right; negative indices start at -1 and proceed to the negative of the length of the sequence, indexing the sequence from right to left. An index that is too large or too small triggers an IndexError:

```
>>> Primes[31]
Traceback (innermost last):
  File "", line 1, in ?
IndexError: tuple index out of range
```

s[i:j], s[i:], s[:j], s[:]
Slice Expressions

These are the slice expressions for sequences, which are used to slice out a subsequence of the sequence.

The fully specified version of this notation provides an index of both the starting and ending points of the subsequence desired. Thus, the s[i:j] notation generates the subsequence of s that starts at index i, and ends just before index j.

```
>>> L = range(15, 100, 7)
>>> L
[15, 22, 29, 36, 43, 50, 57, 64, 71, 78, 85, 92, 99]
>>> L[9:9]
[]
>>> L[9:10]
[78]
>>> L[5:10]
[50, 57, 64, 71, 78]
>>> L[3:-3]
[36, 43, 50, 57, 64, 71, 78]
>>> L[-3:3]
[]
>>> L[5:9000]
[50, 57, 64, 71, 78, 85, 92, 99]
```

```
>>> L[-1000: 1000]
[15, 22, 29, 36, 43, 50, 57, 64, 71, 78, 85, 92, 99]
```

As demonstrated above, slice start and end points are permitted to start "before the beginning" and "after the end" of the sequence, in which case they are assumed to represent the beginning or the end of the sequence, respectively. Furthermore, slices allow the end point to be before or at the start point, which always results in an empty subsequence.

Slices conform to the negative indexing convention. For example, s[1:-1] returns the subsequence of s with the initial and last elements sliced off, but s[-1:1] will always return an empty subsequence, unless the sequence has length 1. Try it!

Slices also allow one or both of the start and end indices to be omitted in which case a missing start point always indicates the beginning of the sequence, and a missing end point represents the end of the sequence.

```
>>> Exclamation = "Cowabunga!"
>>> Exclamation[-3:]
'ga!'
>>> Exclamation[:-3]
'Cowabun'
>>> Exclamation[:]
'Cowabunga!'
```

Slices also define an important convenience for manipulating lists. It is frequently useful in making a copy of a list, in order to be able to modify the copy without messing up the initial list.

```
>>> histogram = [45, 78, 54, 99, 0, 77, 21]
>>> s_hist = histogram[:]
>>> s_hist.sort()      # sort this copy
>>> s_hist             # show the sorted copy
[0, 21, 45, 54, 77, 78, 99]
>>> histogram          # show the unmodified original
[45, 78, 54, 99, 0, 77, 21]
```

To make a separate copy of a list that will not share direct modifications with the original use newlist = oldlist[:].

s * i Sequence Repetition

The "multiplication" notation when applied to an integer and a sequence results in a replication of the sequence.

```
>>> r = range(3, 9, 2)
>>> r
[3, 5, 7]
>>> r * 5
[3, 5, 7, 3, 5, 7, 3, 5, 7, 3, 5, 7, 3, 5, 7]
>>> r * 0
[]
>>> "<>" * 24
'<><><><><><><><><><><><><><><><><><><><><><><><>'
>>> [None] * 10
[None, None, None, None, None, None, None, None, None, None]
```

As demonstrated above s * i produces a sequence of the same type as s, but with the contents of s repeated i times.

Sequence repetition is more than just a cute feature, particularly for lists, because the expression [None]*20 is a standard way to create a list of length 20 which will be filled in with meaningful values later. Sequence repetition can also be used to create "lists of lists" which can be used to emulate generic multidimensional arrays. However, when creating "multidimensional arrays" in Python, be careful not to accidentally share the same list in the array. For example, the following does not create a multidimensional list:

```
>>> BADARRAY = [ [None] * 3 ] * 2
>>> BADARRAY
[[None, None, None], [None, None, None]]
>>> BADARRAY[1][2] = "shared"
>>> BADARRAY
[[None, None, 'shared'], [None, None, 'shared']]
```

As demonstrated, rather than providing an array of two subarrays, BADARRAY provides an array of two references to the same subarray. For this reason the modification to the right sub array was reflected in the left subarray (because they are the same object).

There are several ways to create a **GOODARRAY**:

```
>>> GOODARRAY = [None] * 2
>>> for i in xrange(2):
...     GOODARRAY[i] = [None] * 3
...
>>> GOODARRAY
[[None, None, None], [None, None, None]]
>>> GOODARRAY[1][2] = "not shared"
>>> GOODARRAY
[[None, None, None], [None, None, 'not shared']]
```

Here the for loop makes a new object to represent each row. More generically, we may define:

```
def multi_list(shape, initial_value):
    """recursively create a multi-dimensional array as a list"""
    if shape == []:
        return initial_value
    else:
        this_dimension = shape[0]
        others = shape[1:]
        array = [None] * this_dimension
        for i in xrange(this_dimension):
            array[i] = multi_list(others, initial_value)
        return array
```

For example:

```
>>> GOOD2 = multi_list([3,2], 0)
>>> GOOD2
[[0, 0], [0, 0], [0, 0]]
>>> GOOD2[1][1] = 302.5
>>> GOOD2
[[0, 0], [0, 302.5], [0, 0]]
>>> GOOD3 = multi_list([4], "baby")
>>> GOOD3
['baby', 'baby', 'baby', 'baby']
>>> GOOD3[3] = "maybe next week, 'cause ya see I'm on a losing streak"
>>> GOOD3
['baby', 'baby', 'baby',
 "maybe next week, 'cause ya see I'm on a losing streak"]
>>> GOOD4 = multi_list([2,2,2], 0)
>>> GOOD4
[[[0, 0], [0, 0]], [[0, 0], [0, 0]]]
```

```
>>> GOOD4[0][1][0] = 19
>>> GOOD4
[[[0, 0], [19, 0]], [[0, 0], [0, 0]]]
```

Play with this function if you don't understand how it works. It's a good illustration of recursion—and it's fun too!

`len(s)` Sequence Length

The `len(s)` function returns the length of the sequence s. It is often used in conjunction with a for loop to iterate across the indices of a list. For example, the following function adds an increment to each element of a list:

```
def incr_list(list, incr = 1):
    for index in xrange( len( list ) ):
        list[ index ] = list[ index ] + incr
```

Behold some example usages of this function:

```
>>> L = [6, 9, 1]
>>> incr_list(L)
>>> L
[7, 10, 2]
>>> incr_list(L, -10)
>>> L
[-3, 0, -8]
```

The `len` operation is shared with dictionaries.

`X in s` Sequence Membership Test

The `X in s` truth-valued expression tests whether the object X is equal to a member of the sequence s. For example:

```
Esteemed_Monikers = ("jredford, "lwall", "tchrist", "jar")
if Moniker in Esteemed_Monikers:
   send_reply("Greetings esteemed guest!  Always pleased to see you!")
```

Although the implementation of this test is very efficient for sequences with up to hundreds of simple elements, for very long sequences this test can cause performance problems, because it basically checks to see whether X == E succeeds for each element E of s, until one of the tests succeeds or until they all fail. An alternative approach to accomplish the same result would use a dictionary:

```
# initialize the Esteemed_guest indicator dictionary:
Esteemed_guest = {}
Esteemed_guest["jredford"] = 1
Esteemed_guest["lwall"] = 1
Esteemed_guest["tchrist"] = 1
Esteemed_guest["jar"] = 1
... many more entries ...
# later:
if Esteemed_guest.has_key(Moniker):
    send_reply("Greetings esteemed guest!  Always pleased to see you!")
```

Here the `Esteemed_guest.has_key(Moniker)` test always executes very quickly, regardless of how large the Esteemed_guest dictionary grows. Nevertheless, the membership test expression `X in s` is invaluable, particularly for testing membership in nonhuge sequences (with only up to hundreds of elements).

For example, the following is a reasonable implementation of a function that tests whether an single character string is a numeric digit:

```
def is_numeric_digit(char):
    return (char in "0123456789")
```

for x in s: ... For Loop

The for statement is a special construct designed for iterating over the items of a sequence. Nuances of the for loop construct are described later; for now it suffices to say that the for loop walks through the items of the sequence s, assigning each to the target variable *x*, and then executes the code block of the for loop (which usually uses the target binding in some way).

We have seen a number of uses for the for loop construct, but below we provide some additional examples:

```
>>> def powers_of_2(n):
...     result = [None] * n
...     for i in xrange(n):
...         result[i] = 1 << i
...     return result
```

```
...
>>> powers_of_2(10)
[1, 2, 4, 8, 16, 32, 64, 128, 256, 512]
>>>
>>> def total(sequence_of_num):
...     result = sequence_of_num[0]
...     for item in sequence_of_num[1:]:
...         result = result + item
...     return result
...
>>> total( (9.0, 7.6, -312, 1.2e2, 788L, 5) )
617.6
```

WARNING

There is an important caveat regarding the use of for loops with lists: The program should *never* modify a list that is currently being walked by an active for loop. If a list changes in the middle of a for loop, the behavior of the for loop is undefined. Now, if the items of the list are mutable objects, the program may mutate the items, but the objects in a list that is a target of iteration in a for loop should not be reassigned or moved while the for loop is active. If you wish to allow the program to alter a list during an iteration which passes over the contents of a list, there are at least two permitted alternatives: use a while loop in place of a for loop, or use a for loop that iterates over a fresh copy of the list:

```
# using a while loop to iterate over a list that may mutate:
index = 0
while index < len(list):
    item = list[index]
    ... do something which may modify the list ...
    index = index +1

# using a for loop to iterate over a copy of a list that may mutate
for item in list[:]:
    ... do something which may modify the list ...
```

s + q Sequence Catenation

The "plus" expression applied to sequences catenates the sequences.

```
>>> ("Nixon", "Ford", "Carter", "Reagan", "Bush", "Clinton") + ("Dole",)
('Nixon', 'Ford', 'Carter', 'Reagan', 'Bush', 'Clinton', 'Dole')
```

```
>>> "Kennedy" + ", John Fitzgerald"
'Kennedy, John Fitzgerald'
>>> range(4) + range(-9,-5)
[0, 1, 2, 3, -9, -8, -7, -6]
```

Only sequences of the same type may be catenated, and catenation is not permitted for XRange objects.

tuple(s) Convert to Tuple

The tuple(s) function converts the sequence s to a tuple containing the same objects in the same order. This function is particularly useful for converting lists (which are mutable) to tuples in order to use functions that require tuple (or immutable) arguments.

For example, it is often convenient to convert lists to tuples in order to construct dictionary keys. As mentioned, lists can never be used as keys to dictionaries, but tuples (if they contain only immutables) are often very useful as dictionary keys. Thus, to use the contents of a list (containing immutables) as a key to a dictionary, convert the list to a tuple, and use the tuple as the key:

```
def dict_insert_list(Dict, list, value):
    tup = tuple(list)
    Dict[ tup ] = value

def dict_retrieve_list(Dict, list):
    tup = tuple(list)
    return Dict[ tup ]

def dict_del_list(Dict, list):
    tup = tuple(list)
    del Dict[ tup ]
```

map(None, s) Convert to List

Just as it is occasionally useful to convert an arbitrary sequence to a tuple, so is it occasionally useful to convert an arbitrary sequence to a list, which is most easily accomplished using a special case of the map function map(None, s). The map function in full generality is described as a method for callable objects, but we include this special case here, because it is best thought of as a sequence operation.

```
>>> map(None, "Bambi")
['B', 'a', 'm', 'b', 'i']
>>> map(None, (5,6,7))
[5, 6, 7]
>>> map(None, xrange(3,10,2))
[3, 5, 7, 9]
>>> map(None, [1,2,8])
[1, 2, 8]
```

For example, the following function produces a new tuple containing the values of oldtuple, reversed:

```
def tup_reverse(old_tuple):
    templist = map(None, old_tuple)
    templist.reverse()
    return tuple(templist)
```

This function can be used as follows:

```
>>> T = ("DEC", "IBM", "Microsoft")
>>> tup_reverse(T)
('Microsoft', 'IBM', 'DEC')
```

Actually, there is no requirement that the argument to the `tup_reverse` function must be a tuple: try it with lists and xranges too, but it always returns a tuple.

In addition to these methods which are permitted for all sequences, there are a number of operations which are defined only for each individual type.

Special Intrinsic Operations for String Objects

`ord(c)` ASCII Value of Singleton String

The `ord(c)` function when applied to a string of length one returns the ASCII value (the internal representation) of the character in the string as an integer.

```
>>> ord("a")
97
```

raw_input(), raw_input(prompt)
Line from Standard Input

This function reads a line from the standard input (also known as **sys.stdin** within the module **sys**, excluding the trailing newline that marks the end of the line.

```
>>> raw_input("Type your name: ")
Type your name: Vladimir Lenin
'Vladimir Lenin'
>>> line = raw_input()
That was the year that was.
>>> line
'That was the year that was.'
```

The optional prompt parameter will be used as a prompt string for the input, if it is provided.

The `raw_input)()` function does not attempt to "evaluate" the string as a Python expression, in contrast to the input() function, which does. The `sys.stdin.readline()` method is similar to `raw_input()`, except that `sys.stdin.readline()` includes the line break character(s) as part of the line and the `raw_input(prompt)` automatically provides a prompt for the input.

If the standard input is exhausted, `raw_input` will raise a `EOFError`. If Python is linked with a "readline" utility (such as GNU readline) the user may edit the input line using the readline features!

S % T String/Tuple Substitution

The `S % T`, where `S` is a string and `T` is a tuple, provides a very convenient and efficient formatting notation, similar to the printf convention of the C programming language.

```
>>> format = "%s ate %s apples in %s days and therefore saw %s doctors"
>>> format % ("Lola", 6.5, 8, 1.5)
'Lola ate 6.5 apples in 8 days and therefore saw 1.5 doctors'
```

In the previous format string, each `%s` is a formatting directive which represents a placeholder for the string representation of a value to be placed in the string. The expression `format % tuple` generates a new string resulting from replacing each corresponding directive in format with the string representation of the corresponding value from the tuple (and the number of directives must match the number of values exactly).

This formatting conversion operation improves on printf because data of any type are automatically converted to a reasonable default string representation via the "%s" directive.

```
>>> list = [1,2,5,7]
>>> format = "The list %s contains small prime numbers"
>>> format % (list,)
'The list [1, 2, 5, 7] contains small prime numbers'
```

However, there are occasions where it is useful to specify a specific conversion format that may not match the default conversion provided by Python. To aid in formatting, Python provides the following other formatting directives. These directive notations follow the standard C conventions (with omissions), and the rest of this section may be ignored until you need to read it.

The following directives are defined for numeric conversions:

Example	Result	Description
"%c" % (97,)	'a'	convert int to char
"%f" % (687.987,)	'687.987000'	float without exponent
"%e" % (6786876L,)	'6.786876e+06'	float with exponent
"%g" % (6786876L,)	'6.78688e+06'	float with or without exponent
"%d" % (678.76,)	'678'	signed decimal integer
"%o" % (8976,)	'21420'	octal integer (without leading 0)
"%u" % (-677,)	'4294966619'	unsigned integer
"%u" % (677.8,)	'677'	unsigned integer
"%x" % (255,)	'ff'	hexidecimal integer (without leading 0x)

Whenever a float is interpreted as an integer it is truncated to an integer for the purposes of the conversion. Here the "unsigned integer" representation is given twice to emphasize that a negative value represented as an unsigned integer is usually not intuitively meaningful.

These format directives may be marked with minimum length field and a precision, using the notation. %m.MD, where m is the minimum length, M is the precision, and D is the directive. If the precision is omitted, the notation becomes %mD.

Example	Produces
"%5d" % (12,)	' 12'
"%5d" % (1234567,)	'1234567'
"%4.4f" % (555.872764,)	'555.8728'
"%4.4f" % (5,)	'5.0000'
"%4.4e" % (555.872764,)	'5.5587e+02'
"%3.8g" % (5.6,)	'5.6'
"%8.8s" % ("Peter Robot",)	'Peter Ro'
"%8.8s" % ("Pet",)	' Pet'
"%8.3s" % ("Peter Robot",)	' Pet'

Floating point values will be rounded to present the number of decimal places specified in the precision. Strings are truncated on the right to the length specified by the precision and any extra space required by the minimum length is filled with spaces on the left. For integer values the precision is ignored and the resulting string is as long as needed to represent the value.

Flags may be inserted immediately before the % to alter the default behavior of the directives.

Example	Produces	Discussion
"%-5i" % (12,)	'12 '	"-" forces left justification.
"%+5i" % (12,)	' +12'	"+" forces a sign for positive numbers.
"%05i" % (12,)	'00012'	"0" fills with 0's, not blanks
"% i" % (12,)	' 12'	" " precede positive numbers with a blank. Why ask why?
"%#x" % (12,)	'0xc'	"#" precede octal with 0, hex with 0x.
"%#g" % (12,)	'12.0000'	"#" for g force a decimal point, and don't truncate trailing 0's.

The formatting directives are extremely useful, but they also probably constitute the most boring part of Python.

S % D **String/Dictionary Substitution**

The S % D operation, where S is a string and D is a dictionary is decidedly unboring. In fact it is quite exciting and invaluable.

```
>>> Info = { "Name" : "Alfonzo",
...         "Age": 185.7,
...         "likes": "Bourbon",
...         "hobby": "Sword Fighting",
...         "flaw": "died with his boots on as a youth" }
>>> Format = """
... Greetings %(Name)s!
...     As a fellow aficionado of %(likes)s, I would like
... to invite you to join the Python mailing list.  This
... list is of great interest to people approximately %(Age)s
... years old who practice %(hobby)s.  Please consider joining
... the list, %(Name)s, and I hope to hear from you soon.
... """
>>> print Format % Info

Greetings Alfonzo!

As a fellow aficionado of Bourbon, I would like
to invite you to join the Python mailing list. This
list is of great interest to people approximately 185.7
years old who practice Sword Fighting.  Please consider joining the list,
Alfonzo, and I hope to hear from you soon.
```

Now, this is a huge improvement on printf. Here the Format % Info notation produced a new string by replacing all %(key)s directives in the Format string by the string representation of the value associated with the key in the dictionary Info. A careful inspection of the previous example reveals that the dictionary may include information not used in the format string, but all of the keys requested in the format string must be present in the dictionary.

This notation permits all the other directive formats described above to follow the end of the parenthesized key.

```
>>> Line = "  Stddev=%(sd)#12g Avg=%(av)+12.6f Med=%(md)4.4e"
>>> Data = { "sd": 56432.987, "av": 877.897, "md": 678543 }
```

```
>>> Line % Data
'  Stddev=      56433.0 Avg= +877.897000 Med=6.7854e+05'
```

Use this operation! It makes a lot of work which is normally a pain in the anatomy actually easy and fun, and also FAST.

There are many other standard facilities for manipulating strings that are not officially part of the Python core, discussed elsewhere. In particular, the string, regex, and regsub modules are invaluable for manipulating strings. See the Playing Chapter and the Appendix on Regular Expressions for a discussion of the most important string facilities.

Special Intrinsic Operations for Lists

Lists are the standard mutable sequence type provided by the Python core. They have a number of associated operations not shared by all other built-in sequence types.

`L[i]` = x List Index Assignment

The index assignment statement `L[i]` = x sets the position at index i of the list L to refer to the object x. We have already seen many uses of this statement.

Index assignments that are too large or too negative trigger an `IndexError`.

`L[i:j]` = `L2`, `L[i:]` = `L2`, `L[:i]` = `L2`, `L[:]` = `L2` Slice Assignment

The slice assignment statement modifies the list L in place (i.e., it does not create a new list) by "replacing" the subsequence of L starting at i and ending just before j with the contents of the list L2.

```
>>> L = range(5)
>>> L
[0, 1, 2, 3, 4]
>>> L[1:3] = [9,6]
>>> L
```

```
[0, 9, 6, 3, 4]
>>> L[3:5] = []
>>> L
[0, 9, 6]
>>> L[1:1] = [7,-1,-7]
>>> L
[0, 7, -1, -7, 9, 6]
>>> L[4:] = [1,0]
>>> L
[0, 7, -1, -7, 1, 0]
>>> L[5:3] = [5,4,3]
>>> L
[0, 7, -1, -7, 1, 5, 4, 3, 0]
```

As the previous example demonstrates, if the length of the assigned slice does not match the length of the list value on the right side of the assignment, the elements of the target list are shifted in order to place the new values in the same relative position as the slice they replace. An assignment L[i:j] = L2, where j is at or before i, will cause the right-hand values to be inserted just before the element at index i.

Slice assignment conforms to the negative index conventions supported by the other index-based operations. For example, L[-1:] = L2 effectively removes the last element of L and appends the contents of L2.

```
>>> L = ["Go", "West", "Young", "Man"]
>>> L[-1:] = ["Woman", "or", "Man"]
>>> L
['Go', 'West', 'Young', 'Woman', 'or', 'Man']
```

As shown above, end indices that are omitted or are past the end of the list are assumed to represent the end of the list. Similarly, start points that are too negative or omitted are assumed to represent the start of the list, just as in slice assignment. It is particularly useful to note that L[:] = L2 replaces all content of L with the content of L:

```
>>> L = ["tired", "list"]
>>> L
['tired', 'list']
>>> L[:0] = ["old", "and"]
>>> L
['old', 'and', 'tired', 'list']
>>> L[:2] = ["not", "so"]
```

```
>>> L
['not', 'so', 'tired', 'list']
>>> L[5:] = ["of", "strings"]
>>> L
['not', 'so', 'tired', 'list', 'of', 'strings']
>>> L[:] = ["rested", "list"]
>>> L
['rested', 'list']
```

del L[i] List Index Deletion

This deletes the element of L at list i (in place). It's very similar to L[i: i+1] = [ ] (except that it doesn't work if i is not a valid index; in that case it raises an IndexError).

```
>>> L = ["Lenin", "Trotski", "Stalin"]
>>> del L[1]
>>> L
['Lenin', 'Stalin']
```

del L[i:j] Slice Deletion

The del statement for slices deletes the slice starting at i and ending just before j. This has precisely the same effect as L[i:j] = [ ].

```
>>> L = [2, 4, 8, 16, 32, 64]
>>> L
[2, 4, 8, 16, 32, 64]
>>> del L[1:-1]
>>> L
[2, 64]
```

L.append(x) Append One Element

Add the element x at the end of the list L.

```
>>> L = ["DOS", "OS/2"]
>>> L.append("Linux")
>>> L
['DOS', 'OS/2', 'Linux']
```

```
>>> L.append("NT")
>>> L
['DOS', 'OS/2', 'Linux', 'NT']
>>> L.append("Win95")
>>> L
['DOS', 'OS/2', 'Linux', 'NT', 'Win95']
```

L.count(x) Count Occurrences of an Element

Return the number of elements in L equal to x (i.e., the number of elements E such that E == x).

```
>>> L = ["green", "light", "yellow", "light", "red", "light", "stop!"]
>>> L.count("blue")
0
>>> L.count("light")
3
>>> L.count("yellow")
1
```

L.index(x) Smallest Index of Element Occurrence

Return the smallest index of an element of L which is equal to x, or raise a ValueError if there is no such element.

```
>>> L = [1, 5, 2, 5, 1, 6, 9]
>>> L.index(5)
1
>>> L.index(1)
0
>>> L.index(6)
5
```

L.insert(i, x) Insert x at i

Insert x into L so that it appears at index i; shift the current element at i and all subsequent elements up one index.

```
>>> L = ["pig", "likes"]
>>> L.insert(0, "my")
>>> L
['my', 'pig', 'likes']
>>> L.insert(2, "often")
>>> L
['my', 'pig', 'often', 'likes']
>>> L.insert(4, "truffles")
>>> L
['my', 'pig', 'often', 'likes', 'truffles']
>>> L.insert(16, "when in France")
>>> L
['my', 'pig', 'often', 'likes', 'truffles', 'when in France']
```

The L.insert method does not conform to the negative index convention. Indices at or less than zero are interpreted as the front of the list, and indices past the end of the list are interpreted to mean the end of the list.

L.sort(), L.sort(F) Sort List

The L.sort() function sorts a list in place using the standard comparison function cmp. Due to the generality of the standard comparison function, this operation is remarkably powerful. For example, if we have a list L of tuples containing names and ages

```
>>> L = [ ("Joe",3), ("Stan", 1), ("Lily", 4), ("Stan", 2), ("Joe", 2) ]
>>> L.sort()
>>> L
[('Joe', 2), ('Joe', 3), ('Lily', 4), ('Stan', 1), ('Stan', 2)]
```

then after sorting, the elements will be ordered first by name, then by age, as demonstrated.

If the standard comparison function is not appropriate for a given purpose, a program may provide an alternative comparison function using the alternate calling sequence L.sort(F), where F should be a function of two arguments that returns: F(x,y) negative if x should precede y in the sort order; F(x,y) positive (nonzero) if x should follow y in the order, or F(x,y) zero if the relative ordering of x and y is unimportant. For example, we can re-sort L by age (and not name) as follows:

```
>>> def F(tuple1, tuple2):
...     return cmp( tuple1[1], tuple2[1] )
...
>>> L.sort(F)
>>> L
[('Stan', 1), ('Joe', 2), ('Stan', 2), ('Joe', 3), ('Lily', 4)]
```

There is an additional restriction on the alternative comparison function F—it should represent a linear ordering, that is, F(x,y) should be negative if and only if F(y,x) is positive (nonzero), and whenever F(x,y) and F(y,z) are both negative, then F(x,z) is negative too.

If these conditions are not satisfied, then the behavior of L.sort(F) is undefined. Also L.sort(F) is not guaranteed to be "stable," meaning that sorting a list twice may reorder equivalent elements, for example.

WARNING

L.remove(x) Remove First Occurrence

Remove from L the first element of L that is equal to x.

```
>>> L = ["Jim", "Bob", "Bob", "Joe", "Jim", "Tom"]
>>> L.remove("Bob")
>>> L
['Jim', 'Bob', 'Joe', 'Jim', 'Tom']
>>> L.remove("Tom")
>>> L
['Jim', 'Bob', 'Joe', 'Jim']
```

The L.remove(x) operation only removes one element from the list even if many elements are equal to x, and triggers a ValueError if L contains no element equal to x.

The following function will remove all elements of L equal to x from the list:

```
>>> def RemoveAll(L, elt):
...     try:
...         while 1:  # loop until error
...             L.remove(elt)
...     except ValueError:
...         pass
...
```

```
>>> L = [1,6,4,1,3,5,1,4,1,5]
>>> RemoveAll(L,4)
>>> L
[1, 6, 1, 3, 5, 1, 1, 5]
>>> RemoveAll(L,1)
>>> L
[6, 3, 5, 5]
```

L.reverse() Reverse List

The L.reverse() operation reverses the order of elements of a list in place.

```
>>> L = ["sharks", "eat", "people"]
>>> L
['sharks', 'eat', 'people']
>>> L.reverse()
>>> L
['people', 'eat', 'sharks']
```

range(n), range(m,n), range(m,n,k) Generate Integer Range as List

The range function (related to the xrange function) generates a list of integers:

```
>>> range(5)
[0, 1, 2, 3, 4]
>>> range(5,10)
[5, 6, 7, 8, 9]
>>> range(5, 50, 7)
[5, 12, 19, 26, 33, 40, 47]
```

The range(n) form generates the sequence of integers from 0 to n-1. The range(n,m), form generates the sequence of integers from n up to m-1, and the range(n,m,k) form generates the sequence of integers n, n+k, n+2k, and so forth, until the sequence reaches or exceeds m-1. For the last form, k can be negative, in which case the sequence terminates when it reaches or becomes smaller than m:

```
>>> range(5, 50, -7)
[]
```

```
>>> range(5, -50, -7)
[5, -2, -9, -16, -23, -30, -37, -44]
```

The result of range(n), where n is negative, produces an empty list, as does the result of range(n, m) where n is larger than m. Similarly range(n,m,k) produces an empty list when k is positive and n is greater than m, or when k is negative and n is less than m.

The range function is frequently useful for generating a sequence to be used as the object of iteration of a for loop:

```
>>> employees = ["Sam", "Norm", "Rebecca", "Woody"]
>>> odd_employees = []
>>> for index in range(1, len(employees), 2):
...     odd_employees.append( employees[index] )
...
>>> odd_employees
['Norm', 'Woody']
```

However, as mentioned above, the xrange function is generally better for this purpose when the range may be large, because it does not allocate elements until they are needed.

The range function has advantages over the xrange function in some circumstances. Particularly, the list result of the range function can be modified in arbitrary ways, whereas an XRange object can never be modified. Consider the following, which we present without explanation:

```
>>> odd_employees = []
>>> odd_indices = range(1, len(employees), 2)
>>> odd_indices
[1, 3]
>>> odd_indices.append(2)        # Rebecca is kinda odd too!
>>> odd_indices
[1, 3, 2]
>>> for index in odd_indices:
...     odd_employees.append( employees[index] )
...
>>> odd_employees
['Norm', 'Woody', 'Rebecca']
```

Special Intrinsic Operations for XRanges

xrange(n), xrange(m,n), xrange(m,n,k)

The xrange function is similar to the range function, but produces an XRange object (which only generates an integer when it is indexed) rather than a physical list containing all the indices of the range (which may consume, potentially, a great deal of memory for large ranges).

```
>>> xrange(7)
(0, 1, 2, 3, 4, 5, 6)
>>> xrange(7, 9)
(7, 8)
>>> xrange(7, -7, -3)
(7, 4, 1, -2, -5)
```

See the range function for an explanation of the calling sequence for xrange, because these two functions have precisely the same interpretations for their calling sequences. Again, we emphasize that it is preferable to use xrange() in place of range() whenever a program requires a linear sequence of integers, but will not need to modify the sequence—most notably, for use in for loops.

R.tolist()

If R is an XRange object, then R.tolist() generates a list object containing the same integers in the same order. This function has the same effect as map(None, R).

Intrinsic Operations for Files

Permanent data is usually stored in files on a file system. Most users of computers have some idea of what a file is—a collection of data that resides somewhere in the computer in such a way that the data persists, even if it is not associated with any running application, and even if the machine that holds the file is shut down and restarted at a later time.

Python views standard files as sequences of characters which may be read or written as strings. Furthermore, each file has an associated "seek position" that indicates where the next character to read from or write to lies in the sequence of characters that constitutes the file.

open(name), open(name, mode), and open(name, mode, bufsize) Open a File

The open function provides the standard way to obtain a new file object. An open(name) with only the name argument will open the file with the given name for read-only access. The optional mode parameter allows a file to be opened explicitly for read write or append (modes "r," "w," and "a," respectively). In addition the open function supports an update flag "+" and a binary flag "b" that are not meaningful on all platforms (although b is allowed on all platforms, and is ignored where it makes no sense).

The optional buffer size parameter specifies the desired buffer size for the file. After a file is opened, its seek position is initially at the start of the file, except for append mode where the seek position is initial at the end of the file.

f.read(), f.read(n) Read From File

The read operation reads characters from the file starting at the current seek position, returning a string. Without the optional integer argument, f.read() will read the entire remaining contents of the file as a string. If the integer parameter is present, f.read(n) will read n characters starting from the current seek position, but stopping at the end of the file if it is encountered. The seek position of the read file is left just after the last character read. If a read() is performed at the end of a file, then the empty string is returned, and this is the only case where a read returns an empty string except for f.read(0).

`f.readline()` Read Line from File

The `readline` operation acts like the `read` operation, but stops reading after the first newline encountered, or after the last character of the file, whichever comes first.

`f.readlines()` Read Remaining Lines from File

Reads all lines from the current seek position to the end of the file, returning a list of lines. The assignment `lines = f.readlines()` is very much like the statement sequence:

```
lines = []
while 1:
   ln = f.readline()
   if ln:
      lines.append(ln)
   else:
      break
```

The seek position moves to the end of the file after a successful call to `f.readlines()`.

`f.write(S)` Write String to File

The write operation writes the string `S` at the current seek position. The seek position is left at the end of `S`.

`f.writelines(L)` Write List of Strings to File

The writeline operation writes a list of strings to the file. Do not be confused by the name: no line separators or other characters are added to the strings in the list.

`f.seek(n), f.seek(n, m)`
Move File Position

The seek operation moves the seek position for the file. By default `f.seek(n)` moves the seek position to the absolute seek position n. If the optional parameter m is provided, it indicates that the seek position should move:

```
if m=0: to the absolute position n,
if m=1: move from the current position forward n places.
if m=2: seek to the position n places from the end of the file.
```

Negative n values are only meaningful if m is 1 or 2.

`f.tell()` Get File Position

Return the position of the current seek position of the file as an integer.

`f.flush()` Write Buffered Data Now

The flush operation forces the operating system to write written data for the file to the physical device (usually a disk). For performance reasons, data written to a file may remain cached in memory for a period of time before an explicit flush is requested. Files are automatically flushed when they are closed or when Python exits, unless Python crashes—which, of course, never happens :-).

`f.isatty()`
Test Whether File is a tty Device

This predicate returns true or false value indicating (roughly) whether the file "looks like" a keyboard or a terminal. A program may use this test to decide whether the program is interacting with a live user (if isatty is true), or whether the program is running as a noninteractive process.

`f.close()` Close File

Shut down the file object and release any system resources associated with this access to the file. To access the file again, the program will need to use another file object. A `close` always flushes the file. A closed file object will not allow any other operations, except for a redundant `close`.

Playing with files is great fun in Python. Try out these operations interactively, but be careful not to clobber any files containing important information!

> The `sys` module contains the special files `sys.stdin` and `sys.stdout`, the standard input and standard output of the process, respectively.

NOTE

Intrinsic Operations for Callable Objects

Classes, functions, methods, and built-in functions and methods are all callable objects, and if a `__call__` method is defined for an instance, an instance can be a callable object too. All objects, including callable objects, are "first class" and may be stored in variables or structures or passed as arguments to other callable objects.

There are a number of special operations that may be applied to any callable object.

f (...) Function Call

Any expression followed by parenthesized argument list sequence represents a function call.

```
>>> def info(a=1, b=2):
...     return "a=%s, b=%s, a+b=%s" % (a, b, a+b)
...
>>> info()          # no arguments
'a=1, b=2, a+b=3'
>>> info(6)         # one positional argument
'a=6, b=2, a+b=8'
>>> info(6,3)       # two positional arguments
'a=6, b=3, a+b=9'
>>> info(b = -90)   # one keyword argument
'a=1, b=-90, a+b=-89'
>>> info(b = -90, a = -120) # two keyword arguments
'a=-120, b=-90, a+b=-210'
```

As demonstrated above, callable objects may accept optional arguments with default values that may be omitted in a function call, and arguments may also be identified by keyword name instead of by position. As we shall see, the combination of keyword name with default values is an extremely useful convenience. In any call all positional parameters must precede all keyword parameters. Keyword style calling sequences are allowed even if no default values are given.

The following calls to info are invalid, however:

```
info(1,2,3)   # too many arguments (TypeError).
info(c=2)     # no such parameter (KeyError).
info(1, a=1)  # multiply defined value for a (TypeError).
info(a=1, 3)  # keyword argument precedes positional (SyntaxError).
```

apply(f, tuple), apply(f, tuple, dict)
Apply Function to Dynamic Arguments

The apply function allows the argument sequence to a function call to be constructed at run time. The tuple argument should list all the positional parameters for the call and the dictionary should contain all keyword/value pairs for the call. Consider the following function and the for loop that invokes the function using apply:

```
>>> def promo(nm, sl="Mr.", aw="A BRAND NEW CAR", date="Today"):
...     print """
...     Dear %s %s:
...         This note is to inform you that you have almost certainly
...     won %s!!! Just send back your order form by %s.
...         Sincerely, Joe Schmoe. """ % (sl, nm, aw, date)
...
>>> Suckers = [
        ("Smith", {}),
        ("Jones", {"sl":"Miss"}),
...     ("Skip", {"aw": "AN ALL PURPOSE LANGUAGE", "date": "Yesterday"})]
>>> for (name,dict) in Suckers:
...     apply(promo, (name,), dict)
...

    Dear Mr. Smith:
        This note is to inform you that you have almost certainly
    won A BRAND NEW CAR!!! Just send back your order form by Today.
        Sincerely, Joe Schmoe.
```

```
Dear Miss Jones:
    This note is to inform you that you have almost certainly
won A BRAND NEW CAR!!! Just send back your order form by Today.
    Sincerely, Joe Schmoe.

Dear Mr. Skip:
    This note is to inform you that you have almost certainly
won AN ALL PURPOSE LANGUAGE!!! Just send back your order form by
Yesterday.
    Sincerely, Joe Schmoe.
```

Here the for loop uses the `apply` function to dynamically execute the equivalent of:

```
promo("Smith")
promo("Jones", sl = "Miss")
promo("Skip", aw = "AN ALL PURPOSE LANGUAGE", date = "Yesterday")
```

The `apply` function is extremely powerful, as we shall see.

`filter(f, seq)`, `filter(None, seq)`
Filter Sequence by Function

The filter function applies a predicate `f` to each member of a sequence `seq`, returning a list of those elements that tested true. If the test function is `None`, the "true" elements of the sequence are returned.

```
>>> filter(None, [ 1, 0, "this", "", {}, {0:0}, {"three":3}] )
[1, 'this', {0: 0}, {'three': 3}]
>>>
>>> def mult_of_3(n):
...     return (n % 3) == 0
...
>>> filter(mult_of_3, [1,6,3,6,1,7,9,0,12,13,-9])
[6, 3, 6, 9, 0, 12, -9]
```

`map(f, seq)`

The `map` function applies a transformation function `f` to each member of a the sequence `seq` returning a list of transformed values.

```
>>> from string import upper, lower
>>> l = ["Free", "Software", "inside"]
>>> map(upper, l)
['FREE', 'SOFTWARE', 'INSIDE']
>>> map(lower, l)
['free', 'software', 'inside']
```

As mentioned, if the first argument to map is None, then the result is the input sequence translated to a list format (or copied, if it was a list to begin with). You can think of map as implemented as follows

```
def my_map(transform, seq):
    result = []
    for elt in seq:
        result.append( transform(elt) )
    return result
```

except that the real map function runs faster and permits the first argument to be None.

reduce(f, sequence)
reduce(f, sequence, init)

This cute function is not used very often in practice. It is equivalent to:

```
dummy = {} # a uniquely identifiable dummy reference

def my_reduce(function, sequence, init= dummy):
    if init is dummy:
        init = sequence[0]
        sequence = sequence[1:]
    for elt in sequence:
        init = function(elt, init)
    return elt
```

We don't encourage the use of reduce too much, because it is very easy to think an operation that uses reduce is clever and efficient, when in fact it is very slow, especially if the function builds large structures. Hard-core functional programming fans will like reduce very much and will also know when its use is appropriate.

The following is a disastrous way to build a large string from a list of strings:

```
def concat(s1, s2):
    return s1 + s2

big_string = reduce(concat, big_list_of_string, "")
```

Don't do this: It will recopy the first string in the list once for each element of the list, the second string one less time than that, and so forth. Use `joinfields` instead:

```
import string
big_string = string.joinfields(big_list_of_string, "")
```

The `joinfields` function will copy each substring of the list exactly once.

Intrinsic Operations for Objects with Dynamic Attributes

Classes, instances, and modules all have dynamic attributes, and a number of functions and notations allow programs to manipulate the attributes of objects of these types. Classes and instances conform to inheritance rules for attribute retrieval, as described in greater detail below, but attribute assignment and deletion is only done in the local namespace of an object—never in any inherited name space.

In this section, we leave the discussion somewhat brief and abstract, but the following sections detail the use of attributes and inheritance with further examples.

The static attribute `s.A` notation along with the `getattr` and `hasattr` functions may be used with any object with attributes even if those attributes may not be modified (such as in the case of file objects and objects of other types), but they are listed in the context of dynamic attributes for uniformity of presentation.

`vars(S)` Dump Object Local Name Space

This function returns a dictionary mapping names to values for the local namespace of an object, for example:

```
>>> class Programmer:
...     eyes = "red"
...     clothes = "rumpled"
...     does_he_she_care = 0
...
>>> vars(Programmer)
{'eyes': 'red', '__doc__': None, 'does_he_she_care': 0, 'clothes': 'rumpled'}
```

`S.A` Static Attribute Retrieval

The `S.A` notation retrieves the value for the attribute `A` of the object `S`. For instances and classes, this expression may trigger a search for an inherited attribute value when there is no such attribute defined locally in the name space for `S`.

NOTE

Attribute retrieval inheritance rules: If `S` is an instance of class `C` and the attribute `A` is not assigned in the local name space for `S`, then `S.A` will evaluate to `C.A`, or fail if there is no such attribute of `C`. If `C.A` turns out to be an unbound method, the method binds to the instance `S`. Note that the search for `C.A` may result in a search of the superclasses of `C`, as described below.

If `S` is a class declared

```
class S(S1, S2, S3): # S1, S2, S3 are the ordered superclasses of S.
    ...
```

and the attribute `A` is not assigned in the local name space for `S` then `S.A` will evaluate to `S1.A` if it is defined, or otherwise `S2.A` if it is defined, or otherwise `S3.A` if it is defined. In any case, if no local or inherited value can be found for the attribute `A`, the `S.A` expression will trigger an AttributeError. Note that the search for `S1.A` may cause a search of the attributes of the superclasses of `S1`, too.

S.A = x Static Attribute Assignment

This assignment sets the value of the attribute A of object S to the value x in the local name space for S. Attribute assignment only effects the name space of S, not any other name space inherited by S:

```
>>> class Record:
...     fname = "joe"
...     lname = "schmoe"
...
>>> Record.fname
'joe'
>>> r = Record()
>>> r.fname
'joe'
>>> r.fname = "sue"
>>> r.fname
'sue'
>>> Record.fname
'joe'
```

Here the instance r inherits r.fname from Record.fname until the local assignment r.fname = "sue" overrides the inherited value. The assignment does not alter the value of Record.fname but merely, however.

del S.A Static Attribute Deletion

This statement deletes the attribute A in the local name space for S, if present, and leaves any inherited value for S.A unchanged. Continuing the previous example:

```
>>> del r.fname
>>> r.fname
'joe'
>>> del r.fname
Traceback (innermost last):
  File "<stdin>", line 1, in ?
AttributeError: delete non-existing instance attribute
```

`delattr(S, name)` Dynamic Attribute Deletion

`getattr(S, name)` Dynamic Attribute Retrieval

`setattr(S, name, value)` Dynamic Attribute Assignment

`hasattr(S, name)` Dynamic Attribute Test

The first three of these are, respectively, the dynamic translations:

Dynamic Notation	Static Translation
delattr(S, "A")	del S.A
getattr(S, "A")	S.A
setattr(S, "A", 1)	S.A = 1

However, when the `name` string is not a literal string, there is no general way to translate, for example `getattr(S, name)` into the static notation. These dynamic attribute access functions provide great power, as will be seen.

The `hasattr(S, name)` returns true if S has an attribute of name name.

`dir(S)` Dump Local Names

This function returns the names from the namespace of S as a list of strings.

Simple Minded Multiple Inheritance Example

In this section, we give an unmotivated and abstract example of inheritance, designed for extreme simplicity. We will see many motivated examples in the balance of the book.

To illustrate the inheritance mechanism for class and instance attributes, consider the following class hierarchy with this diagram:

```
     Top

Left   Right │ superclasses,
             │ in left/right order.

  Bottom     │
```

and the Python declarations

```
class Top:
    left = "Top Left"
    top = "Top Top"
    bottom = "Top Bottom"
    right = "Top Right"

class Left(Top):
    left = "Left Left"
    bottom = "Left Bottom"

class Right(Top):
    bottom = "Right Bottom"
    right = "Right Right"

class Bottom(Left, Right):
    bottom = "Bottom Bottom"

def dump(thing):
    return (thing.left, thing.top, thing.bottom, thing.right)
```

Alright. This is a classic completely unmotivated academic example, but at least it's terse. Let's dump out some of these classes and see what attributes they inherit:

```
>>> for x in (Top, Left, Right, Bottom):
...     print x.__name__, dump(x)
...
Top ('Top Left', 'Top Top', 'Top Bottom', 'Top Right')
Left ('Left Left', 'Top Top', 'Left Bottom', 'Top Right')
Right ('Top Left', 'Top Top', 'Right Bottom', 'Right Right')
Bottom ('Left Left', 'Top Top', 'Bottom Bottom', 'Top Right')
```

Not surprisingly, whenever a class (say, Bottom) has no local name for an attribute (say Bottom.top), it inherits the attribute from one of its superclasses (in the case of `Bottom.top` from `Top` via the direct superclass `Left`). Note that `Bottom` inherits nothing from its `Right` superclass because `Left` defines the attributes `left` locally and both `top` and `right` are inherited from `Top` before the inheritance search ever reaches `Right`, which is searched last.

Nevertheless, we may dynamically add a new attribute to Right and immediately see it inherited by Bottom, as follows:

```
>>> Right.r_local = "new right attribute"
>>> Bottom.r_local
'new right attribute'
```

As described, instances of these classes inherit any attribute values they do not define locally from their class (which may in turn inherit from superclasses):

```
>>> Bt = Bottom()
>>> dump(Bt)
('Left Left', 'Top Top', 'Bottom Bottom', 'Top Right')
>>> Bt.left = "my own left"
>>> dump(Bt)
('my own left', 'Top Top', 'Bottom Bottom', 'Top Right')
>>> dump(Bottom)
('Left Left', 'Top Top', 'Bottom Bottom', 'Top Right')
```

As we can see, assignments to the local namespace of `Bt` do not affect the namespace of its class `Bottom`, but they may prevent `Bt` from inheriting `Bottom.left` when `Bt.left` is defined in `Bt`'s local name space.

The present authors find unmotivated examples such as this unsatisfying, and hence we apologize. Nevertheless, we hope this simple case gives the reader insight into the inheritance mechanism.

Instance Methods and the Automatic Binding of self

There is an important nuance regarding attributes of instances. Consider the following:

```
import string

class string_accumulator:
```

```
def __init__(self):
    self.list = [""]
def append(self, string):
    self.list.append(string)
def dump(self):
    if len(self.list) == 1:
        return self.list[0]
    s = string.joinfields(self.list, "")
    self.list = [s]
    return s
```

This class efficiently accumulates long sequences of strings and dumps out their concatenation on demand. Lets examine the attributes of this class and the attributes of an instance of this class:

```
>>> sa = string_accumulator()
>>> string_accumulator.append
<unbound method string_accumulator.append>
>>> sa.append
<method string_accumulator.append of string_accumulator instance at 123840>
```

 Note that `sa.append` and `string_accumulator.append` are not the same! The second is the generic method for all instances of `string_accumula-tor`, but the first is the generic method made specific to the instance sa.

NOTE

More generally the attributes of an instance x that evaluate to methods of a class are automatically bound with the instance x as the first argument of the method (conventionally named `self`). Thus, we can name the bound methods of `sa` and use them as follows:

```
>>> eater = sa.append
>>> spitter = sa.dump
>>> for x in range(100, 110):
...     eater( `x` )
...
>>> spitter()
'100101102103104105106107108109'
```

Try it! Experimentation is the best way to get a handle on these concepts.

Intrinsic Operations for Modules

Modules provide the highest-level name spaces for naming Python objects, and
they have a number of special operations devoted to them.

NOTE Modules in Python are dynamic, not static, as in most other common programming languages. This is very nice for cross-platform and multiconfiguration
development, because a Python program can dynamically test the environment
and load the functionality appropriate for that environment, or available in that
environment. For example:

```
try:
    # try to get high performance set operations as builtins
    import kjbuckets
except ImportError:
    # kjbuckets not unavailable; use a slower implementation
    import mySets
    kjbuckets = mySets
```

Remember that it's perfectly alright to try to use a module that's not there, provided you can back off to an alternate that will work.

`import` M **Module Import**

This operation imports the module as a name in the current name space (usually
the namespace of the current module). If the module has not been loaded before,
this will result in a search for the module and an initialization of the module. If
the module already exists, however, it will not be re-initialized or reloaded.

`from M import X,Y,Z,` `from M import *` **Import Names from Module**

This operation imports a sequence of names from the module M as local names
in the current name space. As before, this will result in a search for the module
and an initialization for M only if M has not already been loaded. Only use this
form for the names you need and/or for modules M that have already been
debugged and tested, because this form of importing destroys the utility of the
`reload` operation.

`reload(M)` **Reload a Module**

This operation reloads a previously loaded module M and reinitializes the module. This operation is primarily useful for debugging, where the source for the module M is changed and the programmer wishes to obtain the new version of M without restarting the interactive Python interpreter.

As mentioned above, although reload will re-create the module, it will not replace names imported *from* the module into other modules.

WARNING

The `reload(M)` function requires an existing module (or an expression which produced a module, whereas the `import` statements require module names. If an interactive `import` fails try modifying the source file for the module and then type

NOTE

```
import M
reload(M)
```

to guarantee that the module is reloaded from the source file.

`__import__(name)`
Dynamically Import a Module by Name

This is the dynamic version of the `import` statement. `__import__("regex")` is equivalent to `import regex`, but in contrast to the `import` statement `__import__` permits programs to import modules named by dynamic strings. This function is obscure and rarely needed.

The statement `import regex` is precisely equivalent to the assignment `regex = __import__("regex")`.

NOTE

Intrinsic Operations for None

There aren't any! That's why it's called None.

Fancy Intrinsic Operations for Executing Data (Careful!)

Python supports a number of built-in functions which allow data to be executed as parts of a program. These functions are dangerous for many applications and should be used with great care.

 Especially in the context of networked applications, these functions should be used with great caution. In particular only code from trusted sources should ever be evaluated, unless the module executing the code runs under Python's restricted execution mode.

Behold the functions used for compiling and executing data, we will not discuss them in detail, but instead refer the reader to the standard library manual and the reference manual that come with the Python distribution.

```
>>> input("hello? ")
hello? 23 - 9
14
>>> C = compile("oct(123)", "", "eval")
>>> exec C
>>> eval(C)
'0173'
>>> D = {}
>>> execfile("cowboy.py", D)
>>> D.keys()
['COWBOY', 'Cowboy_fn', '__builtins__', 'COWGIRL']
```

The statement `exec` and the functions `eval`, `execfile`, and `input` are quite powerful and useful if properly used, but they must be used with caution.

What Next?

At this point we have covered most of the Python language, either explicitly or by example, but there are some issues of syntax and control constructs that need more careful explanation. These issues are covered in the next chapter.

CHAPTER FIVE

SYNTAX AND CONTROL

We have already covered a lot of the syntax for Python in the process of discussing the semantics above, so some of the summary below will simply refer to previous sections. However, there are a number of points which fit best in a separate presentation on syntax. We also discuss the primary control constructs in detail as follows.

Expressions

A Python expression is a piece of syntax which returns a Python object, and which may be used as the right side of an assignment or in other constructs which permit entries for values (such as in argument lists for function calls).

Behold the universe of Python expressions:

Names: Any name, regardless of the object the name names, is an expression that returns the object named by the identifer. As described above, Python uses scoping rules to decide whether an name is local, global, or a name for a standard built-in object. For example, the right sides of all the assignments below are name expressions with various scopes:

```
>>> x = None # the right side of this assignment is a built in name
>>> y = len  # same here.
```

```
>>> z = y     # The right side of this assignment is a global name
>>> def f():
...     x = y # Since y is not local, it is global
...     z = x # But x is local, since it is assigned here.
...     w = range # range is not local, not global,
...               # but it names a standard built in.
...
...
```

Literals: Instances of ints, longs, floats, and strings may be created using literal notations, as in the right sides of the following assignments:

```
>>> sq_string = 'a single quoted string'
>>> dq_string = "a double quoted string"
>>> tsq_string = '''a triple single quoted string'''
>>> tdq_string = """a triple double quoted string"""
>>> cat_string = "an " 'adjoined' """ sequence """ "of" ''' strings'''
>>>
>>> decimal_int = 6395         # doesn't start with 0
>>> octal_int = 05347          # starts with 0
>>> hexadecimal_int = 0x79ee1a # starts with 0x or 0X
>>>
>>> decimal_long = 8776234100921896L  # ends with L or l
>>> octal_long = 077123667542L
>>> hexadecimal_long = 0xffe3a99d6000fL
>>>
>>> usual_float = 2.777779
>>> final_dot_float = 5567.
>>> leading_dot_float = .0005
>>> exponent_float_no_dot = 666e24
>>> exponent_float_w_dot = 6.66e26
>>> neg_exponent_float = 34.9e-11
```

Many of these notations will be familiar to many readers, who may feel free to skip parts of the section below which describes each of these notations in gruesome detail.

   Parentheses: Any expression may be placed in parentheses to form a parenthesized expression:

```
>>> ("Where do we go from here?  Which is the way that's clear?")
"Where do we go from here?  Which is the way that's clear?"
```

As in basic high school algebra, parentheses force the syntax within the parentheses to be evaluated as a single expression, which may override the normal rules of precedence for operators. For example, the addition of parentheses cause the following two expressions to evaluate differently:

```
>>> 4.5 * 6.7 - 2.9 * 3.1
21.16
>>> 4.5 * (6.7 - 2.9) * 3.1
53.01
```

In this case, multiplication normally has higher precedence than subtraction, but by placing parentheses around the subtraction we force the subtraction to occur first, before the multiplications.

In general (just as in many other languages and common mathematical notations) it is a good idea to use parentheses on expressions liberally in order to explicitly indicate the intended computation for an expression. Expressions that rely on operator precedence can be confusing and can easily be in error. For example, many prefer

```
((x is None) and (y < 3)) or (not D.has_key(name))
```

over

```
x is None and y < 3 or not D.has_key(name)
```

even though they represent precisely the same computation to Python.

Tuples: In a normal expression, context commas between expressions construct tuple objects containing the values associated with the expressions:

```
>>> "milk", "onions", "oat meal", "pickled pigs feet"
('milk', 'onions', 'oat meal', 'pickled pigs feet')
```

The problem with using the comma notation alone for constructing tuples is that commas are also used in other contexts in Python, such as in function argument lists, in list display notations, and in dictionary display notations. Thus, to avoid confusion, it is preferable to use "redundant" parenthesizes in comma separated lists of expressions to create tuple objects, and to also parenthesize any complex expression within the list. For example, we would prefer

```
((x * 2), (y - 5), (z / 7))
```

over

```
x * 2, y - 5, z / 7
```

even though these expressions are equivalent, as we see in the following interaction:

```
>>> (x, y, z) = (8.5, 1e-3, 7.8e3)
>>> ( (x * 2), (y - 5), (z / 7) )
(17.0, -4.999, 1114.28571429)
>>> x * 2, y - 5, z / 7
(17.0, -4.999, 1114.28571429)
```

NOTE

The following notations for create singleton and empty tuples:

```
>>> p = (1,)    # singleton tuple
>>> print p, len(p)
(1,) 1
>>> p = ()      # empty tuple
>>> print p, len(p)
() 0
>>> p = (1)     # an integer, not a tuple
>>> print p, len(p)
1
Traceback (innermost last):
  File "<stdin>", line 1, in ?
TypeError: len() of unsized object
```

List displays: Square brackets enclosing a comma-separated list of expressions define an expression which creates a new list containing the values associated with each of the expressions. For example:

```
>>> ["Norm", "Woody", "Sam", "Kramer"]
['Norm', 'Woody', 'Sam', 'Kramer']
>>> [ord, map, apply]
[<built-in function ord>, <built-in function map>, <built-in function apply>]
>>> def f(tuple):
...     (a, b) = tuple
...     return (b, (a+b))
...
>>> [ f((1, 1)), f(f((1, 1))), f(f(f((1, 1)))) ]
[(1, 2), (2, 3), (3, 5)]
```

Here the last list generated is a list of three tuples, which some readers may recognize as related to the famous Fibonacci sequence.

Dictionary displays: A curly brackets notation creates new dictionary objects:

```
>>> { 0.5: -1, 0: 0, 2: 1, 4: 2 }
{0: 0, 0.5: -1, 2: 1, 4: 2}
>>> { None: "unknown", 1: "unit", 0: "false" }
{0: 'false', 1: 'unit', None: 'unknown'}
>>> { "ls": "dir", "cp": "copy", "cd": "cd" }
{'cp': 'copy', 'cd': 'cd', 'ls': 'dir'}
>>> { (0,0) : "origin",
...   (0,1) : "upper left",
...   (1,0) : "lower right",
...   (1,1) : "upper right" }
{(1, 1): 'upper right', (1, 0): 'lower right', (0, 0): 'origin',
 (0, 1): 'upper left'}
```

The general form for the dictionary display notation is

```
{ key1: value1, key2: value2, ..., keyn: valuen }
```

where the keys and values are each expressions.

 In display notations, "redundant" trailing commas are permitted.

NOTE

Standard String Conversion: A special expression notation

```
` expression `
```

(an expression bracketed by back ticks) allows arbitrary Python values to be converted into string values. See the section on Generic Built-In Methods for more information on this notation. This is short-hand for `repr(expression)`.

Attribute expressions: Many objects have "attributes" which can be retrieved using the notation

```
expression.attribute
```

Most notable among the objects which have attributes are modules, classes, and class instances.

```
>>> import string
>>> string.letters # attribute letters of module string
'abcdefghijklmnopqrstuvwxyzABCDEFGHIJKLMNOPQRSTUVWXYZ'
```

Other Python objects sometimes have attributes too. For example, lists and dictionaries have built-in methods named by attribute notation. See the section on objects with dynamic attributes for more information regarding inheritance and attribute access.

Subscript expressions: The expression `Structure[expression]` retrieves a single element from a dictionary or sequence. See the discussion of special methods for dictionaries and sequences above.

Slice expressions: The expressions `L[:]`, `L[n:m]`, `L[n:]`, `L[:m]` are each slice expressions which construct a subsequence of a sequence. See the discussion of built-in operations for sequence elements for more information regarding slice expressions.

Calls: The expressions `f(a,b,c)`, `f(name="Lonny", age=5)`, and `f(name, age=5, gender="male")` are all call notations which may be used with callable objects. See the discussion of special methods for callable objects for more information on function calls.

The "usually arithmetic" expressions: The following notations allow traditional arithmetic notations in Python when applied to numeric values. Some of the notations have special meanings when applied to other types, such as strings or sequences, as noted in the section on each individual type.

Notation	Normal Interpretation
x + y	numeric addition (sequence catenation)
x - y	numeric subtraction
x * y	numeric multiplication (sequence repetition)
x / y	numeric division
x % y	numeric modulus (string substitution)

The bit manipulation expressions: The following notations allow bit manipulations see the section on special methods for integers and longs.

```
~m,  m >> n. m << n, m & n, m ^ n, m | n
```

Truth-valued expressions (logical operations and comparisons): The ordinal comparison expressions

```
X < Y, X > Y, X <= Y, X >= Y, X != Y
```

all evaluate to the truth values true (1) or false (0). Furthermore, comparisons may be chained. Thus `0 <= X < Y < 1.0` and `0<=X and X<Y and Y<1.0` have the same intuitive reading (although because X is evaluated precisely once in the former, they have a slightly different semantics).

The operators

```
X is Y, X is not Y
```

test identity, and also evaluate to truth values. The truth-valued operators

```
X in S, X not in S
```

test sequence membership.

Literals

String Literals

A string literal expression generates a string object. There are several forms for string literals:

```
string1 = 'The Lion Sleeps Tonight'
string2 = "You Can't Always Get What You Want"
string3 = \
"""The play "The Effect of Gamma Rays on Man In
   the Moon Marigolds" isn't as technical as it may sound"""
string4 = '''You say "Yes,"  I say "No."'''
```

The values assigned with string1 and string2 are single-quoted strings. Single-quoted strings proceed from the first single (double) quote mark to the next unescaped single (double) quote mark. Quote marks may be inserted inside a single quoted string by preceding them with a backslash:

```
>>> print 'You can't always get what you want' # this won't work
  File "<stdin>", line 1
```

```
    print 'You can't always get what you want'
                     ^
SyntaxError: invalid syntax
>>>
>>> print 'You can\'t always get what you want' # but this will work.
You can't always get what you want
```

The values assigned to string3 and string4 are triple-quoted strings, which may include explicit line breaks and form feeds, and hence are convenient for formatting long multiline texts.

The backslash-newline sequence in a string literal can aid in formatting longish text as well. For example, instead of:

```
Lyric = """To avoid complication
    she never kept the same address.
In conversation
    she spoke just like a baroness."""
```

(which doesn't look right) we can write the more readable

```
Lyric = """\
To avoid complication
    she never kept the same address.
In conversation
    she spoke just like a baroness"""
```

to precisely the same effect. A backslash-newline sequence in a string literal is ignored and omitted from the string, which in the above literal allows us to format the string exactly as we want it to print.

To construct long strings that may consist of a single huge line string values may be appended implicitly by adjoining them. For example

```
>>> x = "hello" "world"
>>> x
'helloworld'
>>> too_long = (  # this needs parens to make it into a multiline expression.
...     "This is a string that contains no newlines, but we can write"
...     " it on multiple lines by adjoining strings in parentheses."
...     " Alternatively, we could also use string addition (catenation)"
...     " or even string.join or string.joinfields as we have seen,"
...     " but the present method is the preferred approach, in the case where"
...     " all the strings to catenate are literals.")
```

String literals also support standard "escape sequences" which represent special characters. Any character can be written using the "octal escaped representation" of the form "\DDD" where "DDD" is the three digit octal representation for the ascii value associated with the character. For example, "\141" is another way to write the string "a". In addition a number of common characters have special representations:

Name	Escaped Form	Equivalents
bell (alert)	"\a"	"\007"
backspace	"\b"	"\010"
horizontal tab	"\t"	"\011"
newline (line feed)	"\n"	"\012"
vertical tab	"\v"	"\013"
form feed	"\f"	"\014"
carriage return	"\r"	"\015"
double quote	"\""	"\042" or '"'
apostrophe	"\'"	"\047" or "'"

Many of these string conventions are borrowed from ANSI C language conventions for string representation. Hexadecimal representations are also remitted, which allows any number of digits. Try "\x0006f".

Integer Literals

Integer objects may be created using three alternative representations. For example, the following are all ways of creating the same integer value:

```
>>> 943   # the usual decimal representation (base 10)
943
>>> 01657 # a leading zero indicates octal representation (base 8)
943
>>> 0x3af # a leading 0x indicates hexadecimal representation (base 16)
943
```

Decimal integer literals are a sequence of digits that doesn't start with a zero. Most programmers use this representation exclusively because decimal notation is the notation people use in day-to-day life.

As a relatively obscure feature, Python allows hexidecimal and octal integer literals as well as decimal integer literals. Once in a while (especially when using primitive subroutine libraries that require single integers to represent several bit fields) it is useful to create integers using octal (base 8) or hexidecimal (base 16) notation, which are indicated by a leading zero (followed by octal digits which are the normal digits except for 8 and 9) or a leading "0x" followed by hexidecimal digits (which include the usual digits as well as the hex digits ABCDEF (either in upper- or lowercase), respectively.

For example, the following expressions produce equivalent lists of integers in decimal, octal, and hexidecimal, respectively:

```
>>> [0, 1, 2, 3, 4, 5, 6, 7, 8, 9, 10, 11, 12, 13, 14, 15, 16, 17]
[0, 1, 2, 3, 4, 5, 6, 7, 8, 9, 10, 11, 12, 13, 14, 15, 16, 17]
>>> [00, 01, 02, 03, 04, 05, 06, 07, 010, 011, 012, 013,
...  014, 015, 016, 017, 020, 021]
[0, 1, 2, 3, 4, 5, 6, 7, 8, 9, 10, 11, 12, 13, 14, 15, 16, 17]
>>> [0x0, 0x1, 0x2, 0x3, 0x4, 0x5, 0x6, 0x7, 0x8, 0x9, 0xa,
...  0xb, 0xc, 0xd, 0xe, 0xf, 0x10, 0x11]
[0, 1, 2, 3, 4, 5, 6, 7, 8, 9, 10, 11, 12, 13, 14, 15, 16, 17]
```

If you don't already understand hexidecimal and octal representations, you may never need to understand them, so we won't talk more about them here, except to mention that integer values may be converted back to string octal or hexidecimal string representations using the standard built in functions hex and oct.

```
>>> hex(943)
'0x3af'
>>> oct(943)
'01657'
```

Python normal converts integers to decimal representations for printing.

Long Integer Literals

Long integers may be of arbitrary size and are constructed by appending an L to an integer expression, as in 9999999999999999999L. Lowercase "el" also tags a long integer, but it looks a lot like a "one," so we avoid using this notation.

Floating Point Literals

Floating point values are indicated by an exponent or a decimal point somewhere in the representation. The following are all equivalent floating point values

```
>>> 10.0, 1e1, 1e+1, 0.1e+2, 100.0e-1
(10.0, 10.0, 10.0, 10.0, 10.0)
```

It is worth noting that although `class` and `def` statements create and name class and function (or method) objects, respectively, they do not "return" a value, and thus are not expressions.

Operator Precedence

We advise you not to think too hard about operator precedence—use a lot of parentheses instead. But for those that are interested, here is the order of precedence:

Notation	Description
(x), [a,b], {a: b} `a`	Parentheses, Displays, string conversion
s[i]	Subscript
x.ID	Attribute reference
~a	Bit inversion
+a, -a	Unary plus and minus
a * b, a / b, a % b	Multiplication, division, remainder
+, -	Addition and subtraction
i << j, i >> j	Bit shifting
i | j, i & j, i ^ j	Bitwise operations
A < B, A >= B, etc.	Comparisons (some omitted)
not A	Negation
A and B	Conjunction
A or B	Disjunction

The precedence shown is from highest to lowest, meaning that operations listed earlier bind tighter than those listed lower. For example,

```
a + b >> i . x & j
```

is equivalent to

```
((a + b) >> (i.x)) & j
```

Variables and Scoping

In contrast to values, which always have types in Python, variables never have types—a Python variable names an arbitrary object. Syntactically, a Python variable is a name which is not subordinate to an object via the dot notation. For example, in the statement

```
TEXT = string.upper(text)
```

x, string, and TEXT are all variables, but upper refers to an attribute of the object associated with the string variable.

There is precisely one exception where an unqualified name is not a variable—when it's a keyword specifier in an argument list. Consider the following function:

```
def decision(person, shoe_size=10, IQ=100):
    if shoe_size>IQ:
        print "Fire", person
    else:
        print "Promote", person
```

By using Python keyword arguments (described in greater detail below) we can invoke this function with the arguments out of order, among other conveniences, but the keyword names used to accomplish this feat are not variables, strictly speaking. For example, in the following invocations, none of the references to person, shoe_size, and IQ are variables.

```
decision("Paul", IQ=150)
decision(person="Sonny", IQ=7, shoe_size=17) # just kidding, Congressman.
decision(shoe_size=9, person="George")
```

In general, a complete Python program can use the same variable names many times to name many different objects, and Python distinguishes the different variables with the same name using scoping rules. Python's scoping rules are similar in spirit to those of the C programming language or other lexically scoped languages.

When the Python interpreter encounters a variable X, it decides that the variable is one of the following.

```
X is a local variable in a function F.
X is a local variable in a method M.
X is a local variable in a class C.
X is a global variable of the current module.
X is a global standard intrinsic variable.
No such X.
```

We now examine the conditions under which Python reaches each of these determinations.

X is a local variable in a function F:

In this case the variable reference is enclosed in the function definition for F, and X is assigned somewhere within the definition for F. For example,

```
def F( ... ):
    ...
    # due to the following assignment ALL references to X
    # inside the definition for F are local:
    X = value
    ...
```

To illustrate this mechanism, consider the following programming mistake which has been known sometimes to occur:

```
>>> def falala(repititions):
...     print "Fa",
...     range = range(repititions)
...     for count in range:
...         print "La",
...     print
...
>>> falala(8)
```

```
Fa
Traceback (innermost last):
  File "<stdin>", line 1, in ?
  File "<stdin>", line 3, in falala
NameError: range
```

Apparently Python could not find the value of range. Now range is a standard intrinsic function: Why wasn't it found?

In this case, in the statement

```
range = range(repitions)
```

we tried to initialize a local variable called range using the range function. However, thanks to this very same assignment, ALL references to range inside the function definition are considered local references—even the function call on the right side of the assignment! Thus, in attempting to evaluate range(repititions), Python found that the local variable range had not been initialized. A two-character change suffices to correct this error:

```
>>> def falala(repititions):
...     print "Fa",
...     range1 = range(repititions)
...     for count in range1:
...         print "La",
...     print
...
>>> falala(8)
Fa La La La La La La La La
```

By assigning to range1 instead, the reference to range is not inferred local, and Python uses the standard range function from the standard built-in module, as desired.

All arguments in a function definition are considered local variables to a function also. Thus, the following function also includes a scoping error:

```
>>> def checklength(list, len):
...     if len(list)!=len:
...         return "length is wrong"
...     else:
...         return "length is okay"
...
```

```
>>> checklength(["an","example","list"], 2)
Traceback (innermost last):
  File "<stdin>", line 1, in ?
  File "<stdin>", line 2, in checklength
TypeError: call of non-function
```

Again, this error may be corrected by replacing the len argument with a name that doesn't "shadow" the built-in function len:

```
>>> def checklength(list, length):
...     if len(list) != length:
...         return "length is wrong"
...     else:
...         return "length is okay"
...
>>> checklength(["an","example","list"], 2)
'length is wrong'
```

Local and global variables of the same name never interfere with each other: Assigning to a global will not change a local variable of the same name, and assigning to a local will not change a global of the same name.

Local variables can also be created by import statements executed within a function definition:

```
def F( ... ):
    ...
    # by virtue of this ``import'' FTPlib becomes a local variable
    # within the definition of ``F'':
    import FTPlib
    ...
    # by virtue of this ``from... import...'' statement ``joinfields''
    # becomes a local variable of ``F'':
    from string import joinfields
    ...
```

Local variables that are used before they have been assigned a value cause the interpreter to raise a NameError—Python does not try to guess what value the variable was meant to have (unlike some languages the reader may have seen):

```
>>> x = 16
>>> def F():
...     y = x
...     x = 1
```

```
...
>>> F()
Traceback (innermost last):
  File "<stdin>", line 1, in ?
  File "<stdin>", line 2, in F
NameError: x
```

Here x is a local variable of F() (unrelated to the global variable assigned above the definition for F) which is used before it is assigned. In our experience, languages that try to guess values for uninitialized variables sometimes guess the wrong value at very bad times.

x Is a Local Variable in a Method M

This is essentially similar to the previous case, except in the context of a method definition. In this case the variable reference for X is enclosed within the method definition for M and X is assigned somewhere in the definition for M. For example as in:

```
class C( ... ):
  ...
  def M( ... ):
      ...
      # due to the following assignment all references to X
      # inside the def are local:
      X = value
      ...
```

Just as in function definitions, argument names in method declarations become local variables of the method, and import statements within a method definition create local variables as well. (Actually, as far as the parser is concerned, function defs and method defs are the same construct in different contexts.)

x Is a Local Variable in a Class C

Class declarations also define a local scope that exists only while the class object is being created.

```
class C( ... ):
  ...
    # Due to the following declaration all references to X
```

```
# inside the class statement are local.
X = value
...
Y = X + 1
```

The local variables of class creation become attributes of the class object after the class has been created. Hence, for example, after the class C has been created, the values associated with the variables X and Y assigned in the class statement above may be identified by. C.X and C.Y, respectively.

X **is a Global Variable of the Current Module**

Any variable which is not a local variable of one of the types listed above is either a global variable or an intrinsic name or an erroneous variable which does not exist. A reference to X which is not local refers to the global variable X of the current module, if there is such a variable in the current module. Modules usually initialize their global variables using assignment, function definition, class definition, or by importing a named object from another module:

```
# this creates a module global variable HTTPlib,
# naming the module defined in the HTTPlib.py source file
#
import HTTPlib

# this creates global variables split and upper naming objects
# of the same name initialized in the module string.
#
from string import split, upper

# this creates a module global variable X
#
X = 40

# this creates a module global variable F naming a function:
#
def F():
    # since X is neither an argument to F, nor assigned in F,
    # it is the global X initialized above
    return X + 1

# this creates a module global variable C naming a class:
```

```
#
class C:
    # here Y is local to class creation and X is global to the module
    Y = 3 * X
```

x Is a Global Standard Intrinsic Variable

Any variable which is not a local variable and which does not exist in the current module may refer to an attribute of the `built-in` module. The built in module is always searched last, and usually contains variables naming objects (such as `None`, the error object `NameError`, and the length function `len`) which are generally useful in Python programming.

NOTE As far as the parser and the compiler are concerned, there are only two scopes: global and local. The difference between a module global and an intrinsic global is determined at run time—if X is not local and doesn't match a currently defined module global, the interpreter searches the intrinsic namespace.

No Such x

If X is neither a local variable, a global variable of the current module, nor a standard intrinsic name, then there is no such variable, and the reference to X will trigger a NameError. For example:

```
>>> list = [X, Y, Z]
Traceback (innermost last):
  File "<stdin>", line 1, in ?
NameError: X
```

Here the variable X appears at the global level in the Python interactive interpreter (which executes in the module __main__), and because there was no X in __main__, and there is no standard built-in object named X, Python complained that there was no such X.

Variable references that appear within a function or method or class definition may also be *nonexistent* if they have not been assigned in the declaration and do not exist in the current module, and do not name a standard built-in object:

```
>>> def addtoX(N):
...     return X + N
...
>>> addtoX(5)
Traceback (innermost last):
  File "<stdin>", line 1, in ?
  File "<stdin>", line 2, in addtoX
NameError: X
```

The distinction between different kinds of local variables given above is provided for pedagogical purposes only: All local scopes are essentially the same. Local variables are created during the execution of a function, method, or during the creation of a class object and "disappear" after the execution has completed. Module global variables, in contrast, exist for the life of the module, or until they are explicitly deleted from the module.

Local variables of different class or function or method declarations do not interfere with each other. For example, in the following snippet of code none of the different assignments of X will effect the other X values:

```
# X as a module global
X = 99

# X as a function argument (local)
def F(X):
    ...

# X imported from another module within a function local scope
def G():
    from M import X
    ...

class C:
    # X as a class definition local
    X = "San Diego"

    def M1(self):
        # X as a method local
        X = None
```

The local variables of the SAME function, invoked more than once, do not interfere with each other either, as we will see under the section on recursion.

As a test, why will the following incr function always fail?

```
X = 0
def incr():
    X = X + 1
    return X
```

Try it!

Declarations (def, class, and global)

Unlike many programming languages, where large chapters can be devoted solely to the different types of declarations the language requires, Python only has three simple declarations: the def statement declares a function or (within a class declaration) a method of a class; the class statement declares a class object; and the global declaration declares a sequence of variables to have global scope.

We have seen examples of the class and def statements, but for fun we give an example of another function definition using def:

```
def factorial(n):
    "The number of ways N different objects can be arranged in a line."
    if n in (0,1):
        return 1L # use longs: factorials get BIG fast!
    else:
        return factorial(n-1) * n
```

This statement defines a function and names it factorial. Function and method declarations using def permit a number of interesting forms for declaring arguments, which we describe below.

We also give another class statement:

```
from math import sqrt

class Quadratic:

    """The quadratic a*x^2 + b*x + c.
       Do you remember high school algebra? I didn't; I asked Alex Kononov."""

    def __init__(self, a, b, c):
        (self.a, self.b, self.c) = (a, b, c)
        ds = self.discriminatesq = b*b - 4*a*c
        divisor = 2*a
```

```
    if ds>0:
        d = self.discriminate = sqrt(ds)
        self.roots = [ ( -b + d )/divisor, ( -b - d )/divisor ]
    elif ds==0:
        self.roots = [ -b/divisor ]
    else:
        self.roots = [] # an empty tuple (no real valued roots)

def apply(self, x):
    "compute the quadratic function at x"
    return self.a * x * x + self.b * x + self.c
```

This statement creates a class and names it Quadratic. For even more fun the initialization method for the class (__init__) computes the real valued roots of the quadratic form, if there are any. We will talk more about classes in the following paragraphs.

Most interesting at this point is the global declaration—it's interesting because it suggests that WE LIED SHAMELESSLY IN THE SECTION ON VARIABLES AND SCOPE. In particular, you can always specify that a variable that would normally be treated as a local variable should be interpreted as a global variable by declaring it global. We feel that because they are hardly ever really necessary, global variable declarations are an obscure feature of Python that should be avoided, but we describe them here anyway.

Python variables do not have fixed types, so they do not have type declarations. A Python variable is "created" the first time it is assigned. Normally a variable assignment creates a variable within the present scope—either within a local scope of a class or def declaration when the assignment is contained in such a declaration or within the global scope of the current module otherwise.

However, a variable declared global in a function or method has global scope in the current module. For example,

```
>>> count = 0  # a global variable
>>> def newcount():
...     global count # memo to Python: use the global variable count
...     save = count
...     count = count + 1
...     return save
...
>>> newcount()
0
```

```
>>> newcount()
1
>>> newcount()
2
>>> count
3
```

Here we declared the count variable global, so even though it is assigned in the function newcount, it retains global scope in the current module, and changes to count within the function are preserved from one invocation of newcount to the next.

Declaring variables global can sometimes be useful, particularly in debugging—but experience shows it is a bad idea to modify global variables generally speaking. The newcount example above provides a plausible use for a global declaration—using a global variable to generate a sequence of integers—but even here we feel it would be a better style to use class instances instead, because multiple instances would allow the creation of an arbitrary number of counters whereas newcount uses just one. The following is more agreeable to our eyes:

```
>>> class counter:
...     def __init__(self, initial=0):
...         self.count = initial
...     def new(self):
...         save = self.count
...         self.count = save + 1
...         return save
...
>>> newcount = counter().new
>>> newcount()
0
>>> newcount()
1
>>> othercount = counter().new
>>> othercount()
0
>>> othercount()
1
>>> newcount()
2
>>> othercount()
2
```

Even in the context of debugging, declaring variables global can often introduce new bugs beyond the ones that you are trying to find. In particular, programmers are confused sometimes by global variables "shared" between modules. For example, suppose we have a module Employees containing:

```
Num_employees = 0
```

And inside another module called Human_Relations we have the function:

```
from Employees import Num_employees

def hire_person(name):
    global Num_employees
    Num_employees = Num_employees + 1 # yuck!
    ...
```

In this case, the Human_Relations.hire_person function will fail (miserably) to
modify the value of Employees.Num_employees, because the statement

```
from Employees import Num_employees
```

does not create a shared variable between the two modules. Instead it creates a
new variable called Num_employees in the Human_Relations module, using
the present value of Employees.Num_Employees. Subsequent changes to the
value of this new variable are not reflected in a change to
Employees.Num_Employees, because the variables are distinct. If you find this
discussion confusing…good—your confusion suggests that you should avoid
modifying global variables, as we say.

If you avoid altering global values, you automatically avoid the possibility
of this confusion. Isn't that nice? But if you really insist, you can even declare a
sequence of variables global.

```
def f():
    global name, age, iq, num_ears, tail_length, snout_width
    ...
```

Oops. We lied again! Not all local variables can be declared global. Python
prevents function argument variables from being global, as we see below:

```
>>> def global_test_wont_work(x):
...     global x
```

```
...      return x
...
SyntaxError: name is local and global
```

NOTE Strictly spoken, only `global` is a declaration. The `def` and `class` constructs are statements that may be placed inside functions and executed dynamically, just like any other statement.

Assignments

The Python assignment statement is quite general and convenient. It can be simple like

```
X = ord("g")
```

Or it can unpackage a complex structure built from tuples and lists as in

```
(eye, [dorsal, gill], tail) = fish
```

Here if `fish` had the value `(2, [4.5, 6], "wide")` then we have

```
>>> dorsal, tail, eye, gill
(4.5, 'wide', 2, 6)
```

In particular, one may swap the value of X and Y like so:

```
(X, Y) = (Y, X)
```

Furthermore, assignments can be chained where each of the targets (left sides) for the assignments are assigned from the same right-hand value:

```
>>> person = (name, [iq, sal], job) = ("jake", [100, 2000], "fence")
>>> person, name, iq, sal, job
(('jake', [100, 2000], 'fence'), 'jake', 100, 2000, 'fence')
```

Unlike various languages that derive more directly from the C language, in Python, assignments are not expressions because they are statements that do not produce a value. Thus, in Python the statement

```
if (x = 0):
    raise "hell", "why the heck did you do that? x can't be 0!!!"
```

is a syntax error, not a horrible bug that won't show up until after the product has been in the field for half a year. This one feature of Python has prevented more bugs than we can name, in our humble experience.

The `if` Statement

The `if` statement allows Python to make simple decisions based on conditions of the program. A very simple example of an `if` statement is:

```
if name in ["foo", "bar"]:
   year = raw_input("What year did you graduate from MIT? ")
```

If statements also allow multiway branching, either just in two directions:

```
if age<18:
   raise AgeError, "You can't see the pictures that reside herein!"
else:
   send_filth()
```

or multiway branching using one or more `elif` clauses which may optionally be combined with an else clause as well.

```
if user_agent == "mozilla":
   send_java()
elif user_agent == "explorer":
   send_VBscript()
elif user_agent == "grail":
   send_Python()
else:
   send_default_html()
```

Loops (`while`, `for`, `break`, and `continue`)

There are two standard loop constructs in Python: the `while` and the `for` statement. The most general loop is the `while` loop which executes the body of the loop so long as the start condition evaluates to a `true` value.

As a silly example, the following function finds an int power of 2 greater than n:

```
def larger2power(n):
    p = 1
    while p<n:
        print "nope: %s < %s" % (p,n)
        p = p * 2
    return p
```

This rather talkative function executes as follows:

```
>>> larger2power(123)
nope: 1 < 123
nope: 2 < 123
nope: 4 < 123
nope: 8 < 123
nope: 16 < 123
nope: 32 < 123
nope: 64 < 123
128
```

If we want to be fancy, we could also use bit shifting to emulate multiplication by 2, but under certain conditions a bit shift may cause a value to "shift off the end" and become negative. We can test for this extreme condition using an else clause to a while loop.

```
def larger2power(n):
    p = 1
    while p>0:
        if p>n:
            break # we found a larger 2 power!
        p = p << 1
    else:
        print "p <= 0, did you give me a long?"
        return
    print "%s is a power of 2 greater than %s" % (p, n)
```

Here the loop terminates "normally" when the if statement determines that p has grown larger than n and in this case a break statement will terminate the loop without executing the else clause.

```
>>> larger2power(88)
128 is a power of 2 greater than 88
```

But if p becomes negative or zero, the while condition p>0 becomes false, terminating the loop and executing the else clause.

```
>>> larger2power(9999999999999L)
p <= 0, did you give me a long?
```

As demonstrated, there are actually several ways to terminate a `while` loop: If the `while` test becomes false the loop terminates and any `else` clause of the loop executes; if a `break` enclosed immediately in the loop executes, the loop terminates, not executing the `else` clause; also, if a `return` is executed anywhere inside the loop, the loop terminates; or if an unhandled error occurs in the loop, the loop terminates, and the else clause is not executed.

NOTE   The `else` clause on a loop executes only when the loop terminates normally without a `break` or `return` or the occurrence of an uncaught exception.

Thus, there is yet another way to define `larger2power` using errors and `returns` to terminate the loop:

```
def larger2power(n):
    p = 1
    while 1:
        if p>n:
            return p
        elif p<0:
            raise ValueError, "n too large: %s" % (n,)
        else:
            p = p<<1
    else:
        print "can't get here from anywhere"
```

Here the last print statement is unreachable code, because the `while` condition can never become false, and the only way an `else` statement to a loop is ever executed is if the `while` condition becomes false. The above `while` loop will only terminate via the `raise` or `return` statements. This implementation works as follows:

```
>>> larger2power(444444)
524288
>>> larger2power(44444444444444444L)
Traceback (innermost last):
  File "<stdin>", line 1, in ?
  File "<stdin>", line 7, in larger2power
```

```
ValueError: n too large: 44444444444444444L
```

There is another control construct that effects the behavior of loops: the `continue` construct.

```
def larger2power(n):
    p = 1
    while 1:
        if p<0:
            raise ValueError, "n too large %s" % n
        elif p<=n:
            p = p << 1
            continue
        return p
```

The `continue` construct short-circuits the execution of a loop body back up to the top of the loop. In the above example, the `continue` statement indicated prevented the `return` from executing until p is large enough. The `continue` and `break` constructs can be useful in short tight loops, because they can make loops faster and easier to read because they reduce the need for state variables. But these constructs should be avoided in longer looping constructs, because a human reader can fail to notice them, and become hopelessly confused—especially because `break` and `continue` always refer to the nearest enclosing loop, which easily may be confused with some other enclosing loop by the weary programmer.

The `for` loop can be regarded as an optimization of the `while` loop for iterating over sequences. For example, the following function uses a `for` loop to print out a well-known nursery rhyme:

```
Verse_data = [
  ("Mary had a", "little lamb", "whose fleece was white as snow"),
  ("And everywhere that", "Mary went", "that lamb was sure to go"),
  ("It followed her to", "school one day", "which was against the rules"),
  ("It made the children", "laugh and play", "to see a lamb at school")]

def mary():
    for verse in Verse_data:
        (lead, refrain, cadenza) = verse
        print lead + " " + refrain
        print "   " + refrain
        print "     " + refrain
```

```
print lead + " " + refrain
print "    " + cadenza
print
```

Here the variable of the loop `verse` binds to each member of `Verse_data` in turn, and the statements of the loop body execute for each member. For example, in the third iteration, `verse` receives the binding:

```
verse = ("It followed her to", "school one day", "which was against the
rules")
```

And the loop body prints:

```
It followed her to school one day
   school one day
     school one day
It followed her to school one day
   which was against the rules
```

NOTE The elements of the target of a for loop may be unpacked into several variables just like a multiple assignment, and hence we could have written

```
for (lead, refrain, cadenza) in Verse_data:
    print ...
```

directly. Remember that the variables must always exactly match each member of the target for the unpacking to succeed, however.

Of course `for` loops are not always child's play. The following function computes the union of the elements of a sequence of sequences.

```
def lists_union( Seq_of_Seq ):
    D = {}
    for Seq in Seq_of_Seq:
        for elt in Seq:
            D[elt] = elt
    return D.keys()
```

We may use this function, for example, as follows:

```
lists_union(["Wherefore", "art", "thou?"])
['u', 'e', '?', 'W', 'o', 'a', 'h', 't', 'f', 'r']
```

This function will fail for some sequences of sequences: why?

NOTE

The `for` loop permits `else` clauses and `break` and `continue` constructs, just like the `while` loop. Again the `else` clause only executes if control reaches the end of the loop without a `break`.

For example, the following function trims a sequence of words at the first word that includes a period.

```
def sentence(word_sequence):
    for index in range(len(word_sequence)):
        if "." in word_sequence[index]:
            break
    else:
        raise ValueError, "no period found"
    return word_sequence[:index+1]
```

If no period is found, the `else` clause will raise a `ValueError`.

```
>>> sentence(["Never", "say", "never.", "Again."])
['Never', 'say', 'never.']
>>> sentence(["Always", "say", "always"])
ValueError: no period found
```

Function and Method Definition and `return`

Functions and Methods of classes are defined using the same `def` construct, of form:

```
def NAME( FORMAL_ARGUMENTS ):
    DEFINITION_BLOCK
```

This presentation has already provided many examples of function definitions. For simplicity, we will refer to functions in the forgoing instead of constantly repeating "function or method" even though all the commentary about functions applies to both functions and methods.

When the function expression is called

```
NAME( ACTUAL_ARGUMENTS )
```

the actual arguments are bound to the formal arguments as local variables of the function NAME and the DEFINITION_BLOCK is executed.

The definition block may execute a return statement to explicitly return a value for the calling function expression. If control "drops off the end" of a function, the implicit return value of the function is None.

Python provides very exciting extended calling sequence conventions for functions: Functions may provide arguments with default values; functions may accept an arbitrary number of arguments; functions may be called with their arguments "out of order" using keyword names; functions may accept arbitrary collections of named keyword arguments. These features together greatly aid in making programs and interfaces remarkably short, clear, and flexible. We now discuss each of these possibilities.

Default Values for Arguments

It is often the case that a function may require parameters that frequently have the same value. In this case, the function definition may allow the calling program to omit the usual values by providing the usual value as a default:

```
def donate(amount = 10, kind = "deductible"):
    print amount, kind
```

here we may call the donate function with no arguments to use all defaults, or we may give one or both arguments:

```
>>> donate()
10 deductible
>>> donate(5)
5 deductible
>>> donate(1000, "bribe")
1000 bribe
>>> donate(kind = "tip")
10 tip
```

The last call illustrates how a keyword argument (described below) may override only a specific default value, and leave the others alone.

WARNING

Never mutate a default value for a function argument. Any mutations performed to a default argument will persist to the next call of the function, and this is usually a very confusing occurrence. For example, observe

```
>>> def funny(x, list=[]):
...     list.append(x)
...     return list
...
>>> funny(1)
[1]
>>> funny(2)
[1, 2]
>>> funny(3)
[1, 2, 3]
```

Despite its bizarre nature, this feature is indispensable "once in a blue moon," so it is a permanent part of Python. Due to this feature, it is usually best to avoid using mutable values such as lists or dictionaries as default values—use None instead and override the value explicitly in the function body.

```
>>> def boring(x, list=None):
...     if list is None:
...         list = [] # make a new list if one wasn't given...
...     list.append(x)
...     return list
...
>>> boring(1)
[1]
>>> boring(2)
[2]
>>> boring(3, [5,6])
[5, 6, 3]
```

Arbitrary Length Argument Sequences

A function may accept an arbitrary sequence of arguments by providing a "catch-all" sequence argument *arg, which must follow all named arguments.

```
def stats(init = 0.0, *others):
    print init, others
    total = init
    for x in others:
        total = x + total
    print "total %s, avg %s" % (total, total/(1+len(others)))
```

Here the `stats` function may be called with zero or more arguments, for example, as follows:

```
>>> stats()
0.0 ()
total 0.0, avg 0.0
>>> stats(4.0)
4.0 ()
total 4.0, avg 4.0
>>> stats(4.1, 5.4, 3, 4, 9)
4.1 (5.4, 3, 4, 9)
total 25.5, avg 5.1
```

If the first argument is provided, it is bound to the `init` formal parameter to `stats`. Any additional arguments are collected as a tuple and bound to `others`. If there are 1 or fewer arguments the others tuple will be empty.

Keyword Calling Sequence

Keywords are much more exciting than arbitrary argument sequences. In many applications, such as graphical interfaces, it is frequently the case that an operation can possibly accept many arguments, most of which usually have reasonable defaults. In Python, a function may provide as many arguments with as many defaults as it pleases, and the program that uses that function can override only those specific arguments that need to have nondefault values:

```
def print_text(text="Hello", font="h", color="blue", size=6,
               family="atomic", bgcolor="white", style="bold"):
    print text, font, color, size, family, bgcolor, style
```

This silly text function pretends to display a text object on some sort of graphic display, but actually just prints out its arguments to the terminal. We may override any collection of the parameters given by using, or not using the appropriate keyword names to name them:

```
>>> print_text( style="em", color="crimson")
Hello h crimson 6 atomic white em
>>> print_text()
Hello h blue 6 atomic white bold
>>> print_text("Goodbye", bgcolor="pink")
Goodbye h blue 6 atomic pink bold
```

Here the `keyword=value` argument must have `keyword` as the name of one of the formal parameters to the function called, and all keyword pairs must follow all positional arguments.

Arbitrary Named Keyword Arguments

It is possible for a function to accept an unrestricted set of keyword/argument pairs, by using a "keyword catch-all" argument of form `**arg`, which must follow all named arguments. All keyword pairs not associated with another parameter of the calling sequence will show up in the catch-all argument as dictionary entries. For example,

```
def Person(name="bob", age=33, **other_info):
    print name, age, other_info
```

Here the calling program may provide up to two positional arguments, but nearly any sequence of keyword arguments imaginable:

```
>>> Person(sex = "not often")
bob 33 {'sex': 'not often'}
>>> Person(gender="f", name="Shirley", job="clerk")
Shirley 33 {'gender': 'f', 'job': 'clerk'}
>>> Person("bob", 45, name="fred")
Traceback (innermost last):
  File "<stdin>", line 1, in ?
TypeError: keyword parameter redefined
```

Hmmm…why did the last call result in an error?

Functions may accept an arbitrary number of positional arguments and an arbitrary collection of keyword arguments at the same time, but this is usually confusing. We avoid mixing the two. Python resolves calls that involve defaults and keyword arguments "the only way that makes sense"—for a formal definition of this concept, please see the Python reference manual.

The following class makes a "replacement" for a function that prints a trace of all calls to the function through the replacement.

NOTE

```
class FTracer:
    def __init__(self, fn):
        self.fn = fn
```

```
    def __call__(self, *args, **kargs):
        print "calling", (self.fn, args, kargs)
        return apply(self.fn, args, kargs)
```

We may use an instance of this class to trace the `min` function as follows:

```
>>> m2 = FTracer(min)
>>> m2(1,2,0,3)
calling (<built-in function min>, (1, 2, 0, 3), {})
0
>>> m2("apples", "oranges")
calling (<built-in function min>, ('apples', 'oranges'), {})
'apples'
>>> m2(name="joe")
calling (<built-in function min>, (), {'name': 'joe'})
Traceback (innermost last):
  File "<stdin>", line 1, in ?
  File "<stdin>", line 6, in __call__
TypeError: this function takes no keyword arguments
```

The `FTracer.__call__` method permits arbitrary calling sequences by catching both sequential arguments in `*args` and keyword arguments in `**kargs` and passing them down to the traced function using `apply`.

Class Definition

Previous discussion has provided a number of examples of `class` definitions. A `class` statement creates a new class object with associated attributes and methods.

```
class Bag:
    default_to_zero = 1

    def __init__(self):
        self.D = {}

    def insert(self, key):
        D = self.D
        try:
            D[key] = D[key] + 1
        except KeyError:
            D[key] = 1

    def howmany(self, key):
```

```
   try:
      return self.D[key]
   except KeyError:
      if self.default_to_zero:
         return 0
      else:
         raise KeyError, "no such element in this bag"
```

The Bag class implements a simple data structure for counting collections of objects, using one attribute default_to_zero and three methods __init__, insert, and howmany. We may use the Bag class, for example, as follows:

```
>>> B = Bag()
>>> for c in "that was the world that was then":
...    B.insert(c)
...
>>> B.howmany("w"), B.howmany("t"), B.howmany("X")
(3, 6, 0)
```

Here B = Bag() implicitly used the Bag.__init__ method to initialize the Bag instance B.

Classes may be organized into class hierarchies, where each class provides a sequence of (previously defined) superclasses.

```
class NoDefault:
   """Mixin to force an error on howmany of absent key."""
   default_to_zero = None

class SeqArgs(Bag):
   """A bag that initializes from a sequence automatically."""
   def __init__(self, seq):
      Bag.__init__(self)
      for elt in seq:
         self.insert(elt)

class MultiArgs(SeqArgs):
   """A bag that initializes from an arbitrary length argument list."""
   def __init__(self, *args):
      SeqArgs.__init__(self, args)

class MyFavoriteBag(NoDefault, MultiArgs):
   """Initializes from arbitrary argument list, doesn't default to 0"""
   pass
```

Here the `NoDefault` class may be used to simply override the value of `default_to_zero` in any subclass of `Bag`, thus forcing the `Bag.howmany` function to raise an error on a key that hasn't been inserted into the Bag. The `SeqArgs` and `MultiArgs` classes provide variations for initializing a bag, each explicitly calling the initializer of the superclass using the fully specified calling sequence, for example, `Bag.__init__(self)` in `SeqArgs`.

A *mixin* is a class which may be combined with another base class in order to override parts of the base class behavior. For a subclass to get the mixin behavior, the mixin must precede the base class in the inheritance search. Generally, this means that a subclass that uses two mixins to alter the behavior of a base class should have a declaration similar to

```
class subclass(mixin1, mixin2, base_class):
    ...
```

Here the `base_class` is listed last to guarantee that the behaviors of the mixins are preferred.

We may use `MyFavoriteBag` as follows:

```
>>> M = MyFavoriteBag(5,6,3,5,3,5,3,6,8,4,3,4,32,7)
>>>
>>> M.howmany(5), M.howmany(3), M.howmany(32)
(3, 4, 1)
>>> M.howmany(0)
Traceback (innermost last):
  File "<stdin>", line 1, in ?
  File "<stdin>", line 18, in howmany
KeyError: no such element in this bag
```

Exceptions (`raise` and `try`)

Python handles exceptional conditions and run-time errors in programs conveniently and easily using named exceptions. An exception in the simplest case represents an error condition that prevents a computation from completing. Such exceptions can occur within built-in or intrinsic operations, or they may be explicitly `raised` by Python code using

```
raise Exception, value
```

where the value is optional.

If an exceptional condition is not anticipated by the program, an exception will terminate the process, but if the program expects an exception, the program may specify finalization actions which must take place before exiting a block of code using `try ... finally` or the program may "catch" the exception using

```
try:
    ... Code that may raise Exception ...
except Exception, variable:
    ... Code that does something appropriate after Exception ...
```

Here the `except` clause effectively cancels the exceptional condition and allows the program to continue normally after the `except` block executes.

By using the exception mechanism, the Python program may essentially focus on the "sunny day" scenario and yet handle unusual (i.e., exceptional) conditions outside the main logic of the code. This approach greatly simplifies the logic of programs that interact with external systems in complex ways, and which therefore have many possible failure conditions.

The `raise` statement triggers an error which causes the Python program to search for an exception handler to handle the error.

```
>>> My_Error = "sorry fella"
>>> def four_over(n):
...     if n==0:
...         raise My_Error, "this should be a standard error, but hey!"
...     return 4.0/n
...
>>> four_over(9)
0.444444444444
>>> four_over(0)
Traceback (innermost last):
  File "<stdin>", line 1, in ?
  File "<stdin>", line 3, in four_over
sorry fella: this should be a standard error, but hey!
```

Here in the evaluation of `for_over(0)` the `raise` statement explicitly triggered a `My_Error`. The Python interpreter failed to find any exception handler to handle this error, so the control returned all the way to the top level of the interpreter where the error was reported.

We can catch an error occurring during the execution of a program using a try .. except statement.

```
def four_over_or_None(n):
    try:
        return four_over(n)
    except My_Error, value:
        print "caught", My_Error, value
        return None
```

Here, if the four_over function raises a My_Error error, the except clause will catch the error and the associated value, printing them before returning the value None.

```
>>> print four_over_or_None(7)
0.571428571429
>>> print four_over_or_None(0)
caught sorry fella this should be a standard error, but hey!
None
```

More generally current operation terminates once control returns to the Python main loop and the Python interpreter terminates each active code block from the most recent back to the oldest until it finds an except clause that handles the error. If an appropriate except clause is found, the control flow resumes at the beginning of that clause. During the search for an exception handler, the interpreter may encounter finally clauses, which are executed before the search for an except handler resumes.

WARNING

The except clause matches string errors by object identity, not by value, so the following does not work:

```
>>> try:
...     four_over(0)
... except "sorry fella":
...     print "caught"
...
Traceback (innermost last):
  File "<stdin>", line 2, in ?
  File "<stdin>", line 3, in four_over
sorry fella: this should be a standard error, but hey!
```

Here the literal value `"sorry fella"`, although equal to `My_Error` was a different object, so the `except` clause failed to handle the error. (The object identity convention allows different modules to accidentally give errors the same values without interfering with each other.)

We can also perform cleanup actions whether or not an error has occurred using the `try .. finally` variant of the `try` statement. The finally clause is normally used to perform actions which release system resources or return some object to a consistent state. Here is a silly example:

```
start_stove()
try:
    boil_eggs()
finally:
    turn_off_stove()
```

Here the `turn_off_stove()` action should be initiated, regardless of whether the `make_scrambled_eggs()` action was successfully completed.

The Python interpreter always executes the `finally` clause when a `try .. finally` statement terminates (except if something really drastic happens, e.g., someone unplugs the computer, in which case the `finally` clause will not execute). Even `try .. finally` clauses that terminate due to a `break` or `continue` or `return` inside the `try` statement will execute their `finally` clauses, as in the following extremely silly example:

```
def make_cakes(number):
    cakes = []
    for cake_num in range(number):
        start_stove()
        try:
            cake = None
            for thing in refrigerator:
                if isa_cake(thing):
                    refrigerator.remove(thing)
                    cake = thing
                    break # break of inner loop
            if cake:
                cakes.append(cake)
                continue # continue of outer loop, finally will execute
            if len(eggs) < 3:
                raise ValueError, "not enough eggs" # finally will execute
```

```
        visit(store) # what the heck
        return cakes + buy_cakes(number - cake_num) # finally executes
    finally:
        turn_off_stove()
```

The `finally` and the `except` clauses may not be mixed in the same `try` statement, but a `try .. except` statement may include many `except` clauses and an optional `else` clause as well.

```
import sys

def divide_check(x,y):
    try:
        result = x/y
    except ZeroDivisionError:
        print "can't divide by 0"
    except TypeError:
        print "x and y can't be combined via the / operator"
    except:
        print "unexpected error!", sys.exc_type, sys.exc_value
    else:
        print "division successful!", result
```

Here the `else` clause executes if the body of the `try` statement completes with no error, and the `except` statements handle the error listed, except for the last `except` statement which handles any error not handled before it. We can test all but the generic handler easily.

```
>>> divide_check(1.0,3)
division successful! 0.333333333333
>>> divide_check(4.0, 0.0)
can't divide by 0
>>> divide_check(5, None)
x and y can't be combined via the / operator
```

With a bit of trickery we can also test the generic `except` clause:

```
>>> class silly:
...     def __div__(self, other):
...         raise IOError, "fooled you!"
...
>>> divide_check( silly(), silly() )
unexpected error! IOError fooled you!
```

An except clause may also handle a number of exceptions, if they are listed as a single tuple.

```
try:
    do_something_complicated()
except (IndexError, KeyError, IOError):
    import sys
    print "uncaught simple error! %s: %s" % (sys.exc_type, sys.exc_value)
    print "ignoring the error..."
```

The attributes of the sys module sys.exc_type and sys.exc_value hold the type and associated value of the current exception during the execution of an except or finally block. Outside an except or finally block, sys.exc_type and sys.exc_value are normally undefined, but their most recent values can be found in sys.last_type and sys.last_value.

Exceptions are invaluable, but they can be abused. As the name implies, use of exceptions should deal with exceptional conditions and should not be used to implement the "normal" flow control of a program.

Also, complex execution sequences enclosed in try ... except constructs should be managed with great care. For example, a KeyError caught after a complex operation may not have occurred where a programmer presumes it had, and a corrective action that corrects the wrong problem might be disastrous. Be sure to use the else clause of an except statement to isolate the problem as closely as possible. For example, don't do this:

```
# example of what not to do:
try:
    egg1, egg2, egg2 = eggs[:3]
    del eggs[:3]
    meal = scramble(egg1, egg2, egg3)
    self.serve(meal, recipient=spouse)
except ValueError: # not enough eggs?
    go_out(self, spouse)
```

because the ValueError may have occurred in scramble. Instead, isolate the problem using an else clause:

```
try:
    [egg1, egg2, egg2] = eggs[:3]
except ValueError: # not enough eggs!
```

```
        go_out(self, spouse)
    else:
        del eggs[:3]
        meal = scramble(egg1, egg2, egg3)
        self.serve(meal, recipient=spouse)
```

Here the except clause will only respond to the case where there weren't enough eggs, as intended.

Object-Oriented Exceptions

Type hierarchies can group classes of related errors via object-oriented error handling. For example, the following class hierarchy structures possible reasons network resource cannot be accessed by a user.

```
class RecoverableAccessProblem:
    """There is a problem accessing this object, but recovery is possible."""

class FatalAccessProblem:
    """There is a problem accessing this object, and no way to recover."""

class ObjectUnavailable:
    """Object unavailable for unknown reason"""
    def __init__(self, reason):
        self.reason = reason

class ServerNotResponding(ObjectUnavailable):
    """Server not communicating, object cannot be served."""

class NoSuchObject(ObjectUnavailable, FatalAccessProblem):
    """Server reports that there is no such object."""

class AuthenticationProblem(ObjectUnavailable):
    """Authentication for access to this object failed"""

class YourBannedCreep(AuthenticationProblem, FatalAccessProblem):
    """You -- and you specifically -- cannot access this object"""

class PasswordRequired(AuthenticationProblem, RecoverableAccessProblem):
    """Please provide user and password to access this object."""
```

Instances of these classes can be used as errors (with no associated value) in raise statements:

```
def do_something_dangerous():
    # Kick any user who tries this function.
    raise YourBannedCreep("get outa my server, now!")
```

Handlers that catch this error may catch it by using any of its superclasses as an error name:

```
def test():
    try:
        do_something_dangerous()
    except FatalAccessProblem, instance:
        print "fatal access problem", instance
        print "documentation: ", instance.__class__.__doc__
        print "reason given: ", instance.reason
```

Here the test( ) function produces the following:

```
>>> test()
fatal access problem <YourBannedCreep instance at 1237b0>
documentation:  You -- and you specifically -- cannot access this object
reason given:  get outa my server, now!
```

A sequence of except clauses will trigger only the first except clause that matches the error.

One common way that object-oriented exceptions are used is to emulate an if..elif..else statement over the possible superclasses of an object:

```
try:
    # do one of the following based on the class of object.
    raise object
except Vegetable:
    object.throw_away() # wouldn't want to eat a vegetable!
except Edible:
    self.eat(object) # but we'll eat anything else that's edible
except Audible:
    object.play()
except:
    if not object.fights_back(self):
        self.poke(object, soft_cushions)
    else:
        self.apologize(object)
```

Recall that the final unqualified except will handle any exception not handled by the other except clauses.

Miscellaneous

There are a number of statements we have not explicitly explained here:

pass: The pass statement is a "no operation" statement which may be inserted wherever a statement is required, but the program need perform no action. A common use for pass is as a null body to a class definition which inherits all behaviors from its superclasses:

```
class Tubular(Groovy, OkeyDokey, Swell):
    pass
```

del: The del statement may be used to delete attributes, entries, items, and slices from objects of appropriate types. These operations are covered under the discussion of each type, in turn, above. The del variable "undefines" a local variable or removes a global variable.

print: The print a, b, c statement produces a printable representation of the values for a, b, and c separated by single spaces. To print more directly to the standard output (for example, to nuke the spaces) use sys.stdout.write, but be sure to convert the arguments to write to strings. A print statement with a trailing comma will print no newline, otherwise the print statement always ends by printing a newline.

import and **from .. import**: The variants of the import statement are used to bring names associated with one module into another module. These are covered in detail under the discussion of built-in methods for modules.

exec: The exec statement is used to execute data as part of a Python program. We will not discuss this statement here, except to note that it can be dangerous to exec data obtained from an arbitrary source, especially within networked applications. Please see the standard reference manual of the Python distribution for more information regarding the exec statement.

CHAPTER SIX

MORE GOODIES

This chapter deals in some corners of Python that didn't fit nicely in other chapters, and it also alerts the reader to some possible difficulties that may arise.

Symbolic Constants

Every module automatically contains three read-only attributes which could act as symbolic constants:

1. __name__: The name of the module as it is known to Python. Normally modules can only have one of two names—either the name of the ".py" file that the module came from, or __main__ if the module was invoked as the main program, using `python file` or `python < file`.

2. __doc__: The documentation string for the module. This is a the value of the literal string at the top of the module, or `None` if no doc string was provided for the module.

3. __builtins__: The "standard built-ins" dictionary used by the module to provide standard built-in services. Usually all modules use the same built-in dictionary, but in the important special case of "untrusted" programs running under secure execution mode certain modules may use special variants of the built in dictionary, which limit the system resources available to the module. For example, it is possible to prevent an untrusted program from being able to read or write files, by using a standard built in dictionary variant which prevents file accesses.

The `if __name__ == "__main__"` Convention

At the bottom of a Python module source file it is common to see something like:

```
if __name__ == "__main__":
    Server_Launch()
```

or even more commonly, something like:

```
if __name__ == "__main__":
    selftest()
```

The function of these entries is to specify how the module should behave if it runs as the "main program."

Generally a module can be used in two contexts: as a module that is subordinate to a main program, or as the main program itself.

If a module is invoked as the main program, then it will have the name `__main__` instead of the standard name for the program. In this case the module could have some special code that launches an application. If the module has a reasonable interpretation as a main program then the result of running the module as `__main__` could be an interesting application, such as an internet server or client. Modules that do not have any compelling interpretations as a main program (for example, those that provide simple library services) frequently run some sort of self test procedure when run as `__main__`, in order to provide an easy way to aid in testing the module after the module has been modified. The

```
if __name__ == "__main__":
    ...
```

conditional is used to launch the "application interpretation" of a module.

Generally speaking, avoid abusing this feature: "real" applications should not be launched from within a complex module source file, but should be launched from a special module file that is only meant to be used as a `__main__` program. This "launch stub" approach allows the logic modules to be byte-compiled easily, and also prevents the possibility of loading a module "twice," a possibility explained in the next section.

N O T E   It is always a good idea to provide a test module associated with every module you write—this test module should exercise the main features of every interesting aspect of the module. Even in the case where a module performs complex interactions with some foreign interface, in Python it is extraordinarily easy to write "stub" functions or object implementations that allow the logic of a module to be tested in "stand-alone mode." For example, the Python modules mentioned in the chapter on embedding Python generally have self-test functionality that tests the modules even when the Python interpreter is not embedded under the NSAPI—usually by providing "fake" stub implementations of the NSAPI interface. A good testing discipline can speed up your programming progress immensely, and because it's so easy to test Python modules, there is no excuse for not doing it.

How to Load a Module Twice, and Why You Shouldn't

As mentioned above, a module can either be subordinate to a main program, or it can act as the main program itself. There is another possibility also: The same module source file can initialize a __main__ module and another module using the standard name. This can lead to catastrophe.

For example, if module A.py contains

```
print "loading A as", __name__
import B
```

and module B.py contains

```
print "loading B as", __name__
import A
```

Then loading A.py from the command line gives:

```
>>> import A
loading A as A
loading B as B
```

This is fine, because each module was loaded once.

But running A.py as a main program gives:

```
% python A.py
loading A as __main__
```

```
loading B as B
loading A as A
```

Here the B module imported A from A.py, but after A.py had already been loaded as __main__. In more complex cases, this can cause grief, because any class C defined in A.py will be created twice, once as __main__.C and another time as A.C. Without going into great detail let it suffice to say that it is best to avoid this possibility by using a "stub module" to launch any application that has complex interrelationships among modules.

The "Pound Bang Hack"

Many Python utilities and library functions begin with a line that looks something like this:

```
#!/usr/local/bin/python
...
```

This is the UNIX "pound bang hack" which allows the script source file to be run as a stand alone executable. Basically when (most versions of) UNIX attempt to run a file as an executable, the loader looks at the first two bytes, and if they are #!, the loader presumes that the file is a script and the rest of the first line gives a path to the program used to interpret the script.

Because this first line just happens to be a Python comment also, it is ignored and completely harmless on non-UNIX systems.

NOTE The #! hack only works for scripts which have been made executable, for example,

```
% chmod +x asciicvt.py
% asciicvt.py
```

Conditional Operator

Some C programmers may miss the ? operator. Do not pine: cheer up! The ((x and [val]) or [val2])[0] code fragment is equivalent to x ? val : val2 from C and C-like languages. If you don't know C, don't worry about this tiny point.

Standard Input and Output

A Python program may interact with the standard input and output using `raw_input()` and `print`, respectively, but these operations do not really give complete control to the programmer—for example, `print` inserts extra spaces that a programmer may not want. To interact with a the standard input and output directly as file objects, use the `sys.stdout` and `sys.stdin` standard file object values of the `sys` module.

Byte Compilation

A python module source file `mymodule.py` when it is imported (not as `__main__`) the first time is generally translated into a byte compiled representation `mymodule.pyc`. A byte-compiled module may be loaded quickly by Python without any parsing, and hence byte compilation is extremely important for larger and more complex Python applications that need to start up quickly.

The byte compilation of `mymodule.py` will only succeed if the file system allows the creation of `mymodule.pyc`. If the `mymodule.pyc` file cannot be created, then the Python interpreter will have to reparse `mymodule.pyc` every time it `imports` the module, and if the module is large, or if many modules have this problem, the extra parsing can become a serious performance problem. To compile all the files of a directory use the python script

```
% python LIB/compileall.py DIRECTORY
```

Where `LIB` is the directory containing the Python libraries (including `compileall`) and `DIRECTORY` is the directory containing `.py` that require compilation. Of course the user running `compilall` must have write permission on the `DIRECTORY`.

If the interpreter finds both the byte-compiled `mymodule.pyc` file and the source `mymodule.py`, the file with the most recent time stamp will be used. Thus, a new `mymodule.py` file will override an obsolete `mymodule.pyc` file.

For companies that may wish to deliver Python modules as part of a product that uses Python in some way, the modules may be delivered in byte compiled form only, to protect proprietary Python source code. For bullet-proof safety it is even possible to use Python to encrypt code objects or byte streams, but we will not discuss this possibility in this book. Look to the section on cryptographic modules in the standard library manual.

The Module Search Path `sys.path`

Every Python interpreter instance maintains a module search path in `sys.path` which gives a sequence of directories the interpreter searches in order to find modules that are not part of the interpreters compiled image (i.e., either Python source `.py` modules, or byte-compiled Python source modules `.pyc`, or dynamically linked object modules). The module search path is normally initialized from an environment variable named PYTHONPATH.

In some cases (most notably for CGI scripts) it may not be possible to rely on the presence of the PYTHONPATH environment variable, or if it is present it may not be possible to be sure it has the correct value. In this case a Python program may explicitly override or modify the `sys.path` value using list modification operations or even complete reassignment, for example,

```
import sys
sys.path.insert(0, "/usr/me/mypython/lib") # search my library first!
```

Memory Management

Python uses a reference count memory management scheme. Usually this means that the Python programmer need not think about managing memory—objects are deallocated when they are no longer in use and kept around so long as they are accessible by some part of a program.

There are occasions, however, where it is natural for a Python program to create circular references:

```
class Person:
    def __init__(self, name):
        self.name = name
        self.parents = []
        self.children = []
    def engender(self, childname):
        child = Person(childname)
        child.parents.append(self)
```

```
        self.children.append(child)
    def expire(self):
        del self.name, self.parents, self.children
```

Here a `Person` object `P` that engenders a `child` creates a circular reference:

```
>>> p = Person
>>> p = Person("George")
>>> p.engender("Walt")
>>> p.name, p.children[0].name, p.children[0].parents[0].name
('George', 'Walt', 'George')
>>> p is p.children[0].parents[0]
1
```

In this case, the circular references stemming from the object p must be explicitly broken (for example, using the `expire` method) before the program disposes of p, otherwise p and the other objects on the path of the circular reference will not be reclaimed.

This possible problem appears distressing to some at first, but it's amazing how rarely circular references actually occur in real applications. The most compelling use for circular references is in graphical windowing systems where a window and its parent have references to each other—but because windows are always explicitly erased from the screen at some point, the destruction of circular references is natural in this domain.

Various enthusiasts have experimented with adding fully general garbage collection to Python, but the general consensus is that this addition would reduce Python's portability, make it harder to embed Python in other systems or extend Python with external interfaces, and possibly make the interpreter run slower. For now, Python programmers must remember to explicitly break circular references, primarily for long-running tasks that cannot afford any memory leaks. Short-running tasks (like filters and CGI scripts) probably can afford the odd uncollected object.

Local Scopes Don't Nest

As a somewhat obscure feature, Python allows functions to be defined within other functions, and classes to be defined within functions, and functions to be defined within methods of classes that have been defined within functions, and so forth. Many programmers never use this capability, and if feel you are one of them, feel free to skip this section.

The remaining readers, who feel they might use this capability, should understand that local scopes do not nest. For example, the following function doesn't work:

```
>>> def compose(f, g):
...     def composition(x):
...         return f(g(x))
...     return composition
...
>>> from math import *
>>> floorlog = compose(floor, log)
>>> floorlog(32666)
Traceback (innermost last):
  File "<stdin>", line 1, in ?
  File "<stdin>", line 3, in result
NameError: f
```

Here the intuitive intent of the h = compose(f,g) function is to create a new function h where h(x) computes f(g(x)). The reason the function call floorlog(32666) failed, however, was that the local variables f and g of the compose function are not available within the definition of the embedded function definition for result.

Do not despair!

There are two standard ways to pass values from an "outer" local scope into an "inner" local scope. The first way is to use default arguments. Values for default arguments to a function or method are evaluated in the enclosing scope for the function or method, so we can "fix" the compose function as follows:

```
>>> def compose(f, g):
...     def composition(x, last = f, first = g):
...         return last( first(x) )
...     return composition
...
>>> floorlog = compose(floor, log)
>>> floorlog(32666)
10.0
```

Another standard fix would use "callable class instances" in place of functions:

```
>>> class Compose:
...    def __init__(self, last, first):
...        self.last = last
...        self.first = first
...    def __call__(self, x):
...        return self.last( self.first(x) )
...
>>> floorlog = Compose(floor, log)
>>> floorlog(32666)
10.0
```

This last solution uses a bit of class magic mentioned briefly later in the chapter.

Recursion

A wise man once said that recursion was invented by really smart people to make the rest of us feel stupid, and there is something to this assertion. Nevertheless, when you really get going in object-oriented programming you will find yourself righting recursive programs without even being aware of it. A recursive function or method is a function which "calls itself" (directly or indirectly) in its own definition.

Python, like all good modern languages, supports recursion nicely. In the section on sequence repetition, we already used recursion to define a function which creates a multidimensional array of arbitrary dimensions.

To illustrate another user of recursion consider the following example which employs recursion in addition to a fancy trick often associated with recursion called "memoization." The doc string immediately below the def describes what the function computes, in true Python style.

```
"Memoized computation of combinations"

Known_Combinations = {}

def Combinations(n, k):
    "How many ways can you choose k things from a sack of n things?"
    if k>n:
        raise ValueError, "not enough things in the sack: " + ` (n, k) `
    try:
        # use known value, if available
        return Known_Combinations[ (n, k) ]
```

```
except KeyError:
    # Not known.  Oh well, I guess we'll actually have to do some work:
    if n==k or k==0:
        # there is only one way to pick all or none of them
        result = 1L
    else:
        # otherwise we can divide the possibilities
        # into those which pick the first object, and those which don't
        including_first = Combinations(n-1, k-1)  # Recursive!
        excluding_first = Combinations(n-1, k)   # Recursive!
        result = including_first + excluding_first
    # remember this result for possible future use
    Known_Combinations[ (n, k) ] = result
    return result
```

This `Combinations` function is recursive because it "calls itself" in its own definition (twice!).

 In a recursive function local variables may be "in use several times" when the function has called itself, but because a function call creates a new name space for each call, the value assigned to the variable `including_first` in the highest function call will not be altered by assignments to `including_first` in lower function calls, for example.

Recursive functions like this one that call themselves more than once can sometimes be horribly inefficient—and this one would be horribly inefficient if we hadn't "memoized" it. Memoization here uses a mutable global variable `Known_Combinations` to store the previously computed combinations. Consequently in the process of computing `Combinations(30,12)`, we will evaluate `Combinations(10,5)` at most once, whereas without memoization, we would evaluate same a horrifying number of times (exercise: exactly how many times?). Of course we exhorted you not to modify global values earlier, but never mind—you know what they say about foolish consistency!

All right. If you insist we can come up with a memoization trick that doesn't use global variables—and in fact make memoization generic at the same time. We leave readers to figure how this works for themselves, except to provide the standard advise: play with it!

```
class Memoizer:
    """Memoizes a function: This only works for positional argument
        sequences containing only immutables."""
```

```
    def __init__(self, function):
        self.f = function
        self.Known = {}

    def __call__(self, *args):
        """This is the magic __call__ method, used when an instance
           is called as a function."""
        K = self.Known
        try:
            return K[args]
        except KeyError:
            # darn! This is a new argument sequence.
            result = apply(self.f, args)
            # remember the result, for possible future use.
            K[args] = result
            return result

# example usage
def Combinations(n, k):
    "Combinations computation, simple and SSSLLLOOOWWW"
    if k>n:
        raise ValueError, "not enough things in the sack"
    if k==0 or n==k:
        return 1L
    else:
        return Combinations(n-1, k-1) + Combinations(n-1, k)

# Now clobber the named function with its memoization
Combinations = Memoizer(Combinations)
```

Voila! No mutable globals in sight. Don't get carried away with memoization, however, because if you memoize a function that is never called twice with the same arguments, you'll just make Python do a lot of extra work. Meanwhile the memoization dictionary self.Known may get awfully big!

Class Instance Magic

Instances of a class can be made to "look like a sequence" to Python. For example, the following class looks like a sequence which actually evaluates a function at each index:

```
class FSeq:
    def __init__(self, function, lower, upper, delta=1.0):
        self.function = function
```

```
        self.lower = lower
        self.upper = upper
        self.delta = delta
        if len(self)<0:
            raise ValueError, "bad params %s %s %s" % (lower,upper,delta)
    def __len__(self):
        return int((self.upper - self.lower)/(self.delta*1.0))+1
    def __getitem__(self, index):
        if index<0 or index>len(self):
            raise IndexError, "index too large"
        return self.function( self.lower + index * self.delta )
```

Here is an example usage of this class:

```
>>> import math
>>> F = FSeq(math.sin, 0, 1, 0.3)
>>> for x in F:
...     print x,
...
0.0 0.295520206661 0.564642473395 0.783326909627
>>> F[0]
0.0
>>> len(F)
4
```

The ability to make class instances respond to built-in constructs and functions like indexing and `len` is extremely convenient. For example, using this magic a program that was designed to operate on "in core" sequences can be modified to operate on indexed file structures (that look like just another sequence) with little or no change.

We will occasionally use the magic methods that allow an instance to emulate a core Python type, explaining the techniques used as the need arises, but for now we will briefly describe the more important of these methods.

A `Class` may define the following magic methods:

`__init__(self, ... )`

- The standard initialization (almost always used).
- Return value is ignored.
- This function is implicitly invoked by `Class( ... )`.

`__del__(self)`

- Finalization on deallocation.
- Return value is ignored.
- This function is implicitly invoked when the last reference to self is broken.

`__repr__(self)`

- Readable string representation.
- Should return a string.
- This function is implicitly invoked by `` `self` ``, `repr(self)`, or `"%s" % self`, and in a few other cases.

`__str__(self)`

- Printable string representation.
- Should return a string.
- This function is implicitly invoked by `print self`.

`__cmp__(self, other)`

- Comparison.
- Should return an integer, and should define a total order within the class in the same manner as the intrinsic `cmp`.
- This function is implicitly invoked by `<=` and `list.sort` and other operations that implicitly or explicitly use `cmp`

`__hash__(self)`

- Hash value computation.
- Should return an integer, preferable producing a different integer for each instance.

- This function is implicitly invoked when `self` is archived in a hash based structure, such as a dictionary. While `self` resides in a hashed structure the `__hash__` value must remain constant or the resulting behavior may be undefined.

`__call__(self, ... )`

- Function call interface for instances.
- May return anything.
- This function is implicitly invoked whenever `self` is called as a function, either explicitly as `self( ... )` or implicitly via `map` or `apply` or similar operations.

`__getattr__(self, name)`

- Attribute retrieval.
- May return anything.
- The interpreter calls `self.__getattr__("attr")` to evaluate `self.attr`, but only when `self.attr` is not defined in the local name space or by inheritance.

`__setattr__(self, name, value)`

- Attribute assignment.
- Return value is ignored.
- The interpreter always calls `self.__setattr__(self, "attr", value)` to execute `self.attr = value` if this method is available. This one is tricky!

`__delattr__(self, name)`

- Attribute deletion.
- Return value is ignored.
- Called implicitly by `del self.attr`.

```
__len__(self)
```

- Length of structure.
- Must return an integer.
- Called implicitly by `len(self)`.

```
__getitem__(self, item)
```

- Called implicitly by `self[item]`.

```
__setitem__(self, item, value)
```

- Called implicitly by `self[item] = value`.

```
__delitem__(self, item)
```

- Called implicitly by `del self[item]` Index accesses.

Furthermore, there are numerous special methods for defining the "numeric" operations, for example `__add__(self, other)` defines a `self + other` operation. Also methods such as `__setslice__` allow classes to interact with the slicing notations. Please consult the standard Python reference manual for a precise discussion of all of these methods and the precise rules for using them.

NOTE   The default implementation for `__setattr__` is roughly equivalent to:

```
def __setattr__(self, name, value):
    self.__dict__[name] = value
```

Most alternate implementations for `__setattr__` interact directly with `self.__dict__` like this at some point, in order to store local state for `self`.

Documentation Strings

Python allows functions, classes, methods, and modules to be adorned with documentation strings, as illustrated in the following module:

```
"""My module mymod.py.
   Actually it doesn't do anything interesting, so this doc string
   is short."""

def my_fun(**args):
    """Return keyword pairs as a dictionary.
       this function will not accept any positional arguments."""
    return args

class my_Record:
    """Dynamically accept arbitrary keyword arguments and initialize
       them as attributes of the self instance."""
    def __init__(self, **args):
        for (name, value) in args.items()
            setattr(self, name, value)
    # no other methods.
```

Here each of the triple-quoted strings are documentation strings which may be examined interactively at run time.

```
>>> print my_fun.__doc__
Return keyword pairs as a dictionary.
       this function will not accept any positional arguments.
>>> my_fun(x=1, y=2)
{'y': 2, 'x': 1}
```

Syntactically, the doc string of a module is the literal string occurring at the top of the module, if there is one. Similarly, the doc string for a class or method or function is the literal string at the top of the `class` or `def` declaration, if there is one.

As shown, doc strings can be examined from the interactive interpreter. Documentation strings are also useful for generating automatic documentation from source code and for aiding in fancy debugging and development tools such as class browsers. Many Pythoners believe doc-strings will become even more important in the future, so it's a good idea to provide at least a short doc-string with each module, class, function, and method you write that is important.

CHAPTER SEVEN

GENERATING HTML: A CASE STUDY IN DYNAMIC OBJECTS

In this chapter, we will create and discuss a Python library for automatically generating HTML documents. Writing this chapter was a lot of fun because the final module uses some of Python's Big Guns, particularly: keyword arguments, `getattr`, `setattr`, apply, multiple inheritance, and class mixins. But because that's a lot to swallow at once we will first do it the wrong way—the way we would be forced to do it in a less-flexible programming language. After getting frustrated with the false start, we will analyze how to improve our approach, and solve the problem simply and elegantly using more advanced techniques.

The techniques implemented in this chapter are suitable for use in production systems, even though we will not implement all of HTML with all of the possible proprietary extensions floating around the Net. We claim that the general framework developed here is solid and that readers can easily adapt the framework by generating their own subclasses of classes developed here in order to generate HTML elements or HTML special features not directly implemented in this chapter.

This chapter will not describe the automatic generation of HTML FORMs, but will defer all discussion of forms to the chapter on CGI programming. Nevertheless, the techniques described here may be easily extended for the generation of FORM and INPUT elements as well.

What HTML Looks Like

HTML stands for HyperText Markup Language, and a very simple HTML document looks something like this:

```
<HTML>
<HEAD>
<TITLE>
Example HTML
</TITLE>
</HEAD>
<BODY>
This is a very simple example.
</BODY>
</HTML>
```

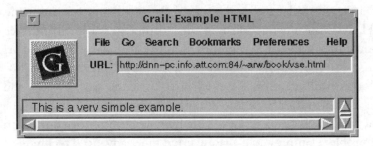

Figure 7.1 Presentation of a very simple HTML document.

Now that's a lot of typing for such a simple example. Happily, we didn't type it. Instead we got Python to type it for us by entering in the interactive interpreter:

```
>>> from HTMLfmt import *
>>> doc = HTML("Example HTML", "This is a very simple example.")
>>> print doc
 ... Python printed the document shown above here ...
```

This chapter will describe how we defined the HTML class that enabled this simplification as well as describe much more interesting classes that allow us to generate, for example:

```
>>> Text = """
...    HTML Tag | Description
...    P        | Paragraph Marker
...    BR       | Line Break
...    PRE      | Preformatted Text
... """
>>> Table = H_Table_Pipe_TBlock(Text)
>>> doc = HTML("Some HTML Tags", Table)
>>> print doc
<HTML>
<HEAD>
<TITLE>
Some HTML Tags
</TITLE>
</HEAD>
<BODY>
<TABLE BORDER>
  <TR>
      <TH>HTML Tag </TH>
        <TH>Description</TH>
    </TR>
  <TR>
      <TD>P</TD>
        <TD> Paragraph Marker</TD>
    </TR>
  <TR>
      <TD>BR</TD>
        <TD> Line Break</TD>
    </TR>
  <TR>
      <TD>PRE</TD>
        <TD> Preformatted Text</TD>
    </TR>
  </TABLE>
</BODY>
</HTML>
```

The previous example gives an example of a document containing an HTML
TABLE, which is a prime candidate for automatic generation because TABLEs
are very hard to create by hand. In fact most of the HTML examples shown in
this chapter were generated with the help of Python (because using Python
saved us a lot of typing).

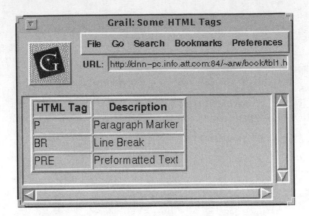

Figure 7.2 A document that contains a table.

Why Would Anyone Need Programs that Generate HTML?

Unless you've been living in a remote primitive cabin on a mountain in Montana for the last several years, you will know that HTML has become the Lingua Franca for sharing, retrieving, and distributing information on the Internet and beyond, so we won't spend too much time justifying HTML itself. Furthermore, although we like to use programs to generate static documents, you may prefer not to because there are various user-friendly graphical tools around that will help you do this easily. Where programmatic generation of HTML is indispensable is for reformatting existing data, or for generating HTML dynamically.

If you want to generate documents on the fly, in response to a user request (for example, in response to a CGI POST to your web site, as discussed later in this book) then you may need to write a program to generate a document appropriate to the request.

Furthermore if you wish to present existing data that is not already formatted in HTML on a Web site, you will probably want to translate the non-HTML format into some sort of an HTML representation, and if you need to do the translation often (say, once every three minutes, or once each for 50,000 files of the same format), we would advise you to write a program that automates the task.

For example, a site which hopes to list the current weather conditions, based on information retrieved from the National Weather service once an hour, might wish to place the information into a complicated HTML table, like the example given above or worse, and the only reasonable way to accomplish this translation would be to use a special purpose program to reformat the data.

So How Does HTML Work?

For a more detailed description of HTML and all its features, you could take a look at some of the following Web locations that we have found useful:

```
http://www.ncsa.uiuc.edu/General/Internet/WWW/HTMLPrimer.html
http://www.well.com/user/millenn3/
http://www.exclamation.com/htmlinfo/
```

Alternatively, you can probably find even better sites if you poke around some of the major Web indices and search engines out there. Nevertheless, for the purposes of this chapter, it is useful to review the basics of HTML at a very high level.

HTML is a formal language that segments a text file into areas of text that are intended to be presented in different ways. HTML presentation tools (such as Netscape Navigator or Grail) read in the text, identify the special HTML marks that indicate how the text is to be presented, and attempt to faithfully present the text as directed. The marks that bound areas of text in HTML are called *tags*, which usually come in pairs: a begin tag of form <TAGNAME ...> (sometimes with attributes) and an end tag of form </TAGNAME>. For example, if we examine the Python generated HTML document:

```
<HTML>
<HEAD>
<TITLE>
General Comments
</TITLE>
</HEAD>
<BODY>
<DL>
 <DD>apples<DT>
```

```
    Shouldn't be compared to oranges.
 <DD>oranges<DT>
    Not comparable with apples
  </DL>
</BODY>
<HTML>
```

We see a number of HTML tag pairs that bound segments of text, the biggest of which is the pair <HTML>..</HTML> which bounds the entire HTML document. Within the HTML tag pair there are two sections set off by two other sets of tag pairs: <HEAD>..</HEAD> identifies information about the document that is not intended to be directly displayed in the document itself, and a <BODY>..</BODY> pair that highlights the body of the document intended for display. There are a number of other tags in this document, which we shall describe briefly when we get around to generating them, but we will note here that not all tags come in <TAG>..</TAG> pairs. For example, the list element <DD> tag has no associated </DD>. Furthermore, notice that start tags frequently can specify attributes such as the BORDER and CELLSPACING attributes in <TABLE BORDER CELLSPACING=4>

Our goal, for the remainder of this chapter will be to develop a Python library that not only saves typing but also allows programs to dynamically construct arbitrary HTML representations for arbitrary data, easily.

For example, given a file comments.txt containing the text

```
General Comments
apples
Shouldn't be compared to oranges.
oranges
Not comparable with apples.
```

we can use the library constructed in this chapter to help easily construct the example document given above. In particular, the following module (run as the main script) will convert the contents of the file comments.txt to the example HTML document, writing the HTML text into comments.html:

```
# module DLdemo.py
from HTMLfmt import *

def DLdemo(infilename, outfilename):
    # read in the infile as TITLE followed by header/body lines.
```

```
    infile = open(infilename, "r")
    Title = infile.readline()[:-1] # Get title first (discard newline)
    Pairs = []
    while 1: # now read header/body to the end (as single lines)
        header = infile.readline()
        body = infile.readline()
        newpair = ( header[:-1], body[:-1]) # discard newlines
        if body:
            Pairs.append(newpair)
        else:
            break # terminate input when empty body is read.
    infile.close()
    # do formatting (using HTMLfmt.py conveniences)
    dllist = PairsDL(Pairs)  # make a DL list from the pairs
    doc = HTML(Title, dllist)# put it in an HTML document
    # output the formatted HTML
    outfile = open(outfilename, "w")
    text = `doc`  # convert document to string
    outfile.write(text)
    outfile.close()

if __name__=="__main__":
    DLdemo("comments.txt", "comments.html")
```

This program could be shortened considerably, but at the expense of readability, so we leave it in the more verbose form. This module is generic in the sense that it is not specific to the silly example in "comments.txt," and we can use it to convert any document (named, say, anydoc.txt) of format

```
This is the TITLE
This is Header 1
This is the content associated with Header 1
This is Header 2
This is the content associated with Header 2
...etcetera...
...Etcetera...
```

to an HTML document containing a display list (DL) element via the function call

```
>>> from DLdemo import DLdemo
>>> DLdemo("anydoc.txt", "anydoc.html")
```

thus generating the file anydoc.html with the content

```
<HTML>
<HEAD>
<TITLE>
This is the TITLE
</TITLE>
</HEAD>
<BODY>
<DL>
 <DD>This is Header 1<DT>
    This is the content associated with Header 1
 <DD>This is Header 2<DT>
    This is the content associated with Header 2
 <DD>...etcetera...<DT>
    ...Etcetera...
   </DL>
</BODY>
</HTML>
```

Furthermore, we can use the same function to automatically convert as many files as we please.

Also, when the marketing guys in the company decide it would be much cooler to present the same information using tables instead of display lists, we can modify two lines in the DLdemo module

```
...
# do formatting (using HTMLfmt.py conveniences)
table = apply(VerySimpleTable, (Title,) + tuple(Pairs))
doc = HTML(Title, table)
...
```

and run all 20,000 **.txt** files through this function to generate html documents containing tables instead. For example, from **anydoc.txt** producing

```
<HTML>
<HEAD>
<TITLE>
This is the TITLE
</TITLE>
</HEAD>
<BODY>
<TABLE BORDER>
  <TR>
      <TD>This is Header 1</TD>
```

```
          <TD>This is the content associated with Header 1</TD>
      </TR>
   <TR>
      <TD>This is Header 2</TD>
         <TD>This is the content associated with Header 2</TD>
      </TR>
   <TR>
      <TD>...etcetera...</TD>
         <TD>...Etcetera...</TD>
      </TR>
   <CAPTION ALIGN="bottom">This is the TITLE</CAPTION>
   </TABLE>
</BODY>
</HTML>
```

the mind boggles at the fun we can have!

But the tools we will use in the final module will take advantage of some very powerful Python features that will require a gentle introduction and motivation. Therefore, rather than launching into the fully general approach, let's do it the wrong way first and see why more horsepower is needed.

A False Start: Generating TABLEs the Wrong Way

Before we do it right, let's make some mistakes. This presentation actually follows the historical development of the module discussed in this chapter. We first spent about an hour developing a perfectly good solution that worked fine, but we noticed that we were repeating the same patterns of code over and over, so we scrapped our perfectly good small Python program that worked great, and started over in order to obtain a more flexible and general solution. Actually there was another intermediate attempt omitted here, better than the first, that we also scrapped when we realized we could do even better.

This mode of operation—writing a small working Python program, and then scrapping it to do better—is very common among Python programmers and less common elsewhere. It's easy to start over with Python because Python programmers can frequently solve seemingly difficult problems very quickly with very short programs. This leads the programmer to a mode of operation where, by trying and discarding various approaches in very quick sequence, they rapidly converge on powerful and general approaches to solving problems using Python. This contrasts greatly with the programming styles of programmering using more rigid, turgid, verbose, and less usable languages—here programmers must often stick to a half-witted, but working, approach with grim tenacity, because they know it would be horribly difficult to start over or improve the code. Some of the present authors know they have been grimly tenacious in the past; you can change too.

All the development described in this chapter, including backtracking, took a total of only two days, and even though it was done very quickly, the result is suitable for use in production systems, we modestly claim. Programming really doesn't need to be tiresome and difficult—as you will realize once you've used Python.

The Problem: What is an HTML Table?

In order to generate TABLEs, first we need to understand the syntactic structure of TABLEs. Let's take a look at another complete HTML TABLE before we proceed to analyze the syntax of TABLEs:

```
<TABLE BORDER>
   <TR> <TH>upper left </TH> <TH> upper right</TH> </TR>
   <TR> <TD>lower left</TD>  <TD>lower right</TD>  </TR>
   <CAPTION ALIGN="bottom">A TABLE</CAPTION>
   </TABLE>
```

Syntactically an HTML table (as HTML source text) appears as follows:

```
<TABLE ...table attributes...>
   ...line 1...
   ...line 2...
   ...etcetera...
   </TABLE>
```

That is, it is a sequence of lines bounded by the `<TABLE ...>...</TABLE>` tag pairs. The lines themselves must be composed of rows bounded by the `<TR>...</TR>` tag pairs:

```
<TABLE BORDER>
   <TR>...Content of line 1...</TR>
```

```
<TR>...Content of line 2...</TR>
<TR>...etcetera...</TR>
</TABLE>
```

Each line must consist of row elements marked off by either table heading tag pairs <TH>..</TH> indicating that the item is a TABLE HEADING (which normally is presented in bold font) or by a normal Table entry tag pair <TD>..</TD> (which is presented in the default font).

Extra whitespace and newlines inside a table (and in HTML generally) is discarded, so the actual look of the HTML source for a table may have little relationship to how it is presented by a browser.

The situation is more complicated than the above explanation indicates, however, because TABLE, TR, TD, and TH tags can all take attributes, which indicate various formatting parameters. For example, a TD attribute may indicate that this element of the row is to span three columns (rather than the default of one column) and that it is to span two rows. Furthermore, TABLEs themselves may be elements of other tables. For example, the following TD table element requests to span multiple rows and columns and contains a TABLE as its content:

```
<TD ROWSPAN=2 COLSPAN=3>
 <TABLE BORDER>
    <TR> <TD>Dave</TD> <TD>Sara</TD> <TD>Wendy</TD> </TR>
    <TR> <TD>Shushan</TD> <TD>Ty</TD> <TD>Elmo</TD> </TR>
    <CAPTION ALIGN="bottom">Our People.</CAPTION>
 </TABLE>
</TD>
```

Here the first <TD ...> matches the last </TD> and everything in between specifies a table to be treated as one element within another table. For example, the following document includes a table that contains the table given above.

```
<HTML>
<HEAD>
<TITLE>
The cool guys
</TITLE>
</HEAD>
<BODY>
<TABLE BORDER>
```

```
<TR>
    <TD ROWSPAN=2 COLSPAN=3><TABLE BORDER>
        <TR> <TD>Dave</TD> <TD>Sara</TD> <TD>Wendy</TD> </TR>
        <TR> <TD>Shushan</TD> <TD>Ty</TD> <TD>Elmo</TD> </TR>
        <CAPTION ALIGN="bottom">Our people</CAPTION>
    </TABLE></TD>
        <TH>Cool Internet Services</TH>
  </TR>
<TR> <TD>All you need</TD> </TR>
<TR> <TD>When you need it.</TD> <TD>How you need it.</TD>
    <TD>real cool.</TD> <TD>The right price.</TD> </TR>
</TABLE>
</BODY>
</HTML>
```

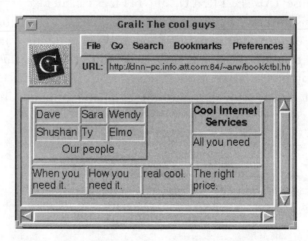

Figure 7.3 Marketing types prefer complicated tables like this one.

Also, TABLEs may optionally contain a CAPTION element, as the example demonstrates. So in attempting generating HTML with generic tools, the problem gets complex quickly.

The Strategy: Self-Formatting Objects

Ultimately our HTML generator will produce strings. For generating HTML, the most obvious way to produce these strings would be to write a bunch of functions that produce strings directly, perhaps like:

```
from string import joinfields
# this is NOT the way to do it...
def dumb_Table(list_of_lines):
    return "<TABLE>" + joinfields(list_of_lines, "\n") + "</TABLE>"
```

Now, as experienced Python programmers, we didn't even consider this approach, because we knew at some point many of the HTML fragments we intended to generate would share common behaviors, and that we would ultimately like to generate them dynamically and incrementally.

Object classes share common behavior much more easily than do functions, using inheritance, and class instances can be easily modified dynamically and incrementally, whereas string results of function calls cannot. So although the example function given above appears simple and intuitive, it will be much more useful to develop a class structure to implement HTML elements.

Let's illustrate the advantage of class instances over functions with a brain-dead example which may be more accessible than full-blown HTML. Consider the following related function and class definitions:

```
# this is not so nice.
def Cowboy_fn(name, horse=None):
    """This function is short, but not very flexible"""
    if horse:
        horseinfo = " and my horse's name is " + horse
    else:
        horseinfo = "" # if no horse, no horseinfo...
    return "Howdy, I'm %s%s." % (name, horseinfo)

# this is nicer!
class COWBOY:
    """instances of this class may be modified dynamically!"""
    name = "Dave" # most cowboy's are named Dave
    horse = None  # by default, assume no horse
    horseinfo = "" # ...and no horseinfo

    def __init__(self, name=None, horse=None):
        if name:
            self.name = name # override default name only if name is given
        if horse:
            self.horse = horse # and similarly...

    def __repr__(self):
        if self.horse:
            self.horseinfo = " and my horse's name is " + self.horse
```

```
        return "Howdy, I'm %s%s." % (self.name, self.horseinfo)

# With classes we can use inheritance to share behavior!
class COWGIRL(COWBOY):
    name = "Sue" # most cowgirls are named Sue
```

For the moment, we defer the explanation of the COWBOY.__repr__ method. Here the Cowboy_fn function and the COWBOY class accomplish similar purposes in basic usage:

```
>>> from cowboy import *
>>> print Cowboy_fn("Walt", "Sandy")
Howdy, I'm Walt and my horse's name is Sandy.
>>> print COWBOY("Walt", "Sandy")
Howdy, I'm Walt and my horse's name is Sandy
```

However, The important difference is that the COWBOY class generates an instance that we can modify dynamically. For example, we can use all defaults, and then later add a horse and a nondefault name:

```
>>> cb = COWBOY()
>>> print cb
Howdy, I'm Dave.
>>> cb.name = "Johnboy"
>>> print cb
Howdy, I'm Johnboy.
>>> cb.horse = "Trixie"
>>> print cb
Howdy, I'm Johnboy and my horse's name is Trixie.
```

Furthermore, once we have a class, we can create similar classes that share common behaviors easily and without recopying code, as we did in the definition of the COWGIRL class.

```
>>> cg = COWGIRL()
>>> print cg
Howdy, I'm Sue.
>>> cg.horse = "Old Foggy"
>>> print cg
Howdy, I'm Sue and my horse's name is Old Foggy.
```

But wait! There are even more advantages!

The Magic of __repr__

The COWBOYs class uses the __repr__ magic instance method to inform Python how to convert instances of COWBOY to a string, for example, for printing.

By default, Python doesn't know any generic way to convert the instances of a class to a string, so the default conversion is useful for debugging, but not for any other interesting purpose:

```
>>> class x:
...     def __init__(self, a):
...         self.a = a
...
>>> xx = x(1)  # create an instance of x.
>>> xx         # echo it.
<x instance at 1236d8>
```

Here the class x does not indicate how instances should be converted to strings, so the default result of echoing the instance xx just indicates that xx is a member of the class x. Boring!

A class, however, may define a __repr__ function that informs Python how an instance of a class should be converted to a string, overriding the default conversion:

```
>>> class x:
...     def __init__(self, a):
...         self.a = a
...     def __repr__(self):
...         return "x(%s)" % (self.a,)
...
>>> xx = x(1)
>>> xx
x(1)
```

Here the __repr__ method of the instance xx essentially produces a string "x(1)" which could be read back in to Python to produce a value similar to xx.

The more interesting COWBOY.__repr__ method generates a greeting (as a string) when an instance of COWBOY is converted to a string, and the string produced indicates the current state of the name and horse instance attributes.

Class Attribute Defaults

Note that for both the name and horse attributes, defaults are defined in the COWBOY class as COWBOY.name == "Dave" and COWBOY.horse == None. Thus, any instance cb of COWBOY with no specific named attribute defined will evaluate cb.name to "Dave" by default.

```
>>> cb = COWBOY()
>>> (cb.name, COWBOY.name)
('Dave', 'Dave')
>>> cb.name = "Hopalong"    # define cb.name locally
>>> (cb.name, COWBOY.name)
('Hopalong', 'Dave')
```

As demonstrated above, defining a specific value for cb.name does not change the default value COWBOY.name. As we shall see, many HTML elements have tons of defaults, so defining default values at the level of a class will be very convenient.

Just-In-Time Formatting

Finally, the string representation for a COWBOY instance is only constructed when it is needed using the COWBOY.__repr__ method (for example, for printing) using the current values for the attributes or defaults of the instance.

```
>>> cb = COWBOY()
>>> print cb
Howdy, I'm Dave.
>>> cb.name = "Jeremia"
>>> print cb
Howdy, I'm Jeremia.
>>> cb.horse = "Moses"
>>> print cb
Howdy, I'm Jeremia and my horse's name is Moses.
```

This allows COWBOY instances to be modified dynamically, and those modifications to automatically be reflected in the string representation.

Furthermore, we define the COWGIRL class to be a subclass of the COWBOY class, inheriting all defaults and methods of COWBOY except for the name default value, which we override. As we shall see, many HTML classes will have definitions nearly as simple as the COWGIRL declaration.

Hence in order to take advantage of class inheritance, and default attribute values and the magic __repr__ method, we opt to generate HTML entities as Python class instances that format themselves using a __repr__ method, instead of the obvious strategy of developing functions that produce strings. This strategy allows great flexibility, simplicity, and code sharing.

The Wrong TABLE Class Definition

In pursuit of our stated strategy, we first define a TABLE class which produces a "self-formatting TABLE instance," as follows. (We omit most doc-strings for brevity). We choose to start with the TABLE class, because it is the hardest to implement and will show up the difficulties of this somewhat simple-minded approach the soonest.

The TABLE HTML element has a number of options: It can have a border, or the border may be omitted; cells can have specified or default padding; and cells can have specified or default spacing. These options are indicated in HTML source via the inclusion of exclusion of the BORDER, CELLSPACING, and CELLPADDING option in the start tag. For example,

```
<TABLE>...</TABLE>
<TABLE BORDER>...</TABLE>
<TABLE CELLPADDING=2>...</TABLE>
<TABLE CELLSPACING=3 BORDER>...</TABLE>
```

Hence, in our class definition, we specify that these options should be omitted by default (indicated by a value of None). Furthermore, a TABLE may optionally include exactly one CAPTION element, which we omit by default in the class definition as well. All of the defaults may be overridden by providing a value for the appropriate argument to the TABLE.__init__ initialization function. Hence, the definition of the TABLE class commences as follows:

```
from string import joinfields
from types import *            # get some useful tools...

class TABLE:
   BORDER = None        # defaults for TABLE HTML attributes (omit).
```

```
CELLSPACING = None
CELLPADDING = None
Lines = () #  default to an empty sequence of lines.
CAPTION = None  # default to no caption.

def __init__(self,
             Lines=None,
             CAPTION="",
             BORDER=None,
             CELLSPACING=None,
             CELLPADDING=None):
    # override defaults only if values are given
    if Lines: self.Lines = Lines
    if CAPTION: self.CAPTION = CAPTION
    if BORDER: self.BORDER = BORDER
    if CELLSPACING: self.CELLSPACING = CELLSPACING
    if CELLPADDING: self.CELLPADDING = CELLPADDING
    # gosh! that was a little repetitive!
```

The __init__ initialization function for the TABLE class mirrors the COW-BOY example given above—the default values defined by the TABLE class will be overridden by an instance only if the values are specified in the argument list.

The Lines argument to TABLE.__init__ should be a sequence of lines for the table, each properly formatted using <TR>...</TR> because we do not define the TABLE class to do this formatting automatically. Similarly the CAPTION value should be properly formatted as <CAPTION>...</CAPTION>, because we will not accomplish this formatting directly in the TABLE class either.

Before defining a TABLE.__repr__ method, we define a helper method TABLE.headstring that just generates the start tag (including any options, if they are given) for the table.

```
# class TABLE continued...
   def headstring(self):
       """create table head, adding optional parameters if present
          eg headstring = "<TABLE BORDER CELLPADDING=3>"
       """
       D = { "bd": "", "cp": "", "cs":"" }
       if self.BORDER: D["bd"] = " BORDER"
       if self.CELLSPACING: D["cs"] = " CELLSPACING=" + `self.CELLSPACING`
       if self.CELLPADDING: D["cp"] = " CELLPADDING=" + `self.CELLPADDING`
       # hmmm... that was a little repetitive too!
       return "<TABLE%(bd)s%(cp)s%(cs)s>" % D
```

The TABLE.headstring method uses a dictionary D to define the substitutions for the BORDER, CELLSPACING, and CELLPADDING options, using empty strings by default, and then if any of the attributes BORDER, CALLSPACING, or CELLPADDING are meaningful for self (the instance) the empty substitution is replaced by " BORDER" or " CELLSPACING=n" or " CELLPADDING=m", respectively. Finally the result of the method is computed via "<TABLE%(bd)s%(cp)s%(cs)s>" % D, which generates a start tag using the substitutions given in D.

We may now define the TABLE.__repr__ method using the TABLE.headstring method:

```
# class TABLE continued...
   def __repr__(self, indent=""):
       # get the headstring as the first line to return
       resultstrings = [ self.headstring() ]
       # get the line strings (convert each line to string representation
       #   and store them all in resultstrings, pass any indenting down).
       for line in self.Lines:
           # try to use the .__repr__ with an indent
           try:
               rep = line.__repr__(indent)
           except:
               # Whoops!  line.__repr__(indent) didn't work!
               rep = str(line)
           resultstrings.append( rep )  # store it.
       if self.CAPTION:
           resultstrings.append( self.CAPTION )
       resultstrings.append("</TABLE>")
       return joinfields(resultstrings, "\n" + indent)
```

NOTE Note that the for loop, which converts each element of self.Lines to a string, is a bit elaborate. The reason is that we want to permit elements of self.Lines to be either simple strings or members of other types or class instances that define a __repr__ method with an optional string parameter line.__repr__(indent). Close inspection reveals that TABLE.__repr__ itself permits an optional indent parameter: We will explain this parameter later.

We also use str(line) to convert line elements to strings (if line.__repr__(indent) fails) in order for the line to contain something other than a string value. We use `str(line)` rather than `repr(line)` because if line happens to be a string, `repr(line)` would enclose the string value in an extra pair of quotes, whereas `repr(line)` does not.

Now the TABLE class definition is complete. As a matter of habit, whenever possible we always define a self-test function for any class or function we define in Python. This habit is extremely useful, both to illustrate the use of the program fragment in a (sort of) working example and to provide "regression testing" in case we decide to modify the class or function later.

```
def testTABLE():
    print "testing TABLE() to stdout"
    # make some literal string lines
    L1= "<TR> <TD> line 1 </TD> </TR>"
    L2= "<TR> <TD> line 2 </TD> </TR>"
    L3= "<TR> <TD> line 3 </TD> </TR>"
    # create a TABLE instance using the lines, options, and a CAPTION
    T = TABLE( ( L1, L2, L3 ),
                CAPTION = "<CAPTION>various lines</CAPTION>",
                CELLSPACING = 4,
                BORDER = 1)
    print `T`   # print the standard string conversion for T
```

In particular, the `testTABLE()` function generates the following:

```
>>> from table0 import *
>>> testTABLE()
testing TABLE() to stdout
<TABLE BORDER CELLSPACING=4>
<TR> <TD> line 1 </TD> </TR>
<TR> <TD> line 2 </TD> </TR>
<TR> <TD> line 3 </TD> </TR>
<CAPTION>various lines</CAPTION>
</TABLE>
```

Let's test the TABLE class further using interactive Python. First define some lines for a table, as strings, and then create a table:

```
>>> r1 = "<TR> <TD> a line </TD> <TR>"
>>> r2 = "<TR> <TD> another line </TD> <TR>"
>>> T = TABLE( [r1, r2] )
>>> print T
```

```
<TABLE>
<TR> <TD> a line </TD> <TR>
<TR> <TD> another line </TD> <TR>
</TABLE>
```

Note that the printed representation for T has no options on the </TABLE> start tag (in TABLE.headstring, all the option substitutions defaulted to the empty string).

Now we experiment with the formatting of the start tag <TABLE...> by specifying a CELLSPACING:

```
>>> T.CELLSPACING=2
>>> print T
<TABLE CELLSPACING=2>
<TR> <TD> a line </TD> <TR>
<TR> <TD> another line </TD> <TR>
</TABLE>
```

Here the specified CELLSPACING forced the " CELLSPACING=2" to be inserted into the start tag by TABLE.headstring.

Now let's add a caption to T and see what the result looks like:

```
>>> T.CAPTION = "<CAPTION>Fascinating</CAPTION>"
>>> print T
<TABLE CELLSPACING=2>
<TR> <TD> a line </TD> <TR>
<TR> <TD> another line </TD> <TR>
<CAPTION>Fascinating</CAPTION>
</TABLE>
```

Finally, just what the heck does the optional indent argument to the __repr__ function do? Let's try it:

```
>>> print T.__repr__("   ") # call __repr__ directly with an indent.
<TABLE CELLSPACING=2>
   <TR> <TD> a line </TD> <TR>
   <TR> <TD> another line </TD> <TR>
   <CAPTION>Fascinating</CAPTION>
   </TABLE>
```

Aha! By providing an indent (three spaces) to `T.__repr__` the instance T automatically formats itself to be indented three spaces. Actually, `T.__repr__()` indented all lines but the first, because after playing around with the module, we discovered that it worked best to assume that the indenting of the first line was handled elsewhere.

We will define all HTML elements to allow optional indenting, in order allow complex elements to indent their components. The intension is to make the resulting HTML source will be easier for a human reader to understand (Mozaic and Grail and other programs that format HTML documents will ignore the extra whitespace).

A difficulty with the TABLE class is that it required all the rows within the TABLE to be formatted properly. In order to define an automatic way to format table rows, we proceed to define a TR class modeled on the TABLE class given above. Unfortunately, careful examination of the TR class will give experienced programmers a familiar sick feeling:

```
class TR:
    """A whole lot like TABLE, but not close enough!"""
    ALIGN = None     # option defaults (omit)
    VALIGN = None
    NOWRAP = None
    items = () # default to an empty sequence of items

    def __init__(self,
                items = None,
                ALIGN = None,
                VALIGN = None,
                NOWRAP = None):
        if items: self.items = items
        if ALIGN: self.ALIGN = ALIGN
        if VALIGN: self.VALIGN = VALIGN
        if NOWRAP: self.NOWRAP = NOWRAP

    def headstring(self):
        D = { "al": "", "va": "", "nw": "" }
        if self.ALIGN: D["al"] = " ALIGN=" + `self.ALIGN`
        if self.VALIGN: D["va"] = " VALIGN=" + `self.VALIGN`
        if self.NOWRAP: D["nw"] = " NOWRAP"
        # help!  my fingers are getting tired!
        return "<TR%(al)s%(va)s%(nw)s>"
```

```
    def __repr__(self, indent):
        """Standard string conversion, again. Looks very familiar!"""
        # get the headstring...
        resultstrings = [ self.headstring() ]
        # convert each element of self.items (much like as in TABLE)...
        for elt in self.items:
            try:
                rep = elt.__repr__(indent)
            except:
                rep = str(elt) # Whoops!...
            resultstrings.append(rep)
        resultstrings.append("</TR>")
        return joinfields(resultstrings, " ") # yawn!
# this is SOOOO boring, there's got to be a better way!
```

As the final comment indicates, the definition of the TR class is distressingly familiar—it's just the TABLE class with different attributes! Unfortunately the similarity is not close enough that we may directly inherit behaviors from the TABLE class because the names of the attributes of TABLE and those of TR differ, and hence the methods of TABLE won't find the right attributes when they try to manipulate a TR instance.

In a less dynamic language that doesn't allow dynamic attribute access (like Java and C++ don't), we would be completely stuck: We would have to continue writing very similar boilerplate code over and over, and should we later discover that the boilerplate is flawed, we'd have to make innumerable error-prone revisions to all the classes we defined, thus entering a seemingly endless test, edit, test, edit, test, edit, cycle... Help!

Happily we are not using a less dynamic language! We are using Python, with its arsenal of dynamic features we can draw on to maximize code sharing and minimize tedious error-prone repetition. To this end, let's give up on this deadly tedious approach and start over with a high-powered improved solution.

The Right Way to Generate Tables (and the rest of HTML)

Let's back off a bit and analyze the problem. The TR and TABLE classes we defined the wrong way had several places where tedious repetition entered the equation. The first were the __init__ functions which looked roughly like this

```
def __init__(self, arg1=Default1, ..., argn=Default2):
    if arg1: self.arg1 = arg1
    ...
    if argn: self.argn = argn
```

It seems what we need is some way to wrap all the argument/value pairs of the calling sequence into a single structure and assign all of the arguments by looping over the structure. We can do exactly this in Python, by using the keyword argument dynamic calling sequence in combination with the `setattr` dynamic attribute assignment function.

The next place where tedium reigned supreme was in the `headstring()` methods that each initialized a dictionary to provide empty string substitutions associated with attributes, and then overrode the defaults, something like this:

```
def headstring( ... )
    D = { ... default empty substitutions ... }
    if self.arg1: D["arg1"] = " arg1=" + `self.arg1`
    ... etcetera etcetera ad infinitum ...
    if self.argn: D["argn"] = " argn=" + `self.argn`
```

Apparently we need to loop over the names of attributes, extracting the associated values of the attributes from the `self` instance. The Python `getattr` function will help us do this nicely.

The Surprising Power of `getattr` and `setattr`

The `setattr (object, name, value)` accepts an `object`, a string `name`, and a `value` and attempts to set the attribute named by `name` of `object` to the `value`. Roughly speaking

```
setattr(object, "attribute", value)
```

is a less readable way to write `object.attribute = value`, but

```
setattr(object, name, value)
```

is the only official way to dynamically set an attribute of an object. Intuitively it is similar to the pseudo-Python assignment:

```
object.<string associated with name> = value
```

As a stupid example, if we want to set the attributes a, b, c, d, e, and f of X all to None, we could write

```
X.a = None
X.b = None
X.c = None
X.d = None
X.e = None
X.f = None
```

or, if we want to be cute, we could write:

```
for name in ("a", "b", "c", "d", "e", "f"):
    setattr(X, name, None)
```

The setattr function is good for more than cute tricks, however, because it allows Python programs to implement highly flexible features that normally require some sort of complicated trickery (like templates, or code generation) in less dynamic languages, as follows.

The getattr (object, name) function is the dual to the setattr function, it gets the attribute of the object named by the string value of name, if there is one, or raises an AttributeError otherwise. Roughly

```
getattr(object, "attribute")
```

is a less readable way to write the expression object.attribute but

```
getattr(object, name)
```

is the only official way to dynamically retrieve the value associated with an attribute of an object. Intuitively it is similar to the pseudo-Python expression:

```
object.<string associated with name>
```

Furthermore, for classes and class instances, getattr (object, name) will search the inheritance hierarchy associated with the object in order to find a value associated with the string value of name in the "nearest" superclass of the object, unless the object itself defines the value.

For a stupid example, if we want to print the values of the attributes a, b, c, d, e, and f of X, we could write

```
print X.a
print X.b
print X.c
print X.d
print X.e
print X.f
```

or if we wanted to be cute we could write:

```
for name in ("a", "b", "c", "d", "e", "f"):
    print getattr(X, name)
```

Again, getattr (object, name) is good for far more than trickery like this silly printing example, which is demonstrated soon.

Dynamic Keyword Arguments for HTML

A function or method may accept an arbitrary number of keyword/value pairs in its calling sequence by including an **Arg argument in the declaration of the calling sequence, which will evaluate to a dictionary containing those keyword/argument pairs that were not associated with other arguments, which may appear in the declaration.

Consider the function:

```
def KDict(**pairs):
    return pairs
```

This function effectively defines an alternative way to declare dictionaries that map strings to objects:

```
>>> KDict(one = 1, two = 2, three = 3)
{'one': 1, 'three': 3, 'two': 2}
>>> KDict(CAPTION="<CAPTION>yes!</CAPTION>", CELLSPACING=30)
{'CAPTION': '<CAPTION>yes!</CAPTION>', 'CELLSPACING': 30}
```

Here the KDict function accepts any set of associations between keywords and values, converting them to a dictionary mapping the keyword names to the associated value.

WARNING

Note that because the `KDict` function defines no way to interpret positional arguments (that don't have keywords), the call will raise an error whenever `KDict` is called with positional arguments:

```
>>> KDict(3, ears = 2)
Traceback (innermost last):
  File "<stdin>", line 1, in ?
TypeError: too many arguments
```

More interestingly, consider the class:

```
class Record:
    def __init__(self, **pairs):
        for (name, value) in pairs.items():
            setattr(self, name, value)
```

This class defines a generic `Record` constructor which will construct an instance containing precisely those attributes specified as name/value keyword arguments to the constructor. The `Record.__init__` initialization function accepts any sequence of keyword/value pairs in the calling sequence in the dictionary pairs, and then iterates through the items of the dictionary (using `pairs.items()`) setting each. For example,

```
>>> r = Record(one = 1, two = 2, three = 3)
>>> r.one, r.two, r.three
(1, 2, 3)
>>> dir(r)
['one', 'three', 'two']
```

Thus, the `Record` instance r has exactly three attributes: one, two, and three respectively, associated with the values 1, 2, and 3.

```
>>> r2 = Record(CAPTION="<CAPTION>yes!</CAPTION>", CELLSPACING=30)
>>> r2.CAPTION, r2.CELLSPACING
('<CAPTION>yes!</CAPTION>', 30)
>>> dir(r2)
['CAPTION', 'CELLSPACING']
```

the Record instance r2 has only two attributes, CAPTION and CELLSPAC-ING, with the values specified in the keyword/value pairs of the calling sequence.

```
CAPTION="<CAPTION>yes!</CAPTION>", CELLSPACING=30
```

Furthermore, the `Record` class is a convenient way to create instances with whatever attribute names we please, and we will use precisely this capability to simplify class definitions for generating HTML.

The `HTMLfmt` Module Done Right

As usual, the `HTMLfmt` module we develop below will use tools imported from Python libraries, so we import these tools at the top of the module for later use.

```
import string
from string import joinfields, splitfields, lower
from types import *
```

The type and string modules and the functions imported from the string module have all been explained earlier, and we will assume the reader understands them in this chapter.

Defining a Superclass for all HTMLElements

Now let's use dynamic attribute features and keyword arguments to capture the repeating code we saw in our aborted attempt to generate HTML. We capture the most important features in a "virtual superclass" `HTMLElement`, which is not intended to be used directly; it is only used to define common behaviors among all its (many) subclasses.

We will assume that all initialization for `HTMLElements` uses keyword arguments exclusively, and use the keyword/value pairs blindly to initialize the attributes of `HTMLElement` instances, just as in the Record example given above.

```
class HTMLElement:
    """Virtual superclass, provides common functionality"""

    def __init__(self, **NamedArgs):
        """Copy non-false given named arguments as attributes of self.
           To allow positional calling sequences or default values,
           this initializer should be overridden by subclasses, see examples.
        """
        for (name, value) in NamedArgs.items():
            if value:
                setattr(self, name, value)
```

This method mirrors both initialization functions defined for the TABLE and TR classes in our aborted attempt, except by using keyword named arguments and `setattr` the initialization has been made generic.

The `HTMLElement.__init__` method has two deficiencies: It doesn't support any positional arguments, and it does not check that the attribute names make sense. We will correct these deficiencies by always overriding this method in subclasses with an `__init__` method that allows positional arguments and "calls up" to `HTMLElement.__init__( ... )` using only the keyword arguments appropriate to the subclass.

Defining a Headstring Method for all HTML Elements

Next, we aim for a generic way implement the headstring method, i.e., we aim to generate HTML start tags such as

```
<DD>
<TABLE BORDER CELLPADDING=3>
<TR ALIGN="left" VALIGN="middle">
```

for any HTML element in a generic way, just as our aborted implementations of TABLE and TR each generated their own start tags using a headstring method in a nongeneric way.

Although the formats for these start tags are similar, the attributes they use for each HTML element will differ by subclass. Hence, the superclass `HTMLElement` must assume that any instance using the `HTMLElement.head-string` method provides some information regarding the attributes to use in the start tag. In particular, `HTMLElement.headstring` will assume that the following default values have been redefined, if needed:

```
# class HTMLElement continued
   HTML_Attributes = () # defaults to no attributes
   HTML_Tag_Marks = ()  # defaults to empty sequence
   Tag_Format = "** UNKNOWN TAG FORMAT **"
```

Here `self.HTML_Attributes` should provide a sequence of attribute names that correspond to the optional entries in the start tag. For tables, the appropriate sequence would be

```
("BORDER", "CELLSPACING", "CELLPADDING")
```

and for TR (table row) elements the appropriate sequence would be

```
("ALIGN", "VALIGN", "NOWRAP")
```

Some of the HTML_Attributes are peculiar in that they occur as simple flags and have no associated values, and these special attributes are assumed to be listed in self.HTML_Tag_Marks. For example, the NOWRAP flag of the TR element has no associated value (e.g., <TR NOWRAP VALIGN="top">), so self.HTML_Tag_Marks value for all TR instances should be ("NOWRAP",) —a singleton tuple.

Finally, recall that our aborted implementations of TABLE and TR each used the magical format strings

```
"<TABLE%(bd)s%(cp)s%(cs)s>"
"<TR%(al)s%(va)s%(nw)s>"
```

respectively, to specify the escaped format sequence for the start tag. These format strings now must be specified as self.Tag_Format by each subclass of HTMLElement, but using the real attribute names rather than abbreviations. Thus, for TABLE and TR elements

```
"<TABLE%(BORDER)s%(CELLPADDING)s%(CELLSPACING)s>"
"<TR%(ALIGN)s%(VALIGN)s%(NOWRAP)s>"
```

are, respectively, the appropriate values for self.Tag_Format.

Assuming the constants self.HTML_Attributes, self.HTML_Tag_Marks, and self.Tag_Format have been specified by the subclass, we may proceed to define a generic HTMLElement.headstring method:

```
# class HTMLElement continued
   def headstring(self):
       """create an HTML Tag starter, eg <TABLE BORDER CELLPADDING=3>"""
       Dict = {}
       # default all HTML_Attribute associations to empty string.
       Atts = self.HTML_Attributes
       for name in Atts:
           Dict[name] = ""

       # override the empty defaults for non-null values
```

```
    simplemarks = self.HTML_Tag_Marks
    for name in Atts:
        try:
            value = getattr(self, name)
        except AttributeError:
            pass # no value defined... skip this name.
        else:
            if value: # only redefine the substitution for non-false values
                if name in simplemarks:
                    Dict[name] = " " + name
                elif type(value) == StringType: # double quote string values
                    Dict[name] = ' %s="%s"' % (name, value)
                else: # otherwise use default string conversion for values
                    Dict[name] = ' %s=%s' % (name, value)

    # return transformed Tag_Format using Dict for escaped substitutions
    return self.Tag_Format % Dict
```

As with `HTMLElement.__init__`, the `HTMLElement.headstring` method mirrors both headstring methods defined for the TR and TABLE classes in the aborted attempt, except that by using sequences of attribute names and `getattr` the method has been made generic.

The `HTMLElement.headstring` function first defines all substitutions in `Dict` for each HTML Attribute to be empty and then tests each such attribute name from `self.HTML_Attributes` to see if the name is defined as an attribute of self, using `getattr(self, name)`. If there is no such attribute, the AttributeError is caught and the name is skipped, but if the attribute is defined, the else clause of the try statement executes. If the value associated with the attribute is nonfalse, the substitution in Dict for that attribute is replaced. The substitution for a simple mark is simply, e.g., BORDER for the case of the BORDER attribute of TABLEs, but for other attributes that require values, the substitution is, e.g., `CELLSPACING=3` for the case of the CELLSPACING attribute of TABLEs.

We are not entirely sure that the explanation above is a better explanation than the Python explained. For readers that find this magic confusing, please experiment with these concepts using interactive Python. Python's dynamic features are extremely powerful, but for the programmer unused to such power they can appear a bit bizarre. Only experience will cure the confusion for sure. Play with it!

A __repr__ Method for Some HTML Elements

Now we proceed to define a __repr__ method for HTML Elements. Just as in our aborted example, this is the formatting method that achieves the ultimate goal of translating a given instance of HTMLElement into a string representation as HTML, suitable for inscription in a complete HTML document, and for presentation by a browser.

For generality the definition of HTMLElement.__repr__ assumes that the content of the element consists of some sort of sequence, and because this is not always the case, some subclasses will simplify the implementation by completely overriding this method.

Just as the HTMLElement.headstring method required information about the subclass, so HTMLElement.__repr__ needs to know what the end tag for this element should look like (if it has one), how to get the sequence of strings to insert between the start tag and the end tag, and how each string in the sequence should be separated, one from the next. This information is assumed to be given by self.end_tag, self.body_list(indent), and self.body_sep, respectively, which are given the following default values:

```
#class HTMLElement continued...
    end_tag = ".** UNKNOWN TAG FORMAT end **"
    body_sep = ""
    def body_list(self, indent=""):
        return [] # default to empty body list
```

For the TABLE and TR elements the appropriate values for end_tag will be </TABLE> and </TR>, respectively. The body_sep for both TABLE and TR should be a newline, because both TABLEs and table rows sometimes get large enough that each element of the body should be placed on separate lines by default. For TABLEs, the self.body_list(indent) method will yield the sequence of rows inside the table, followed by the CAPTION, if there is one.

Assuming the values self.end_tag, self.body_list(), and self.body_sep have been defined appropriately, we proceed to define HTMLElement.__repr__ as follows:

```
#class HTMLElement continued...
    def __repr__(self, indent=""):
```

```
"""Standard string conversion for HTML Elements"""

# indent the body a little further than self.
indent2 = indent + "  "
list = self.body_list(indent2)

# collapse all components of list into a single string,
#   inserting the head and end_tag to the first and last element,
#   and if body_sep includes a newline, indent everything.
#
sep = self.body_sep
if "\n" in sep:
    # use separator plus indentation, if separator includes newline
    # NOTE: these values were magically determined by experimentation.
    sep = sep + indent
    headsep = "\n" + indent
    endsep = "\n" + indent2
else:
    endsep = headsep = ""
# now insert the header with a newline if the separator has one.
if self.Tag_Format:
    head = self.headstring()
    try:
        list[0] = "%s%s%s" % (head, headsep, list[0])
    except IndexError:  # whoops! list is empty!
        list = [ head + headsep ]
# now insert the end tag with a newline if the separator has one.
if self.end_tag:
    list[-1] = "%s%s%s" % (list[-1], endsep, self.end_tag)
# finally join all elements of the list using the (indented) separator.
return joinfields(list, sep)
```

The only thing confusing about this method is the apparently arbitrary decisions regarding when to introduce extra whitespace. These decisions were decided via experimentation using our aesthetic judgment, with the goal of producing HTML source output that could be interpreted by a human as well as by a machine. Your mileage may vary.

NOTE

Rather than prepending and appending start and end tags to the list returned by `self.body_list()`, respectively, we glue them onto the first and last element of the list. This is important because the tags should not be separated from the rest of the list by the `self.body_sep` separator, in some cases. We actually had this nuance wrong in the initial version of this class: We discovered our error during debugging. Of course that was the only bug we found! (Right!)

Now our generic HTMLElement superclass is complete and ready for use. You cannot do anything useful with HTMLElement except create subclasses from it. This class serves the purpose of defining useful common behaviors for many of the classes defined further on, to allow code-sharing and to simplify the definition of the other classes.

Subclasses of HTMLElement must redefine the __init__ function (calling HTMLElement.__init__ as part of the initialization), provide a suitable value for Tag_Format, and end_tag and either redefine __repr__ directly or provide an appropriate redefinition of body_list method to define the body to appear between the start and end tags of the element. Furthermore, subclasses may or may not want to redefine body_sep, HTML_Attributes, and HTML_Tag_Marks as appropriate.

The TABLE Class, a Better Implementation

For example, we may now proceed to define the TABLE class as a subclass of HTMLElement, and all we need to do is override the __init__ method, the body_list methods, and redefine certain constant values used by the superclass.

```
class TABLE(HTMLElement):
    # by default, use an empty sequence of Lines
    Lines = ()
    CAPTION = None
    HTML_Attributes = ("BORDER", "CELLSPACING", "CELLPADDING")
    HTML_Tag_Marks = ("BORDER",) # singleton tuple!
    Tag_Format = "<TABLE%(BORDER)s%(CELLPADDING)s%(CELLSPACING)s>"
    end_tag = "</TABLE>"
    body_sep = "\n"

    # override superclass initialization method
    #
    def __init__(self,
                 Lines=None,
                 CAPTION=None,
                 # default to always use a border (nonstandard)!
                 BORDER=1,
                 CELLSPACING=None,
                 CELLPADDING=None):
        """TABLE initialization, provide default values and
           translation of positional initialization to named format.
```

```
    """
    # Call the superclass initialization, but give keyword naming
    # and default values.
    HTMLElement.__init__(self,
            Lines=Lines,
            CAPTION=CAPTION,
            BORDER=BORDER,
            CELLSPACING=CELLSPACING,
            CELLPADDING=CELLPADDING)
    # Now if self.Lines is neither a list nor a tuple
    # assume it's a mistake.
    if not (type(self.Lines) in (TupleType, ListType)):
        raise ValueError, "self.Lines must be tuple or list"
```

This redefined __init__ function doesn't seem to do much, but in fact it does a lot. The `HTMLElement.__init__` method accepts any keyword/name pairs sent in its argument list, but does not accept any positional arguments at all. The `TABLE.__init__` method, by contrast, specifies the exact sequence of arguments suitable for TABLE HTML elements and their relative positions as positional arguments, as well as their default values if they are omitted.

The call to `HTMLElement.__init__` associates each of the keywords

```
Lines CAPTION BORDER CELLSPACING CELLPADDING
```

with the values of the variables of the same name. This looks a little weird at first to the noninitiated, we freely admit.

NOTE The `self` instance must be explicitly passed to the superclass initializer `HTMLElement.__init__` in order to explicitly bind `self` to the unbound class method.

Now we must describe how to obtain a list of strings that define the interior of a TABLE, by redefining `body_list`.

```
# class TABLE continued...
   def body_list(self, indent=""):
       """Table body list generator.
          Generate the list of lines in the table, indented as specified.
          Add the caption at the end, if given.
       """
```

```
    # copy self.Lines into from_seq, force list representation.
    from_seq = map(None, self.Lines)
    # append the caption, if it's available
    if self.CAPTION:
        from_seq.append(self.CAPTION)
    # convert all objects of from_seq to strings, and put them in result
    nresults = len(from_seq)
    result = [None] * nresults
    for index in xrange(nresults):
        line = from_seq[index]
        rep = Indent_Thing(line, indent)
        # this function is responsible for indentation past first newline
        result[index] = indent + rep
    return result
```

Now we are done! The TABLE class is fully functional, and we may interactively type, for example:

```
>>> from HTMLfmt import *
>>> line1 = "<TR><TD>one element row</TD></TR>"
>>> line2 = "<TR><TD>two element</TD><TD>row</TD></TR>"
>>> T = TABLE([line1, line2])
>>> print T
<TABLE BORDER>
  <TR><TD>one element row</TD></TR>
  <TR><TD>two element</TD><TD>row</TD></TR>
  </TABLE>
```

Whoops! We lied! We left out an important piece that we haven't explained yet: TABLE.body_list uses the Indent_Thing function, defined thusly, with the help of the constants OK_STR and OK_SEQ:

```
# the sequence of types with an okay str(x) conversion for formatting HTML
OK_STR = (IntType, FloatType, LongType, StringType)

# the sequence types that may automatically be converted to
# instances of the Seq class, reasonably.
OK_SEQ = (ListType, TupleType)

def Indent_Thing(The_Thing, indent=""):
    try:
        # Assume The_Thing is an instance with a __repr__ function
        # that permits indentation.
        return The_Thing.__repr__(indent)
    except:
        # Didn't work!... If it's a string, use it, indenting any newlines.
```

```
Thing_type = type(The_Thing)
if Thing_type == StringType:
    if "\n" in The_Thing:
        # for strings with newlines add indenting after newlines
        list = splitfields(The_Thing, "\n")
        return joinfields( list, "\n" + indent )
    else:
        return The_Thing
elif Thing_type in OK_SEQ:
    # if the Thing is an appropriate sequence type
    # convert it to an HTML sequence, and return indented __repr__
    seq = apply(Seq, tuple(The_Thing) )
    return seq.__repr__(indent)
elif Thing_type in OK_STR:
    # for appropriate types return standard string conversion
    return str(The_Thing)
else:
    raise TypeError, "Thing type not good for HTML: " + `Thing_type`
```

The purpose of `Indent_Thing` is strictly cosmetic (but since it makes the output more readable, it also helps with debugging). `Indent_Thing(object, indent)` attempts to produce a string from an arbitrary Python object indented by the indent parameter. This helps, for example, make it easier to read TABLEs that occur within TABLEs in HTML source files by indenting the embedded TABLE to a deeper level than the outer TABLE.

`Indent_Thing` uses a convention we introduced in our previous aborted implementation: All classes defined in this module allow an optional indent argument to their standard string conversion functions `self.__repr__(indent)`. Indent thing first tries to evaluate the __repr__ function with the indentation argument, and if the evaluation fails for any reason, it checks the type of the object, and does something appropriate. For the case of the table T the `self.__repr__(indent)` call will succeed:

```
>>> print T.__repr__("     ")
<TABLE BORDER>
        <TR><TD>one element row</TD></TR>
        <TR><TD>two element</TD><TD>row</TD></TR>
    </TABLE>
```

Note that just as in the aborted example the indentation only effects lines after the first, following the uniform assumption that the first indent is handled elsewhere .

If `The_Thing` is a string, however, the call `The_Thing.__repr__(indent)` will raise an `AttributeError`, and the `except` clause of the `try` statement will execute. For strings, any newline in the string is replace by a newline followed by the indent:

```
>>> S = """The things that pass
... for knowledge
... I can't understand!"""
>>> print Indent_Thing(S, "      ")
The things that pass
      for knowledge
      I can't understand!
```

If `The_Thing` is a list or a tuple (with type listed in `OK_SEQ`), then the object is converted into an instance of the `Seq` class, which we will define next. Alternatively, if `The_Thing` is an `int` or a `long` or a `float` (with type listed in `OK_STR`), it is converted to a string using the default string conversion, but any object of any other type is rejected, and `Indent_Thing` raises a `TypeError`.

Before we proceed to define the `Seq` class used by `Indent_Thing`, let's play with the TABLE class a little more, by fiddling with the TABLE instance T we created earlier.

```
>>> T.CAPTION="<CAPTION>not all rows are equal</CAPTION>" # add caption
>>> print T
<TABLE BORDER>
  <TR><TD>one element row</TD></TR>
  <TR><TD>two element</TD><TD>row</TD></TR>
  <CAPTION>not all rows are equal</CAPTION>
  </TABLE>
>>> T.CELLPADDING = 5 # add CELLPADDING
>>> print T
<TABLE BORDER CELLPADDING=5>
  <TR><TD>one element row</TD></TR>
  <TR><TD>two element</TD><TD>row</TD></TR>
  <CAPTION>not all rows are equal</CAPTION>
  </TABLE>
>>> T.BORDER = None # disable the BORDER
>>> print T
<TABLE CELLPADDING=5>
  <TR><TD>one element row</TD></TR>
  <TR><TD>two element</TD><TD>row</TD></TR>
```

```
<CAPTION>not all rows are equal</CAPTION>
</TABLE>
```

We will get around to showing how to produce TABLEs within TABLEs and special kinds of TABLEs later, but we need to define the TR (table row) and TH/TD (table entry) elements first.

 Note that we have defined TABLE(...) to generate a TABLE with a BORDER by default, because most tables that contain text look stupid without a border. Of course this default can explicitly be disabled, as demonstrated above.

The Seq Class, Just a Sequence of HTML

Once in a while in the life of an HTML hacker, one just wants a sequence of HTML elements or plain text not enclosed inside any larger HTML structure. To this end we define the Seq class as a "fake" HTML element which has no tags, and simply displays its content separated by newlines. This can be useful, for example, to construct plain text to surround a table.

```
>>> S = Seq("Text before the Table.", T, "Text after the table.")
>>> print S
Text before the Table.
<TABLE CELLPADDING=5>
     <TR><TD>one element row</TD></TR>
     <TR><TD>two element</TD><TD>row</TD></TR>
     <CAPTION>not all rows are equal</CAPTION>
   </TABLE>
Text after the table.
```

The definition of the Seq class is straightforward, except that it defines two class attributes Seq.seq_prefix and Seq.seq_tail, both as the empty string. These attributes will be used when we create subclasses of the Seq class that require the elements of the sequence to be separated by tags of one sort or another, as we will see.

```
class Seq(HTMLElement):
    Tag_Format = end_tag = ""
    body_sep = "\n"
    seq_prefix = seq_tail = ""
```

```
def __init__(self, *sequence):
    HTMLElement.__init__(self, sequence = sequence)

def body_list(self, indent=""):
    sq = self.sequence
    nresults = len(sq)
    result = [None] * nresults
    pre = self.seq_prefix
    tail = self.seq_tail
    for index in xrange(nresults):
        elt = sq[index]
        rep = Indent_Thing(elt, indent)
        result[index] = "%s%s%s" % (pre, rep, tail)
    return result
```

The only other thing to notice in the definition of the Seq class is that the __init__ function accepts an arbitrary number of positional arguments (but no keyword/value arguments). This is convenient when a program defines a fixed length sequence of HTML elements.

Seq and the `apply` Function

It is sometimes convenient to construct a sequence of HTML elements of arbitrary length. We already saw this in the Indent_Thing function, which included the line:

```
seq = apply(Seq, tuple(The_Thing) )
```

In this case, The_Thing was a sequence (either a list or a tuple) whose length was unknown. Because there is no way to explicitly call Seq(...) with an argument list of unknown length, Indent_Thing used the apply function, which, like getattr and setattr, is one of Python's dynamic features.

Essentially the expression

```
apply( F, (1,2,3,4) )
```

is a less-readable way to write

```
F(1,2,3,4)
```

However, if Tup is a tuple, then the only official way to express

```
F( ...the contents of Tup... )
```

uses the apply function expression

```
apply( F, Tup )
```

The `apply` function can only be used with tuples, so if L is a list, we must use
`tuple(L)` to convert the list to a tuple in order to translate the contents of the list
into an appropriate form for apply, as does `Indent_Thing`. Note that
`tuple(Tup)` will return the tuple Tup itself.

Some Sequence-like Constructs

For the purposes of generating HTML, in Python a lot of HTML constructs
can be formulated as subclasses of the Seq class. In particular, there is no reason to define an individual paragraph, when a sequence of paragraphs of arbitrary length will suffice:

```
class P_Seq(Seq):
    """A sequence of simple paragraphs"""
    seq_prefix = "<P>"
    seq_tail = "</P>"
    body_sep = "\n\n" # two newlines, for readability
```

That was short and sweet, wasn't it? It can be used as follows (using the TABLE
instance T we created earlier:

```
>>> P = P_Seq("Paragraph before T", T, "Paragraph after T.")
>>> print P
<P>Paragraph before T</P>

<P><TABLE CELLPADDING=5>
     <TR><TD>one element row</TD></TR>
     <TR><TD>two element</TD><TD>row</TD></TR>
     <CAPTION>not all rows are equal</CAPTION>
   </TABLE></P>

<P>Paragraph after T.</P>
```

Now we see why the `Seq` class defined and used the apparently unnecessary `seq_prefix` and `seq_tail` attributes: they were needed by subclasses of Seq that required each element of the sequence to be adorned, in this case, by `<P>..</P>`. Note that in the preceding example, the table T has also been enclosed in a paragraph.

By creating simple subclasses of `Seq`, we can create other common HTML sequence-like constructs.

```
class BR_Seq(Seq):
    """A sequence broken by BR break line tags"""
    body_sep = "<BR>\n"

class HR_Seq(Seq):
    """A sequence broken by HR horizontal rules.
       HTML attributes for this member are not implemented."""
    body_sep = "<HR>\n"
```

These classes generate sequences of elements separated by broken lines and horizontal rules, respectively.

Numbered and Unnumbered HTML Lists as Sequences

The `Seq` class paradigm also captures HTML list constructs, but only the numbered <UL> and unnumbered list <OL> constructs, because the display list <DL> construct is more complex and requires special handling. However, the <UL> and <OL> constructs each permit special options in the start tags (TYPE for UL and TYPE and START for OL), so the implementation of these classes requires the redefinition of the initialization method __init__:

```
class UL(Seq):
    """Unordered list (bullet list)."""
    Tag_Format = "<UL%(TYPE)s>"
    end_tag = "</UL>"
    HTML_Attributes = ("TYPE",) # singleton
    seq_prefix = "<LI>"  # optional LI attributes not supported here.
    # default TYPE
    TYPE = None
    # override init
    def __init__(self, sequence, TYPE=None):
```

```
        HTMLElement.__init__(self, sequence = sequence, TYPE=TYPE)
        if len(self.sequence)<1:
            raise ValueError, "HTML List must have elements"
        self.TYPE = Check_Attribute(self.TYPE, ("disc", "circle", "square"))

class OL(UL):
    """Ordered (numbered) list."""
    Tag_Format = "<OL%(TYPE)s%(START)s>"
    end_tag = "</OL>"
    HTML_Attributes = ("TYPE", "START")

    def __init__(self, sequence, TYPE=None, START=None):
        HTMLElement.__init__(self, sequence = sequence,
                             TYPE=TYPE, START=START)
        # check TYPE and sequence, assume START is correct...
        if len(self.sequence)<1:
            raise ValueError, "HTML List must have elements"
        # allow self.TYPE to be the integer 1, if so convert it.
        if self.TYPE == 1:
            self.TYPE = "1"
        self.TYPE = Check_Attribute(self.TYPE, ("1", "i", "a", "A"))
```

These two classes both redefine the __init__ method in order to accept the options TYPE and START and also change some formatting parameters, but aside from that inherit all behavior from the Seq class.

Both of these classes check that the value of self.TYPE appears in a specific sequence of allowed values, using the Check_Attribute function, given below:

```
def Check_Attribute(value, possibilities):
    """Utility function for checking string attribute values.
       Return false values unchanged, otherwise
       if the value is in possibilities after lower conversion,
       return it as lower case, else raise TypeError.
    """
    if not value:
        return value
    newvalue = lower(value)
    if not (newvalue in possibilities):
        raise TypeError,\
        "%s not one of %s" % (value, possibilities)
    return newvalue
```

Hmmm... There is a small bug (feature) hidden here. We challenge the reader to find it and fix it!

Let's look at some example lists that can be generated from the OL and UL classes:

```
>>> u = UL(["hickory", "dickory", "doc"], TYPE="Disc")
>>> print u
<UL TYPE="disc">
<LI>hickory
<LI>dickory
<LI>doc
  </UL>
>>> o = OL(["Peter Peter Pumpkin Eater",
...         Seq("Mice", u), "Old King Cole"], TYPE=1)
>>> print o
<OL TYPE="1">
<LI>Peter Peter Pumpkin Eater
<LI>Mice
  <UL TYPE="disc">
    <LI>hickory
    <LI>dickory
    <LI>doc
      </UL>
<LI>Old King Cole
  </OL>
```

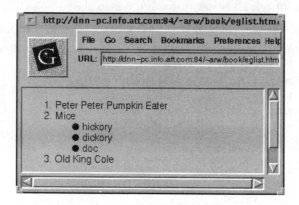

Figure 7.4 Some silly lists.

Display Lists (Labeled Lists)

HTML also allows lists to be associated with textual labels via the DL (display list) element. Because each entry in a display list has a label and a body associated with the label, the DL element is more complicated than a simple sequence, so we implement it as a direct subclass of `HTMLElement`.

```
class DL(HTMLElement):
    """A display list. Arguments should be a sequence of pairs.
        eg: DL( ["Bob","No kids"],
                ["Sue", DL(("Tom","No kids"), ("Tim","No kids") ) ] )
        or  apply(DL, pairtuple)
    """
    # the COMPACT attribute is not implemented (it's hardly used).

    Tag_Format = "<DL>"
    end_tag = "</DL>"
    body_sep = "\n"

    # override init
    def __init__(self, *pairs):
        # check the Body
        try:
            for pair in pairs:
                if len(pair) != 2:
                    raise ValueError
        except:
            raise ValueError, "Body must be Sequence of pairs"
        HTMLElement.__init__(self, Body=pairs)

    def body_list(self, indent=""):
        """DL body list gives
            <DD>title<DT>
                <indent>entry
        for each (title, entry) pair of the body."""
        Body = self.Body
        nBody = len(Body)
        result = [None] * nBody
        indent2 = indent + "  "
        for index in xrange(nBody):
            thisone = Body[index]
            (title, entry) = (thisone[0], thisone[1]) # allow non-tuple thisone
            Ititle = Indent_Thing(title,indent)
            Ientry = Indent_Thing(entry,indent2)
            result[index] = " <DD>%s<DT>\n%s%s" % (Ititle, indent2, Ientry )
        return result
```

The DL class redefines the __init__ method, as usual, but also checks the elements of the argument pairs to make sure that the argument really is a list of pairs. To complete the definition, we redefine the body_list method, which formats both the title and the entry for each pair in self.Body, with the entry indented a little further in than the title. As usual the Tag_Format, end_tag, and body_sep are also redefined for instances of this class.

The document string at the top of the class definition gives an example usage for the DL class. Let's try it:

```
>>> dl = DL( ["Bob","No kids"],
...          ["Sue", DL(("Tom","No kids"), ("Tim","No kids") ) ] )
>>> print dl
<DL>
 <DD>Bob<DT>
    No kids
 <DD>Sue<DT>
    <DL>
     <DD>Tom<DT>
        No kids
     <DD>Tim<DT>
        No kids
     </DL>
 </DL>
```

Alternate Initialization for Classes

Languages like java and C++ sometimes allow classes to be initialized in many different ways by specifying alternative initialization functions in a class definition. Python only permits one initialization method for any given class, but Python functions may be used to define other ways to create an instance of the class.

For example, the DL element bears a striking resemblance to the Python dictionary type—in some sense they both map keys to values. In some circumstances, it might be convenient to convert a dictionary to a display list, so we define an "alternate display list generator" as a Python function that performs the conversion:

```
def DictDL(Dict):
    """Convenience: produce a sorted DL from dictionary items."""
    items = Dict.items()
    items.sort()
    return apply(DL, tuple(items))
```

We can use this function, for example, as follows:

```
>>> Dict = {"kittens": "cute, furry, not edible",
...         "rabbits": "cute, furry, delicious with garlic",
...         "frogs": "little green slimy things, taste like chicken"}
>>> dl = DictDL(Dict)
>>> print dl
<DL>
 <DD>frogs<DT>
    little green slimy things, taste like chicken
 <DD>kittens<DT>
    cute, furry, not edible
 <DD>rabbits<DT>
    cute, furry, delicious with garlic
  </DL>
```

More Stuff for TABLES

Of course the various sorts of HTML lists are relatively uninteresting compared to TABLEs, and because we haven't defined classes for table rows (TR) or table entries (TD and TH) we haven't really disposed of the TABLE problem yet.

The table row element TR is a lot like a sequence, but for the sake of some trivial customization we define it as a direct subclass of HTMLElement, rather than as a subclass of Seq:

```
class TR(HTMLElement):
    """TR: Table Row for a TABLE"""
    HTML_Attributes = ("ALIGN", "VALIGN", "NOWRAP")
    HTML_Tag_Marks = ("NOWRAP",) # singleton tuple
    Tag_Format = "<TR%(ALIGN)s%(VALIGN)s%(NOWRAP)s>"
    end_tag = "</TR>"
    body_sep = "\n"
    # default to no row elements
    row_elements = ()
    # default to no ALIGN or VALIGN
    ALIGN = VALIGN = None

    # override superclass initialization method
    def __init__(self,
                 row_elements = None,
                 ALIGN = None,
                 VALIGN = None,
                 NOWRAP = None):
```

```
    """TR initialization function"""
    # I'm getting the hang of this!
    HTMLElement.__init__(self,
            row_elements = row_elements,
            ALIGN = ALIGN,
            VALIGN = VALIGN,
            NOWRAP = NOWRAP)
    # check ALIGN and VALIGN for validity, if given
    (self.ALIGN, self.VALIGN) = Check_ALIGNS(self.ALIGN, self.VALIGN)

def body_list(self, indent=""):
    """TR body_list generator.
       Indent each row element in sequence a little farther in.
       Quite similar to TABLE.body_list.
    """
    re = self.row_elements
    nresults = len(re)
    result = [None] * nresults
    for index in xrange(nresults):
        row_elt = re[index]
        rep = Indent_Thing(row_elt, indent)
        # This function is responsible for indenting rep
        # up to first newline
        result[index] = indent + rep
        indent = indent + "  " # 2 spaces more for next one.
    return result
```

Most of this is similar to examples given before, except that the initialization function checks the **ALIGN** and **VALIGN** attributes for valid values using the following function:

```
def Check_ALIGNS(ALIGN, VALIGN):
    """Both TR and TD have the same possible values for ALIGN and VALIGN,
       so we make this a utility function."""
    newALIGN = Check_Attribute(ALIGN, ("left", "center", "right"))
    newVALIGN = Check_Attribute(VALIGN, ("top", "middle",
                                         "bottom", "baseline"))
    return (newALIGN, newVALIGN)
```

As we shall see, the table element TH and TD classes will use this function also.

The only other peculiarity of TR is that it formats each entry of the row on a new line with each subsequent entry indented a little further. Again, because HTML formatters ignore whitespace, this extra indenting is strictly intended to improve the readability of the HTML output.

```
>>> tr = TR(["<TD>a</TD>", "<TD>b</TD>", "<TD>c</TD>"])
>>> print tr
<TR>
  <TD>a</TD>
    <TD>b</TD>
      <TD>c</TD>
  </TR>
```

Because a table row can have quite a few entries which can each be quite large (for example, they can be other tables), each TR entry is listed on its own line, but to indicate the relative position of the subsequent entries, one entry is indented a little further than the last.

Multiple Inheritance: A Mixin

To complete all the components needed to construct a TABLE, we need to define the TH and TD table entry elements. However, we defer the direct definition of TH and TD for a bit in order to factor out some common functionality that TH and TD share with many other HTML elements.

Many HTML elements are simple annotations around a single block of text, and for these the general HTMLElement.__repr__ function is overkill. For this reason we provide a "mixin" class that can be used to override the HTMLElement.__repr__ function with a simpler and more efficient replacement, HTMLSingleEntry:

```
class HTMLSingleEntry:
    """Another virtual superclass for subclasses with simple bodies
       containing only one element.
       Assumes subclass has self.Text which represents the one body entry.
       This is a mixin that should be listed before HTMLElement.
    """
    # __repr__ requires self.Text to be defined, so we define it
    # to be empty string by default.
    Text = ""

    def __repr__(self, indent=""):
        ItemString = Indent_Thing(self.Text, indent)
        head = self.headstring()
        endtag = self.end_tag
        if "\n" in self.body_sep:
            return "%s%s\n%s%s\n%s%s" % (
```

```
            indent, head, indent, ItemString, indent, endtag)
    else:
        return "%s%s%s" % (head, ItemString, endtag)
```

As mentioned in the doc string for HTMLSingleEntry, any subclass that uses this mixin as a superclass must list HTMLSingleEntry before HTMLElement (or one of its subclasses) so that the search for the __repr__ function will find HTMLSingleEntry.__repr__ before HTMLElement.__repr__. Furthermore, HTMLSingleEntry assumes that the single-body element associated with the self-instance is always given by self.Text, so this convention must be followed by any subclass.

This class includes some mysterious format strings which are used to format the output nicely with extra whitespace. We came up with them after several iterations of experimentation and testing, and we have no desire to try to justify them here.

Using the Mixin to Define TD

By combining HTMLSingleEntry with HTMLElement we may define a class to handle the TD table element by simply defining constants which specify the extraordinary number of options supported by this HTML element, and then redefining the __init__ method in the standard fashion:

```
class TD(HTMLSingleEntry, HTMLElement):
    """A Table entry (no one knows why it's called TD)"""
    HTML_Attributes = ("ROWSPAN", "COLSPAN", "ALIGN", "VALIGN",
                       "NOWRAP", "WIDTH")
    HTML_Tag_Marks = ("NOWRAP",) # singleton tuple
    Tag_Format = \
      "<TD%(ROWSPAN)s%(COLSPAN)s%(ALIGN)s%(VALIGN)s%(NOWRAP)s%(WIDTH)s>"
    end_tag = "</TD>"
    # use default body_sep
    # default ALIGNments None
    ALIGN = VALIGN = None

    # override initialization
    def __init__(self,
                 Text,
                 ROWSPAN = None,
                 COLSPAN = None,
                 ALIGN = None,
```

```
                VALIGN = None,
                NOWRAP = None,
                WIDTH = None):
    """TD initialization function."""
    # yawn.
    HTMLElement.__init__(self,
                Text = Text,
                ROWSPAN = ROWSPAN,
                COLSPAN = COLSPAN,
                ALIGN = ALIGN,
                VALIGN = VALIGN,
                NOWRAP = NOWRAP,
                WIDTH = WIDTH)
    # check ALIGN and VALIGN for validity, if given
    (self.ALIGN, self.VALIGN) = Check_ALIGNS(self.ALIGN, self.VALIGN)
```

WARNING

For full generality, we include all the standard options of the TD element, but programs that generate many tables or truly large tables and which never use these options and do not require complex Text values may prefer to use a simple function such as

```
def sTD(Text):
    return "<TD>%s</TD>" % Text
```

in place of the TD class to speed up the generation of the HTML text.

The class that corresponds to a CAPTION element of a TABLE is even simpler, but quite similar:

```
class CAPTION(HTMLSingleEntry, HTMLElement):
    """CAPTION for a TABLE"""
    HTML_Attributes = ("ALIGN",) # singleton tuple
    Tag_Format = "<CAPTION%(ALIGN)s>"
    end_tag = "</CAPTION>"
    # use default body_sep
    # default alignment, None
    ALIGN = None

    # override initialization
    def __init__(self, Text, ALIGN=None):
        """CAPTION initialization... just calls superclass init"""
        HTMLElement.__init__(self, Text=Text, ALIGN=ALIGN)
        # check that align is either "top" or "bottom"
        self.ALIGN = Check_Attribute(self.ALIGN, ("top", "bottom"))
```

Then to test out a TD, TR, CAPTION, and TABLE we add the following self-test function:

```
def testTD():
    print "Testing TD"
    # create a bunch of TD elements
    TD0 = TD("alpha", COLSPAN=3, ALIGN="left", VALIGN="middle")
    TD1 = TD("beta", NOWRAP=1)
    TD2 = TD("gammaglobulin", WIDTH=90)
    # put them in a Table
    T = TABLE( ( TR( ( TD0, TD1, TD1, TD("alphabetical") ) ),
                TR( ( TD2, TD("Sigma Nu"), TD0, TD("nusworthy") ) )
              ),
                CAPTION("If Troy Donohue can be a movie star..."),
                CELLSPACING = 9,
                BORDER=1)
    print `T`
    print
```

Here `testTD()` produces the following output:

```
Testing TD
<TABLE BORDER CELLSPACING=9>
  <TR>
      <TD COLSPAN=3 ALIGN="left" VALIGN="middle">alpha</TD>
        <TD NOWRAP>beta</TD>
          <TD NOWRAP>beta</TD>
            <TD>alphabetical</TD>
  </TR>
  <TR>
      <TD WIDTH=90>gammaglobulin</TD>
        <TD>Sigma Nu</TD>
          <TD COLSPAN=3 ALIGN="left" VALIGN="middle">alpha</TD>
            <TD>nusworthy</TD>
  </TR>
  <CAPTION>If Troy Donohue can be a movie star...</CAPTION>
  </TABLE>
```

The TH element is remarkably similar to the TD element (which is not surprising because a TH represents a table entry in a bolder type), so we can define a class to represent this HTML element easily by subclassing the TD class:

```
class TH(TD):
    """TH is just like TD, but with a different name,
```

```
    syntactically speaking"""

Tag_Format = \
  "<TH%(ROWSPAN)s%(COLSPAN)s%(ALIGN)s%(VALIGN)s%(NOWRAP)s%(WIDTH)s>"
end_tag = "</TH>"
# everything else is the same, even __init__!
```

Isn't object-oriented programming cool?

As an inspection of the testTD function indicates, it is sometimes an unpleasant task to construct a TABLE directly from the default initializers for TABLE, TR, TD, TH, and CAPTION, especially when the result need not take advantage of all the special options and tags defined by these elements. Happily, we can greatly simplify the task of creating tables by defining specialized functions which produce various specialized TABLEs.

Some Simple Functions that Generate
TABLEs

First, we can eliminate the need to create each table row TR instance in the table body, if the table rows do not require any special formatting options.

```
def SimpleTable(Captionbody, *Lines):
    TRlines = map(TR, Lines)
    Cap = CAPTION(Captionbody, ALIGN="bottom")
    return TABLE( TRlines, Cap )
```

The SimpleTable function assumes that Captionbody is the element to use as the CAPTION for the table, and the remaining arguments (collected in the Lines variable) are sequences of TD element instances. The Lines are converted to TR elements (via map) before being placed in a new table.

The following function illustrates the use of SimpleTable:

```
def testSimpleTable():
    print "testing SimpleTable"
    TH1 = TH("Odd")
    TH0 = TH("Even")
    TD1 = TD("One = 1")
    TD0 = TD("Zero = 0")
    T = SimpleTable("Some Bits",
                    [TH0, TH1],
```

```
                              [TD0, TD1])
        print `T`
        print
```

It produces the following output:

```
testing SimpleTable
<TABLE BORDER>
  <TR>
      <TH>Even</TH>
        <TH>Odd</TH>
    </TR>
  <TR>
      <TD>Zero = 0</TD>
        <TD>One = 1</TD>
    </TR>
  <CAPTION ALIGN="bottom">Some Bits</CAPTION>
  </TABLE>
```

Furthermore, if the elements of each row of the table will always be simple TD elements with no special characteristics, we can define a function which makes creating tables even easier:

```
def _TDmapper(sequence):
    """internal helper for VerySimpleTable"""
    return map(TD, sequence)

def VerySimpleTable(Captionbody, *Lines):
    """Like SimpleTable, but automatically format each
       sequence of Lines to be a TD element"""
    TDLines = map( _TDmapper, Lines )
    return apply(SimpleTable, (Captionbody,) + tuple(TDLines) )

# an abbreviations
VST = VerySimpleTable
```

Here the elements of each of the Lines are converted to TD elements before being formatted into a table by the SimpleTable function defined above. We also define VST as an abbreviation for VerySimpleTable, for fun.

The following self-test function illustrates the use of VerySimpleTable:

```
def testVerySimpleTable():
    print "testing VerySimpleTable"
```

```
    T = VerySimpleTable("Opinion",
                        ["Open", "Proprietary"],
                        ["good", "bad"])
    print `T`
    print
```

This function produces the following output:

```
<TABLE BORDER>
  <TR>
      <TD>Open</TD>
        <TD>Proprietary</TD>
    </TR>
  <TR>
      <TD>good</TD>
        <TD>bad</TD>
    </TR>
  <CAPTION ALIGN="bottom">Opinion</CAPTION>
  </TABLE>
```

There is no end to the ways we can develop methods for specialized table construction. For example, the `VerticalDictTable` will produce a table from a Python dictionary, formatted vertically and the subsequent `HorizontalDictTable` also translates a dictionary to a table, but horizontally.

```
def VerticalDictTable(CaptionBody, Dict):
    """from a Dictionary create a Table of form
            key1 value1
            key2 value2
        etcetera"""
    Dictitems = Dict.items()
    Dictitems.sort()
    return apply(VerySimpleTable, (CaptionBody,) + tuple(Dictitems))

def HorizontalDictTable(CaptionBody, Dict):
    """from a Dictionary create a Table of form
            key1    key2    ...
            value1 value2  ...
        etcetera"""
    keys = Dict.keys()
    keys.sort()
    nkeys = len(keys)
    values = [None] * nkeys
    for i in xrange(nkeys):
```

```
        values[i] = Dict[ keys[i] ]
    return VerySimpleTable(CaptionBody, keys, values)
```

Let's examine the objects these functions produce:

```
>>> Dict = { "Gopher" : "What's that?",
...          "Chat": "Too much fun",
...          "HTTP": "World Wide Wait" }
>>> vdt = VerticalDictTable("Vertical!", Dict)
>>> print vdt
<TABLE BORDER>
  <TR>
      <TD>Chat</TD>
        <TD>Too much fun</TD>
    </TR>
  <TR>
      <TD>Gopher</TD>
        <TD>What's that?</TD>
    </TR>
  <TR>
      <TD>HTTP</TD>
        <TD>World Wide Wait</TD>
    </TR>
  <CAPTION ALIGN="bottom">Vertical!</CAPTION>
  </TABLE>
>>> hdt = HorizontalDictTable("Horizontal", Dict)
>>> print hdt
<TABLE BORDER>
  <TR>
      <TD>Chat</TD>
        <TD>Gopher</TD>
          <TD>HTTP</TD>
    </TR>
  <TR>
      <TD>Too much fun</TD>
        <TD>What's that?</TD>
          <TD>World Wide Wait</TD>
    </TR>
  <CAPTION ALIGN="bottom">Horizontal</CAPTION>
  </TABLE>
```

As an exercise, we challenge the reader to make variants of these dictionary formatting functions that force the keys to appear in bold face (using the TH element).

Some Self-Formatting Table Classes

Another way to simplify TABLE creation is to create subclasses of the TABLE class that "know how to format themselves" (whatever that means). Let's look at an example:

```
class Table_WLines(TABLE):
    """Given a list of white separated lines, generate
       a table containing the components of each line as
       an entry, with each line in a separate line of the table.
    """

    def __init__(self,
                 Lines=None,
                 CAPTION=None,
                 BORDER=1,
                 CELLSPACING=None,
                 CELLPADDING=None):
        Lines = self.Translate_Lines(Lines)
        # Now initialize self as a table, with the translated lines
        TABLE.__init__(self,
                 Lines=Lines,
                 CAPTION=CAPTION,
                 BORDER=BORDER,
                 CELLSPACING=CELLSPACING,
                 CELLPADDING=CELLPADDING)

    def Translate_Lines(self, Lines):
        """Translate the list of Lines into a Table Rows"""
        result = []
        for line in Lines:
            rowseq = []
            splitline = self.split(line) # break white separated components
            for component in splitline:  # make each component into TD
                rowseq.append( TD(component) )
            # make the row sequence into a TR, put in result
            result.append(TR(rowseq))
        return result

    def split(self, line):
        """Delegate to string.split, subclasses may do something else..."""
        return string.split(line)
```

This class automatically creates a TABLE from a sequence of white separated strings. The usage of the class looks something like this:

```
>>> tw = Table_WLines(["Instant Software", "Instant Headache"])
>>> print tw
<TABLE BORDER>
  <TR>
      <TD>Instant</TD>
        <TD>Software</TD>
    </TR>
  <TR>
      <TD>Instant</TD>
        <TD>Headache</TD>
    </TR>
  </TABLE>
```

This initialization for the class accepts Lines as a sequence of unformatted strings, unlike the TABLE superclass which requires a sequence of formatted table rows. The unformatted lines are split on whitespace and each white separated substring is formatted into a TD element, and for each line the resulting sequence of TD lines is grouped into a TR row. The resulting sequence of rows is then formatted as a TABLE using the TABLE initializer.

The functionality of this class could have been implemented as a function, but now that it is implemented as a TABLE we can use multiple inheritance and mixins to define classes with related functionality.

A Text-Block/Table Mixin

One mixin we can use with `Table_WLines` is `Table_TBlock` which redefines the `Translate_Lines` method to expect a block of text rather than a list of lines.

```
class Table_TBlock:
    """Table Text Block mixin for Table_WLines or subclasses.
        This mixin expects a Lines as a block of text, which will be split at
        newlines into a line list (with surrounding whitespace ignored).
        The resulting split lines will be formatted into a table by
        self.Table_Line_Class which must be a superclass of self
        defined by the class that uses this mixin.
    """
```

```
def Translate_Lines(self, Lines):
    """Assume Lines is a text block:
       strip surrounding whitespace, split on newlines,
       and delegate remaining processing to
       self.Table_Line_Class.Translate_Lines( ... ).
    """
    strip = string.strip(Lines)
    split = string.splitfields(strip, "\n")
    return self.Table_Line_Class.Translate_Lines(self, split)
```

This mixin splits the block of text given by Lines on newlines and then hands the result to another Translate_Lines function. Because this is a generic mixin that can be combined with many different classes, it requires the class that should process the resulting list of lines to be given by self.Table_Lines_Class. For example, we mix Table_TBlock with Table_WLines as follows:

```
class Table_WBlock(Table_TBlock,  Table_WLines):
    """Format a block of text into a table (no header).
       each element assumed white separated"""
    Table_Line_Class = Table_WLines
```

The resulting derived class will then format a block of text by splitting the text on newlines and then formatting each white separated element of each line as a table element, as shown in the following example:

```
>>> block = """ $29.95 USA
...             $39.50 Canadian"""
>>> Twb = Table_WBlock(block)
>>> print Twb
<TABLE BORDER>
  <TR>
      <TD>$29.95</TD>
        <TD>USA</TD>
    </TR>
  <TR>
      <TD>$39.50</TD>
        <TD>Canadian</TD>
    </TR>
  </TABLE>
```

A Table/Separator Mixin

We can also define mixins that redefine the way `Table_WLines` splits each line.

```
class Table_Sep_Lines:
    """Mixin for Table_WLines and subclasses.
       Instead of recognizing whitespace as separating
       fields, split each line using self.field_sep
       (which must be defined by the subclass using the
       mixin).
    """
    # Remember back in Table_WLines we defined self.split...
    # We factored out this operation in order to be able to
    # override it here!
    def split(self, line):
        """split line using self.field_sep"""
        return string.splitfields(line, self.field_sep)

# subclass mixins that define some common separators
class Table_Pipe_Lines(Table_Sep_Lines):
    field_sep = "|"
class Table_Colon_Lines(Table_Sep_Lines):
    field_sep = ":"
class Table_Tilde_Lines(Table_Sep_Lines):
    field_sep = "~"
```

`Table_Sep_Lines` and its subclasses redefine the `Table_WLines.split` method to split on a specified field separator given by self.field_sep rather than on whitespace.

By using these mixins we may create a class that accepts a block of text, splitting each line into rows, and splitting each row by colons.

```
class Table_Colon_TBlock(Table_Colon_Lines, Table_WBlock):
    pass # nothing needs to be declared!
```

For example, `Table_Colon_TBlock` may be used as follows:

```
>>> block = """ Group : Pass Word : Number : Members
            bin::2:root,bin,daemon
            sys::3:root,bin,sys,adm
            adm::4:root,adm,daemon   """
>>> Cap = CAPTION("The /etc/groups file")
>>> tctb = Table_Colon_TBlock(block, Cap)
```

```
>>> print tctb
<TABLE BORDER>
  <TR>
      <TD>Group </TD>
        <TD> Pass Word </TD>
          <TD> Number </TD>
            <TD> Members</TD>
    </TR>
  <TR>
      <TD>        bin</TD>
        <TD></TD>
          <TD>2</TD>
            <TD>root,bin,daemon</TD>
    </TR>
  <TR>
      <TD>        sys</TD>
        <TD></TD>
          <TD>3</TD>
            <TD>root,bin,sys,adm</TD>
    </TR>
  <TR>
      <TD>        adm</TD>
        <TD></TD>
          <TD>4</TD>
            <TD>root,adm,daemon</TD>
    </TR>
  <CAPTION>The /etc/groups file</CAPTION>
  </TABLE>
```

Are you getting the "power of mixins rush"? We are. We always do. It's a shame some other languages don't support multiple inheritance.

Making the First TABLE Row Bold

We can also subclass the Table_WLines class to create a new class that assumes that the first line of the table is intended to be a title line, and hence formats each element of the first line as a TR element, rather than a TD element, so that the elements of the first line will appear in boldface print.

```
class H_Table_WLines(Table_WLines):
    """Similar to Table WLines, but make first line use TH"""
    def Translate_Lines(self, Lines):
        first = Lines[0]
```

```
        firstseq = []
        splitline = self.split(first)
        for component in splitline:
            firstseq.append(TH(component)) # note, make TH's here not TD
        firstresult = TR(firstseq)
        others = Table_WLines.Translate_Lines(self, Lines[1:])
        return [firstresult] + others
```

We can now use this class directly, for example:

```
>>> htw = H_Table_WLines(["OpenDoc OLE CORBA",
...                        "Good Bad Ugly"])
>>> print htw
<TABLE BORDER>
  <TR>
      <TH>OpenDoc</TH>
        <TH>OLE</TH>
          <TH>CORBA</TH>
    </TR>
  <TR>
      <TD>Good</TD>
        <TD>Bad</TD>
          <TD>Ugly</TD>
    </TR>
  </TABLE>
```

Or, we can combine `H_Table_WLines` with the mixins for Table_WLines.

```
class HPipeBlock(Table_TBlock, Table_Pipe_Lines, H_Table_WLines):
   Table_Line_Class = H_Table_WLines # needed by Table_TBlock
```

(This class doesn't appear in the library, we just made it up interactively!) The `HPipeBlock` class then (because it uses `Table_TBlock`) expects the `Lines` to be a block of text separated into rows by newline characters, and (because it uses `Table_Pipe_Lines`) separates each element of each row by splitting on pipe characters and (because it uses `H_Table_WLines`) expects the first line to represent a title for the table which should be formatted in bold. That's a lot of functionality for such a small class definition!

We can use `HPipeBlock`, for example:

```
>>> Text = """
... File    | Description
... README  | General information, read this first
```

```
...    PY.tar.gz  |  The Python distribution, tarred, gzipped
...    """
>>> hpb = HPipeBlock(Text, CAPTION("The Files"))
>>> print hpb
<TABLE BORDER>
  <TR>
      <TH>File       </TH>
         <TH>  Description</TH>
    </TR>
  <TR>
      <TD>README     </TD>
         <TD>  General information, read this first</TD>
    </TR>
  <TR>
      <TD>PY.tar.gz </TD>
         <TD>  The Python distribution, tarred, gzipped</TD>
    </TR>
  <CAPTION>The Files</CAPTION>
  </TABLE>
```

The BODY of an HTML Document

The BODY of an HTML document can take a number of arguments, so we define a class to make it easy to modify the parameters of the body of a document. To this module a BODY is just another HTML element that includes a single entry, even though the Text of the BODY can be very large.

```
class BODY(HTMLSingleEntry, HTMLElement):
    """BODY block of an HTML document.
       the Text parameter represents entire document body."""

    HTML_Attributes = ("BACKGROUND", "BGCOLOR", "TEXT", "LINK",
                       "VLINK", "ALINK")
    Tag_Format = \
    "<BODY%(BACKGROUND)s%(BGCOLOR)s%(TEXT)s%(LINK)s%(VLINK)s%(ALINK)s>"
    end_tag = "</BODY>"
    body_sep = "\n"

    def __init__(self,
                 Text,   # this can be HUGE!
                 BACKGROUND=None,
                 BGCOLOR=None,
                 TEXT=None,
                 LINK=None,
```

```
                    VLINK=None,
                    ALINK=None):
        # boilerplate, don't do anything special, assume values are valid.
        HTMLElement.__init__(self,
                    Text=Text,
                    BACKGROUND=BACKGROUND,
                    BGCOLOR=BGCOLOR,
                    TEXT=TEXT,
                    LINK=LINK,
                    VLINK=VLINK,
                    ALINK=ALINK)
    # BODY can use all default methods, other than __init__
```

For example, we can create a BODY like so:

```
>>> D = { "DNS": "Domain Name Service",
...       "NFS": "Network File System",
...       "TLA": "Three Letter Acronym" }
>>> dl = DictDL(D)
>>> b = BODY(dl)
>>> b.BGCOLOR = "#00ff00" # add a background color.
>>> print b
<BODY BGCOLOR="#00ff00">
<DL>
 <DD>DNS<DT>
    Domain Name Service
 <DD>NFS<DT>
    Network File System
 <DD>TLA<DT>
    Three Letter Acronym
  </DL>
</BODY>
```

Generating Entire Documents

As far as this library is concerned, an entire HTML document is just another
HTMLElement, so we define a class for it, just like the others, but for convenience we define the HTML element to always include a TITLE and a HEAD
element, because this is traditional.

```
GENERIC_HTML_FMT= """\
<HTML>
<HEAD>
```

```
<TITLE>
%(TITLE)s
</TITLE>
%(MiscHead)s
</HEAD>

%(Body)s
</HTML>
"""

class HTML(HTMLElement):
    """An entire HTML document.  It takes "fake" attributes
         TITLE -- the title for the document.
         MiscHead -- Additional stuff besides the TITLE to appear in HEAD
            (eg, BASE, ISINDEX, LINK, METAs, NEXTID etcetera).
            Without extending the current library this should probably
            always be a string.
         Body -- the BODY of the document, can be any of HTML element,
            or just a string, if you so desire.  If it isn't an instance
            of the Body class, it will be converted to one.
      TITLE and Body are required arguments.
      """
    MiscHead = None # default for self.MiscHead

    # boilerplate: override __init__
    def __init__(self, TITLE, Body, MISCHEAD=None):
        HTMLElement.__init__(self, TITLE=TITLE, Body=Body, MISCHEAD=MISCHEAD)
        # convert Body if needed:
        try:
            raise self.Body
        except BODY:    # this will catch the error, if Body is a BODY inst.
            pass # okey dokey.
        except:         # this will catch all other cases
            # convert the Body to a BODY instance
            self.Body = BODY(Body)

    # override __repr__ for this special case.
    def __repr__(self, indent=""):
        """Printable representation of an HTML document.
           ignores the optional indentation parameter."""
        Dict = {"TITLE": self.TITLE, "Body": self.Body, "MiscHead":""}
        # if MiscHead is defined, use it.
        if self.MiscHead:
            Dict["MiscHead"] = self.MiscHead
        return GENERIC_HTML_FMT % Dict
```

This class is different from the others in that it does most of its "own work" after initialization, and in that it automatically includes the other elements TITLE and HEAD. In particular, it defines its own HTML.__repr__ that uses the constant format string GENERIC_HTML_FMT as a template for constructing the document representation, with the TITLE, MiscHead, and BODY members inserted in the template.

NOTE

Note that HTML.__init__ uses Python's object-oriented exception handling to convert any Body value that is not an instance of the BODY class (or an instance of a subclass of BODY) into a BODY instance.

The HTML class can be used to format other HTML entities into a complete HTML document, like so:

```
>>> Title = "The Usual Document Types"
>>> Commentary = """
... <H1>Document Types</H1>
... In addition to plain text one often finds other document
... types on the web.  Among the common formats are the following.
... """
>>> Block = """
... Kind of Document ~ Format often used ~ Format less usual
... Static Images ~ GIF or JPEG ~ TIFF or BMP
... Sound ~ AU or WAV ~ SND
... Moving Images ~ MPEG ~ QT or MOV
... """
>>> class myTable(Table_TBlock, Table_Tilde_Lines, H_Table_WLines):
...     Table_Line_Class = H_Table_WLines
...
>>> table = myTable(Block)
>>> doc = HTML(Title, HR_Seq(Commentary, table))
>>> print doc
<HTML>
<HEAD>
<TITLE>
The Usual Document Types
</TITLE>
</HEAD>
<BODY>
  <H1>Document Types</H1>
  In addition to plain text one often finds other document
  types on the web.  Among the common formats are the following.
```

```
    <HR>
<TABLE BORDER>
    <TR>
        <TH>Kind of Document </TH>
            <TH> Format often used </TH>
                <TH> Format less usual</TH>
    </TR>
    <TR>
        <TD>Static Images </TD>
            <TD> GIF or JPEG </TD>
                <TD> TIFF or BMP</TD>
    </TR>
    <TR>
        <TD>Sound </TD>
            <TD> AU or WAV </TD>
                <TD> SND</TD>
    </TR>
    <TR>
        <TD>Moving Images </TD>
            <TD> MPEG </TD>
                <TD> QT or MOV</TD>
    </TR>
    </TABLE>
</BODY>
</HTML>
```

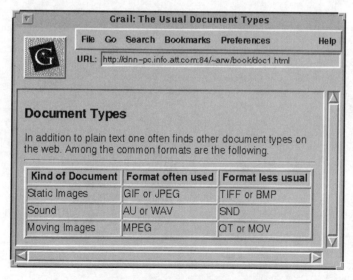

Figure 7.5 A generated document with a TABLE.

Summary

At this point we end our discussion of generating HTML. We have left out a lot, but we have conquered many of the hairiest aspects of HTML, simply and elegantly using some of Python's powerful dynamic features—notably multiple inheritance, dynamic attribute access (`getattr` and `setattr`), first-class functions (`apply`), and dynamic keyword arguments. We will revisit an important aspect of HTML, FORMs, in the chapter on CGI programming.

CHAPTER EIGHT

CGI PROGRAMMING

CGI stands for the "Common Gateway Interface" which has become one of the most popular techniques for providing and propagating dynamic information across the Internet. This chapter describes the major features of CGI programming and gives examples of implementing CGI programs using Python.

Let's introduce the basics of HTTP. HTTP, the "Hyper-Text Transmission Protocol," defines a mechanism that allows a client program to request data from a server program, and the server program to transfer a stream of data to a client program in response to the request. For example, when a user presses the "What's cool" button on the Netscape Navigator Client Program, Navigator retrieves the object `http://home.netscape.com/home/whats-cool.html`. More precisely, the Navigator client uses HTTP to contact the server named `home.netscape.com` listening on the standard HTTP port 80, in order to request the document `/home/whats-cool.html`:

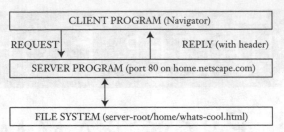

Here the server program recognizes the requested object as corresponding to a fixed file on the file system and sends the contents of the file back to the client program, prepending a response header with additional information about the data, such as its intended interpretation as `text/html`.

A CGI interaction essentially uses a short-lived program that dynamically produce an object in response to a request instead of simply retrieves a file.

A CGI program, such as `/big/arw/public_html/book/cgi/test.cgi` is launched by an HTTP server program when a client (such as a browser program) requests an object, such as

`http://dnn-pc.info.att.com:84/~arw/book/cgi/test.cgi`

In its most common usage, the CGI mechanism allows Web site to deliver a graphical form to a browser that a user may fill in with data that is delivered to a CGI program on the same site. The CGI protocol can be used to provide remote database access, to distribute data across the planet, and as a tool in electronic commerce. Most of our readers have probably already interacted with CGI programs as clients, for example, by submitting a query to a Web site search engine.

How CGI Works

Some of our readers can think of CGI interactions as performing a "simple stateless remote procedure call" invoked by a client and processed by a remote host. Roughly speaking, the content of an HTML form submitted by a user to a browser program is translated by the browser program into an encoded string representation. For example, when the user presses GO FOR IT!, the browser might translate the following form (Figure 8.1):

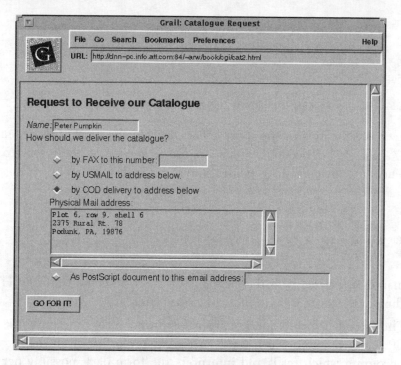

Figure 8.1 An example form.

into a message containing the contents of the form that looks like this:

```
POST /test.cgi HTTP/1.0
User-agent: Grail/0.3b2
Content-type: multipart/form-data;
            boundary="192.11.95.133.151.4652.835022488.30632"

--192.11.95.133.151.4652.835022488.30632
Content-Type: text/plain
Content-Disposition: form-data; name="customer"

Peter Pumpkin
--192.11.95.133.151.4652.835022488.30632
Content-Type: text/plain
Content-Disposition: form-data; name="medium"

OVERNIGHT
--192.11.95.133.151.4652.835022488.30632
```

```
Content-Type: text/plain
Content-Disposition: form-data; name="snailaddress"

Plot 6, row 9, shell 6
2375 Rural Rt. 78
Podunk, PA, 19876
--192.11.95.133.151.4652.835022488.30632--
```

Here we see the data of the form encoded using the most verbose `multi-part/form-data` encoding, which has the advantage of being easy to read. The encoding includes three fields: `customer` with value `Peter Pumpkin`, `medium` with value `OVERNIGHT` and `snailaddress` with value:

```
Plot 6, row 9, shell 6
2375 Rural Rt. 78
Podunk, PA, 19876
```

The names associated with the elements of the form come from the HTML encoding of the form, which will be described later.

The encoded form contents are transmitted across the network to an HTTP server program which usually passes the information in the form to a CGI program which reads and interprets the form data, possibly performs some appropriate action (such as inscribing the request for a catalogue in a file), and generates a response in HTML which is transmitted back to the client browser and presented to the user. The dynamically generated response might look something like:

```
HTTP/1.0 200 OK
Date: Monday, 17-Jun-96 21:49:10 GMT
Server: NCSA/1.3
MIME-version: 1.0
Content-type: text/html

<HTML><HEAD><TITLE>
   Thank You Peter Pumpkin!
</TITLE></HEAD>
<BODY>
   We will dispatch a catalogue by overnight mail to
<PRE>
```

```
Plot 6, row 9, shell 6
2375 Rural Rt. 78
Podunk, PA, 19876
</PRE>
    By noon today. COD.
</BODY></HTML>
```

The standard Python distribution provides a `cgi` module that allows easy implementation of CGI programs. In particular, the `cgi` module provides a very nice programming interface that hides many of the details of the CGI mechanism from the programmer. Nevertheless, it is often useful to understand what happens beneath the surface when implementing CGI programs, so this chapter will discuss some of the hidden details of the CGI mechanism, as well as the high-level view provided by the `cgi` module.

Following a CGI Request

Let's look more closely at how a CGI interaction proceeds. The simplest case is a CGI program that is associated with a simple URL (Universal Resource Locator), such as

```
http://dnn-pc.info.att.com:84/~arw/book/cgi/test.cgi
```

This kind of simple request usually corresponds to a simple hot link in an HTML document instead of the more interesting case of an HTML form. For example, the following trivial (and technically illegal) HTML document includes a link that will launch `test.cgi`.

```
Press
<A HREF="http://dnn-pc.info.att.com:84/~arw/book/cgi/test.cgi">
here
</A>
To see the output from <STRONG>test.cgi</STRONG>.
```

To the user this document might be presented by a browser looking like the following (Figure 8.2):

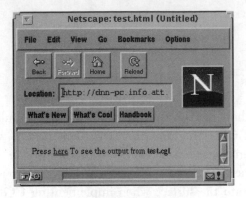

Figure 8.2 A document with a hot link that launches a CGI program.

The URL that identifies the CGI program is interpreted as follows:

```
protocol:        http
host:            dnn-pc.info.att.com
port:            84
resource (URI):  ~arw/book/cgi/test.cgi
```

When the user requests that a browser retrieve an object associated with this URL (by clicking on the **HREF link**), the browser connects to the server program on the host machine (in this case, dnn-pc.info.att.com) using the port number 84 (if the port number is omitted, the standard HTTP port 80 is used) which should communicate using the HTTP protocol. If there is a server waiting on the given machine and port, the browser sends a request message to the server that might look like this:

```
GET /~arw/book/cgi/test.cgi HTTP/1.0
Connection: Keep-Alive
User-Agent: Mozilla/2.0 (X11; I; SunOS 5.4 sun4m)
Host: dnn-pc.info.att.com:84
Accept: image/gif, image/x-xbitmap, image/jpeg, image/pjpeg, */*
```

The final line of the message is blank—this empty line indicates the end of the "request header." In more general circumstances, more information (such as "post data") may follow the header.

When the server receives this request it attempts to identify an object to return to the client that matches the resource name

```
/~arw/book/cgi/test.cgi
```

In our case we have configured the server in question to interpret the **.cgi** extension to always identify an executable cgi program, so the server will attempt to execute a program in order to generate an "object" that responds to the request as the standard output of the program. For other extensions such as **.gif** the server may not execute a program, but simply deliver a file prefixed with a header.

Furthermore the server understands the **/~arw** prefix as an abbreviation for the full path

```
/big/arw/public_html
```

So in an attempt to generate a response to the CGI request, the server will try to execute a program called

```
/big/arw/public_html/book/cgi/test.cgi
```

and capture the standard output of the program as the response to the request.

In this case, we use the following Python program to implement test.cgi:

```python
#!/usr/local/bin/python
print "Content-type: text/html" # identify response as HTML
print # end of headers
print "hello"
# dump the environment of the program as preformatted text
print "<PRE>"
import os
for (x,y) in os.environ.items():
    print x, ":", y
print "</PRE>"
```

WARNING

A CGI program must be executable in order for it to run. Under UNIX this means that the program should have been marked executable via a command like

```
% chmod +x test.cgi
```

and the first line

```
#!/usr/local/bin/python
```

is needed to indicate that this program is to be interpreted by the Python interpreter. Furthermore the directory containing the program must be readable by the world because HTTP servers generally run CGI programs using as a low privileged user such as *nobody* as a security precaution to prevent damage to the system by a faulty CGI program that allows a malicious request to do nasty things.

NOTE

Because a CGI program usually runs as a nonprivileged user in a special environment, the PYTHONPATH environment variable may not be set, or it may be set to a value the programmer cannot control, and hence the sys.path value for the Python interpreter may not refer to directories containing modules needed by the program. Even worse, the sys.path for a CGI program may contain a path which finds a module /usr/local/lib/python/mymodule.py that was not the intended implementation /usr/home/Pete/MyPyLib/mymodule.py. A CGI program may explicitly modify sys.path to make sure that the interpreter will find the correct modules required by the program.

```
import sys
sys.path.insert(0, "/usr/home/Pete/MyPyLib")
```

The above example inserts the directory /usr/home/Pete/MyPyLib at the front of sys.path, making sure that the interpreter searches this directory first when attempting to locate external modules. In general, a CGI program should import the standard sys module and insert all needed directories at the front of sys.path before importing any other modules.

WARNING

Python CGI programs often get quite sophisticated and often use many modules (20 modules is not uncommon). It is especially important that all modules used by CGI programs be byte compiled (usually with the exception of the main CGI "executable" modules themselves) in order to allow the interpreter to import the compiled versions of the modules, rather than requiring the interpreter to reparse and recompile the modules for each CGI request. Byte-compiled modules are generally useful, but they are especially important for CGI programs because CGI programs are short lived and therefore need to start up quickly. Furthermore, because CGI programs usually have no write permissions on important directories, the CGI process itself rarely will be able to create the .pyc byte code files.

To force the creation of the .pyc byte code files required by CGI programs, log in as a user with write privileges on the directories that contain the modules used by the programs and run a program which imports each of the modules:

```
import cgi
import HTMLfmt
```

```
import MIMEtools
import calendar
...
```

When the server runs `test.cgi`, it provides information about the request to the program as environment variables, and this is why we wrote the `test.cgi` program to dump its environment, which is given by `os.environ` in Python. In the more general case additional information may be given as standard input to the program as if it had been typed by an interactive user on the keyboard.

In this case the server initializes the following environment variables to the following values for `test.cgi`:

Variable Name	Value
GATEWAY_INTERFACE	CGI/1.1
SCRIPT_NAME	/~arw/book/cgi/test.cgi
SERVER_SOFTWARE	NCSA/1.3
SERVER_PROTOCOL	HTTP/1.0
REMOTE_ADDR	192.11.95.133
SERVER_NAME	dnn-pc.info.att.com
REMOTE_HOST	dnn-pc
HTTP_CONNECTION	Keep-Alive
SERVER_PORT	84
HTTP_HOST	dnn-pc.info.att.com:84
REQUEST_METHOD	GET
PATH	/usr/sbin:/usr/bin
HTTP_ACCEPT	image/gif, image/x-xbitmap, image/jpeg, image/pjpeg, */*
QUERY_STRING	(empty)
HTTP_USER_AGENT	Mozilla/2.0 (X11; I; SunOS 5.4 sun4m)

with empty standard input.

That's a lot of information. The variables with names that begin HTTP_ are all copied directly from the request itself, and the others are generated by the server program. Most CGI programs ignore most of these environment parameters, but they are available in case they are useful. For example, a CGI program that generates an image may want to examine HTTP_ACCEPT (if it is available) in order to provide an image that the client browser is guaranteed to understand (perhaps in this case preferring an image of the image/gif format to an image of type image/tiff).

A new instance of a CGI program process is created for every request. This means that a CGI program does not automatically have any information about the current state of the system or what has happened in the past—it is "stateless" and must obtain all information about its current context by examining environment variables, reading files, or explicitly drawing information from other system resources.

To create "stateful" CGI type applications, possibly consider developing a separate specialized server program, or using other techniques such as an ILU object server.

The task of the CGI program test.cgi is to respond to the request using the information provided by the environment (and in the more general case perhaps also using information sent as standard input). The response must be sent back to the server program as the standard output, and the response must explain what type of information is being sent back by providing a Content-Type header line. Usually the Content-Type produced by a CGI program is text/html, but some CGI programs may generate text/plain or image/jpg or some other type of data identified by some other Content-Type. In any case the CGI program must print a line such as

```
Content-type: text/html
```

followed by a blank line to indicate the end of the response headers before generating the body of the reply.

A CGI program may provide any number of header lines, but the Content-type header is required and the sequence of headers must be terminated by a blank line before writing the actual content.

After the blank line that marks the end of the headers, the CGI program should print to standard output text that serves as the response to the request. The server program normally prepends a number of headers to the request and sometimes may process the response in other ways as well. In the case of `test.cgi` the full response generated by the Server looks like this:

```
HTTP/1.0 200 OK
Date: Monday, 17-Jun-96 21:49:10 GMT
Server: NCSA/1.3
MIME-version: 1.0
Content-type: text/html

hello
<PRE>
GATEWAY_INTERFACE : CGI/1.1
SCRIPT_NAME : /~arw/book/cgi/test.cgi
SERVER_SOFTWARE : NCSA/1.3
SERVER_PROTOCOL : HTTP/1.0
REMOTE_ADDR : 192.11.95.133
SERVER_NAME : dnn-pc.info.att.com
REMOTE_HOST : dnn-pc
HTTP_CONNECTION : Keep-Alive
SERVER_PORT : 84
HTTP_HOST : dnn-pc.info.att.com:84
REQUEST_METHOD : GET
PATH : /usr/sbin:/usr/bin
HTTP_ACCEPT : image/gif, image/x-xbitmap, image/jpeg, image/pjpeg, */*
QUERY_STRING :
HTTP_USER_AGENT : Mozilla/2.0 (X11; I; SunOS 5.4 sun4m)
</PRE>
```

NOTE Everything up to and including the MIME-version line are headers generated by the server program, and the remainder of the response is the standard output of test.cgi—a content type header followed by a blank line followed by hello followed by a dump of environment variables enclosed in a PRE preformatted text HTML tag pair.

The full response is then sent back to the client browser and formatted by the browser for presentation to the user. In this case the formatted response looks like Figure 8.3:

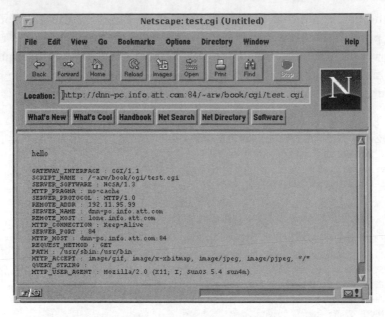

Figure 8.3 The output of test.cgi as the user sees it.

The CGI Life Cycle

Thus, in general, a CGI Request usually navigates the following life cycle:

ACTOR	ACTION
User	Presses a hotlink or submits a form.
Client browser	Generates a request based on the user action and transmits the request to the server program.
Server program	Recognizes the request as a CGI request based on the name or location of the request, prepares an environment and standard input for CGI program, and launches a new CGI program for this request.
CGI program	Interprets the request using the environment variables and possibly the standard input, and generates a Content-type header and a response to the request as standard output.

The Program may also perform other actions such as writing data to a file or database. When the CGI program is done with this one request it terminates.

Server program   Receives the output generated by the CGI program adding a number of standard headers to form a complete HTTP response, and transmits the response to the back to the Client Browser.

Client browser   Receives the response and (in the case of an HTML response) formats the response and presents it to the user.

User   Admires the response, calls in the spouse and kids, and decides to send lots of money to your company.

Honestly, the final step in this process is not guaranteed.

NOTE

In the life cycle shown, all of the actors were long lived (we hope) except for the CGI program which is created especially for handling the request and which terminates after it has done its job. The short-lived nature of CGI programs make simple CGI applications relatively robust and easy to implement compared to complex long-lived server processes. However, the lack of state information shared between different instances of a CGI program and the overhead associated with having a separate process for each request can be problematic for some applications. Nevertheless, even complex search engine applications that handle thousands of hits per hour can be implemented well within the CGI model.

GET Requests with Query Strings

A CGI request may provide additional information beyond the resource name, including parameters for the request such as name/value pairs. There are two main techniques used to give additional information to a CGI program in a request: by providing a query string attached to the resource name in a GET request, or by providing additional information following the request headers in a POST request. The GET style request allows a simple and convenient way to provide a small amount of information, with the advantage that the request may be "hard-coded" into an URL, or generated from a FORM within an HTML document (POST requests, by contrast cannot be hard-coded into an URL).

For example, a simple `month.cgi` program may require a year and a month in order to generate a textual representation for the days of a given month, and these two simple parameters may be provided as a query attached to a GET request. In particular, a user may request a presentation for August 2014, by pressing a hot link specified by

```
Press <A
HREF="http://dnn-pc.info.att.com:84/~arw/book/cgi/month.cgi?M=August&Y=2014">
here
</a>
for the month of August, 2014.
```

Here the attached query string `M=August&Y=2014` explicitly identifies the particular year and month requested.

Alternatively, the user can interact with a form such as

```
<FORM ACTION="http://dnn-pc.info.att.com:84/~arw/book/cgi/month.cgi"
      METHOD="GET">
Month: <SELECT NAME="M">
       <OPTION>January<OPTION>February<OPTION>March
       <OPTION>April<OPTION>May<OPTION>June
       <OPTION>July<OPTION>August<OPTION>September
       <OPTION>October<OPTION>November<OPTION>December
       </SELECT>
Year: <INPUT NAME="Y">
<INPUT TYPE="SUBMIT">
</FORM>
```

to dynamically select any month and year that seems amusing. The `METHOD="GET"` attribute of the FORM tag indicates that the data from the form should be attached as a query string to the ACTION URL, just as in the earlier hotlink example, except that the string is constructed dynamically by the browser client program when the user submits the FORM.

Thus, for example, the following HTML document contains both a hot link and a FORM that trigger the `month.cgi` CGI program, in each case formatting the month and year information as GET style parameters.

```
<HTML><TITLE>Month query</TITLE>
<BODY>
<FORM ACTION="http://dnn-pc.info.att.com:84/~arw/book/cgi/test.cgi"
      METHOD="GET">
```

```
Month: <SELECT NAME="M">
       <OPTION>January<OPTION>February<OPTION>March
       <OPTION>April<OPTION>May<OPTION>June
       <OPTION>July<OPTION>August<OPTION>September
       <OPTION>October<OPTION>November<OPTION>December
       </SELECT>
Year: <INPUT NAME="Y">
<INPUT TYPE="SUBMIT">
</FORM>
<HR>
Press <A
HREF="http://dnn-pc.info.att.com:84/~arw/book/cgi/month.cgi?M=August&Y=2014">
here
</a>
for the month of August, 2014.
</BODY></HTML>
```

This HTML document (Figure 8.4) has the following appearance in a client browser.

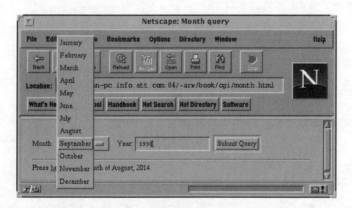

Figure 8.4 Interactive appearance of a month query HTML document including a FORM element and a hot link.

When the user presses the **Submit Query** button, the browser transmits a request to the server program that looks like this:

```
GET /~arw/book/cgi/month.cgi?M=September&Y=1998 HTTP/1.0
Connection: Keep-Alive
User-Agent: Mozilla/2.0 (X11; I; SunOS 5.4 sun4m)
Host: dnn-pc.info.att.com:84
Accept: image/gif, image/x-xbitmap, image/jpeg, image/pjpeg, */*
```

The end of the headers, which is also implicitly the end of the GET request is indicated by a final blank line.

As shown, the parameters from the form appear after a ? at the end of the URL requested on the GET line. When the Server program decides that this request must be handled by the CGI program month.cgi it also recognizes the extra information after the ? as GET style CGI parameters and prepares an environment that includes a QUERY_STRING containing everything after the ? marker:

```
QUERY_STRING : M=September&Y=1998
```

The server program then launches the month.cgi CGI program using the prepared environment. The CGI program must interpret the QUERY_STRING and produce an appropriate response for the user. In this case, we will implement month.cgi to produce the following response:

```
Content-type: text/html
<HTML><TITLE>A Month</TITLE><BODY>
For M=September&Y=1998 your month is:
<PRE>
    September 1998
Mo Tu We Th Fr Sa Su
    1  2  3  4  5  6
 7  8  9 10 11 12 13
14 15 16 17 18 19 20
21 22 23 24 25 26 27
28 29 30
</PRE>
<HR> Thanks for your interest!
</BODY></HTML>
```

When presented in a browser, this response might look like Figure 8.5:

NOTE For this example, we will use the way-cool calendar module that comes with the standard Python distribution.

```
>>> calendar.month_name.index("August")
8
>>> calendar.prmonth(2014, 8)
      August 2014
Mo Tu We Th Fr Sa Su
             1  2  3
 4  5  6  7  8  9 10
```

```
11 12 13 14 15 16 17
18 19 20 21 22 23 24
25 26 27 28 29 30 31
```

We will not discuss this module in great detail, but we'll let the reader figure it out!

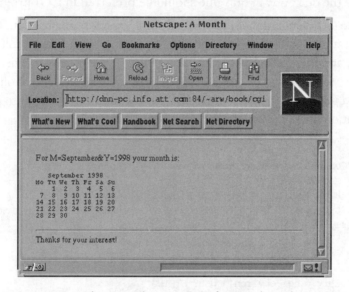

Figure 8.5 A document that presents a formatted month to a user dynamically generated by `month.cgi`.

WARNING

Strictly for the purposes of illustrating the details of GET requests we will directly parse the input string in the `month.cgi` program. This is a mistake, in general, because the `cgi` module provides much more general tools for handling all styles of requests and many possible encodings. Use this example to understand the workings of the CGI mechanism, but do not imitate it; implement real CGI programs using the excellent `cgi` module.

We now describe the implementation of `month.cgi` The `month.cgi` program begins with a documentation string and a bunch of `imports`, as usual.

```
#!/usr/local/bin/python

"""A `month' cgi program that parses its arguments directly.
   Real cgi programs should use the cgi module."""

import cgi, calendar, string
```

Here we introduce the cgi module, but we will only use it here to obtain the cgi.environ information, which is usually identical to the os.environ used in test.cgi above. The cgi.environ value sometimes may differ from the os.environ variable on some platforms and environments, so for portability the cgi.environ value should be preferred in CGI programs.

The go() function defines the main flow of logic for the program. If no error conditions are encountered, go() prints a Content-type header, followed by a blank line, and then proceeds to parse the QUERY_STRING environment variable using the getMY(query) function. The calendar.prmonth function translates the derived numerical month and year parsed by getMY(query) into a calendar representation for the month in the given year.

```
def go():
    print "Content-type: text/html" # identify response as HTML
    print # end of headers
    print "<HTML><TITLE>A Month</TITLE><BODY>"
    # use a try/finally block to guarantee that the document is terminated
    # properly
    try:
        # eg query = "M=April&Y=1987"
        try:
            query = cgi.environ["QUERY_STRING"]
        except KeyError:
            print "Sorry, I need a QUERY_STRING"
            raise SystemExit
        (year, month) = getMY(query)
        print "For", query, "your month is:"
        print "<PRE>"
        try:
            calendar.prmonth(year, month)
        finally:
            print "</PRE>"
    finally:
        print "<HR> Thanks for your interest!"
        print "</BODY></HTML>"
```

The most interesting thing about the go() function is its use of the try error handling statement. The outermost try...finally guarantees that Thank you for your interest will always show up at the end of the document, even if the function terminates early due to an error condition. The first inner try...except terminates the CGI program if no QUERY_STRING is available in the CGI environment. The second inner `try..finally` guarantees that the printed `PRE` tag will be terminated under any circumstances—even if `calendar.prmonth(year, month)` fails.

NOTE Proper use of Python error handling can greatly simplify the implementation of robust CGI programs, especially when these programs require logging and complex interactions with external systems. Explicit checking for all the possible things that could go wrong and the specification of handling or finalization under error conditions can be extremely difficult using other languages or tools that do not provide convenient error handling.

The `getMY(query)` function extracts the month and year from the `query`, translating them to integer values.

```
def getMY(query):
    """from query="M=April&Y=1987" return (1987, 4), for example."""

    # eg pairs = ["M=April", "Y=1987"]
    pairs = string.splitfields(query, "&")
    if len(pairs)<2:
        print "<br>gimme more data please! "+`pairs`
        raise SystemExit
    M = Y = None
    for pair in pairs:
        # eg name = "M", value = "April"
        [name, value] = string.splitfields(pair, "=")
        if name == "Y":
            Y = value
        if name == "M":
            M = value
    # if we don't have both the month and the year something's wrong
    if (not Y) or (not M):
        print "<br>Hmmm... I just don't like that query: "+`(Y,M)`
        raise SystemExit
    # convert the month name to a numeric month
    try:
        month = calendar.month_name.index(M)
    except ValueError:
        print "<br>OOPS: No such month (!) "+ `M`
        raise SystemExit
    # convert the year to a number
    try:
        year = string.atoi(Y)
```

```
except ValueError:
    print "<br>OOPS: year isn't a number (!) " + `Y`
    raise SystemExit
return (year, month)
```

We will not trace the logic of this function in great detail as it is somewhat straightforward and tedious. We note, however, that at a number of places the function may reach a condition where the CGI process cannot produce a normal response, such as when it determines that a month name is invalid, and in these cases it will terminate the CGI process by raising a `SystemExit` exception. The `SystemExit` exception causes the computation to terminate except that any outstanding `finally` clauses will execute.

Of course the `go()` function is meant to be used as the main program, launched via the standard `if __name__=="__main__":` convention.

```
if __name__=="__main__":
    go()
```

N O T E

A CGI program can often be easily tested from a command line interface by defining the environment variables needed by the interface. For example under UNIX using the ksh shell we can type:

```
% export QUERY_STRING="M=September&Y=1998"
% month.cgi
Content-type: text/html

<HTML><TITLE>A Month</TITLE><BODY>
For M=September&Y=1998 your month is:
<PRE>
     September 1998
Mo Tu We Th Fr Sa Su
       1  2  3  4  5  6
 7  8  9 10 11 12 13
14 15 16 17 18 19 20
21 22 23 24 25 26 27
28 29 30
</PRE>
<HR> Thanks for your interest!
</BODY></HTML>
```

In the case of month.cgi, only the QUERY_STRING environment variable was required, but generally speaking, other CGI programs will need at least the REQUEST_METHOD environment variable as well.

We can also test the behavior of the program under error conditions in this manner:

```
% export QUERY_STRING="M=Setember&Y=1998"
% month.cgi
Content-type: text/html

<HTML><TITLE>A Month</TITLE><BODY>
<br>OOPS: No such month (!) 'Setember'
<HR> Thanks for your interest!
</BODY></HTML>
```

If a CGI program "just doesn't work," try testing it from the command line. If the response generated from a command line test appears correct, the problem may be with file system permissions, or the problem may have to do with the configuration of the server program.

Using the `cgi` Module

As we've pointed out, a CGI program should use the `cgi` module to parse its arguments. There are two main advantages to using the `cgi` module.

1. The GET method is only one of the ways that information may be passed to a CGI program. The `cgi` module will automatically detect which method is being used and parse the data appropriately, allowing the CGI program to extract the information using a common procedural interface regardless of the method used.

2. The GET method and others do not pass the data submitted by the user unmodified; for technical reasons some of the characters are "quoted" and must be programmatically "unquoted" before they will appear as the user intended. For example the sequence 1987 + 2 will appear in a GET request as 1987+%2B+2 in the QUERY_STRING because both SPACE and + are characters with special meanings. The `cgi` module will automatically unquote any quoted data for a CGI program.

So, let's examine how we can modify the month.cgi program to use the `cgi` module. Here is the improved month2.cgi which will work with POST multipart of URL encoded requests as well as with GET requests.

```python
#!/usr/local/bin/python

"""A `month' cgi program that uses the cgi module to parse its arguments."""

import cgi, calendar, string

def go():
    print "Content-type: text/html" # identify response as HTML
    print # end of headers
    print "<HTML><TITLE>A Month</TITLE><BODY>"
    try:
        try:
            # have the cgi module parse the data for you...
            form = cgi.FieldStorage()
            MField = form["M"] # extract the M and Y fields
            YField = form["Y"]
        except (KeyError, TypeError):
            print "Sorry, I need both Month and Year"
            raise SystemExit
        # get the values of the fields
        try:
            M = MField.value
            Y = YField.value
        except AttributeError: # multiple values...
            print "Sorry, Multiple months or multiple years are not allowed."
            raise SystemExit
        # convert the month name to a numeric month
        try:
            month = calendar.month_name.index(M)
        except ValueError:
            print "<br>OOPS: No such month (!) "+ `M`
            raise SystemExit
        # convert the year to a number
        try:
            year = string.atoi(Y)
        except ValueError:
            print "<br>OOPS: year isn't a number (!) " + `Y`
            raise SystemExit
        print "For", (M,Y), "your month is:"
        print "<PRE>"
        try:
            calendar.prmonth(year, month)
        finally:
            print "</PRE>"
    finally:
        print "<HR> Thanks for your interest!"
```

```
    print "</BODY></HTML>"
if __name__=="__main__":
    go()
```

Compared to `month.cgi`, this program requires less mechanics for parsing the query, because the `cgi.FieldStorage` class does most of the work. Also, this implementation is more robust because it will reject invalid query strings that specify, for example, more than one month.

The `cgi.FieldStorage` class provides a general interface for extracting parameters from a CGI request, regardless of the method used by the request. For any given CGI program, only one `FieldStorage` instance should be created (because the first instance may consume the standard input). The resulting object

```
    form = FieldStorage()
```

has a dictionary interface, and the result of `form[fieldname]` gives a container object containing the value for value associated with the `fieldname`. It is actually possible that a single fieldname will correspond to more than one value, in which case `form[fieldname]` gives a list of container objects for values associated with that name. If there is no value associated with `fieldname`, then `form[fieldname]` triggers a `KeyError`, or possibly if the query string is invalid a `TypeError`.

NOTE

If there is only one value associated with `fieldname`, the object given by

```
    x = form[fieldname]
```

provides a container for the value associated with `fieldname`. The value itself may be obtained by

```
    v = x.value
```

The reason the `cgi` module provides containers for values instead of the values directly is that very advanced versions of the CGI protocol allow field entries to have additional associated information beyond the value, and using container objects to encapsulate the values as well as the other information allows all variants of the protocol to have a uniform interface to Python CGI programs.

A program may distinguish between single- and multiple-valued fields by testing the type of form[fieldname], which will be ListType only if there is more than one value.

```
from types import ListType
...
try:
    x = form[fieldname]
except KeyError:
    # fieldname has zero values
    pass
except TypeError:
    # the query string had an invalid format
    raise ValueError, "I expect a valid query string!!!"
else:
    if type(x) != ListType:
        # fieldname has one value
        thisvalue = x.value
        process(thisvalue)
    else:
        # fieldname is associated with multiple values
        for container in x:
            thisvalue = container.value
            process(thisvalue)
```

As shown, if form[fieldname] raises a KeyError then the query string was valid but the fieldname was absent, but if form[fieldname] raises a TypeError, the request did not provide a valid query string.

NOTE

In month2.cgi the M and Y fields each required exactly one value, so we used the following strategy to signal error conditions for invalid inputs

```
try:
    MField = form["M"]
    YField = form["Y"]
except (KeyError, TypeError):
    # error condition: no value for required field M or Y
    ...
try:
    M = MField.value
    Y = YField.value
except AttributeError:
```

```
# error condition: if the .value attribute was absent then
# one of YField of MField was a list indicating multiple values...
...
```

The month2.cgi program may now be used in place of the month.cgi program. Furthermore, month2.cgi may be used where the month.cgi program would fail, because month2.cgi can handle other CGI methods in addition to the GET method, thanks to the cgi module.

The month2.cgi program can also be tested from the command line if the QUERY_STRING environment variable is provided and the REQUEST_METHOD environment variable is set to GET.

```
% export QUERY_STRING="M=August&Y=1991"
% export REQUEST_METHOD="GET"
% month2.cgi
Content-type: text/html

<HTML><TITLE>A Month</TITLE><BODY>
For ('August', '1991') your month is:
<PRE>
     August 1991
Mo Tu We Th Fr Sa Su
          1  2  3  4
 5  6  7  8  9 10 11
12 13 14 15 16 17 18
19 20 21 22 23 24 25
26 27 28 29 30 31
</PRE>
<HR> Thanks for your interest!
</BODY></HTML>

% export QUERY_STRING="M=July"
% month2.cgi
Content-type: text/html

<HTML><TITLE>A Month</TITLE><BODY>
Sorry, I need both Month and Year
<HR> Thanks for your interest!
</BODY></HTML>

% export QUERY_STRING="M=Julio&Y=1990"
% month2.cgi
Content-type: text/html
```

```
<HTML><TITLE>A Month</TITLE><BODY>
<br>OOPS: No such month (!) 'Julio'
<HR> Thanks for your interest!
</BODY></HTML>
```

URL Encoded POST Requests

GET style requests can only pass a limited number of parameters to a CGI program because the HTTP standard limits the size of the GET line to a reasonable maximum length. It is often useful to send a very large amount of data to a CGI program, however, and POST requests are designed to allow such large transfers.

POST requests come in two variants. The old version uses the "URL encoding" approach which encodes information in a manner similar to the way GET requests encode information, except that the parameters are provided after the request header. The new version uses a multipart MIME message. Let's look at the old method first.

A standard POST method defaults to an "URL encoded POST," which is specified in an HTML form by setting METHOD="POST", for example:

```
<FORM ACTION="http://dnn-pc.info.att.com:84/~arw/book/cgi/month.cgi"
      METHOD="POST">
Month: <SELECT NAME="M">
       <OPTION>January<OPTION>February<OPTION>March
       <OPTION>April<OPTION>May<OPTION>June
       <OPTION>July<OPTION>August<OPTION>September
       <OPTION>October<OPTION>November<OPTION>December
</SELECT>
Year: <INPUT NAME="Y">
<INPUT TYPE="SUBMIT">
</FORM>
```

This FORM has exactly the same appearance to the user as a FORM that uses the GET method, only the technique for delivering the data differs.

When the user submits this form, the browser sends a request to the server program that looks something like this.

```
POST /~arw/book/cgi/month2.cgi HTTP/1.0
Referer: http://dnn-pc.info.att.com:84/~arw/book/cgi/monthP1.html
Connection: Keep-Alive
```

```
User-Agent: Mozilla/2.0 (X11; I; SunOS 5.4 sun4m)
Host: dnn-pc.info.att.com:5001
Accept: image/gif, image/x-xbitmap, image/jpeg, image/pjpeg, */*
Content-type: application/x-www-form-urlencoded
Content-length: 17

M=February&Y=1976
```

There are two things to note in this request. The first line specifies that the method of the request is POST, and the requested object /~arw/book/cgi/month2.cgi includes no encoded query and no ? marker. Instead the request header includes a Content-length field, and after the blank line that ends the request headers we see the request body M=February&Y=1976.

Essentially a POST request moves the parameters for the request out of the header section of the request and into the body of the request that follows the blank line at the end of the header. The data from the form is encoded precisely as in the GET request, but there is no limitation on the amount of data which may be sent in the body. The value for the Content-length header happens, not coincidentally, to be exactly the length of the data given in the body of the message, which we can verify interactively using the Python interpreter.

```
>>> len("M=February&Y=1976")
17
```

NOTE   At this point, it is useful to give a general description for an HTTP request. Contemporary HTTP requests all have the following format:

```
METHOD OBJECT HTTP-VERSION
FIELD: VALUE
FIELD2: VALUE2
FIELDN: VALUEN

BODY DATA ...
MORE BODY DATA ...
```

The first line of the request identifies the method for the request, the object requested, and the HTTP version for the request. Subsequent lines up to the first blank line provide additional header information, formally encoded using the RFC-822 Internet Mail header encoding. After the first blank line a request may optionally include additional information as the "body" of the request. GET requests always have an empty body, and POST requests use the body to encode the data being POSTed. Early prototypes of the HTTP protocol had different formats than this, but support for these earlier versions is not important in practice anymore.

Default "URL encoded" POST requests always provide a `Content-length` header which indicates the exact number of bytes provided in the body. The protocol needs to know where the data ends because otherwise the Server program or the CGI program may block forever attempting to read data that will never arrive.

When the server program receives this request, it reads and parses the header for the request, recognizes the request as a POST request, and identifies `/~arw/book/cgi/month2.cgi` as a CGI object to be processed by the program `/big/arw/public_html/book/cgi/month2.cgi`. The server program then launches `month2.cgi` providing a number of environment variables and sending the body of the request as the standard input for the program.

In particular, when the `month2.cgi` program starts, it receives something like the following environment variable values:

```
GATEWAY_INTERFACE :   CGI/1.1
SCRIPT_NAME :         /~arw/book/cgi/month2.cgi
SERVER_SOFTWARE :     NCSA/1.3
HTTP_PRAGMA :         no-cache
SERVER_PROTOCOL :     HTTP/1.0
REMOTE_ADDR :         192.11.95.99
SERVER_NAME :         dnn-pc.info.att.com
REMOTE_HOST :         lone.info.att.com
HTTP_CONNECTION :     Keep-Alive
SERVER_PORT :         84
HTTP_HOST :           dnn-pc.info.att.com:84
REQUEST_METHOD :      POST
HTTP_REFERER :        http://dnn-pc.info.att.com:84/~arw/book/cgi/monthP3.html
PATH :                /usr/sbin:/usr/bin
HTTP_ACCEPT :         image/gif, image/x-xbitmap, image/jpeg, image/pjpeg, */*
QUERY_STRING :
CONTENT_LENGTH :      17
CONTENT_TYPE :        application/x-www-form-urlencoded
HTTP_USER_AGENT :     Mozilla/2.0 (X11; I; SunOS 5.4 sun4m)
```

As usual, most of these environment variables are not of interest to most CGI programs, but note that the QUERY_STRING is empty, the REQUEST_METHOD is POST, and the CONTENT_LENGTH appears in the environment. The body of the request sent to the server appears as the standard input for month2.cgi, namely as

```
M=February&Y=1976
```

In order to produce an appropriate response to this query, the month2.cgi program must examine the environment, determine that this is a POST request with URL style encoding, read the posted data, parse and unquote the representation for the fields the user submitted to the form, and finally produce an appropriate response.

Do we need to modify the month2.cgi implementation given above? No! The cgi module automatically interprets the environment and the standard input correctly, and the existing month2.cgi works just fine for both!

For the purposes of extremely careful professional CGI programs, we just lied. There is one problem that should never occur in a perfect world: If the CONTENT_LENGTH is larger than the actual data in the request a CGI program may hang, awaiting more data that will never arrive, terminating only after the connection is broken. This situation may occur if a client program is buggy or malicious. In general it is a good idea to check the content length, to make sure it is not larger than some reasonable limit, and also to use some mechanism to time-out invalid requests.

Handling Buggy or Malicious POSTs.

To address the issue of possible buggy or spammy requests, we implement yet another variant of the month.cgi program, month3.cgi, which uses UNIX signals to implement a time-out. On non-unix platforms some other method may be needed to implement time-outs. The month3.cgi program is identical to the month2.cgi program except that it includes the following additional declarations:

```
import cgi, calendar, string, signal, sys

def AlarmHandler(number, traceback):
    print "I'm sorry, I was unable to parse your submitted data."
```

```
    raise SystemExit

class myStdin:

    def __init__(self, fp = sys.stdin):
        self.fp = sys.stdin

    def __getattr__(self, name):
        return getattr(self.fp, name)

    def read(self, length, timeout=3):
        list = [""] * length
        fp = self.fp
        # set a sanity timer
        signal.signal(signal.SIGALRM, AlarmHandler)
        # read data to length, 1 char at a time...
        signal.alarm(timeout)
        for i in xrange(length):
            list[i] = fp.read(1)
        # cancel the timer
        signal.alarm(0)
        result = string.joinfields(list, "")
        return result

LENGTH_LIMIT = 400

def GetForm(limit = LENGTH_LIMIT):
    # check the Content_Length if present
    try:
        CL = cgi.environ["CONTENT_LENGTH"]
    except KeyError:
        pass
    else:
        cl = string.atoi(CL)
        if cl>limit:
            print "Wow! that's too much data"
            raise SystemExit
    form = cgi.FieldStorage(myStdin())
    return form
```

Furthermore, the `go()` function is modified to use `GetForm`:

```
def go():
    ...
            # have the cgi module parse the data for you...
            form = GetForm()
    ...
```

The GetForm function first checks the CONTENT_LENGTH if present and judges a size larger than 400 to be invalid for this application. If the CONTENT_LENGTH passes the sanity test, however, GetForm retrieves the form data for the CGI program using cgi.FieldStorage, but using a "wrapper" for the standard input, myStdin().

The myStdin() instance acts just like the ordinary sys.stdin except that UNIX signals guarantee that a read that takes longer than 3 seconds will cause the program to terminate.

NOTE

The magic method definition

```
def __getattr__(self, name):
    return getattr(self.fp, name)
```

guarantees that any attribute or method that is not defined for an instance of myStdin will be "delegated" to self.fp —i.e., the attribute or method self.fp.name will be used whenever self.name is not defined either in the local name space of self or in any superclass of self.

The myStdin.read method reads data from the real sys.stdin one character at a time in order to allow the signals to work properly. Python defers signals that occur in the middle of a read operation for technical reasons, but there is no middle to a single character read.

If the read finishes within 3 seconds, the alarm is canceled, but if the time-out occurs before then, the signal mechanism will call the AlarmHandler signal handler, which prints an apology and exits the application.

We can see the timeout mechanism at work by running the month3.cgi program from the command line and refusing to give it any standard input.

```
% export CONTENT_LENGTH=17
% export REQUEST_METHOD=POST
% export CONTENT_TYPE="application/x-www-form-urlencoded"
% month3.cgi
Content-type: text/html

<HTML><TITLE>A Month</TITLE><BODY>
I'm sorry, I was unable to parse your submitted data.
<HR> Thanks for your interest!
</BODY></HTML>
```

Here, just before printing `I'm sorry...`, the program paused for 3 seconds awaiting the standard input that never arrived.

If on the other hand, we provide standard input (using `echo` because we don't type fast enough), the program will not time-out and proceed normally.

```
% echo "M=February&Y=1976" | month3.cgi
Content-type: text/html

<HTML><TITLE>A Month</TITLE><BODY>
For ('February', '1976') your month is:
<PRE>
    February 1976
Mo Tu We Th Fr Sa Su
                   1
 2  3  4  5  6  7  8
 9 10 11 12 13 14 15
16 17 18 19 20 21 22
23 24 25 26 27 28 29
</PRE>
<HR> Thanks for your interest!
</BODY></HTML>
```

In a similar manner, we can test the mechanism that rejects requests with too large `CONTENT_LENGTH` values:

```
% export CONTENT_LENGTH=8888
% echo "M=February&Y=1976" | month3.cgi
Content-type: text/html

<HTML><TITLE>A Month</TITLE><BODY>
Wow! that's too much data
<HR> Thanks for your interest!
</BODY></HTML>
```

NOTE   To emulate an URL-encoded POST request from the command line, provide environment variables

```
% export REQUEST_METHOD=POST
% export CONTENT_TYPE="application/x-www-form-urlencoded"
% export CONTENT_LENGTH=17
```

except that the `CONTENT_LENGTH` value varies based on the data to be provided to the form. Finally, when invoking the program, provide the URL-encoded data for the test as standard input to the form, for example, using the echo command, or by piping in standard input from a file.

```
% echo "M=February&Y=1976" | month3.cgi
```

Multipart Form Data POST Requests

Multipart POSTs arrived recently in the world of CGI programming, and they are an extremely useful addition because they encode data in a simpler (if more verbose) manner and are generally more appropriate for transferring large amounts of data from a client to a server than URL encoding methods.

To initiate a multipart CGI request an HTML form must specify that the method is METHOD="POST" and the encoding type is ENCTYPE="multipart/form-data", as in the following example:

```
<FORM ACTION="http://dnn-pc.info.att.com:84/~arw/book/cgi/month3.cgi"
      METHOD="POST"
      ENCTYPE="multipart/form-data">
Month: <SELECT NAME="M">
       <OPTION>January<OPTION>February<OPTION>March
       <OPTION>April<OPTION>May<OPTION>June
       <OPTION>July<OPTION>August<OPTION>September
       <OPTION>October<OPTION>November<OPTION>December
       </SELECT>
Year: <INPUT NAME="Y">
<INPUT TYPE="SUBMIT">
</FORM>
```

As before, this form has the same appearance as a similar form that uses GET style encoding, but on submission of the form, data will be delivered to the server program differently.

When the user submits the contents of this form, the request sent by the browser to the server program might look like this:

```
POST /~arw/book/cgi/month3.cgi HTTP/1.0
Referer: http://dnn-pc.info.att.com:84/~arw/book/cgi/monthP4.html
Connection: Keep-Alive
User-Agent: Mozilla/2.0 (X11; I; SunOS 5.4 sun4m)
Host: dnn-pc.info.att.com:5001
Accept: image/gif, image/x-xbitmap, image/jpeg, image/pjpeg, */*
Content-type: multipart/form-data;
```

```
              boundary=--------------------------11842961131639
Content-Length: 238

----------------------------11842961131639
Content-Disposition: form-data; name="M"

March
----------------------------11842961131639
Content-Disposition: form-data; name="Y"

1984
----------------------------11842961131639--
```

Here the header of the request identifies the request as a POST with a Content-type of multipart/form-data and a boundary of

```
--------------------------11842961131639
```

In this encoding the data is provided in the body of the request (following the headers) in separate textual segments using a MIME (Multipurpose Internet Mail Extensions) style format. Each field/value pairs resides in its own segment separated by the boundary. The general form of the request body (after the blank line that follows the header) is

```
--boundary
segment1
--boundary
segment2
--boundary
segmentN
--boundary--
```

where the boundary is identified by the Content-type field given in the request header. The interior boundaries are given by --boundary (the boundary prefixed by two hyphens), and the final boundary is given by --boundary--. All boundaries appear on separate lines.

Each segment within the body consists of a header, which will usually contains a single line indicating that the data in the segment is a named field of a form, and a body which represents the content of the named field. Following the RFC822 tradition, the header within each segment is separated from the body by an empty line.

```
Content-Disposition: form-data; name="FieldName"
```

Field Data: This data may span multiple lines, and may even be a nonprintable stream of bytes that represents an executable program or an image.

The client program is responsible for choosing a `boundary` which does not appear within any of the segments within the body.

When the server program receives this request, it treats it much like any other POST request—the header data is translated to environment variables, and the body of the request becomes the standard input for the CGI program that is tasked with handling the request.

No modifications to `month2.cgi` or `month3.cgi` are needed for these programs to properly handle multipart data, because the `cgi` module handles this format automatically, behind the scenes.

Doing a Professional Job

Although `month2.cgi` and `month3.cgi` will work with the three different input formats, they fail to meet high standards of software engineering practice, because they repeat a great deal of logic that is not specific to the problem at hand. We wrote these programs poorly on purpose in order to give a gentle introduction to the topic of CGI programming, but a real production program should use better modularization to factor out functionality that is generic to many CGI applications.

To give a better example of a CGI implementation, we provide `month4.cgi`.

```python
#!/usr/local/bin/python
"""The "month" cgi program using the generic CGI module."""

import genCGI, string, HTMLfmt, calendar

class monthCGI(genCGI.ParseMixin, genCGI.Verbose_Mixin, genCGI.cgiBase):
    """Subclass of generic CGI handlers for handling the month query."""

    # the program should receive these single valued fields.
    # Superclass methods will place these in self.formdict
    #   for example as {"M":"September, "Y":"1977"}, or abort if
```

```python
    #   either is not present or multiply defined.
    SingleValuedFields = ["M", "Y"]
    Content_length_limit = 1000 # abort if the content length > 1000

    # here is the title
    def get_title(self):
        return "The month of %(M)s of %(Y)s" % self.formdict

    # when the fields arrive, use this method to compute the body
    # of the reply (returning an HTML table).
    #
    def get_body(self):
        M = self.formdict["M"]
        Y = self.formdict["Y"]
        try:
            year = string.atoi(Y)
        except ValueError:
            # Make the error message more self-explanatory.
            # ... a superclass method will catch this exception.
            raise ValueError, "Year must be an integer: " + `Y`
        try:
            month = calendar.month_name.index(M)
        except ValueError:
            raise ValueError, "Invalid month: " + `M`
        # MAKE AN HTML TABLE!
        # get a list of lists representing the month
        days = calendar._monthcalendar(year, month)
        # replace the 0's in calendar with ""
        for row in days:
            for index in range(len(row)):
                if row[index] == 0:
                    row[index] = ""
        # add the day names
        days.insert(0, calendar.day_name)
        # convert days to a tuple
        days = tuple(days)
        # return a table as the calendar
        title = "%s %s" % (M, Y)
        table = apply(HTMLfmt.VerySimpleTable, (title,) + days)
        return `table`

if __name__ == "__main__":
    # Run the standard CGI processing sequence.
    #   this method is implemented in a superclass of monthCGI.
    monthCGI().GO()
```

This implementation improves on the others because it only includes the logic required to compute the response and does not include the standard logic for printing the `text/html` header line, timing out invalid requests, parsing the form, or handling various standard error conditions. The standard part of the processing is handled by the superclasses `ParseMixin`, `VerboseMixin`, and `cgiBase` of the `genCGI` module. This implementation is also much "cooler" than the previous ones, because it returns an HTML TABLE (see Figure 8.6) instead of a block of preformatted text.

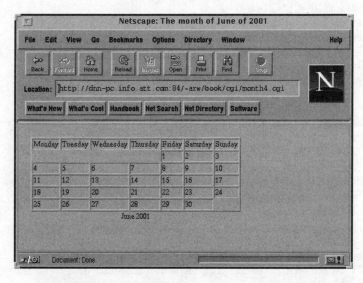

Figure 8.6 A month as a table generated by `month4.cgi`.

A Superclass for `cgi` Programs

The `cgiBase` class of the `genCGI` module provides the bulk of the standard logic required by many kinds of CGI programs, including `month4.cgi`. CGI applications can use some or all of this standard logic by creating a subclass of `genCGI` and using the standard methods that are appropriate but redefining the methods where the standard implementation is not appropriate. We will not describe every facet of the implementation of `cgiBase`, but we will provide a discursive outline.

The primary methods for cgiBase are __init__ and GO.

```
class cgiBase:
  """Superclass for developing CGI processing objects."""

  Content_length_limit = None # set to integer to limit content length
  Form_data_Timeout = 3        # set to None for no timeout
  traceback = 1 # set to zero to disable debug traceback dump.

  def __init__(self, infile=myStdin(sys.stdin), outfile=sys.stdout,
                     environ=cgi.environ):
    self.infile = infile
    self.outfile = outfile
    self.environ = environ

  def GO(self):
    try:
      # perform sanity checks
      self.sanity_check()
      # get the form data
      form = self.get_form()
      # check the form data, prepare response
      self.prepare_response(form)
      # generate the title, otherheaders, and body
      title = self.get_title()
      otherheaders = self.get_otherheaders()
      body = self.get_body()
      send_reply(self.outfile, title, body, otherheaders)
    except CGITerminate:
      # on CGITerminate the process was terminated early, on purpose.
      self.aborted()
    except: # any other error was an accident... report it.
      (type, value) = (sys.exc_type, sys.exc_value)
      self.UnhandledError(type, value, sys.exc_traceback)
    else:
      # normal successful completion.
      self.success()
```

As in month4.cgi, the cgiBase implementation uses a wrapper for the standard input by default to avoid the possibility that badly formed requests may cause the program to block. Subclasses may optionally set Content_length_limit to an integer to limit the size of POSTed content, and the time-out on reading the request data may be redefined or disabled by redefining Form_data_time out.

The GO method performs the standard actions of reading the submitted data and generating a response, primarily by calling other methods that do the "real work" in a standard order. If the GO method completes normally, a standard reply of the form

```
Content-type: text/html
%(otherheaders)s

<HTML><HEAD>
<TITLE>%(title)s</TITLE>
</HEAD>
<BODY>
%(body)s
</BODY></HTML>
```

is sent via standard output as the response to the request, where the values of title, otherheaders, and body are computed by the methods self.get_title, self.get_otherheaders, and self.get_body, respectively. Most subclasses will need to redefine at least get_title and get_body in order to define a response appropriate to the problem at hand.

Any of the methods used by GO may raise a special error CGITerminate, but only after sending a response to standard input in order to terminate the process early (usually after detecting some sort of error condition). Alternatively a method may raise some other error which is handled by the self.UnhandledError method by default.

The standard steps in the computation of GO have the following intended meanings:

self.sanity_check(): This method "hook" allows the program to check for sanity conditions before attempting to read the submitted data. The default implementation checks the CONTENT_LENGTH to make sure it is not too big. Other implementations may examine other entries from the header data, for example, to check authorization parameters. Many CGI programs can use the default implementation.

self.get_form(): This method reads the form data provided to the CGI program. The standard implementation times out the read process if it takes too long.

`self.prepare_response()`: This hook allows programs to perform preliminary computations that need to complete before the remainder the reply can be computed. Its default implementation is only useful for debugging, and most CGI programs should redefine this method.

`self.get_title()`: This hook should return a title for the HTML response. Because the default return value for this method is

```
"Generic CGI script in DEBUG mode"
```

every good CGI script should redefine this method.

`self.get_otherheaders()`: This hook allows other headers in addition to `Content-type: text/html` to be inserted into the response. Most CGI programs may adopt the default implementation, which returns no additional headers, as an empty string.

`self.get_body()`: This hook computes the body of the response. The default implementation for this method is useful only for debugging purposes, so this method must always be redefined by reasonable CGI programs.

`send_reply()`: This function sends the reply, if everything went well.

`self.aborted()`: This will only be invoked if the standard `GO()` sequence raised a `CGITerminate` exception. If this happens, the method that raised the exception should have already sent a response, but `self.aborted` is provided in case a program needs to perform other clean-up actions, such as writing to a log file. The default implementation does nothing.

`self.UnhandledError( ... )`: If the `GO` computation raises an exception other than CGITerminate, then either the error was unexpected or the code that raised the error didn't feel like sending a response (as in `month4.cgi` where the `get_body` method explicitly raises a `TypeError`). The UnhandledError method must send a response to the client and perform any necessary clean-up actions required before terminating. The default implementation is primarily useful for debugging, and hence truly professional CGI programs may wish to redefine this method.

`self.success()`: This hook is provided in case the program needs to perform any final actions (such as writing to a log file) in the case that the process completes successfully. The default implementation does nothing.

Thus, the `cgiBase` captures a great deal of standard logic required for professional CGI programs, but also allows the standard logic to be redefined easily as needed.

The `genCGI` module also provides two additional utility classes: `Verbose_Mixin` which provides verbose diagnostics for debugging purposes, and `ParseMixin` which makes interpreting the form data easier.

The `ParseMixin` class allows subclasses to define two sequences `self.SingleValuedFields` and `self.MultiValuedFields` which indicate what fields the program expects to be provided by the request data. On success the `Parse_Mixin.get_form` method initializes `self.formdict` to provide an easy interface to get the values for the fields where

```
self.formdict[name]
```

returns a single value for declared single-valued fields or a list for declared multiple-valued fields. This mixin also redefines `self.prepare_response` to do nothing (disabling the debug implementation).

WARNING

It has become almost conventional for CGI programs to repeat a great deal of standard logic ad nauseam. Painful experience indicates that this can become a very bad problem, when, for example, the same bug or feature must be fixed in 50 different CGI programs. Use Python's excellent modularity and object-oriented features to avoid the pitfall of cut-and-paste repeated code in all circumstances, and especially in CGI programs.

FORM Input Elements

Most CGI programs answer requests that are initiated from a FORM element in an HTML document. Below is an example HTML document that illustrates some of the more important form elements. Ostensibly this form allows a user to sign up for a free sample of a pet toy or a pet treat.

```
<HTML><TITLE>Order a Sample</TITLE>
<BODY>
<FORM ACTION="http://dnn-pc.info.att.com:84/~arw/book/cgi/FORM.cgi"
      METHOD="POST" ENCTYPE="multipart/form-data">

<H1>Want a free sample?</H1>

<INPUT TYPE="hidden" NAME="CONFIGFILE" VALUE="personal.cfg">

How many pets do you have? <INPUT NAME="NPETS" TYPE="text"> <BR>
Please indicate the kind(s) of Pet(s) you have: <BR>
  <INPUT TYPE="checkbox" NAME="petkind" VALUE="Cat">Cat(s);
  <INPUT TYPE="checkbox" NAME="petkind" VALUE="Dog">Dog(s);
  <INPUT TYPE="checkbox" NAME="petkind" VALUE="Bird">Bird(s);
  <INPUT TYPE="checkbox" NAME="petkind" VALUE="Other">Other kinds.<BR>

What is your favorite color?
  <SELECT NAME="COLOR">
    <OPTION>Green
    <OPTION>Crimson
    <OPTION SELECTED>Brown
    <OPTION>Pink
  </SELECT><BR>

What free sample might you be interested in?
  <INPUT TYPE="radio" NAME="sample" VALUE="treat">a pet treat;
  <INPUT TYPE="radio" NAME="sample" VALUE="toy">a pet toy;
  <INPUT TYPE="radio" NAME="sample" VALUE="surprise">surprise me!<BR>

Your mailing address:<BR>
<TEXTAREA NAME="More" COLS=60 ROWS=5></TEXTAREA><BR>
We have a limited number of free samples and we can only
send you one if you give us your mailing address today!<BR>

Press here to request a free sample:
<INPUT TYPE=SUBMIT NAME="Listing" VALUE="Go For It!"><BR>
Press here to send information as private (but no sample!)
<INPUT TYPE=SUBMIT NAME="Private" VALUE="Private">
<BR>
<INPUT TYPE=RESET>
</FORM>
</BODY></HTML>
```

A browser might present this form to a user like so (Figure 8.7):

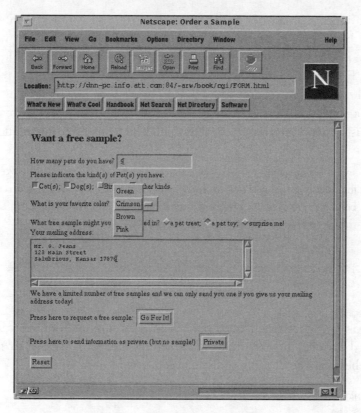

Figure 8.7 Another example form.

The following discussion describes the elements illustrated in this form.

```
<FORM ...> ... </FORM>
```

The FORM tag encloses a section of an HTML document that usually includes various form input elements. The ACTION attribute of a FORM identifies the "object" (usually a CGI program) to receive the form data and return a response. The METHOD specifies the kind of method to use to transfer the data, and the ENCTYPE, if present, specifies the type of encoding for the transferred data.

```
<INPUT TYPE="hidden" NAME="CONFIGFILE" VALUE="personal.cfg">
```

This is an input element of type `hidden` that (usually) is not presented to the user by a browser. The `NAME` and `VALUE` listed, however, will show up as a field/value pair in the request sent by the browser program to the CGI program, however. This input element is often useful to allow HTML forms to provide additional context information to a CGI program—for example, using `hidden` variables a single CGI program may service many different `FORM`s in different ways, by using `hidden` variables to determine which form sent the request.

WARNING

CGI programs must never assume that any data sent by a request is valid, even if the data is associated with a `hidden` variable in a `FORM`, because a request may be sent by a "robot" program, rather than a "real" browser program, and a robot program can send any data it likes.

```
<INPUT TYPE="checkbox" NAME="petkind" VALUE="Cat">Cat(s);
<INPUT TYPE="checkbox" NAME="petkind" VALUE="Dog">Dog(s);
...
```

The `checkbox` input type allows the selection of multiple options for a given name. In the above, the user may send several values for `petkind` or no values at all by checking one or more of the check boxes, or none of them.

```
<SELECT NAME="COLOR">
<OPTION>Green
... <OPTION>Pink
</SELECT><
```

The `SELECT` input type allows the user to select one of a number of options. More generally, the `SELECT` input type may allow a user to select one or more options, but we will not discuss this possibility here. The user may be permitted to select none of the options listed in a select, and CGI programs should take this possibility into account. The value associated with the selected option is the token following the `<OPTION>` tag.

```
<INPUT TYPE="radio" NAME="sample" VALUE="treat">a pet treat;
<INPUT TYPE="radio" NAME="sample" VALUE="toy">a pet toy;
```

Radio button inputs are grouped by `NAME`, and the user is allowed to select only one of the possibilities, or possibly none of them. Essentially the `SELECT` and `radio` input elements present similar functionality, but with a different look.

```
<TEXTAREA NAME="More" COLS=60 ROWS=5></TEXTAREA>
```

A TEXTAREA element allows the user to enter text into a "screen editor" type area of the form. Initial data for the TEXTAREA may be placed between the end of the <TEXTAREA ...> start tag and the start of the </TEXTAREA> end tag.

```
<INPUT TYPE=SUBMIT NAME="Listing" VALUE="Go For It!">
```

Every FORM should have at least one SUBMIT entry to allow the user to actually submit the form. As the example shows, there may be more than one submit button each with an associated name/value pair. The name/value pair associated with a submit button will show up in the request data only if that button was pressed.

There is much more to be said about FORMs and various input tags that may appear in FORMs, but we stop here. A good strategy for developing forms is to do a lot of net-surfing and examine the text of pages that are interesting. If you like a given form, you can use the source for the form you like to develop a similar form, and then use a test program such as test2.py to see how the form translates into a CGI request. Experimenting with CGI programs is extraordinarily fun and easy, once you've got some test tools, and it's also the best way to develop interesting CGI interfaces.

A Simple CGI Program for Our Moderately Complex FORM

This "pet" sample form might be handled by the following CGI script, which appends the data sent in the request to a file and returns a response to the client.

```
#!/usr/local/bin/python
import genCGI, string

PrivateReply = """
  Thanks so much.  We'll keep your data private."""

OfferReply = """
  <H1>Thank you!</H1>
  If there are any free samples left, we'll send
  you one!"""

class Offer(genCGI.ParseMixin, genCGI.Verbose_Mixin, genCGI.cgiBase):
    SingleValuedFields = [ "CONFIGFILE", "COLOR" ]
```

```
MultiValuedFields = [ "petkind", "sample", "More",
                      "Listing", "Private"]
def prepare_response(self, form):
    if self.formdict["Listing"]:
        self.private = 0
        self.formdict["titlehead"] = "Sample Request: "
    elif self.formdict["Private"]:
        self.private = 1
        self.formdict["titlehead"] = "Private submission: "
    else:
        raise ValueError, "Invalid submission!"

def get_title(self):
    return self.formdict["titlehead"] + "Thank You Very Much"

def get_body(self):
    if self.private:
        return PrivateReply
    else:
        return OfferReply

def success(self):
    "append the data to the file name listed in CONFIGFILE"
    items = self.formdict.items()
    items = map(str, items)
    items.append("=====")
    items.append("")
    items = string.joinfields(items, "\n")
    filename = "/tmp/" + self.formdict["CONFIGFILE"]
    out = open(filename, "a")
    out.write(items)
    out.close()

if __name__=="__main__":
    Offer().GO()
```

WARNING

This CGI program derives a filename from the request data and then writes to that file. This is an extremely dangerous thing to do and should only be done with extreme caution. The implementation provided above is not cautious enough because it doesn't check the filename in any way. We should probably add some sanity check like

```
cfg = self.formdict["CONFIGFILE]
if string.find(cfg, "..") or "/" in cfg:
    raise ValueError, "bad configuration file name: "+`cfg`
```

in order to guarantee (at least) that the directory written to is the /tmp directory, as we had intended. Generally speaking, CGI programs should be extremely careful in manipulating strings that derive from request data. Requests can come from programs that may be buggy or malicious, and a bad request handled by a faulty program can damage the computing environment of the CGI program, especially if the program launches subprocesses or interacts with the file system.

Also, avoid using features of Python (or Perl or other dynamic languages) that execute data in CGI programs—such as eval—because a buggy CGI program that uses eval could possibly be tricked by a malicious client into performing arbitrary actions on the server machine.

An entry in /tmp/personal.cfg as generated by this CGI program looks like this

```
('Listing', ['Go For It!'])
('More', ['Mr. G. Jeans\012123 Main Street\012Salubrious, Kansas 17876'])
('petkind', ['Cat', 'Dog', 'Other'])
('Private', [])
('COLOR', 'Crimson')
('sample', ['toy'])
('titlehead', 'Sample Request: ')
('CONFIGFILE', 'personal.cfg')
=====
```

In this CGI program, we have been careful to identify field values that may be absent as "multiple valued fields," even though they may have exactly only one or zero value. Remember that a field which is not selected or filled in by the user may not be sent as part of the request data to a CGI form.

File Upload

Some browsers allow files to be sent to a CGI program via a POST request with a multipart/form-data encoding type. A simple example form for uploading a file from the client to the CGI program might look like this:

```
<FORM ENCTYPE="multipart/form-data"
 ACTION="http://dnn-pc.info.att.com:5001/test.cgi" METHOD=POST>
GIMME A FILE:
 <input name="file" type="file"> <br>
 <INPUT TYPE="submit" VALUE="Send File">
</FORM>
```

The cgi module interface allows files to be treated just like other fields sent in a request, but the module also allows special hooks for reading in file data "on demand" which will be needed only for very large files which will not fit into available memory on the server machine. We will not describe this mechanism here because it is not frequently needed (but when it is needed, it can be a lifesaver).

Generating CGI Forms

The HTMLfmt module described in the chapter on generating HTML includes some conveniences for generating HTML FORMs and their components. We show examples of some of them without further comment here, because they are quite similar to the other HTML elements described earlier.

```
>>> from HTMLfmt import *
>>> S = SUBMIT("Go for it", "goferit")
>>> print S
<INPUT TYPE="SUBMIT" NAME="Go for it" VALUE="goferit">
>>> print TEXTINPUT("Your email address? ", "email", 16)
Your email address? <INPUT TYPE="text" NAME="email" SIZE=16>
>>> sel = SELECT("gender", "female", "male", "decline to state")
>>> print sel
<SELECT NAME="gender">
<OPTION>female
<OPTION>male
<OPTION>decline to state
  </SELECT>
>>> H = HorizontalRadioSeq("x", ("y", "I like it!"), ("n", "I hate it!"))
>>> print H
<INPUT TYPE="radio" NAME="x" VALUE="y">I like it!
<INPUT TYPE="radio" NAME="x" VALUE="n">I hate it!
>>> C = VerticalCheckSeq("sport", ("f", "football"), ("t", "tennis"))
>>> print C
<INPUT TYPE="checkbox" NAME="sport" VALUE="f">football<BR>
<INPUT TYPE="checkbox" NAME="sport" VALUE="t">tennis
>>> F = MultipartFORM("test.cgi",
...       HR_Seq(
...         "what is your gender?",
...         sel,
...         "what sport(s) do you like?",
...         C,
```

```
...         "How do you like this page?",
...         H,
...         S))
>>> print HTML("Write us!", F)
<HTML>
<HEAD>
<TITLE>
Write us!
</TITLE>
</HEAD>
<BODY>
<FORM ACTION="test.cgi" METHOD="POST" ENCTYPE="multipart/form-data">
what is your gender?<HR>
<SELECT NAME="gender">
  <OPTION>female
  <OPTION>male
  <OPTION>decline to state
    </SELECT><HR>
what sport(s) do you like?<HR>
<INPUT TYPE="checkbox" NAME="sport" VALUE="f">football<BR>
  <INPUT TYPE="checkbox" NAME="sport" VALUE="t">tennis<HR>
How do you like this page?<HR>
<INPUT TYPE="radio" NAME="x" VALUE="y">I like it!
  <INPUT TYPE="radio" NAME="x" VALUE="n">I hate it!<HR>
<INPUT TYPE="SUBMIT" NAME="Go for it" VALUE="goferit"></FORM>
</BODY>
</HTML>
```

Summary

The CGI mechanism provides a very convenient way to allow data to be delivered from a client (usually a browser) to a server. This chapter has described the mechanics of various flavors of the CGI protocol as well as Python programs at various levels of sophistication that implement programs for handling CGI requests on a server machine.

We end this discussion with some general comments on CGI programming.

Please remember that there are a lot of reasons a CGI program may not work that have nothing to do with Python, but everything to do with permissions and HTTP server configuration.

1. In order for a CGI program to work, the permissions on the program
    and the directory containing the program must allow the CGI user
    (usually a low-priviledged user like *nobody*) to execute the program.
    Furthermore, the Python interpreter itself must have permissions that
    allow the CGI user to execute it.

2. In order for a CGI program to work the server program must be
    configured to recognize the request as a CGI request. Sometimes
    this is accomplished by configuring the server to recognize a file
    extension such as `.cgi` to identify an object implemented by a CGI
    script. Of course any python modules imported by a CGI program
    must use the conventional `.py` or `.pyc` extensions.

3. A CGI program will be found by the server program only if the server is
    configured to expand the URL for a CGI request to the file system location
    for the program. In our case, the URL `/~arw/book/cgi/test.cgi`
    expanded to `/big/arw/public_html/book/cgi/test.cgi` in the first
    example given in this chapter.

It is always a good idea to successfully run a CGI script from the command line,
using techniques like those demonstrated in this chapter, before complaining to
a harried system administrator that there are problems with an HTTP server
configuration. Command line tests can also be helpful in developing repeatable
tests for CGI scripts in professional environments.

CGI programmers should also think hard about the security concerns related to
their programs. Pay special attention to programs that launch subprocesses or read
or write files and make sure they cannot accidentally or maliciously be confused into
causing harm or exposing sensitive information to an arbitrary client program.
Avoid launching subprocesses when possible. Remember that the client may not be
your friend.

Once the basics are mastered CGI programming is great fun, especially
because the evidence of your work is so tangible when viewed in a browser.
And it's even better when your work is exposed to the entire population of the
Internet—it's a delightful feeling!

CHAPTER NINE

PROTOCOLS

This chapter discusses the use of sockets and Python networking libraries to interface Python programs with programs running on remote machines using communications protocols. As usual, we shall not attempt to exhaustively reconstruct all information available in the documentation of the Python distribution or in the documentation strings of library modules. Instead, we aim to give a useful general introduction to the topic of protocols and how to build protocols using Python.

The socket interface is the tip of a very big iceberg, and many books on network programming spend a lot of space describing the part of the iceberg that lies under the operating system and network ocean. All that ice is very interesting and once in a while useful to understand, but most network programs need only interact with the socket interface tip that pokes above the surface where the applications reside. Thus this chapter discusses only the socket layer and higher, leaving the details of Ethernet packet layout and such to other books (it gets pretty cold down there in the Arctic Ocean!).

A *protocol* is a formalized conversation between two programs (or, sometimes but not often, more than two programs) that may be running on the same machine or on different machines on different continents. A very simple protocol, like HTTP, can often be run by hand on the client side from the interactive Python interpreter, for example, like so:

```
>>> import socket
>>> s = socket.socket(socket.AF_INET, socket.SOCK_STREAM)
>>> s.connect("www.att.com", 80)
>>> s.send("GET /\r\n\r\n")
```

This interaction creates a socket s that talks to an HTTP server program listening on port 80, the default HTTP port, on the machine with the Internet name "www.att.com". The send call sends a very short old-style HTTP request that asks the server to reply with the content of the root page for the server.

```
>>> print s.recv(100)
<html>
<head>
<title>AT&amp;T Home Page</title>
<!-- Coded by Vincent Murphy -->
<!-- Changed by: Ga
```

Here the recv call retrieved the first hundred bytes of the root page printed earlier, so we can see that the server program correctly interpreted our request and served the page. We now get just the next hundred bytes, and then we close the connection.

```
>>> print s.recv(100)
ry Ellison, 15-Mar-1996 -->
<!-- Changed by: Andy Myers, 21-Mar-1996 -->
<!-- #config timefmt="%A, %
>>> s.close()
```

This interaction is a "by-hand" rendering of essentially the same process that a browser program, such as Netscape Navigator, uses to retrieve the contents of the URL http://www.att.com when the user clicks a hotlink that points there, except that the HTML document received is usually presented in a graphical translation rather than as the literal HTML text.

For the preceding interaction—or any interaction involving remote Internet socket connections—to work, the machine on which the interaction runs must have a connection to a network (usually the Internet) that includes the host machine for the remote server program. Furthermore, the network connection must be running.

In the case of a Windows 95 machine registered with an Internet service provider, it is often possible to interact with sockets before the network connection has initialized, because the operating system will attempt to initialize the connection when the socket is created or bound to a remote address—and this may result in the weird effect that the system may ask for a password for the connection automagically in the middle of the interactive session.

We do not have the space (or, honestly, the knowledge) to explain all the possible ways that a machine can be connected to the Internet or other networks and how the connection should be created or initialized. We content ourselves with supposing that readers of this chapter have machines with network connections and that readers know how to start the connection if necessary. If the connection is a commercial Internet service provider readers should also know how to terminate the network connection when they are finished, to avoid excess connect time charges.

The Finger Protocol Client

The basic HTTP protocol, illustrated earlier, is very simple, but there are examples of even simpler protocols. The *finger protocol* provides methods for looking up information about users of remote machines. Essentially, a client that wishes to receive information about a user, say arw, on a remote machine, say cs.rutgers.edu, opens a connection to the server that listens to the well-known finger port (port number 79) and sends the string arw terminated by a carriage-return/newline "\r\n" pair that marks the end of the request. In response, the server program sends back information on the user with the username arw at the machine cs.rutgers.edu.

Here is a Python implementation for a finger client:

```
import socket
import string
FINGERPORT = 79 # well known port for finger

def finger(user, machine, port=FINGERPORT):
    s = socket.socket(socket.AF_INET, socket.SOCK_STREAM) # make a socket
    s.connect(machine, port) # connect it to the server
    s.send(user+"\r\n")       # send the request
    alldata = []              # collect all data sent back in chunks
    while 1:
        data = s.recv(1024)
```

```
    if not data: break
    alldata.append(data)
  s.close()
  return string.joinfields(alldata, "") # return the pasted chunks.
```

The `finger` function defined earlier implements a simple client interaction that retrieves the finger information for a user if there is such a user and such a machine and if that machine has a finger server on the given port.

```
>>> print finger("bob", "cs.rutgers.edu")
Login name: bob                         In real life: Robert Poppins
Directory: /home/bob                    Shell: /bin/ksh
On since Jun 27 10:47:13 on ttyq5 from 135.3.64.77
7 minutes 3 seconds Idle Time
New mail received Wed Jun 12 16:44:01 1996;
  unread since Fri May 24 03:45:01 1996
No Plan.

>>> print finger("frufru", "ftp.berkeley.edu") # no such user.
Login name: frufru                      In real life: ???

>>> print finger("wally", "spam.eggs.com") # no such host
Traceback (innermost last):
  File "<stdin>", line 1, in ?
  File "./finger.py", line 10, in finger
    s.connect(machine, port)
socket.error: host not found

>>> print finger("orb", "www.att.com", 7676) # no server on this port.
Traceback (innermost last):
  File "<stdin>", line 1, in ?
  File "./finger.py", line 10, in finger
    s.connect(machine, port)
socket.error: (146, 'Connection refused')
```

Let's look more closely at the logic of the `finger` function.

```
  s = socket.socket(socket.AF_INET, socket.SOCK_STREAM)
```

This assignment creates a socket object, specifying that it should be an Internet protocol socket (`socket.AF_INET`) that should receive "reliable" stream data (`socket.SOCK_STREAM`). A `SOCK_STREAM` socket requires the underlying networking software to try to ensure that the data received through the socket arrives exactly as it was sent, or failing that, to reliably indicate that an error occurred. Under the Internet protocol, reliable stream sockets are implemented using the *Transmission Control Protocol* (TCP). Beneath TCP, data is transferred as packets, which sometimes get lost, duplicated, or arrive out of order. TCP attempts to correct for any transmission anomalies, using techniques that are not of great concern to most applications programmers, because they almost always work; we will not discuss the TCP mechanisms further. There are other kinds of sockets (such as unreliable datagram sockets) and other underlying protocols that support sockets other than `AF_INET`, but they are beyond the scope of this discussion.

At this point, the socket object `s` is not associated with any network connection.

```
s.connect(machine, port) # connect it to the server
```

The `connect` method of the socket object attempts to establish a connection (a send/receive conversation) with a program residing on the `machine` listening on the given `port`. Behind the scenes, a machine name such as `ftp.berkeley.edu` is translated to a numerical network address, usually using the *Domain Name Server* (DNS) protocol. The DNS lookup is not normally a problem. However, if the DNS system is not configured properly, the name may not be found or finding it may take a long time.

WARNING Delays due to DNS lookups can cause some programs to block, preventing other activities until the name is resolved. These programs may prefer to look up the name separately using an asynchronous DNS lookup. The program would then use a numeric IP address, like `"100.50.200.5"` for the `connect`. See the `http://www.python.org` contributed libraries for tools that allow asynchronous name lookups. Also examine the `Demos/dns` directory of the Python distribution.

Once the `connect` system call completes, the socket object defines a "telephone-like" interface, where the Python interpreter may "talk" to the remote program on the other end of the socket using the `send` method, or the interpreter may "hear" data sent by the remote program using the `recv` system call.

In the case of the finger protocol, the conversation was very simple: the client sent a user name and the remote server program received the name and returned the user information for that name, if there was any information. Our client program then received all the data sent by the remote program until it received an empty string, indicating that the remote connection had been closed.

```
s.send(user+"\r\n")        # send the request
alldata = []               # collect all data sent back in chunks
while 1:
    data = s.recv(1024)
    if not data: break
    alldata.append(data)
s.close()
```

The s.send method sends a string across the connection, and the s.recv method receives data up to a specified size. The data received will be no larger than the maximum amount requested, but if the available data is smaller (but not empty) than the amount requested, recv returns the amount of data available. If—and only if—the other end of the connection closes the connection, the recv returns an empty string.

In general, socket conversations can be more complex than this, involving many back-and-forth transfers or negotiations between the two ends of the connection (like FTP or TELNET), or they may involve the asynchronous and parallel transfer of large amounts of data resembling a shouting match more than a conversation (like IRC chat).

 NOTE The telephone analogy is deceptive, because data sent and received on a socket connection is buffered by the network subsystem, so one program can talk before the other program is ready to hear, or both programs can talk at the same time and later hear what the other said earlier.

 WARNING It is a very bad idea to depend on system buffers to hold too much data, because the buffers can overload, which may cause the connection to be destroyed. Generally, programs that receive data should try to unload the network system buffers as quickly as possible—perhaps storing the data in a list or a file if the program is not ready to process the data yet. Remember that the network buffers are shared by all processes of the system, and in some cases they may be quite limited.

A Finger Server

Of course, we can also implement a finger server using Python, and we will do so with fake user information.

```python
import sys
from socket import *
import string

USERS = {"pete": "Pedro Montalban, supreme ruler of the universe.",
         "juan": "Juan Matamoros, humble servant",
         "janet": "Janet Delacruz: The person who gets things done."}

bad_request = "bad_request"

def main(HOST="", PORT = 79, BACKLOG=5):
    sock = socket(AF_INET, SOCK_STREAM)
    sock.bind(HOST, PORT)
    sock.listen(BACKLOG)
    print "listening on port %s (%s, %s)" % (PORT, `HOST`, BACKLOG)
    while 1:
        connection = (conn, addr) = sock.accept()
        print "connected by %s \nat %s" % connection
        try:
            name = ""
            while not "\n" in name:
                name = name + conn.recv(1024)
                if len(name) > 4000:
                    raise bad_request, "too long"
            name = string.strip(name)
            data = USERS[name]
        except (KeyError, bad_request):
            print "failed request: ", `name`
            conn.send("No such user.")
        else:
            print "good request: ", (name, data)
            conn.send(data)
        conn.send("\r\n")
        conn.close()
```

This `main` function may be launched when the module is run as a script using the following `if __name__=="__main__":` launch code, which also attempts to interpret the first argument as a port number if present.

```
if __name__=="__main__":
    try:
        port = sys.argv[1]
    except IndexError:
        main() # use standard port, if no port is specified.
    else:
        try:
            portnum = string.atoi(port)
        except:
            print "usage: fingersrv.py [host_number]"
            raise SystemExit
        else:
            main(PORT = portnum)
```

We launch this program from the command line on the machine dnn-pc like so, using a nontraditional and unprivileged port number:

```
% fingsrv.py 2222
listening on port 2222 ('', 5)
```

Port numbers lower than 1024 are reserved for well-known and privileged services on many systems, so unprivileged user programs must often use larger port numbers.

N O T E

Now on a separate machine on the network called lone, we may test our finger server by running the finger.py client. (We cannot use a standard finger client program because our standard client cannot connect on port 2222; it always uses the well-known finger port.)

```
>>> from finger import *
>>> finger("juan", "dnn-pc.info.att.com", 2222)
'Juan Matamoros, humble servant\015\012'
```

At the same time, back on dnn-pc we can see the debug print output from the fingsrv.py program that resulted from this interaction.

```
connected by <socket object, fd=5, family=2, type=2, protocol=0>
at ('192.11.95.133', 33674)
good request:  ('juan', 'Juan Matamoros, humble servant')
```

We request information about an invalid user name from lone:

```
>>> finger("lola", "dnn-pc.info.att.com", 2222)
'No such user.\015\012'
```

At the same instant, we see the debug output from `fingsrv.py` on `dnn-pc` as:

```
connected by <socket object, fd=5, family=2, type=2, protocol=0>
at ('192.11.95.133', 33675)
failed request:  'lola'
```

When we wish to terminate the `fingsrv.py` server, we use a keyboard interrupt (**Ctrl-C** on our system), because the server program runs an endless `listen` loop.

Because `fingsrv.py` awaits connections from remote machines instead of actively establishing connections with them, it uses the socket interface quite differently from the finger client program. Let's examine the code more closely.

```
def main(HOST="", PORT = 79, BACKLOG=5):
    sock = socket(AF_INET, SOCK_STREAM)
    sock.bind(HOST, PORT)
    sock.listen(BACKLOG)
    ...
```

The server program creates a socket of the same type as the client program, but rather than `connect`ing the socket to a remote program the server `bind`s the socket object to the `PORT` (which by default would be the well-known finger port 79) on the `HOST`, usually the local host (where the program is running), conventionally named by the empty string `""`. After the `bind`, any program that attempts to `connect` to the local host on the `PORT` will be directed to the `sock` socket object. The `listen` method invocation requests that the network system keep a backlog of up to 5 (by default) pending connections before rejecting connection attempts.

NOTE A `listen`er program can request a backlog as large as it wants of the underlying system, but systems often cannot support more than a small backlog. On many systems a backlog of 5 is the maximum allowed, and requests for a larger buffer of unserviced connections are reduced to the real limit.

The `accept` method accepts an available connection. If there are no available connections, `accept` blocks until a connection is available.

```
    ...
    print "listening on port %s (%s, %s)" % (PORT, `HOST`, BACKLOG)
    while 1:
        connection = (conn, addr) = sock.accept()
        print "connected by %s \nat %s" % connection
        ...
```

The `sock.accept()` method returns a 2-tuple containing a new socket object `conn` and an address pair `addr` for a connection request from a remote client. We will not concern ourselves with the address here. The new `conn` socket is the "telephone" by which our server communicates to the client program that initiated the connection.

NOTE

The `conn` and `sock` sockets should be treated as different objects, even though they are both "sockets." The `sock` socket is used only to listen for new connections. When it "hears" a new connection, it generates a new socket `conn` to serve as the conduit for the connection. Listener sockets such as `sock` should not be used for communicating directly with other programs under the TCP/Stream model.

In general, a listener socket like `sock` can generate new connections while existing connections are active. Multiple connections may be handled by multiple threads within the same program, subprocesses, polling, asynchronous notification, or other multiprocessing techniques.

Our `fingsrv.py` program handles each connection serially, completing the existing conversation before listening for a new connection. The program first receives the user name requested using `conn.recv` and a newline to represent the end of the user name. Once the `name` has been received, the program sends a response to the client using `conn.send` and closes the connection. Not surprisingly, this is the behavior expected of the server by the `finger` client function given earlier.

CGI/HTTP Robot Clients

An HTTP robot program automatically retrieves pages from HTTP servers. There are many different kinds of robots and many different uses for them.

One common use for a robot is as a test device to make sure a Web Server machine and all its components are up and running. A robot of this sort might send a CGI request to your company's Web server once every 15 minutes or so from some remote site and examine the response for certain sanity conditions. If the robot determines the response to be "insane" or if it gets no response, it may think something is wrong and trigger an alarm of some sort—for example, it may make your office mate's pager beep (not yours, we hope).

In this section, we'll examine techniques for sending general CGI requests and receiving responses from a robot program—techniques that could be used as a component of a robot program. In particular, we will describe the implementation for the GETRequest class, which may be used interactively as follows:

```
>>> from requests import GETRequest
>>> machine = "dnn-pc.info.att.com"    # the server to contact
>>> uri = "/~arw/book/cgi/month3.cgi"  # the cgi script to test
>>> params = {"M": "May", "Y": 1977}   # cgi parameters.
>>> port = 84                          # the non-default port number
>>> G = GETRequest(machine, uri, params, port)
>>> print G.retrieve()  # get it!
HTTP/1.0 200 OK
Date: Monday, 08-Jul-96 18:57:39 GMT
Server: NCSA/1.3
MIME-version: 1.0
Content-type: text/html

<HTML><TITLE>A Month</TITLE><BODY>
For ('May', '1977') your month is:
<PRE>
      May 1977
Mo Tu We Th Fr Sa Su
                   1
 2  3  4  5  6  7  8
 9 10 11 12 13 14 15
16 17 18 19 20 21 22
23 24 25 26 27 28 29
30 31
</PRE>
<HR> Thanks for your interest!
</BODY></HTML>
```

As demonstrated, the GETRequest class allows the program to dynamically and conveniently construct CGI GET requests, deliver those requests to a specified server, and retrieve the response to the request as a string. By sub-classing this request, we also allow programs to make POST-style requests and Multipart POST requests in a similar manner.

For greatest flexibility, the `GetRequest` class has a highly modular design. For example, the `retrieve` method relies heavily on other methods and doesn't do much itself.

```
BLOCKSIZE = 8000

class GETRequest:

    blocksize = BLOCKSIZE # overrideable for testing purposes

    def __init__(self, machine, uri, queryDict, port=HTTPPORT):
        self.machine = machine
        self.uri = uri
        self.Dict = queryDict
        self.port = port
        self.sock = None

    def retrieve(self):
        sock = self.connect()
        self.send_request(sock)
        return self.get_reply(sock)

    def connect(self):
        from socket import socket, AF_INET, SOCK_STREAM
        sock = self.sock = socket(AF_INET, SOCK_STREAM)
        sock.connect(self.machine, self.port)
        return sock

    def send_request(self, sock):
        request = self.Request_Format()
        sock.send(request)

    def Request_Format(self):
        return Get_Query(self.uri, self.Dict)

    def get_reply(self, sock):
        reply = []
        while 1:
            data = sock.recv(self.blocksize)
            if not data: break
            reply.append(data)
        sock.close()
```

```
        return string.joinfields(reply, "")

# other methods omitted for now...
```

An examination of this logic reveals a careful method encapsulation of logic shared by the `finger` client function described earlier, but the higher degree of modularity here allows greater flexibility, as we shall see.

But in outline, the finger and HTTP protocols are very similar—a client sends a request and the server responds with a reply. The `Request_Format` method delegates the formation of the request string to the `Get_Query` function. In the example instance `G` created earlier, we have:

```
>>> print G.Request_Format()
GET /~arw/book/cgi/month3.cgi?M=May&Y=1977 HTTP/1.0
User-Agent: test_robot
Accept: */*
```

The `Get_Query` function is defined with the help of the standard `urllib.quote` function that encodes the query string using the URL encoding conventions required by HTTP.

```
def Simple_Request(uri = "/index.html", agent = "test_robot"):
    Dict = {"METHOD":"GET", "URI":uri, "AGENT":agent, "BODY": ""}
    return SIMPLE_REQUEST % Dict

def urlencode_data(Dict):
    """Encode dictionary as an url encoded query string.
       Dict should contain name-->value, where value is
       a list only when the name should have multiple values.
    """
    from urllib import quote
    from types import ListType
    pairs = []
    for (name, values) in Dict.items():
        ename = quote(str(name))
        if type(values) != ListType:
            values = [values]
        for value in values:
            evalue = quote(str(value))
            pairs.append( "%s=%s" % (ename, evalue) )
    return string.joinfields(pairs, "&")

def Get_Query(url, Dict):
```

```
query = urlencode_data(Dict)
uri = "%s?%s" % (url, query)
return Simple_Request(uri)
```

Here the `Simple_Request` function uses the `SIMPLE_REQUEST` string constant, with the value:

```
%(METHOD)s %(URI)s HTTP/1.0
User-Agent: %(AGENT)s
Accept: */*

%(BODY)s
```

The `%(name)s` directives in `SIMPLE_REQUEST` are replaced using string/dictionary substitution.

The `GETRequest` class allows a program to define an arbitrary GET request (regardless of whether the request is a CGI request) and retrieve a response from that request as a string. But not all HTTP requests are GET requests.

We can re-use most of the methods of `GETRequest` to define similar retrieval classes for POST and multipart post requests as follows:

```
class POSTRequest(GETRequest):
    def Request_Format(self):
        return Post_Query(self.uri, self.Dict)

class Multi_Post_Request(GETRequest):
    def Request_Format(self):
        return Multi_Post_Query(self.uri, self.Dict)
```

We omit the definitions for `Post_Query` and `Multi_Post_Query` because they are fairly similar to the `Get_Query` function. Note, however, that `Multi_Post_Query` constructs a multipart MIME message, with the help of the standard `mimetools.choose_boundary` function.

A Polling Robot Event Loop

In general, robot programs may spend a great deal of time waiting for responses to arrive, so robot implementers may want to initiate many requests at once, handling the response data as it arrives. The `select` function allows robots to handle many request connections in a nonblocking style by allowing a program to select those request with available data and respond to those requests, while deferring requests where new data has not arrived yet.

The `select` system call

```
from select import select
(readablelist, writeablelist, errorlist) = \
    select(list1, list2, list3, timeout)
```

uses hidden system magic to determine which members of `list1` have readable data available, which members of `list2` have buffer space for nonblocking writes, and which members of `list3` have "out of band" or error conditions set. The members that pass the respective tests are returned as `readablelist`, `writeablelist`, and `errorlist`, respectively. In general, the `select` system call is most useful for use with sockets. Indeed, on some systems (notably Windows NT and its relatives), only socket objects can be used with `select`.

Select thus allows a program to test a group of sockets, in particular to see which of them has readable data available. The timeout parameter may be omitted, which results in a `select` call that blocks until one or more of the sockets is available. If the timeout parameter is provided, it should be a number indicating the number of seconds that `select` should wait for one of the sockets to become available. In particular, if the timeout parameter is 0 and none of the sockets is ready, `select` will return three empty lists immediately and allow the program to do other work before returning later to check on the sockets.

"Out-of-Band" data is a feature of the TCP protocol that is not implemented consistently across the landscape of the Internet and that seems to be generally avoided and largely historical at this time. When used, it indicates error, abort, or other "alert" conditions, but because it is not often used we won't discuss it in detail. It is probably reasonable to assume that any socket returned in the third list for `select` is in an error state and should be closed.

We define alternate retrieval mechanisms for the `GETRequest` class and its subclasses as follows:

```
# class GETRequest continued...
    def start(self):
        """For use with a non-blocking read event loop."""
```

```
        self.sock = sock = self.connect()
        self.send_request(sock)
        self.data_read = []

    def try_read(self):
        """For use with a non-blocking read event loop.
           returns true when data is done."""
        from select import select
        # make sure self is readable
        (test, dummy1, dummy2) = select([self.sock], [], [], 0)
        for sock in test:
            data = sock.recv(self.blocksize)
            if not data: return 1
            self.data_read.append(data)
        return 0

    def when_done_reading(self):
        """For use with a nonblocking read event loop.
           default implementation just prints the read data.
           If this is used, it will usually need to be overridden.
        """
        data = string.joinfields(self.data_read, "")
        print data

    def selectable(self):
        """the selectable object in self."""
        return self.sock
```

Here, instead of reading all data for the request in a single go, we allow the request to be started using self.start; later reads may be attempted using self.try_read. The try_read method only reads data if data is available and only returns 1 if all data has been read. Until all data is read, the pieces received are collected in self.data_read as a list and the when_done_reading method is provided as a "hook" that should be called when the response is complete. The default implementation for when_done_reading is not terribly useful, but it is provided for testing purposes; this method should probably always be redefined in subclasses in real use, and it should deliver the response data to some appropriate process or destination.

These additional methods, as their doc-strings indicate, are designed to work with a "read-event loop," which we implement as a separate class as follows:

```
class Read_Event_Loop:
    verbose = 0 # override this to get verbose tracing...
```

```
def __init__(self, timeout=1, *readables):
    self.timeout = timeout
    self.init_list = readables
    self.started = {}

def start_all(self):
    init_list = self.init_list
    self.init_list = ()
    for readable in init_list:
        self.start_item(readable)

def start_item(self, readable):
    if self.verbose: print "starting", readable
    readable.start()
    self.started[ readable.selectable() ] = readable

def try_all_readables(self):
    from select import select
    started = self.started
    selectables = started.keys()
    if self.verbose: print "selecting", len(selectables)
    (readavails, dummy1, dummy2) = \
        select(selectables, [], [], self.timeout)
    for readavail in readavails:
        readable = started[readavail]
        if self.verbose: print "reading", readable
        test = readable.try_read()
        if test:
            if self.verbose: print "terminating", readable
            readable.when_done_reading()
            del started[readavail]

def all_done(self):
    return len(self.started) == 0

def go_til_done(self):
    while not self.all_done():
        self.try_all_readables()
```

This class is designed to contain a number of readable request objects in a single structure, archived in the dictionary `self.started`. The `try_all_readables` method is the central method of this class: it tests all readable objects that have been started to see if they have data available, and for those that do have data available, it executes `readable.try_read()`. If `readable.try_read()` returns success, then the `readable` has completed reading the response and is removed from `self.started` after the `readable.when_done_reading()` hook is executed.

The following simple test program demonstrates the use of the `Read_Event_Loop` class:

```
def test(machine="www.att.com",
         uri="/cgi-bin/ATT_WEB/search",
         Dict={"all":"all", "keywords": "Internet services",
               "weight": "weight", "limit": 2},
         port=HTTPPORT):
    """Poke a cgi program using all 3 request formats.
       The cgi program may not recognize all request formats...
    """
    print machine, uri, Dict
    request1 = GETRequest(machine, uri, Dict, port)
    request2 = POSTRequest(machine, uri, Dict, port)
    request3 = Multi_Post_Request(machine, uri, Dict, port)
    Looper = Read_Event_Loop()
    Looper.verbose = 1
    Looper.start_item(request1)
    Looper.start_item(request2)
    Looper.start_item(request3)
    Looper.go_til_done()
```

NOTE

In addition to `select`, there are approaches that allow a program to handle a number of socket connections at once without blocking. On many systems multiple threads may be run in the same process, but multithreaded programming is extremely difficult, even in Python, so attempt this with great caution. The `http://www.python.org` site provides Sam Rushing's portable asynchronous sockets library, which uses native asynchronous socket notification on certain systems and emulates asynchronous notification using `select` on other systems. Of course, it is often possible to handle multiple connections in separate processes, but communications among the processes may become difficult if it is needed, because the processes will not share the same address space.

Custom HTTP Servers in Python

The Python distribution comes loaded with some basic HTTP Server implementations given in library modules `SocketServer.py`,

`BaseHTTPServer.py`, `SimpleHTTPServer.py`, and `CGIHTTPServer.py`. Actually, the `SocketServer` module is not specific to HTTP and can be used as the basis for a wide range of protocol Server implementations.

These modules are fun to play with, and we recommend you give them a try. The `SimpleHTTPServer` module defines an implementation for a simple HTTP server with no CGI capabilities, which you may find useful if you want to run a basic personal server on your workstation. For the adventurous, the `CGIHTTPServer` extends the simple server with CGI script functionality.

By default, both these implementations serve pages using a server-root tree that is rooted at the directory in which the program was started. The `CGIHTTPServer` also allows CGI programs to be placed in subdirectories `/htbin` or `/cgi-bin`. One possible problem with `CGIHTTPServer` is that if a "normal" user launches the server, the server and any CGI programs that the server launches will operate with that user's privileges, unless the user that launched the program has the ability to execute the UNIX `setuid` command.

What is more interesting about these programs/modules is that they may be customized using subclassing and inheritance to perform nonstandard HTTP operations. As a very simple example, the following customization of the `CGIHTTPServer` functionality forces requests that end in the extension `cgi` to be interpreted as CGI scripts:

```python
#!/usr/local/bin/python
import CGIHTTPServer, BaseHTTPServer, SimpleHTTPServer
import string, os

class myHandler(CGIHTTPServer.CGIHTTPRequestHandler):
    cgi_extensions = [ "cgi", "py" ]
    def is_cgi(self):
        """like CGIHTTPRequestHandler.is_cgi, but recognized, eg, test.cgi
           or test.py as a cgi request.
        """
        path = self.path
        qposition = string.find(path, "?")
        if qposition < 0: qposition = len(path)
        cgipath = path[:qposition]
        dotposition = string.rfind(cgipath, ".")
        if dotposition>0:
            extension = cgipath[dotposition+1:]
            if extension in self.cgi_extensions:
```

```
            slashposition = string.rfind(cgipath, "/")
            self.cgi_info = (path[:slashposition], path[slashposition+1:])
            return 1
        # use default if above didn't succeed
        return CGIHTTPServer.CGIHTTPRequestHandler.is_cgi(self)

def test(HandlerClass = myHandler,
         ServerClass = BaseHTTPServer.HTTPServer):
    import sys
    SimpleHTTPServer.test(HandlerClass, ServerClass)

if __name__=="__main__": test()
```

It is also easy to implement custom CGI-like functionality by deriving sub-classes from classes in these modules, for example, to allow the CGI request to be answered within the server process itself. This approach avoids the over-head of spawning a subprocess and allows the CGI functions to share persis-tent state in the server. We leave the implementation of these extensions to the interested reader.

If nothing else, these fairly sophisticated (if shockingly terse) server imple-mentations provide a detailed example of how to implement advanced server functionality using Python. There are two sorts of classes in each of these mod-ules: *server* classes essentially monitor the listening socket for new requests, and *handler* class instances are created to handle requests as they arrive. A variety of mixins are available that modify the behaviors of the servers and handlers. Please see the documentation strings of these modules for more information.

The Standards

Internet protocols are defined by standards documents called rfcs (*requests for comments*). There are many different rfcs at many different levels of standardiza-tion. If you want to write a client or server that implements a standard protocol, you should probably consult the latest rfc on the topic. Any good search engine will point a Web surfer to good sources for the rfc texts, but we have found the Ohio State archive http://www.cis.ohio-state.edu/hypertext/ information/rfc.html to be particularly usable.

Many standard Internet protocols traditionally run on standard well-known ports. Table 9.1 lists some common protocols and their well-known ports.

Table 9.1 Common protocols and their ports.

Protocol/Service	Abbreviation	Well-Known Port
Echo	echo	7
Daytime	daytime	13
File transfer	ftp	21/20
Telnet terminal	telnet	23
Simple mail transport	smtp	25
Trivial file transfer	tftp	69
Finger	finger	79
Domain name service	domain	53
HyperText transfer	http	80/84/8000
NetNews	nntp	119

NOTE The standard protocols are all well and good, but if you are implementing a system where you control both ends of the connection (such as in cooperative games, chat systems, or intranet applications), feel free to diverge from the standard approaches and be creative. And be sure to look into the `marshal` and `pickle` modules for nonstandard, but highly efficient, means to transfer large amounts of formatted data between two Python programs.

A Guide to Other Python Internet Tools

The Python distribution comes with a number of tools for interacting with Internet protocols and other tools (such as mail archives) that follow Internet conventions, in addition to those mentioned earlier.

ftplib.py	FTP client interface
gopherlib.py	Gopher client interface
httplib.py	Simple HTTP client interface
mimetools.py	Utilities for parsing and generating MIME encapsulated multipart mail messages
nntplib.py	NetNews client interface
urllib.py	Generic tools for parsing and retrieving many common Universal Resource Locator objects
rfc822.py	Generic tools for parsing and interpreting rfc 822–style mail headers

These all have standard documentation in the standard Python libraries reference.

There is also a very useful built-in module called `binascii` and an undocumented library module `base64.py` that implements efficient translations for `base64`-encoded binary data to and from ASCII representations.

```
>>> import binascii
>>> x = binascii.b2a_base64("Yond Cassius has a lean and hungry look;")
>>> print x
WW9uZCBDYXNzaXVzIGhhcyBhIGxlYW4gYW5kIGh1bmdyeSBsb29rOw==

>>> print binascii.a2b_base64(x)
Traceback (innermost last):
  File "<stdin>", line 1, in ?
binascii.Error: Incorrect padding
>>> import string
>>> print binascii.a2b_base64( string.strip(x) )
Yond Cassius has a lean and hungry look;
```

The `binascii` module is the lowest-level interface to base 64 and certain other encodings. Note that the output of `b2a` must have the newline stripped off before it will work as input to `a2b`. The `base64` module provides the preferred interface for encoding and decoding `base64` data.

Base 64 encoding encodes arbitrary 8-bit data as 6-bit ASCII representations in short lines that include no white space. This encoding passes unharmed through all but the most unpleasant and finicky mail filter programs, and it is the encoding preferred by most highly functional mail programs to transfer, for example, GIF images via Internet mail. The journeyman Internet programmer will eventually encounter `base64` encoding and will find it delightful that Python automatically includes tools for manipulating this format. We refer the reader to the MIME `rfc` for a precise definition of how base 64 works.

Other related modules that may be of interest are the `uu.py` module, which implements standard `uuencode` and `uudecode` functionality, and the `binhex` module, which allows compression and decompression using Apple Macintosh BinHex encoding.

As mentioned in the appendices, contributed modules are available at `http://www.python.org` and the mirror sites, providing tools for efficient encryption and compression of data that may be useful to Internet programmers, particularly for use in for-pay Internet services or for intranet applications that require data protection. Furthermore, additional client and server prototypes are available as contributed modules.

Many demo programs that implement Internet-based programs are available in the standard distribution in the `Demo` directory, particularly in the `www`, `sockets`, `rpc`, and `dns` subdirectories. These programs may be of direct use if they serve as code examples to help in the development of similar Internet-based applications.

Probably the most sophisticated application in existence, which is implemented only in Python (with no special purpose extensions or interfaces), is the Grail browser by CNRI. At this time, the source for Grail is available for inspection, although the copyright on the source is more restricted than Python's copyright. We recommend the Grail source tree for excellent additional examples of Internet programming.

Summary

Implementing protocols can become an exciting game with Python. If you need to implement sophisticated Internet-based services, or even if you don't, we recommend giving the world of Internet protocol programming a try.

But be warned: It can be addictive.

Chapter Ten

GUI Programming with Python

Graphical user interfaces or GUIs are usually written with an object-oriented programming language such as C++ or Smalltalk and a class library provided with the compiler or by a third party. The class library provides the basic windows and controls need by the GUI and the interface to the underlying operating system. Python is a convenient language for GUI programming because of its simple yet powerful object-oriented features such as classes, multiple inheritance, and virtual functions. Also, because Python is a scripting language, it is quick and easy to change the program and see what the changes look like.

The class library determines what type of GUI objects can be created. All libraries support the usual GUI controls such as buttons, menus, list boxes, scroll bars, edit windows, and labels. There is more variation in how higher-level objects such as windows are created. There may be a specific window class or there may be a way to make a window out of other components. There may or may not be higher classes for the application object, documents, etc.

The event system is the other important component of the GUI class library. All GUI code is event-driven. That is, after the initialization, the GUI code just waits for and responds to events from the user or the GUI system. Some GUI systems call these events *messages*. The user generates events by pressing keys, moving the mouse, pressing mouse buttons, and selecting menu items and operating controls such as buttons. The system generates events when windows are resized, moved out of the way of other windows (an "expose" event), created, or destroyed. The kinds of events tend to be differ greatly for various class libraries and operating systems.

There are currently at least four class libraries available to write GUI code in Python. They are used just like class libraries in C++. You import the class library and create instances of the classes. You can use the base classes directly, or you can create your own classes that inherit from the base classes. You can override some of the base class methods and add additional methods of your own. Most of the Python GUI class libraries are available from www.python.org and are described in the following sections.

Tkinter

Tkinter is a class library based on the Tk Toolkit written by John Ousterhout and published by Sun Microsystems. Tk has been used extensively to write GUI code for UNIX systems running the X Window system. Recently, Sun published versions of Tk that run on 32-bit Windows (NT and 95) and the Macintosh. These versions run with the UNIX (Motif-like) look and feel, but versions are in development that will have the look and feel of the native platform. There is no version for Windows 3.1, but the NT version can be used on 3.1 with Microsoft's Win32s system.

The Tkinter library classes follow the Tk widgets, and classes are available for toplevels, frames, canvases, text screens, and the usual controls such as buttons, menus, list boxes, scroll bars, edit windows, and labels. Messages mirror the X Window events.

WPY

WPY is a class library based on the Microsoft Foundation Classes or MFC, a popular C++ class library. WPY follows MFC rather closely, in both its classes and its messaging system, and it is possible to use MFC documentation to write WPY code. The reverse is also true; it is possible to learn to write C++ MFC code by learning WPY. WPY differs from MFC in that it is a small subset and does not try to implement all of MFC. It also provides a slightly higher-level drawing model, in that the WPY system will maintain the contents of a window instead of calling for the window to be redrawn by the programmer.

WPY programs run natively (using MFC itself) on Windows 3.1x, 32-bit Windows NT and 95, and on UNIX/X using the Tk toolkit.

PythonWin

PythonWin is also based on MFC, but it offers a much more complete and feature-rich interface to MFC. It attempts to expose all of MFC for use by the programmer. It also has special support for Winsock sockets not present in the Python core distribution. It has OLE support built in with interfaces for MAPI, DAO, and Netscape Automation; OCX support is being worked on. PythonWin programs run natively on Windows NT and 95 only.

wxPython

wxPython is a Python interface to wxWindows, a portable GUI toolkit developed at the Artificial Intelligence Applications Institute at the University of Edinburgh. It was designed for cross-platform portability to UNIX/X, Windows 3.1, Windows NT, and the Macintosh. It has its own classes and messaging system, which are quite high level and arguably cleaner than the native APIs on the supported platforms.

There are other Python GUI class libraries available, including the Motif extension, the native Mac interface, and stdwin. Some Python GUI interfaces even explore very experimental and nonstandard approaches such as OpenGL and the Linux CGG library. New developments in this area proceed rapidly, but the interfaces mentioned are particularly stable and useful.

Crash Course on Objects

All these class libraries require object-oriented (OO) programming techniques to be used effectively. Much ink has been spilled on OO; it has been described as the only right way to program and as an overrated technique that is hard to apply properly in practice. We do not claim that OO is the answer to every programming problem, but it is the right way to write a GUI. There is a natural fit between GUIs and objects. Object-oriented programming was discussed in Chapter 4, but we want to go over it again briefly, with examples drawn from GUI objects. Hopefully this will make it all more concrete.

Object-oriented programming is primarily about, well, "objects." An *object* is a "thing" containing data attributes and methods (functions) that operate on the data. To make an object you first need a class. The *class* defines the data and methods and serves to categorize objects according to the kind of object they are. For example, a GUI push-button class would describe a button. Then you make an *instance* of the class that represents the actual button. For example, if CButton is a class, the following code makes two buttons:

```
b1 = CButton()
b2 = CButton()
```

Both buttons b1 and b2 would have data attributes for their size, location, color, and text to display. They would have methods that control how they are drawn and how they change when they are pressed. Other methods would be available to move and resize them and so on.

In addition to classes, instances, data attributes, and methods, there are three main ideas in OO:

- *Encapsulation* means that details are hidden and only certain data attributes and methods are exposed to the user of the object. Our button would have a method to redraw the button in its pushed state, but such a method would probably be hidden from the user, because the GUI is responsible for drawing the button.

- *Polymorphism* means that different objects that have common operations are treated consistently. For example, push buttons, check buttons, and radio buttons are all buttons, so the way the text is set and the way they are positioned on the screen should be the same. But some methods could be different. A check button would have a data attribute or method to return its checked state, but a push button would not.

- *Inheritance* means that data and methods common to two classes are expressed in a common base class. An instance of a class has all its own data and methods plus all the data and methods of all its base classes. For example, GUI buttons are all rectangular and can all be moved, so a possible inheritance scheme would be:

```
class RectangularVisibleObject:
    def MoveObject(self, x, y):
        ....
    def HideObject(self, hidden = 1):
```

```
    ....
class PushButton(RectangularVisibleObject):
    def OnButton(self, event):
        pass
class CheckButton(RectangularVisibleObject):
    def OnButton(self, event):
        pass
    def SetCheckedState(self, check = 1):
        ....
```

Objects of class `PushButton` and class `CheckButton` would each have the common methods `MoveObject()` and `HideObject()`. Only objects of class `CheckButton` would have the `SetCheckedState()` method.

The `OnButton()` method is the method called when the button is pressed. It does nothing because the author of the class library cannot know what the button will ultimately do. To really use the button class, a programmer would derive another class from it and override the `OnButton()` method:

```
class MyPushButton(PushButton):
    def OnButton(self, event):
        print "I've been pushed!"

mybutton = MyPushButton()
```

The `mybutton` object still has all the data and methods that a push button normally has, but the `OnButton()` method has been replaced with a custom version. This is the typical use of any class library. The library is full of complicated premade classes. To use one, create your own class derived from a class in the library. Ignore almost everything about the class, but override a method or two and maybe add some more methods and data attributes. Now you have a customized class that acts just like the base class but has a few extra behaviors. You have reused existing code and customized a base class in a simple, straightforward fashion with a minimum of work. When all this works, OO is great!

Of course, OO has its problems too; it is possible to use the best OO techniques and wind up with a programming mess. OO only works well when the class structure is well designed to fit the problem at hand. The right design is hard to know when you start writing the program. After a few thousand lines of code are written, it becomes clearer what the design should have been, but it becomes harder to change the class structure. It is worthwhile to spend a little extra time in the program design phase to get a really good class structure in place at the start. When OO works, it leads naturally to code reuse and an elegant programming style, and changes are likely to be easier and more robust.

GUI Hello World in Tkinter

Now let's take a look at the inevitable "hello world" program, as written in Tkinter and WPY. Although both are class libraries, the classes and the manner in which events are handled are quite different. Here is the Tkinter version:

```
#! /usr/local/bin/python

from Tkinter import *

class Hello:
  def __init__(self, master):
    self.master = master
    canvas = self.canvas = Canvas(master, height="8c", width="16c")
    canvas.pack(side=TOP)
    canvas.create_text("0.5c", "0.5c", anchor=NW, text="Hello World")
    button = Button(master, text="Quit", command=self.quit_callback)
    button.pack(pady="0.3c", side=BOTTOM)
  def quit_callback(self):
    self.master.quit()

root = Tk()
root.title("Usual Hello World Demo")
hello = Hello(root)
root.mainloop()
```

There is one class `Hello` defined, which is instantiated with `master`, the Tk main window. This main window is the container for the other two Tkinter objects created, a `Canvas` and a `Button`. First the canvas is created with a height of 8 centimeters and a width of 16 centimeters. A canvas is a drawable surface, and its `create_text()` method is called to draw some words on it. The `anchor=NW` indicates that the coordinates refer to the northwest (upper-left) corner of the text. There are other methods available to draw rectangles, lines, circles, and so on. Once an object is drawn on a canvas, the Tkinter system will redraw it itself if necessary. In some other GUIs, the programmer would have to redraw the canvas if, for example, another window covering the canvas were removed.

Next a button is created with text **Quit** and a command `self.quit_call-back` to be called when the button is pressed. The `pady` value adds extra space around the button. The `quit_callback` command is then defined as a method of the class. In Tkinter, you decide which events, such as button presses, you care about and then you specify a function or method to be called when the event occurs. The result, of course, is that the application exits when the button is pressed.

The canvas `pack()` method is called to pack the canvas in the top of the main window, and the button `pack()` method packs the button in the bottom. This "packer" is a powerful Tk geometry manager. Instead of specifying the (x, y) coordinates of the canvas and button, we specify that the canvas goes at the top and the button goes at the bottom of the parent main window. There is no size specified for the main window, so it assumes the size of its contents. This makes layout of controls much easier.

The rest of the code is not within a class. The `Tk()` method creates a Tk main window and calls it `root`. The window title is set to the specified text, and an instance of class `Hello` is created, thus creating and packing the canvas and button. Finally, the `mainloop()` method is called. This starts the event loop, and no further code will be executed except for methods and functions called for events. The main frame with its canvas and button will now appear on the screen until it is dismissed with the **Quit** button.

GUI Hello World in WPY

WPY has classes for "application" and "document" and is generally a higher-level model than Tkinter. Here is the same program in WPY (see Figure 10.1 to see what it looks like when running on Windows 3.11):

```
#! /usr/local/bin/python

import wpy

class MyApp(wpy.CWinApp):
  def InitInstance(self):
    templ = wpy.CSingleDocTemplate(wpy.CDocument, wpy.CFrameWnd, MyView)
    templ.wpyText = "Usual Hello World Demo"
    self.AddDocTemplate(templ)
    self.FileNew()
```

```
    def OnButtonQuit(self, control):
        self.Exit()

class MyView(wpy.CScrollView):
    def OnCreate(self, event):
        b = wpy.CPushButton(self, "Quit")
        self.button = b
        b.Create()
        frame = self.wpyParent
        frame.wpySizeX = frame.wpyOneMeter * 16 / 100
        frame.wpySizeY = frame.wpyOneMeter * 8 / 100
        frame.MoveWindowSize()
    def OnSize(self, rect):
        self.button.WpyPlace(rect, 0.5, 0.8, "s")
    def OnDraw(self, DC):
        pad = DC.wpyOneMeter * 5 / 1000
        DC.DrawText("Hello World", pad, pad)

# Start the application, respond to events.
app = MyApp()
```

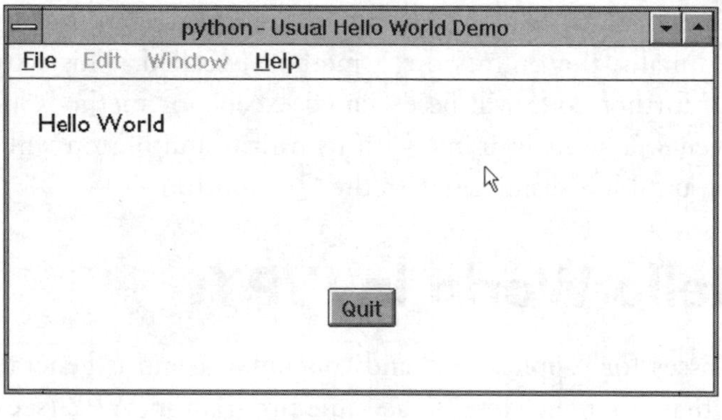

Figure 10.1 "Hello World in WPY.

Let's first look at class MyApp. A WPY program must always create an application object derived from class CWinApp. This object represents the whole application. It must have a method named InitInstance() that creates and registers a "document template" consisting of three classes. The three classes are the document, frame, and view classes for the application. A *document* represents the data in the application that would typically be written to disk. A *view* is the document as displayed in a window. The *frame* is the container of the view, which could also include a menu bar and status bar. A *window* on the screen consists of a frame and a view. For our simple program, we just use the standard document and frame classes CDocument and CFrameWnd, because their default behavior is adequate. But we must always make our own view class, because that class controls what is visible in the window. The last line of InitInstance() calls the application FileNew() method, which creates a new empty document and main window using the three classes we have specified.

Now let's look at the only other class, MyView. When a view object is first created, its OnCreate() method is called. Our version creates a push button with text **Quit**. Next it gets the frame object that is the parent of the view. It sets the frame size to 16 by 8 centimeters and calls the frame's MoveWindowSize() method to set the new frame size.

The OnSize() method is called after OnCreate() and whenever the window size changes. The rect argument gives the current size of the view. Our version places the button's South (lower-center) point at the relative coordinates x = 50%, y = 80% within the view. That is, it places the button at the lower center of the view. We could have done this in OnCreate(), but then the button would not be repositioned if the user changed the window size.

Finally, the OnDraw() method is called to draw the view. The DC argument is the *device context*, the object that receives the drawing commands. In our example, the DC is the view, but a DC can also represent a printer. Our version of OnDraw() just draws text 5 millimeters from the upper-left corner. In a normal MFC program, OnDraw() is called frequently and must be efficient, but WPY acts more like Tkinter, and drawn objects are redrawn by WPY. After the first call, OnDraw() will not be called again unless the programmer calls InvalidateRect() to mark the current view as invalid or the user prints the view, in which case OnDraw() is called with a printer device context.

Note that we have not specified a callback function for our button. Buttons have a default callback name equal to "OnButton" plus their text. In addition, WPY has command routing just like MFC, and the system will search the currently active view, document, frame, and application classes looking for our callback OnButtonQuit. This is a powerful feature, because callbacks can be located in the most convenient class. Our callback will be found in the MyApp class. When it is called, self will have the value of the MyApp instance, so we can call the application exit method. If we had the callback in the MyView class, self would have been the view instance, which might be convenient for mouse events.

The final line of the program actually makes an application object and causes the program to appear on the screen. Note that, except for this line, all code execution is in response to events.

Comparison of Tkinter and WPY

WPY provides its own application model, and programmers are expected to create application, document, frame, and view classes even for simple applications like our example. Tkinter provides no application model, but functions more like a visible-object maker and drawing toolkit. Users of Tkinter should design their own high-level application classes to suit the problem at hand.

In Tkinter, the programmer specifies a function to call for events of interest. WPY attempts to call fixed method names for system events, such as OnSize(), and default method names for controls such as buttons. WPY will search the classes looking for command handlers and will call the method with the appropriate self instance when one is found. If no handler is found, the base class handler is used, and this may have a nontrivial behavior. This makes WPY events more object-oriented.

Tkinter has the packer, a sophisticated geometry manager, and other geometry features. WPY has only the ability to place objects at fixed or relative (x, y) coordinates, so WPY requires layout functions to be written within OnSize().

Cultural aspects are as important as the technical comparison. Tkinter is based on Tk, which is based on the UNIX X Window system. Native Windows look and feel is not yet available, and even if provided, the programming model would not correspond to any Microsoft model. WPY is based on Microsoft's MFC, yet still runs on UNIX/X. Currently, we find that Tkinter is favored by UNIX programmers, and WPY is of interest mostly to PC programmers or those who require a native Windows 3.1 GUI.

An HTML Viewer

We now turn to a more realistic application, an HTML viewer. See Figure 10.2 for a look at the viewer running on Windows 3.11. This program will read in HTML from a file and display it on the screen. If the user clicks an anchor, the HREF (hypertext reference) will be shown in a dialog box. The extensions to really access the net are left as an exercise so we can concentrate on the GUI aspects of the problem. We will use WPY for the GUI. For a more detailed look at Tkinter, see *Programming Python* by Mark Lutz (published by O'Reilly & Associates, ISBN: 1-56592-197-6).

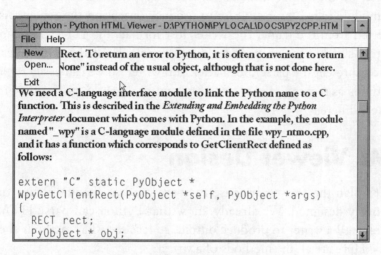

Figure 10.2 Our HTML viewer.

As we saw in Chapter 7, HTML stands for HyperText Markup Language, a platform-independent way to specify the look of documents on the World Wide Web and to connect documents together (with anchors). An HTML document consists of plain ASCII text plus markup tags that describe in a general way how the document should look. Tags usually occur in pairs: a start tag, some enclosed text, and an end tag. For example, this is a level one (big) heading:

```
<h1>This text is really big</h1>
```

There are markup tags for paragraphs, six levels of headings, ordered and unordered lists, preformatted text, horizontal rules, and more. The special anchor tag <a> provides a link to another document. For example, this anchor tag:

```
<a HREF="www.python.org">Python Software Activity</a>
```

will cause the words *Python Software Activity* to appear in blue on many World Wide Web browsers, and clicking the mouse on these words will load the document specified by the HREF value, www.python.org. It is remarkable that such a simple protocol is so generally useful and has provoked such a market frenzy.

Parsing HTML is not particularly difficult, but it is not particularly interesting either. Luckily, Python comes with an HTML parser module htmllib.py, a formatter for the output of the parser called (surprise!) formatter.py, and an output module called DumbWriter to produce output on the screen. As might be expected from the name, the writer just formats the HTML document as ASCII text suitable for output to a dumb terminal. All these modules define classes to represent the parser, formatter, and writer, so we can easily replace and add methods as required, but we need to replace DumbWriter with something completely different.

HTML Viewer Design

First let's plan the classes, because they are hard to change if they turn out to be poorly designed. We already know that Python can parse HTML and ultimately call a writer to produce output, so let's see what methods the writer supports. Here are all the methods of a writer:

```
class CWriter:
  def new_font(self, font):
    # Change the current font to the specified font.
  def new_margin(self, margin, level):
    # Change the current margin to the specified margin.
  def send_label_data(self, data):
    # Print a label such as "1." for a list item.
  def send_paragraph(self, blankline):
    # Finish display of a paragraph, and perhaps add blank lines.
  def send_line_break(self):
    # Break the current line.
  def send_hor_rule(self):
    # Draw a horizontal line.
  def send_literal_data(self, data):
    # Just display the text data without formatting.
  def send_flowing_data(self, data):
    # Form the text data into justified paragraphs and display.
  def new_spacing(self, spacing):
    # Change the current line spacing to the specified spacing.
  def new_styles(self, styles):
    # Change the style.
```

We can see that the writer class is remarkably simple because most of the work was done by the parser and formatter. The basic problem is to have a drawable window for output and the ability to create a few different fonts for headings. Most of the other methods, such as `send_line_break()` and `new_margin()`, just affect the position of the text on the screen. The only real problem is `send_flowing_data()`, which forms stretches of text into paragraphs by breaking lines at blanks when the line would otherwise exceed the window width.

Now let's pick our GUI classes. For the view class, we use `CScrollView`. This handy class provides a drawable surface with automatic scroll bars that appear and disappear as needed. Objects drawn to a `CScrollView` are redrawn by the WPY system when required, so we can just write an `OnDraw()` method that draws the whole document at once. These drawn objects are also class instances, so we can mark the ones that are anchors. That way, when the user clicks the mouse, WPY can search its drawn objects and return the one clicked (if any). If we marked that object as an anchor, we can process the HREF. We will use the `CFont` class to make the fonts to draw on the view.

There is nothing special about the frame, so we will use the stock `CFrameWnd` we used in the "Hello World" example. We do need a document class to represent the HTML document on disk. But we are not changing or interacting with the document, so the class is simple. The application class is mostly the same in any WPY app, so we can almost copy ours from "Hello World."

HTML Viewer GUI Classes
The Application Class

The GUI classes required by our viewer are application, document, frame, view, and menu. Here is the application class, together with the code at the top and bottom of the program:

```
#! /usr/local/bin/python

import wpy, wpycon
import htmllib, formatter, string
from types import *

class MyApp(wpy.CWinApp):
```

```
def InitInstance(self):
  templ = wpy.CSingleDocTemplate(MyDocument, wpy.CFrameWnd, MyView, MyMenu)
  templ.wpyText = "Python HTML Viewer"
  templ.wpyFilter = ("HTML docs [*.htm*]", ".htm*")
  self.AddDocTemplate(templ)
  self.FileNew()
def OnMenuHelpHelp(self, control):
  wpy.AfxMessageBox("This is a very simple html viewer.",
    wpycon.MB_OK | wpycon.MB_ICONINFORMATION)

#
# Other classes go here ....
#

# Start the application, respond to events.
app = MyApp()
```

First we import the WPY module, the HTML parser and formatter modules, and the standard string and types modules. The last line creates the application object as in our "Hello World" example. The application class is almost the same as in "Hello World." The application's `InitInstance()` method specifies the three required GUI classes `MyDocument`, `CFrameWnd`, and `MyView` for creating documents frames and views. The extra `MyMenu` class specifies a menu to use on the frame. The title is "Python HTML Viewer." The `wpyFilter` specifies a file filter to use when opening files for this application. This file filter will limit the initial file choices in the Open File dialog box to files that match the specified pattern. We want to present the user with files ending in .htm and .html, the standard file name extensions for HTML documents.

The `OnMenuHelpHelp()` method is called by one of our menu items; it just puts up a standard dialog box with the specified text. The WPY constants specify a dialog box with a single **OK** button and an informational style.

The Menu Class

A menu in WPY is a class, and the class name is recorded in the document template as shown earlier. Menus do not have any methods except for __init__(). WPY can make the usual menu items such as buttons, check items, radio items, dividing lines, and cascading or popup menus. There are also many prebuilt menu items for the usual **File/Open**, **File/Close**, and other common menu items that seem to part of most applications. Our menu has only **File** and **Help** items with a cascading menu under each. Here is the code:

```
class MyMenu(wpy.CMenu):
  def __init__(self):
    wpy.CMenu.__init__(self)
    file = wpy.MenuFile(self)
    help = wpy.MenuHelp(self)

    wpy.MenuFileNew(file)
    wpy.MenuFileOpen(file)
    wpy.MenuLine(file)
    wpy.MenuFileExit(file)

    wpy.CMenuButton(help, "Help")
    wpy.MenuLine(help)
    wpy.MenuHelpAbout(help)
```

First we call the __init__() method of the base class. Next we create the two items on our menu bar **File** and **Help**. We are using the standard classes MenuFile and MenuHelp for these, so we don't need to specify any text. The parent of these items is self (the menu) because they are top-level menu items.

Next we create a submenu under each top-level menu item. The **File** submenu has items **New**, **Open**, a line for separation, and **Exit**, each with a parent of file. All these are also standard built-in menu items, and they all have built-in handler methods, so we don't need to write our own.

The submenu for **Help** consists of the items **Help**, a line, and **About**. The **Help** submenu item is the only nonstandard menu item, so we must specify its text as **Help**. The handler method used by default is OnMenu plus the names of the menu items needed to reach the item, namely, **Help** from the top-level menu bar followed by **Help** from the submenu. As with buttons, WPY will search GUI classes looking for the handler OnMenuHelpHelp() which, as we saw, is located in the application class.

The Document Class

The document class is very simple because we are not changing or interacting with the document. It mostly just records the file name of the HTML document. Here is the code:

```
class MyDocument(wpy.CDocument):
  def DeleteContents(self):
    self.cur_file = None
  def OnOpenDocument(self, filename):
    self.DeleteContents()
    self.wpyFileName = filename
    self.cur_file = filename
    self.SetModifiedFlag(0)
    self.SetTitle(self.wpyParent.wpyText + " - " + filename)
```

The `DeleteContents()` method is required in any document class, and it is used to initialize the document to an empty state. Our version just records a filename of `None`. The `OnOpenDocument()` method is called with the file name to be opened as a result of the **File/Open** menu command. Recall that we used a default **File/Open** menu handler, and it calls this method. Our version calls `DeleteContents()`, records the file name, sets the "document is modified" flag to **FALSE**, and adds the file name to the title. We need to set the modified flag to **FALSE** so we do not get a "Do you want to save the document" dialog box when we attempt to close the document. Note that we do not need to write a **File/Open** method or many other methods because WPY (and MFC) has many of the usual application behaviors built in.

The View Class

Our view class actually has to do something, namely, parse and draw the document to the screen, so it is a little more complicated. Here it is:

```
class MyView(wpy.CScrollView):
  def OnCreate(self, event):
    frame = self.wpyParent
    frame.wpySizeX = frame.wpyScreenSizeX * 8 / 10
    frame.wpySizeY = frame.wpySizeX / 2
    frame.MoveWindowSize()
  def OnSize(self, event):
    #Re-parse the file if the window size changes
    self.InvalidateRect()
  def OnDraw(self, DC):
    doc = self.wpyDocument
    if not doc.cur_file:
      self.wpyVScrollSize = 0
      self.SetScrollSizes()
      return
```

```
    self.BeginWaitCursor()
    writer = CWriter(self, DC)
    fmt = formatter.AbstractFormatter(writer)
    parser = CParser(fmt)
    file = open(doc.cur_file)
    data = file.read()
    file.close()
    parser.feed(data)
    parser.close()
    self.EndWaitCursor()
    self.wpyVScrollSize = max(self.wpyVScrollSize, self.wpyScreenSizeY)
    self.SetScrollSizes()
  def OnLButtonDown(self, x, y, flags):
    (x0, y0) = self.GetDeviceScrollPosition()
    x = x + x0
    y = y + y0
    drawn = self.GetDrawnObject(x, y)
    if drawn and hasattr(drawn, "anchor"):
      print "anchor: ", drawn.anchor
```

The OnCreate() method just sets the frame size as in the "Hello World" example. We could omit this and the system would use its own default size. The OnSize() method calls InvalidateRect() to mark the view as invalid. This will cause our OnDraw() method to be called to redraw the view. The result is that if the user changes the window size, the HTML document will be reparsed and redrawn to fit the new size.

A view class must always have an OnDraw() method to access the document and draw its contents to the screen. First, if the document is empty (no file name) we set the view size to zero and call SetScrollSizes() to tell the automatic scroll logic our new size. If there is a document, we call BeginWaitCursor() to indicate a lengthy operation. Then we create the parser objects, the writer (our own version), a formatter object using the writer, and a parser object using the formatter. These objects are required by Python's htmllib module. Next we open the file, read its data, and close the file. We then pass the file data to the parser by using its feed() method. We then close the parser, end the wait cursor, and notify the scroll logic of our view's new size. This will cause a scroll bar to appear because we have used a minimum size equal to the screen size.

You may be wondering where the screen output went, because we don't seem to have drawn anything. It turns out that the writer object did the drawing.

When the writer was created, it was passed the view and the device context (DC) so that it could do the drawing itself.

Last, we have the OnLButtonDown() method, which is called when the user clicks the left mouse button. The (x, y) coordinates are the position of the mouse cursor in screen coordinates. Because our view might have been scrolled, we first transform to view coordinates using our scrolled position. Next we retrieve the drawn object (if any) at the mouse cursor position. Recall that when we draw an object such as text to a CScrollView, WPY will redraw the object as required. Here we see that WPY can also search for objects given their coordinates. We are trying to find out whether the user has clicked on a piece of text and whether it might be an anchor. The next line tests to see if an object was found, and if so, it looks to see if the object has an attribute named "anchor." Apparently we will need to create this attribute when we draw anchor text on the screen. Finally, if an anchor is found, we use a Python print statement to put up a dialog box showing the contents of the anchor. Note that using **print** is the easiest way to produce a dialog box in WPY.

HTML Viewer Parser Classes

Now that we have described the GUI classes, we turn to the parser classes. We only have two parser classes, CParser and CWriter. The third formatter class is contained in formatter.py and is used as is.

The Parser Class

You may have noticed that our list of methods for the writer class did not have methods to be called when an anchor is encountered. This is a problem because we want to print anchors in blue text, and we need to know when to turn the blue color on and off. Because the parser knows when it finds an anchor, we need to modify the parser. Here is the code:

```
class CParser(htmllib.HTMLParser):
  def anchor_bgn(self, href, name, type):
    htmllib.HTMLParser.anchor_bgn(self, href, name, type)
    self.formatter.writer.anchor_bgn(href, name, type)
  def anchor_end(self):
    htmllib.HTMLParser.anchor_end(self)
    self.formatter.writer.anchor_end()
```

Hopefully, this kind of change is now second nature. In object-oriented programming, we don't really modify the parser. We create our own parser class, which inherits most of its data attributes and methods from the Python HTML parser. Then we replace the anchor methods with our own versions. Our new anchor begin and end methods first call the base class method and then call the anchor begin and end methods in our writer. Everything happens the same as before except for the extra calls to our writer, and we didn't need to change—or even understand—the Python `htmllib` module.

The Writer Class

The writer is by far the largest class. It is responsible for keeping track of housekeeping data such as the fonts to use and the margin positions, as well as actually doing the drawing to the view. Because this class is somewhat lengthy, we will break it up into pieces. Here is the first piece:

```
class CWriter:
  def __init__(self, view, DC):
    self.view = view
    self.DC = DC
    self.anchor = None
    self.lineHeight = 0
    self.atbreak = 0
    f = self.font = wpy.CFont("roman").Create()
    self.fontDict = {None:f}
    DC.SelectObject(self.font)
    x, y = DC.GetTextExtent("W" * 20)
    x = (x + 19) / 20   # Largest character size
    self.font.sizex = x
    self.font.sizey = self.oldLineHeight = y
    self.indentSize = x * 3
    self.x = self.indent = self.baseIndent = x / 3
    self.y = 0
    self.width = DC.wpySizeX - x
  def anchor_bgn(self, href, name, type):
    if href:
      self.oldcolor = self.DC.SetTextColor((0, 0, 200))
      self.anchor = (href, name, type)
  def anchor_end(self):
    if self.anchor:
      self.DC.SetTextColor(self.oldcolor)
      self.anchor = None
```

The __init__() method is given the view and the device context so the writer can set the view size (for scroll purposes) and draw the output to the DC. We create a roman font to use as the default font and place it into a font dictionary with the key None. It turns out that the formatter uses a font of None to mean a default font. Some font metrics are then recorded, namely, the height of the font to use for line spacing and the width of an uppercase *W* to use for estimating line widths.

The basic indentation is set to one-third the width of *W*, and the amount of additional indentation for each level is set to three times the width of *W*. This is an example of device-independent layout. We must not specify these numbers as, for example, 30 pixels, because we don't know the resolution of the output device. It could be a screen (maybe 70 pixels per inch) or a printer (maybe 300 pixels per inch). By specifying distances in terms of a character size, the output will look more or less the same on any device.

The anchor begin and end methods are called when an anchor is encountered. If the anchor has an HREF (it is a link to another document), the anchor_bgn() method sets the text color to blue and records the old text color. It also sets the anchor attribute of the writer. The anchor_end() method sets the color back to the old color and sets the anchor attribute to None to indicate that we are not in an anchor.

```
#class CWriter:  continued ...
  FontSizeDict = {"h1":48, "h2":36, "h3":24, "h4":20, "h5":18, "h6":16}
  def new_font(self, font):
    # font is None, or the tuple (size, i, b, tt)
    if self.font == font:
      return
    try:
    if self.fontDict.has_key(font):
      self.font = self.fontDict[font]
      self.DC.SelectObject(self.font)
    else:
      size = font[0]
      try:
        height = self.FontSizeDict[size]
      except KeyError:
        height = 0
      if font[3]:
        family = "modern"
      elif size[0] == "h":
        family = "swiss"
      else:
```

```
    family = "roman"
  if font[1]:        # Italic indicator
    family = family + "-italic"
  if font[2]:        # Bold indicator
    weight = wpycon.FW_BOLD
  else:
    weight = wpycon.FW_NORMAL
  f = self.font = wpy.CFont(family, height, weight).Create()
  self.DC.SelectObject(f)
  x, f.sizey = self.DC.GetTextExtent("W" * 20)
  f.sizex = (x + 19) / 20   # Largest character size
  self.fontDict[font] = f
```

The next method, new_font(), is called by the formatter to change the font. The specified font is either None for the default font or a tuple giving the size (a string such as "h1"), a flag for italic, a flag for bold, and a flag for a typewriter text (fixed-width) font. Because tuples can be used as keys in a dictionary, our strategy is to make fonts as required and save them in a font dictionary. When a font request comes in, we look in our dictionary and re-use the font if it exists. Otherwise we make the font.

Take a look at new_font(). First we see if the requested font equals the current font, and if so, we return. Next we see if the requested font is in our font dictionary. If so, we select the font with SelectObject() and return. Otherwise we need to make a new font.

To make a new font we need its family, size, and weight. The family is the string "roman" (a serif typeface), "swiss" (a sans serif typeface), or "modern" (a fixed-width font) plus an optional "-italic" for italic. The size is zero for a default size or the size in points. Weight is one of the weight constants in wpycon such as FW_NORMAL or FW_BOLD. The logic just looks at the requested font data and creates these values. The only trick is that the requested size is a string, so we need FontSizeDict to convert this string to the desired size. We then make the font, select the font for the output device, create the font size information as we did in __init__(), and enter the font into our font dictionary.

```
#class CWriter:  continued ...
  def new_margin(self, margin, level):
    self.send_line_break()
    self.indent = self.x = self.baseIndent + self.indentSize * level
  def new_spacing(self, spacing):
    pass
  def new_styles(self, styles):
```

```
      pass
  def send_label_data(self, data):
    if data == "*":      # default bullet
      w = self.font.sizex * 7 / 10
      x = self.indent - w - w * 4 / 10
      y = self.y - w + self.font.sizex
      self.DC.Rectangle(x, y, w, w)
    else:
      w, h = self.DC.GetTextExtent(data)
      x = self.indent - w - self.font.sizex / 3
      if x < 0:
        x = 0
      self.DC.DrawText(data, x, self.y)
  def send_paragraph(self, blankline):
    self.send_line_break()
    self.y = self.y + self.oldLineHeight * blankline
    self.view.wpyVScrollSize = self.y + 50
  def send_line_break(self):
    if self.lineHeight:
      self.y = self.y + self.lineHeight
      self.oldLineHeight = self.lineHeight
      self.lineHeight = 0
      self.view.wpyVScrollSize = self.y + 50
    self.x = self.indent
    self.atbreak = 0
```

These four methods perform relatively simple formatting tasks. The new_margin() method requests a new margin level (0, 1, 2, ...). The code breaks the current line (if any) and sets the indent to the basic indent plus the level times the indent amount. The new_spacing() and new_styles() methods do nothing and are left as an exercise. The send_label_data() method is used to draw a label for a list item. The data is either the label text such as "1.", "2.", or "*" to indicate an unordered list. If the data is "*", we draw a square with a size determined by the current font size; otherwise we draw the label as is. The label is drawn to the left of the current indent. The send_paragraph() method ends the current paragraph. It breaks the current line and adds some optional blank lines whose height is equal to the most recently used line height. It also sets the view height (for scroll purposes). The send_line_break() method is used to break the current line. It first tests to see if there is a current line (whether the current line has a height). If so, it updates the y position, records the most recent line height, resets the height, and updates the view size. Then it sets the x position to the indent and resets the atbreak flag. We add 50 pixels to the size of the view to provide a little margin at the bottom.

```
#class CWriter: continued ...
  def send_hor_rule(self):
    self.send_line_break()
    self.y = self.y + self.oldLineHeight
    border = self.font.sizex
    pen = wpy.CPen(3, (0, 0, 0)).Create()
    oldpen = self.DC.SelectObject(pen)
    self.DC.MoveTo(border, self.y)
    self.DC.LineTo(self.width - border, self.y)
    self.y = self.y + self.oldLineHeight
    self.DC.SelectObject(oldpen)
    self.view.wpyVScrollSize = self.y + 50
  def send_literal_data(self, data):
    if not data:
      return
    lines = string.splitfields(data, '\n')
    text = string.expandtabs(lines[0])
    for l in lines[1:]:
      self.OutputLine(text, 1)
      text = string.expandtabs(l)
    self.OutputLine(text, 0)
    self.atbreak = 0
```

The `send_hor_rule()` method is called to draw a dividing line across the view. We first break the current line and space downward by the most recent line height. We create a new `CPen` (a drawing tool) with a width of three pixels and a black color. We use `SelectObject()` to select this pen, and we remember the old pen so we can restore it when we are done. Next we move to the start position and draw to the end position. Last, we add more vertical space and restore the old pen.

The `send_literal_data()` method is called for text meant to be displayed without being formatted into justified paragraphs. The text is broken apart into lines with `string.splitfields(data, '\n')`, and any tabs are replaced with blanks. Finally the lines are printed with `OutputLine()`. The last line does not have a line break unless it ends with a newline character.

```
#class CWriter: continued ...
  def send_flowing_data(self, data):
    if not data:
      return
    atbreak = self.atbreak or data[0] in string.whitespace
    text = ""
    pixels = chars = 0
```

```
for word in string.split(data):
  bword = " " + word# blank + word
  length = len(bword)
  # The current line is "text" and its size is
  #    "pixels" pixels plus "chars" characters.
  if not atbreak:
    text = word
    chars = chars + length - 1
  elif self.x + pixels + (chars + length) * self.font.sizex < self.width:
    # Word fits easily on current line.
    text = text + bword
    chars = chars + length
  else:
    w, h = self.DC.GetTextExtent(text + bword)
    if self.x + w < self.width:
      # Word fits.
      text = text + bword
      pixels = w
      chars = 0
    else:
      # Word does not fit.  Output current line.
      self.OutputLine(text, 1)
      text = word
      chars = length - 1
      pixels = 0
    atbreak = 1
  self.OutputLine(text, 0)
  self.atbreak = data[-1] in string.whitespace
```

The send_flowing_data() method is responsible for formatting text into paragraphs by providing line breaks when the text would extend past the right-hand edge of the view. Roughly speaking, it breaks the text into words (at blanks) and keeps adding them to the current line until the line is at its maximum width. Then it outputs the current line and starts a new one. But there are some complications because HTML may change fonts in the middle of a word, thus causing send_flowing_data() to be called for each half. And there are some tricks for efficiency.

The atbreak flag tells us whether or not we are at a word break. A *word break* means we are at a blank between words or at the start of a new line. This flag must be saved between calls to send_flowing_data(). Other methods, such as send_line_break(), may set or unset this flag. If atbreak is false, we are within a word.

We will need to measure the length of the current line to see if it fits within the view. We could call `GetTextExtent()` to return the line size, but this is expensive. Instead, our strategy is to estimate the current line length as the length in pixels we obtained from the last call to `GetTextExtent()`, plus the number of characters we added since then, times the size of W (a large character). The pixel size is zero for a new line, so the estimated size is initially based on the number of characters. Eventually the line will seem to be too large (because we are overestimating its length) so we will need to call `GetTextExtent()` to get the actual length. When we do, this length becomes the length in pixels, and the character count goes to zero. Then we proceed with this better estimate.

Now let's look at the code for `send_flowing_data()` in detail. First, we return if there is no text. Then we set the all-important `atbreak` equal to its current value, or **TRUE** if the data starts with a blank. The current line is `text` with a size of zero pixels and zero characters. We break up the data into words with `string.split()` and loop over the words. Because our words no longer include blanks, we must add back blanks as required. Our first test `if not atbreak` adds the word to the current line if we are not at a break, that is, if we are within a word. Unfortunately, this can cause the word to extend past the right edge, but there seems to be no easy fix. Otherwise, we test to see if the current line size estimate plus the word size fits in the view. If so, we add the word to the line and update the character count. Otherwise, we must measure the exact size of the line plus word with `GetTextExtent()`. If it fits, we add the word to the line and update the line size to the measured pixel size and zero extra characters. Otherwise, we output the current line, make the current line the word, and update the line size to zero pixels and the word length characters.

In all cases, we set `atbreak` to **TRUE** after the first word because we broke the data at white space. But before we return, we set `atbreak` to **FALSE** if the data does not end in white space. If there is a partial line remaining, we print it with `OutputLine()`, but we do not break this line.

```
#class CWriter:  continued ...
  def OutputLine(self, text, linebreak = 0):
    if text:
      o = self.DC.DrawText(text, self.x, self.y)
      if self.anchor:
        o.anchor = self.anchor
```

```
    self.lineHeight = max(self.lineHeight, o.wpySizeY)
    self.x = self.x + o.wpySizeX
if linebreak:
    self.send_line_break()
```

The last method is `OutputLine()`, which will draw the line on the view and optionally break the line. First we draw the text with `DrawText()` and obtain a drawn object corresponding to the text. If we are within an anchor (`self.anchor` is **TRUE**), we create an anchor attribute for the drawn object with a value equal to our anchor data. This will tag the text as anchor text. Next, we update the line height as the largest font height used on the line and update the x position. If `linebreak` is **TRUE**, we break the line.

Summary

In this chapter, we described how Python's object-oriented features make it a convenient language for implementing a graphical user interface. Several class libraries are available for this purpose, and we presented a simple "Hello World" example written using two of them, Tkinter and WPY. A comparison of these examples showed how the available classes and events are different for various GUI models. Because a GUI must be written using object-oriented techniques, we presented a crash course on objects with concrete examples drawn from GUI design.

Next we presented a useful working program, an HTML viewer written using WPY. After a quick review of HTML and a look at Python's `htmllib` parser and formatter, we described in detail the `CWriter` class used to display the parsed HTML and the GUI classes of the viewer. The techniques shown are applicable to a wide class of text formatting and display problems. The interested reader can add network access easily to the HTML viewer (using other Python modules) to make a simple Web browser.

GUIs are not the only programs that are event-driven instead of having straight line logic. Most client-server programs are also event-driven. Python programs that use object-oriented methods work well for many types of event-driven applications.

CHAPTER ELEVEN

EXTENDING PYTHON

This chapter describes how to extend Python with additional built-in methods and types. The extension methods described here can be used to add new basic functionality to Python, or to link Python with external libraries. This chapter serves as an introduction to writing Python extensions, with detailed examples, but it does not intend to replace the standard extensions reference manual of the Python distribution, or the documentation given in the header files, for example, in `abstract.h`. Extension programmers will need to consult these resources in addition to this chapter.

The possible uses for C extensions to Python are limitless. For example, suppose you have applications that use a linear programming library (or a database library, or a text/retrieval system, and so forth) and you wish to give these applications a Web/CGI interface. By interfacing the applications and the library to Python you can create a very powerful tool for rapidly developing CGI programs without the need to write any additional compiled code for each program.

Extending Python is easy, so easy in fact that playing with Python extensions might be an excellent way to learn the C programming language, in particular because a Python/C extension can use Python to handle all input/output considerations (which are extremely tedious and unpleasant implemented directly in C) while the new C language code focuses on implementing algorithms.

Sadly, the topic learning C via Python extensions must wait for some future book. For the present, we will suppose that readers of this chapter are familiar with the C programming language. Although we will not attempt to explain the C programming language or the constructs used in the C program fragments presented below, we will attempt to make our C code painfully readable, and we apologize to expert C programmers who may find this irritating.

On Reading the Python Source: New Names and Old Names

One of the best ways to learn how to extend Python (or how to program in C generally speaking) is by reading and studying examples from the Python source tree and from the Python contributed libraries. One common phrase among the Python community is *Use the Source, Luke*. (And never forget that the source is freely available for reference and even for modification by the truly adventurous.) There is one difficulty, however: The Python source can be confusing because it seems to use two different naming conventions; but it really doesn't.

In the bad old days, Python used a lot of names at the process global level (like `object` and `dictinsert`) that were highly likely to interfere with names from other software packages. This has largely been fixed (although at the present writing, Python 1.3 still has some unfixed names). Now, for example, the old name `dictinsert` has been replaced by the new name `PyDict_SetItemString`, which is more typing, but far less likely to interfere with a name from some other software library, and also more self-documenting.

However, because Python already had an extensive embedded base of users and developers, many of which had their own special purpose Python extensions at the time of the renaming, the old names could not be discarded. Instead the Python source distribution uses the C preprocessor to replace old names with new names in modules that still use the old names, such as many of the standard modules in the Modules directory of the source distribution. The magic header file that affects the renaming is given in the location `Include/rename2.h`. For example, the `rename2.h` file includes the substitution

```
#define dictinsert PyDict_SetItemString
```

to allow modules that use the old `dictinsert` name to compile without modification.

All new modules should use the new naming convention, as we will in the following sections, but to find additional example coding techniques it may be useful to consult Python source modules that use the old naming conventions. In this case, the programmer may need to refer to `rename2.h` in order to translate the old names to new names.

Motivation for Our Extension

The extension module we will describe as follows implements a new Python type that looks something like a hybrid of a string and a file, and which allows the efficient construction and extraction of large sequences of unformated binary data. In particular, we define a `BStream` (byte stream) type that contains a sequence of bytes that may be appended using a write method and extracted using a read method.

```
>>> from bstream import BStream
>>> B = BStream("Hello")
>>> B.write(" World")
>>> B.read(5)
'Hello'
>>> B.to_string()
' World'
```

Note that a read from a `BStream` eliminates the data read.

The reason the new `BStream` type is (arguably) an efficient way to handle byte streams is that the internal implementation is designed to avoid moving data by maintaining an internal buffer that can be up to half empty (or in some cases even more). Thus, writes to the end of the BStream buffer are likely to fit into free space already available in the buffer, and reads from the front of the buffer will usually create extra free space in the buffer, without causing the remaining data in the buffer to be moved. Because `BStream` objects recopy the current data in the object ``exponentially infrequently'', reads and writes to a `BStream` should be fast, on average.

Diagrammatically a BStream object containing the bytes "meaningful data" might have an internal representation that looks like this:

```
bstreamobject:
-------------------------
|(standard python header)|
-------------------------
| valid_start: 8         |
-------------------------
| valid_length: 23       |
-------------------------
| real_length: 32        |
-------------------------
| data ------------------------->"garbage meaningful data garbage "
-------------------------                1         2         3
                   Index ruler:  01234567890123456789012345678901
```

Here the data buffer has 15 bytes of "real" data stored from index 8 up to (but not including) index 23, and the remaining indices (from 0 to 7 and from 23 to 31) are unused areas of the data buffer. Furthermore the 9 free bytes at the end of the buffer may be filled by some future write without the need to shift bytes or resize the data buffer.

With a little cleverness it is possible to use the basic Python types to obtain similar performance characteristics to those provided by BStream objects, but, for example, applications that manipulate large image representations, might find BStreams very convenient, so we proceed with the implementation.

A User's View of Our Extension Module

As mentioned, the Python programmer may view a BStream as a hybrid of a file and a string.

BStream objects are created via the built-in method BStream() which supports a number of calling sequences.

```
>>> from bstream import BStream
>>> big = BStream(10000) # make empty BStream, presized for 10000 bytes
>>> big.to_string()
```

```
''
>>> small = BStream("a little data") # make a BStream copying all of a string.
>>> small.to_string()
'a little data'
>>> tiny = BStream("a little data", 4) # make from string slicing from 4.
>>> tiny.to_string()
'ttle data'
>>> itty_bitty = BStream("a little data", 4, 6) # slice from 4 to 6
>>> itty_bitty.to_string()
'tt'
```

As shown, a BStream may be presized for a given amount of data via BStream(int)—in the example BStream(10000) prepares a BStream that will not need to resize until after 10,000 bytes have been written into the buffer. BStreams may also be initialized from strings, by copying the entire string via BStream(string) or copying the string from the given index via BStream(string, start_index) or copying the string from the given start index to the given end index via BStream(string, start_index, end_index). Just as BStreams may be created by copying strings they may be created by copying other BStreams also:

```
>>> itty2 = BStream(small, 4, 7)
>>> itty2.to_string()
'ttl'
```

Once a BStream B has been created, it has a number of associated methods: B.to_string(...) to convert a BStream to a string, str(B) also converts a BStream to a string, B.read(...) to read from the front of the buffer (returning a string and ``erasing'' the read data), B.write(...) to write to the back of the buffer, len(B) to determine the length of the buffer, B+B2 to create a new BStream catenating the contents of B with the other BStream B2, B[index] to get one character from the buffer, and B[start_index: end_index] to slice the contents of the BStream (generating a new BStream and supporting the standard slicing conventions).

The length, indexing, catenation, and slicing operations are all familiar from the user's perspective, so we will not explain them again now. Instead we focus on the more interesting read, write, and to_string methods.

The read, write, and to_string methods all accept several calling sequences. The read method is similar to the file.read method in that it supports an optional integer argument that defines the maximum size of the data to be read. If the argument is omitted, all of the data is read.

```
>>> B = BStream("Guy L. Steele, Jr.")
>>> B.read(5)
'Guy L'
>>> B.read()
'. Steele, Jr.'
>>> len(B)
0
```

The "basic" calling sequences for `to_string` and) are `B.to_string()` and `B.write(bstream_or_string)`, respectively, but these methods also support two additional integer arguments. In the case of `to_string`, the first integer, if provided, represents the index at which to begin the string conversion, and the other represents the index at which to end the conversion

```
>>> B = BStream("The little fishes of the sea, they sent an answer back to
me")
>>> B.to_string()
'The little fishes of the sea, they sent an answer back to me'
>>> B.to_string(11)
'fishes of the sea, they sent an answer back to me'
>>> B.to_string(11,17)
'fishes'
```

In the case of the `write` method, the second optional argument indicates the index at which to start copying the first argument, and the last indicates where to stop copying, respectively:

```
>>> B2 = BStream("data: ")
>>> B2.write(B, 11, 17)
>>> B2.to_string()
'data: fishes'
>>> B2.write(B, 20)
>>> B2.to_string()
'data: fishes the sea, they sent an answer back to me'
```

The first (and required) argument to `write` may be either a string or another `BStream` (or even the same `BStream`, which possibly made the correct implementation of the `write` method a tad subtle).

Just for Debugging

The following module also provides debugging tools which may be disabled at compile time. With debugging enabled for the module the user may toggle debug printing by calling the debug() method.

```
>>> debug()
>>> test = BStream("a test")
BStream( ... )
BStream: not presized; attempting sliced calling sequence...
empty_bstream(0)
newbuffer(0, 1936990761)
newbuffer: trying to allocate 32
newbuffer: exiting successfully
empty_bstream exiting successfully
bst.write(...)
bst.write(X), copy entire structure
adjust_slice [0 : 6] (0, 6)
adjusted slice = [ 0 : 6 ]
bst.write: congratulations, X is a string
Check_bstream(1189128, 6)
Check_bstream: no modification needed
bst.write: now copying...
copyintobuffer(1189208, 0, 1251876, 0, 6)
bst.write: Successful completion
BStream: successful completion
del <Bstream 1188888> (bstream_dealloc)
>>> debug()
>>> test = BStream("a test")
```

This feature provides an aid to developing or modifying the module, but is not intended to be exposed to real users of the module. The debug method (and all the debug printing code) can be ``erased'' by the C preprocessor by undefining the BSTREAMDEBUG preprocessor flag.

What You Can't Do with a BStream

BStreams are not exactly like strings, even though they have many similarities. In particular, they do not support repetition and they do not provide a meaningful comparison function. The reason these operations are omitted is that

BStreams are meant to be large and it didn't seem reasonable to either repeat or compare such large objects.

BStreams are also not exactly like files. In particular the semantics of the read and write functions are quite different, because it is not possible to write into the middle of a BStream, and because the read operation discards the read data from the internal buffer. Furthermore, BStreams do not support the many other methods supported by file objects, and of course, BStreams have no persistent storage whereas files generally do.

The General Form of an Extension Module

A Python extension module source file generally defines one module, and usually follows a highly standard format. Here we give a very high level view of our C source file bstreammodule.c for the bstream extension module:

```
... HEADER COMMENTS HERE ...
/* include the standard python headers */
#include "Python.h"
... DEBUGGING CODE HERE ...
... C LANGUAGE TYPE DECLARATIONS HERE ...
... TYPE OBJECT FORWARD DECLARATIONS AND TYPE TEST MACROS HERE (IF ANY) ...
... DEFINE INTERNAL UTILITY ROUTINES HERE ...
... PYTHON TYPE METHODS AND TYPEOBJECT STRUCTURE DECLARATIONS HERE ...
... DEFINE MODULE METHODS HERE ...

/* MODULE METHODS STRUCTURE */
static struct PyMethodDef bstr_module_methods[] = {
 /* Function name,     C Language Implementation,  flag (always 1) */
  {"BStream",          (PyCFunction)makeBStream,     1},
#ifdef BSTREAMDEBUG
  /* include the debug method only if debugging is enabled */
  {"debug",            (PyCFunction)bstrdebug,       1},
#endif
  {NULL, NULL}    /* sentinel */
};

/* THE MODULE INITIALIZATION FUNCTION */
```

```
void
initbstream()
{
  Py_InitModule("bstream", bstr_module_methods);
}
```

We will discuss the omitted code fragments presently (except for the header comments), but a few bits of code have not been omitted from this outline, we discuss those now.

The `Python.h` header file declares all functions, constants, and other objects the module may need to communicate with the Python-run time system. This header file is physically located in the Include directory of the Python source distribution.

The final `initbstream()` C function is the entry point that Python uses to create and initialize the extension module. Every Python extension module must define such an init function at the global level. The init function must always call the `Py_InitModule` routine in order to register the Python built- in functions defined in the module using a `PyMethodDef` array structure similar to the `bstr_module_methods` structure given above. A `PyMethodDef` is a structure that provides a Python name string to use as the name for each function, a C function that defines the implementation of the function, and a flag which for the present should always be 1 (for archaic modules it is sometimes 0, and in the future it may be 2 or 3 for all we know)—this flag indicates that Python should use the ``new'' calling sequence conventions for the function. For example, the entry

```
  {"BStream",           (PyCFunction)makeBStream,     1},
```

indicates that the `bstream` module should include the function `BStream`, implemented by the C function `makeBStream`, using the new calling sequence conventions. In the example, we also provide another entry for the ``debug'' function, which is erased by the preprocessor unless `BSTREAMDEBUG` is defined. The final entry of the `PyMethodDef` array must always be

```
  { NULL, NULL }  /* sentinel */
```

because `Py_InitModule` uses these values to detect the end of the array.

Compiling and Linking the Module

For the moment let's suppose we have filled in the blanks above and have a complete Python module that we wish to use. In order for Python to use the module, it must load the functions used by the module and ``find'' the module initialization function. Detailed compilation and linkage issues across the many platforms that Python supports cannot be exhaustively explained in this book, and even if they were explained in this book the material would most likely soon be out of date. Here we will give some hints and examples, but we must defer to the Python distribution, particularly the standard extension reference, the README, and the platform-specific source directories (such as Mac and Nt), for more detailed and up-to-date information on the build procedures and tricks specific to each given platform.

Generally, the compilation of an extension module must use the standard Python include files. The loading or linking of an extension module may also require the Python libraries or object files. Furthermore, Python must execute the module initialization function in order to use an extension module. For dynamically linked modules the Python interpreter will locate the initialization function automatically (by looking for a dynamic library named bstreammodule containing a function called initbstream()—note that the exact names for the library and the initialization function are important in this case—Python will not find them if they are named differently).

For statically linked modules the module initialization function must be declared in the config.c source file and listed in the inittab structure of the config.c source file. In many cases the Python build procedure will create the config.c file with the new module built in, together with an appropriate Makefile automatically, but in other cases the config.c file must be modified ``by hand,'' as described below.

Dynamically Linking an Extension Module to Python

One way to connect the module to Python is to create a dynamically linked library residing in a directory on the Python Path. Python will detect and load such shared libraries automatically when they are needed. The following Makefile constructs a shared library bstreammodule.so from the source bstreammodule.c:

```
# Makefile for building a shared library containing
# the bstream module.  Configured for Solaris using gcc
# and local paths.

CC=gcc -DSOLARIS -Wall

# the src and bld directories for include files and libraries
blddir=              /usr/local/lib/python/lib
srcdir=              /usr/local/include/Py
objdir=              /big/arw/Python-1.3/Objects

# Compiler flags
OPT=           -g
INCLUDES=      -I$(srcdir) -I$(blddir)
DEFINES=       -DHAVE_CONFIG_H
CFLAGS=        $(OPT) $(DEFINES) $(INCLUDES)

all:           bstreammodule.so

bstreammodule.o:      bstreammodule.c
          $(CC) $(CFLAGS) -c bstreammodule.c

bstreammodule.so:     bstreammodule.o
          $(LD) -G bstreammodule.o $(objdir)/abstract.o\
                -o bstreammodule.so
```

Note that our shared library included the object file for the Python abstract object interface, `abstract.o`, because some functions we use from `abstract.c` are not used in the rest of Python (and hence not statically linked to the executable).

Now the `bstreammodule.so` file must be placed in a directory on the Python path for Python programs that will use the `bstream` module. In the search for the module `bstream` when the Python interpreter locates `bstreammodule.so` on the Python path, it will link the dynamic library to the executable process and then locate and execute the initialization function `initbstream()` to create the `bstream` module.

Statically Linking an Extension Module into Python

Another way to connect the module to Python is to rebuild all of Python with the new module compiled in. The easiest way to do this rebuild is to place the new module in the Modules directory of the Python source tree, add an entry for the module in the Modules/Setup file, and globally rebuild Python. For sites with a make utility that support the VPATH feature this automatic rebuild procedure can be effected using local directories that ``shadow" the Python source tree. In some cases, however, it may be necessary to configure and build the Python interpreter by hand with the new module included in the configuration, but even this procedure is straightforward.

Rebuilding from the Modules Source Directory

Rebuilding Python with a new module is extremely easy if you have your own copy of the Python source tree under UNIX, in this case edit the file Modules/Setup (which was generated automatically by the configure script) to reference the module. In our case, we add the lines

```
# my example extension module
bstream bstreammodule.c
```

to the Setup file, and then run make at the top of the source tree to generate a new Python interpreter with the bstream module built in. The rebuild will automatically create a config.c source file that includes the initbstream initialization function, as well as a Makefile that will automatically compile bstreammodule.c and link the resulting object with the interpreter.

In the more general case a new built-in module may reference libraries unknown to the Python distribution. In this case the entry in Modules/Setup must reference any required libraries for the module, for example, like the curses module line

```
curses cursesmodule.c -lcurses -ltermcap
```

which results in a search or the curses and the termcap libraries during the Python build. Furthermore if the module requires header files from directories unknown to the Python distribution then those header files must be listed on the Modules/Setup entry as well, as is done in the standard gdbm entry:

```
gdbm gdbmmodule.c -I/usr/local/include -L/usr/local/lib -lgdbm
```

which causes /usr/local/include to be used as a header file directory during the compile of gdbmmodule.c.

Using View Paths

If you wish to build multiple copies of the Python interpreter with different configurations, or if you don't wish to globally modify the Python source tree, then there are two options: use view paths or build Python by hand.

If you have a make tool that supports the VPATH (``view path'') feature, then consider using view paths. Using view paths each different directory trees can ``shadow'' the global source distribution in order to allow builds of different instances of the Python interpreter with different local configurations. In particular, if we decide to use the $LOCAL directory for testing our bstream module we may run the configure script at the directory $LOCAL to initialize a ``shadow'' tree for the Python source tree and then place the bstreammodule.c.) source file in $LOCAL/Modules and edit the $LOCAL/Modules/Setup file to add a reference to bstreammodule.c as described above. Now a make at LOCAL will build a Python interpreter in the directory $LOCAL including bstreammodule.c but using the global source tree for all other parts of the interpreter.

Please see the Python distribution README file for the latest information on using view paths.

If you do not or cannot use the VPATH feature, then you can build a new interpreter manually using your own Makefile, as described below.

Manual Build

Do not panic; this too is easy (but perhaps not extremely easy). To build a new Python interpreter program containing the new module, you must compile the module and create and compile a config.c file that lists the entry point for the module. These then must be compiled and linked with the Python main program in Modules/main.c, the Python path function in Modules/getpythonpath.c, and the standard Python libraries, which under UNIX are Modules/libModules.a, Python/libPython.a, Objects/libObjects.a, and Parser/libParser.a. The following is a makefile which does this compilation for the bstreammodule.c module under Solaris using the gcc compiler, building the target MyPython:

```
# Makefile for building a special Python interpreter containing
# the bstream module.  Uses a local config.c.
# Uses gcc under Solaris 2.
CC=gcc -DSOLARIS -Wall

# the src and bld directories for include files and libraries
blddir=         /usr/local/lib/python/lib
srcdir=         /usr/local/include/Py

# Compiler flags
OPT=            -g
INCLUDES=       -I$(srcdir) -I$(blddir)
DEFINES=        -DHAVE_CONFIG_H
CFLAGS=         $(OPT) $(DEFINES) $(INCLUDES)

# Libraries (must be in this order!)
MYLIBS=         $(blddir)/libModules.a \
                $(blddir)/libPython.a \
                $(blddir)/libObjects.a \
                $(blddir)/libParser.a

# MODLIBS, LIBS and SYSLIBS that match $(blddir)/Modules/Makefile
MODLIBS=        $(LOCALMODLIBS) $(BASEMODLIBS)
LIBS=           -lsocket -lnsl -ldl
SYSLIBS=        -lm -lc
ALLLIBS=        $(MYLIBS) $(MODLIBS) $(LIBS) $(SYSLIBS)
ADDITIONAL=     $(blddir)/main.o config.o getpath.o bstreammodule.o

all:        MyPython

MyPython:       bstreammodule.o config.o getpath.o
                $(CC) $(ADDITIONAL) $(ALLLIBS) -o MyPython

bstreammodule.o: bstreammodule.c
                $(CC) $(CFLAGS) -c bstreammodule.c

config.o:       config.c
                $(CC) $(CFLAGS) -c config.c

getpath.o:
                $(CC) $(CFLAGS) -c $(blddir)/getpath.c -o getpath.o
```

NOTE Some or all of the absolute paths in this Makefile may have to be altered for your installation.

As mentioned, the `config.c` source file used by thepreceding `Makefile` must list the initialization function for the `bstream` module. We created an appropriate `config.c` file manually by copying the generated `config.c` file from `Modules/config.c` and adding the following lines:

```
...
/* ADDED BY HAND: external declaration for the entry point */
extern void initbstream(); /* inserted */
...
struct {
      char *name;
      void (*initfunc)();
} inittab[] = {
...
/* ADDED BY HAND: inittab line for the entry point */
      {"bstream", initbstream}, /* inserted */
...
      {0, 0}
};
```

The `config.c` source file is the only file that needs to be modified by hand, and only the lines marked as inserted need to be added. The `getpath.c` file must be compiled in the local directory, but it need not be modified.

Now the Details of the Extension Implementation

We now delve into the details of the implementation of the `bstream` module by examining the code of `bstreammodule.c`. We will follow a conceptual top-down approach to explaining the module (which translates roughly into reading the actual text of the C source from the bottom up). We begin by examining the implementations for the built-in functions of the module, and proceed to present deeper details of the module as they arise. Thus, for example, we will refer to the function `bstreamwrite` before it is defined and present its definition after introducing structures and functions that follow the `bstreamwrite` definition in the actual `bstreammodule.c` source file.

Implementing Functions in an Extension Module

A Python extension module generally contains functions and (sometimes) constants. This section will discuss the definition of functions in an extension module. Please refer to `Modules/mathmodule.c` for an example of how to create constants (but since `mathmodule.c` uses old naming conventions, also consult `rename.h` to translate the old names to new names). In the present case, the `bstream` module defines only one "real" function, `BStream()`, and another ``fake'' function for debugging `debug()`. Let's examine the implementation of `BStream()` after a short discussion of the general properties of extension functions.

Built-in functions declared in C always have the same calling sequence. This calling sequence, as we shall see, is identical to the calling sequence for methods to built-in types. The standard C declaration for a built-in function always looks like:

```
static PyObject *
builtin_function(self, args)
   PyObject *self;
   PyObject *args;
{
   ... Actions of the function here ...
}
```

The (equivalent) ANSI C declaration looks like:

```
static PyObject *
builtin_function(PyObject *self, PyObject *args)
{
   ... Actions of the function here ...
}
```

A built-in function can return NULL, with a Python error set if it encounters an error condition; otherwise, it must return a (non NULL) Python object reference, with no Python error set.

Of the two standard arguments to a built-in function the `self` argument is rarely used—the `self` argument represents the module object itself, in case the reader wants to know, and there is usually no reason to mess with the module in a simple function. As we shall see, for methods of built-in types, the `self` argument is almost always used, by contrast.

The other argument, `args`, is a tuple containing the arguments to the function. Thus, for example, the Python level call

```
>>> X = BStream(1000)
```

appears at the C level as a call to `MakeBStream(self, args)` where self is the `bstream` module object and `args` is a tuple containing the Python integer 1000. Generally the first thing a built-in function must do is parse its argument sequence in order to translate the `args` object into its components. Let's examine how the `makeBStream` C implementation for `BStream` parses and uses its arguments. In the case of makeBStream, the function must try to parse its arguments in several different ways, because `BStream( ... )` supports several different calling sequences.

```
static PyObject *
makeBStream(self, args)
     PyObject *self, *args;
{
  bstreamobject *result;
  PyObject *write_result;
  int length, calltest;

  bstDPRINT(("BStream( ... )\n"));  /* debug print */
  /* Is the calling sequence BStream(int)?  */
  calltest = PyArg_ParseTuple(args, "i", &length);
  if (calltest) {
    bstDPRINT(("BStream(%d), make empty presized\n", length));
    result = empty_bstream(length);
    if (!result) { return NULL; } /* empty_bstream failed, error is set */
  } else {
    /* clear the python error from PyArgParseTuple */
    PyErr_Clear();
    /* All other calling sequences are identical to bstream.write().
       create a smallest bstreamobject and use b.write to insert data. */
    bstDPRINT((
      "BStream: not presized; attempting sliced calling sequence...\n"));
    /* make a smallest bstream */
    result = empty_bstream(0);
    if (!result) { return NULL; } /* failed, error is set. */
```

```
    /* Now use the bst.write method.
       bst.write handles all other calling sequences and checks. */
  write_result = bstreamwrite(result, args);
  if (!write_result) {
    bstDPRINT(("BStream: bst.write failed. Aborting...\n"));
    /* discard the result */
    Py_XDECREF(result);
    /* return failure, assume error is set */
    return NULL;
  }
  /* dispose of the result returned by bst.write */
  Py_XDECREF(write_result);
  }
  bstDPRINT(("BStream: successful completion\n"));
  return (PyObject *) result;
}
```

We have modified the actual code slightly to eliminate some white space. The bstDPrint(...) lines provide debug printing when debugging is enabled. To see the function in action, we can run BStream from Python with debugging enabled:

```
>>> from bstream import *
>>> debug()
>>> Y = BStream(100) # integer calling sequence
BStream( ... )
BStream(100), make empty presized
empty_bstream(100)
newbuffer(100, 1802266989)
newbuffer: trying to allocate 128
newbuffer: exiting successfully
empty_bstream exiting successfully
BStream: successful completion
>>>
>>> X = BStream("this") # string calling sequence
BStream( ... )
BStream: not presized; attempting sliced calling sequence...
empty_bstream(0)
newbuffer(0, 1969581667)
newbuffer: trying to allocate 32
newbuffer: exiting successfully
empty_bstream exiting successfully
bst.write( ... )
bst.write(X), copy entire structure
```

```
adjust_slice [0 : 4] (0, 4)
adjusted slice = [ 0 : 4 ]
bst.write: congratulations, X is a string
Check_bstream(1168600, 4)
Check_bstream: no modification needed
bst.write: now copying...
copyintobuffer(1168640, 0, 1231532, 0, 4)
bst.write: Successful completion
BStream: successful completion
>>>
>>> X = BStream("this", "that", 1) # invalid call
BStream( ... )
BStream: not presized; attempting sliced calling sequence...
empty_bstream(0)
newbuffer(0, 1802266989)
newbuffer: trying to allocate 32
newbuffer: exiting successfully
empty_bstream exiting successfully
bst.write( ... )
bst.write() UNRECOGNIZED CALLING SEQUENCE
BStream: bst.write failed. Aborting...
del <Bstream 1168880> (bstream_dealloc)
Traceback (innermost last):
  File "<stdin>", line 1, in ?
TypeError: illegal argument type for built-in operation
```

In these traces, we see some debug print statements from the makeBStream function, and others from functions called by makeBStream that will be presented further down.

Reading the makeBStream function from top to bottom (but ignoring bstDPRINT(...)), it works as follows. First makeBStream attempts to interpret the arguments, args, as a single integer using PyArgs_ParseTuple

```
calltest = PyArg_ParseTuple(args, "i", &length);
```

which works something like the standard C scanf function, as explained below.

If the arguments match the "i" signature then the single integer from args is written into the length variable and calltest is set to 1 (true). In this case makeBStream uses the utility function empty_bstring(...), defined below, to make a bstream object of the requested length

```
result = empty_bstream(length);
```

The empty_bstream call may fail, returning NULL, for example, no memory is available, in which case makeBStream presumes a Python error has been set, returning the standard error result NULL to the caller. Otherwise, makeBStream returns the new bstream object.

If the arguments do not match the "i" signature, makeBStream attempts to interpret args to represent one of the calling sequences

```
BStream(string_or_bstream)
BStream(string_or_bstream, i)
BStream(string_or_bstream, i, j)
```

essentially by allowing the built-in bstream.write method of bstream objects (which has the same calling sequence) to do most of the work. But first makeBStream clears the Python error set by the failed call to PyArgs_ParseTuple via PyErr_Clear(), and then it makes a smallest bstream, again using

```
result = empty_bstream(0);
```

returning NULL if empty_bstream fails. If all goes well, makeBStream uses the built in method bstreamwrite (presented below):

```
write_result = bstreamwrite(result, args);
```

to parse the arguments args and write the data into the new bstream object. If the write succeeds, then the new bstream object is returned, but if the write failed, NULL is returned, presuming that bstreamwrite set a Python error.

Note the Py_XDECREF(...) calls. These are required for managing memory in Python. In particular, if the call to bstreamwrite(...) succeeds, makeBStream calls Py_XDECREF(write_result) in order to discard the result object returned by bstreamwrite. Alternatively, if bstreamwrite(...) fails, makeBStream calls Py_XDECREF(result) in order to allow Python to deallocate the new bstream, because it is no longer needed.

Managing Reference Counts

Python uses a reference counting discipline to manage memory. At the level of Python programming, all reference counting goes on behind the scenes, but at the level of extension modules, reference counting must be done explicitly.

Each Python object is associated with an integer reference count which indicates the number of references held by other structures to that object. While the reference count is above zero, Python keeps the object in memory, but when the reference count reaches zero, Python deallocates the object and frees any memory associated with that object for future use. Python's simple memory management scheme is one reason why it ports so easily to just about any computing platform and fits cleaning inside just about any software environment.

Extension modules must take care to correctly manage reference counts for the objects they manipulate, and in practice this is very easy. Failure to correctly manage reference counts may cause Python to malfunction: Too many reference counts will result in unreclaimed unused objects, causing a memory leak, and too few reference counts may result in an invalid object reference which might cause Python to crash.

Python follows a uniform approach to reference counting. Think of a function as having two sorts of references: "New references" are owned by the function until they are stored in a permanent structure or returned, and "old references" are not owned by the function and must be discarded. When a function returns, all references held by the function must be old references except for the return value of the function which must be a new reference.

Here are the rules for manipulating new and old references:

1. The arguments given to a function, or initialized by `PyArgs_ParseTuple` are all old references.

2   The result returned by other functions, if not NULL, will be a new reference. For example, a function result that is ignored must be DECREFed.

    ```
    /* try to call logger.error("No space left on device")
       and ignore the return value, or any error. */
    temp = Py_Object_CallMethod(logger,
            "error", "s", "No space left on device");
    if (temp == NULL) { PyErr_Clear(); } /* ignore error */
    XDECREF(temp); /* discard the result (even if it was NULL) */
    ```

    (**)

3. Calls to other functions do not alter the new or old status of the arguments to the function call. (**)

4. Only new references may be explicitly stored in a permanent structure. The action of storing the new reference converts the new reference into

an old reference. If the storage operation overwrites an existing reference, then the existing reference must be DECREFed. For example, if data is an old reference that we wish to store in record->info, we proceed as follows:

```
Py_XINCREF(data);      /* convert data to a new reference */
temp = record->info;   /* remember the existing reference */
record->info = data;   /* store data, overwriting temp */
Py_XDECREF(temp);      /* DECREF the overwritten reference */
/* data is now once again an old reference */
```

5. Only old references may be explicitly overwritten by assignment. For example, if X is a new reference, it must be DECREFed before it is overwritten:

```
XDECREF(X);
X = Y;
```

6. The return value of a function must be NULL (with an error set) or a new reference (with no error set).

7. When a function returns, all other references held by the function must be old references, aside from the return value. If a function returns NULL with an error set, all references held by the function must be old references.

8. An old reference X may be converted into a new reference by Py_XINCREF(X). A new reference X may be converted into an old reference by Py_XDECREF(X). For both Py_XINCREF(X) and Py_XDECREF(X), X may be NULL.

9. Never ever explicitly free a properly initialized Python object reference—use XDECREF.

Thus, the C extension programmer must keep track of which references are new and which are old and follow these guidelines. With a bit of practice, this discipline becomes nearly as automatic as breathing.

The assumptions marked (**) are violated on rare occasions by Python internal functions that should never be used by extension modules and that are not mentioned at all in this book. Do not use these functions; they are not intended for use in extension modules.

The (**) assumptions, however, are never violated by the C-level abstract object interface, (defined in `abstract.c` and `abstract.h`), which provides access to most of the Python internals you will need. By all means use the abstract object interface, it's fabulous.

PyArg_ParseTuple

`PyArgs_ParseTuple` provides the standard way to parse the arguments sent to a built-in function or method. This function is a lot of fun because it makes life so easy. It is also possible to parse the arguments structure directly, but we won't discuss this possibility.

`PyArgs_ParseTuple` allows multiple arguments and optional arguments to be extracted from an argument structure using a `scanf`-type argument sequence. For example, to parse the alternate calling sequences:

```
a_function(object, index, string)
a_function(object, index)
a_function(object)
```

where the string may include the embedded null characters, use:

```
static PyObject *a_fun(self, args)
  PyObject *self, *args
{
  PyObject *the_object;
  char *str;
  int strlength, index, test;
  index = 0                 /* default index */
  str = (char *) NULL;    /* default string */
  strlength = -1          /* default string length */
  test = PyArg_ParseTuple(args, "O|is#",
                      &the_object, &index, &str, &strlength);
  if (!test) { return NULL; } /* invalid calling sequence */
  ...
}
```

Here the format string `"O|is#"` indicates that the function expects the calling sequence to start with an arbitrary object, optionally followed by an integer, optionally followed by a string which may contain null characters (and hence requires an explicit length parameter to indicate where the string ends). When

PyArg_ParseTuple(...) executes, if the arguments do not match the requested calling sequence, the return value, test, will be zero and a Python TypeError will be set automatically.

If args does match the requested calling sequence, then the_object will be initialized to an old object reference for the first argument; if two arguments are given, the index variable will be set to the value of the Python integer (otherwise index will retain its default value of 0); and if three arguments are given, then the str and strlength variables, respectively, will be initialized to the value of the Python and the length of the string, respectively (otherwise they will retain their default values of NULL and -1, respectively).

Thus, for example, the calling sequences following will result in the associated listed values (where undef indicates that the value is indeterminate).

Python Call	the_object	Index	str	Length	Test
a_fun(None)	Py_None	0	NULL	-1	1
a_fun(1,1,4)	undef	undef	undef	undef	0
a_fun("a",5,"b")	PyObject * for "a"	5	"b"	1	1
a_fun(None, 59)	Py_None	59	NULL	-1	1

Results of PyArg_ParseTuple for a_fun

Note that the second example call was an invalid calling sequence that left the_object, index, str, and length undefined but returned test as 0. The first and third example calling sequences did not provide all possible arguments and left the remaining arguments with their default values.

We refer the reader to the extensions reference distributed with the Python distribution for the various formats acceptable to PyArgs_ParseTuple, but we will explain the formats we use in the forgoing as they arise.

It is important to remember that any Python object reference initialized via PyArg_ParseTuple is an old reference, and hence, for example, if one of the parsed objects is used as the return value to the a_fun, first it must be INCREFed in order to make it a new reference first.

Also, a Python extension must never modify a string (`char *`) initialized by `PyArg_ParseTuple` because the string returned is not a copy of the string in the `PyStringObject`—it is a pointer to the internal buffer of the string object. Python requires Python string objects to be immutable, but the C programmer has the ability to violate this requirement—don't do it. Modifying a character sequence within a Python string object may cause Python to break or misbehave in distressing ways.

Standard Debugging Tricks

Python extensions are very easy to debug, given that we're programming in C, because you can use the interactive interpreter to aid in the debugging process, especially if you build in debugging aids in the C code.

Here is a standard trick used for compiling in debug print statements when wanted, and automatically erasing them at compile time when not wanted. The idea is that the code may include statements of the form

```
bstDPRINT(("this is an int %d", i));
```

which will translate into

```
if (DebugLevel) printf("this is an int %d, i);
```

if `BSTREAMDEBUG` is defined, but will disappear if `BSTREAMDEBUG` is not defined. Furthermore, if debug printing is enabled, the module will include a function

```
>>> bstreammodule.debug()
```

which will toggle debug printing on or off from Python on demand.

 NOTE This trick may not work under all environments, Using `printf`'s may not be advisable if Python is run under certain graphical user interfaces, because `printf`'s won't work. This trick should be used for Python under interactive console mode only.

Here is the magic precompiler hooks and code which enable the magically disappearing toggleable debug print statement.

```
/* uncomment this to enable debug printing, comment it to disable */
#define BSTREAMDEBUG 1

#ifdef BSTREAMDEBUG

/* toggle this truth valued variable to enable/disable printing */
static int DebugLevel = 0; /* debug printing off by default */

/* Python built in method to accomplish the toggling of debug printing: */

static PyObject * bstrdebug( PyObject *m, PyObject *a)
{
  /* ignore the arguments *a, because we don't care about them... */
  if (DebugLevel) { DebugLevel = 0; }
  else { DebugLevel = 1; }        /* silly, I know, but I like it. */
  /* incref Py_None because it will be the return value */
  Py_INCREF(Py_None);
  return Py_None; /* return "No value" (but no error either) */
}

/* define or nullify bstDPRINT() macro, depending on BSTREAMDEBUG flag */
#define bstDPRINT(x) if (DebugLevel) printf x

#else
#define bstDPRINT(x) {}
#endif
```

Note that the `bstrdebug` function is an extension method that always returns `Py_None`—the standard return value meaning "no value," identical to the `None` constant in Python programming. Never use `NULL` as a return value for a built-in method or function unless a Python error has been set. Always use `Py_None` to represent ``No return value,'' and `INCREF` it as you would any "old" reference.

Python Errors in C

Standard Python errors are available to the extension module, but they must be handled explicitly. A module may also define its own errors in addition to the standard ones (look to the `audioop.c` source for an example, but notice that audioop.c uses the old naming conventions). In the present module, we will only invoke the standard errors because they fit nicely with the problem at hand.

Python errors for an extension module have the standard Python error name prefixed by PyExc_, for example, PyExc_TypeError or PyExc_IndexError. An error may be signaled by an extension module via the function:

```
PyErr_SetString(PyExc_ValueError, "number must be positive")
```

Here PyErr_SetString takes an error object and a string to use as the associated value for the error. Normally after setting an error, an extension function or method immediately exits returning a NULL, or in a few cases some other invalid value that indicates an error has occurred. It is conventional that any function in an extension module that returns an error value must have set a Python error before returning, thus allowing the calling function to detect the error and exit without setting an error.

WARNING

If a function ignores an error, the function should call PyErr_Clear() to explicitly clear the error before proceeding. Failure to clear an error may cause some other part of Python to detect the error at some later time, with arbitrary results.

There are a number of other functions and considerations related to error handling in extension modules (mostly fairly obscure ones), and we refer the reader to the extension manual of the Python distribution for discussion of these.

WARNING

Please remember, however, that the normal rules of reference counting do not apply to error objects. Error objects should never be INCREFed of DECREFed.

Implementing a New Python Type

One of the most exciting and fun aspects of developing a Python extension module is the possibility of making brand new suped-up data structures available to the Python interpreter, by defining new extension types. Many Python modules never need to create a new type and fulfill their purpose excellently using only module level functions like BStream given above. But new types are fun, useful, and more interesting to write.

An extension type may be a simple optimization that provides some capability in a (hypothetically sometimes) faster implementation than Python permits, as with the bstream type we define as follows. Alternatively a new Python type may provide Python with an opaque interface to an external structure. For example, the Netscape Server API uses a C structure called a *pblock* (for parameter block), and to make parameter block structures available to the Python programmer a good approach would be to "wrap" pblocks up inside a new Python pblockobject type and associate appropriate built-in methods to pblockobjects that correspond to the official interfaces to pblocks specified in the NSAPI.

By defining new Python types, just about any data structure can be made available to Python easily and conveniently.

The General Form for Creating a Python Type

A definition for a Python type generally consists of a number of standard elements in a standard order:

```
The Structure Definitions
The Type Object Forward Reference
The Type Test Macro
Internal Utility Routines Related to Objects of the Type
Methods for The Type
Possibly Declarations of Special Methods Structures
Definition of the Type Object for the Type
```

In general, some of these elements may be omitted, but in the case of bstreamobjects, they are all included.

Thus, to begin, we must define the C language data structure that implements a bstream, using appropriate C language structural definitions:

```
#define BSTREAMMINSIZE 32
#define BSTREAMSHRINK 4

typedef struct bstreamobject {
```

```
        /* every Python type must include a standard header */
        PyObject_HEAD
        int valid_start;  /* where the real data starts in the buffer */
        int valid_length; /* where the real data ends in the buffer */
        int real_length;  /* the actual length of the buffer */
        char *data;       /* the buffer */
} bstreamobject;
```

This declaration defines a C language `struct` data type for implementing Python `bstream` objects. Because `bstreams` must be manipulated by Python, they must include certain standard members, such as the object's reference count and the reference to the type object that defines the standard interfaces to the object (declared as follows). These standard members are defined by the macro `PyObject_HEAD` which must always precede other members in the structure that defines the object.

Now we must define a forward reference for the type object to associate with all `bstreamobjects`. Every python object must be associated with a type object which essentially encapsulates a bunch of functions Python programs may use to access the object. The address of the type object is required by any function that creates a new `bstreamobject`, but the declaration of the type object itself must use references to the C language functions that define the interfaces to `bstream` objects! Something has to come first, so by convention we define the type object as a forward reference before the C functions, and complete the definition of the type object later.

```
staticforward PyTypeObject bstreamtype;
```

The `staticforward` macro expands to a forward reference that may differ depending on which platform and compiler compiles the module. It will always produce a declaration that permits the use of references to the `bstreamtype` object before it is declared.

Next it's good style to define the type test macro. It is frequently necessary to test the type of an object in a Python extension function, so it is usually convenient to define a type-test macro for any new python type, which we define for `bstream` objects as follows.

```
#define is_bstreamobject(op) ((op)->ob_type == &bstreamtype)
```

The Type Object for all BStreams

The declarations for a bunch of C functions that define the ways a Python program may access the new type usually follow the type test macro, and the `bstreammodule.c` source follows this convention. But for the moment let's defer the functions and display the declaration of the type object associated with all `bstreams`. This declaration refers to a number of functions and objects we will define and explain later.

```
statichere PyTypeObject bstreamtype = {
  PyObject_HEAD_INIT(&PyType_Type)
  0,
  "bstream",                      /*tp_name*/
  sizeof(bstreamobject),          /*tp_basicsize*/
  0,                              /*tp_itemsize*/
  (destructor)bstream_dealloc,    /*tp_dealloc*/
  0,                              /*tp_print*/
  (getattrfunc)bstream_getattr,   /*tp_getattr*/
  0,                              /*tp_setattr*/
  0,                              /*tp_compare*/
  (reprfunc)bstream_repr,         /*tp_repr*/
  0,                              /*tp_as_number*/
  &bstream_as_sequence,           /*tp_as_sequence*/
  0,                              /*tp_as_mapping*/
  0,                              /*tp_hash*/
};
```

As mentioned above, the `bstreamtype` object defines a collection of functions for accessing `bstreamobjects`. But it also defines a number of other standard members: A standard header via `PyObject_HEAD_INIT`; a dummy value that is always zero, a name for this type, `"bstream"`; a basic size for the type, `sizeofbstreamobject`; and an item size for the type, of zero. The two zero entries are used for fairly elaborate Python types, and should be set to zero by almost all extension programmers. The type name `"bstream"` defines how the type object will print out, and the `basicsize` should always be the size of the structure that implements the object. The `statichere` macro, like `staticforward`, is a macro which makes this declaration work under the zillions of environments that Python supports.

As shown above, this implementation only defines a few of the ways the type can be accessed by Python: The destruction method to use to destroy a bstream `bstream_dealloc`, the attribute method to use to retrieve an attribute of a `bstream` `bstream_getattr`, and the conversion method to convert a `bstream` to a string representation `bstream_repr`. Furthermore, the `bstream_as_sequence` structure referenced in the `bstreamtype` defines a collection of methods used for accessing a `bstream` as if it were a sequence.

To complete the description of the new `bstream` type, we must provide definitions for the functions and structures used in the declaration of `bstreamtype`, which becomes the goal for the remainder of this chapter.

Where are the `write` and `read` and `to_string` operations? Glad you asked.

How Python Accesses Built-In Methods: getattr for Types

When a Python statement, say,

```
>>> B.write("7 horses")
```

is executed, the expression `B.write` is evaluated first, which if successful produces the write attribute of the object B. For built-in types the type generally provides a `getattr` function for retrieving attributes and methods.

In the present case, all `bstream` objects share the following `getattr` function:

```
static PyMethodDef bstreammethods[] = {
/* python name           (C type) C name               flag (always 1) */
  {"write",              (PyCFunction)bstreamwrite,      1},
  {"read",               (PyCFunction)bstreamread,       1},
  {"to_string",          (PyCFunction)bstreamtostring,   1},
  {NULL,           NULL}         /* sentinel */
};
/* THE STANDARD GETATTR FOR NAMED METHODS */
static PyObject *
bstream_getattr(bstr, name)
    bstreamobject *bstr;
    char *name;
{
  return Py_FindMethod(bstreammethods, (PyObject *)bstr, name);
}
```

The `bstream_getattr` function maps attributes of `bstream` objects (like `B.write`) to their C-level implementation (like `B.bstreamwrite`) in a standard manner using the `Py_FindMethod` library function and an additional `PyMethodDef` table `bstreammethods` declared for the purpose. Note that the module function table `bstr_module_methods` and the type method table `bstreammethods` have precisely the same declaration format.

Between the `makeBStream` definition, the `bstreamtype` declaration and the `bstreammethods` declaration, there are a number of functions and structures we have used but have not yet defined, and we will not present all of them in this chapter. We refer the reader to the `bstreammodule.c` source file for the remainder.

We present and explain:

`empty_bstream`	The internal function for creating a bstream.
`bstreamwrite`	The write method.
`bstreamread`	The read method.
`bstreamdealloc`	The deallocator.
`bstream_as_sequence`	The sequence methods structure.

We also present certain internal helper functions as the need arises, omitting helper functions that are not of particular interest.

We have chosen to implement a relatively complex data type in order to demonstrate some of the fancier tricks used in writing Python extensions. Many or most extension modules may be much simpler than the forgoing.

NOTE

Making a bstream

The `makeBStream` function given above used an internal routine `emtpy_bstream` to create `bstreamobjects`. The `read` and `write` methods will also need the ability to resize the `data` buffer within a `bstreamobject`, so we factor the creation of `bstreamobjects` and their buffers into two separate operations, neither of which are used outside the module.

```
static char * newbuffer(minsize, size)
     int minsize; int *size;
{
  int thesize = BSTREAMMINSIZE;
```

```
  int nextsize;
  char *result;
  bstDPRINT(("newbuffer(%d, %d)\n", minsize, *size));
  /* find thesize, as power of 2 larger than minsize */
  while (thesize <= minsize) {
    nextsize = thesize + thesize;
    if (nextsize < thesize) {
        return (char *) PyErr_NoMemory(); }/* integer overflow! */
    thesize = nextsize;
  }
  bstDPRINT(("newbuffer: trying to allocate %d\n", thesize));
  /* allocate a string of size thesize */
  result = (char *) calloc(sizeof(char), thesize);
  if (!result) {
    PyErr_NoMemory();    /* allocation failure */
    return NULL;
  }
  *size = thesize;
  bstDPRINT(("newbuffer: exiting successfully\n"));
  return result;
}
```

Note that `newbuffer` only creates buffers of size a power of 2, in order to automatically provide extra space, eliminating the need for frequent resizes. Note that `newbuffer` may set a memory error using `PyErr_NoMemory()` if `calloc` fails or if the requested size was too large.

Using the `newbuffer` function, we may define `empty_bstream` as follows:

```
static bstreamobject *
empty_bstream(min_len)
    int min_len;
{
  bstreamobject *result;
  bstDPRINT(("empty_bstream(%d)\n", min_len));
  /* create a new structure to return */
  result = PyMem_NEW(bstreamobject, 1);
  if (!result) { return (bstreamobject *) PyErr_NoMemory(); }
  /* initialize structure members for result */
  result->valid_length = 0;  /* update when data is entered into buffer */
  result->valid_start = 0;   /* update when data is removed from buffer */
  /* initialize result->real_length and result->data
     using utility routine newbuffer defined above. */
  result->data = newbuffer( min_len, &(result->real_length) );
  /* if buffer allocation failed, deallocate result, assume error is set */
```

```
if (!(result->data)) {
  PyMem_DEL(result);
  return NULL;
}
/* EVERY PYTHON STRUCTURE MUST BE ASSOCIATED WITH ITS TYPE */
result->ob_type = &bstreamtype;
/* INITIALIZE THE REFERENCE COUNT FOR THE NEW OBJECT */
_Py_NewReference(result);
bstDPRINT(("empty_bstream exiting successfully\n"));
return result;
}
```

The `empty_bstream` function creates a new `bstreamobject`, initializing its members and allocating its `data` buffer properly. Note that if any operation fails after the `result` object has been allocated, the `result` is explicitly deallocated via `PyMem_DEL`. This explicit deallocation is permitted (in fact required) because the `result` object is not yet a properly initialized Python object, and hence is not subject to the reference counting discipline yet. If all goes well, the `result` object becomes a properly initialized Python object at the end of the function after its `ob_type` member has been initialized to the `bstreamtype` shared type object for all `bstreams` and after the reference count for `result` has been initialized by `_Py_NewReference(result)`.

Every new Python object must have an `ob_type` type object reference and a properly initialized reference count.

NOTE

Writing Into a bstream object

The `bstreamwrite` function writes data into a `bstream` buffer—its moderately complex logic involves mostly error checking and bookkeeping required by the various calling sequences.

In `bstreamrite` below the single call to
`PyArg_ParseTuple(args, "O|iO", &from_object,`
`                        &start_index, &end_index_object);`

NOTE　supports all calling sequences for the `write` operation. Some of the logic following this call is included only to provide debug print statements that echo the arguments provided to the function.

```
static PyObject * bstreamwrite(self, args)
    bstreamobject *self; PyObject *args;
{
  PyObject *from_object, *end_index_object;
  PyStringObject *from_py_string;
  bstreamobject *from_bstream, *dummy;
  char *from_string;
  int start_index, end_index, calltest, from_len,
      from_start;
  bstDPRINT(("bst.write..)\n"));
  /* set some default values */
  start_index = 0;  /* by default start copying from start of argument */
  from_py_string = NULL;  /* set this to argument if argument is a string */
  from_bstream = NULL; /* set this to argument if argument is bstream */
  end_index_object = NULL;

  /* Check the calling sequence:  Look for
         bst.write(X) or bst.write(X, n) or bst.write(X, n, m)
     where n and m are integers and X can be anything (for now) */
  calltest = PyArg_ParseTuple(args, "O|iO",
                &from_object, &start_index, &end_index_object);
  if (!calltest) { return NULL; }
  /* analyze the arguments */
  if ((start_index == 0) && (end_index_object==NULL)) {
    bstDPRINT(("bst.write(X), copy entire structure\n"));
    /* later use length of from_object as end_index */
  } else {
    if (end_index_object != NULL) {
      /* get the end_index as an integer */
      if (!PyInt_Check(end_index_object)) {
      PyErr_SetString(PyExc_ValueError, "bst.write: end must be integer");
      return NULL;
      }
      end_index = PyInt_AsLong(end_index_object);
      bstDPRINT(("bst.write(X,%d,%d), write slice\n", start_index,
end_index));
    } else {
      bstDPRINT(("bst.write(X,%d), write from start\n", start_index));
    }
  }
  /* C equivalent of Python: from_len = len(from_object)  */
  from_len = PyObject_Length(from_object);
  if (from_len < 0) {
    /* negative length indicates an error occurred */
    return NULL;  /* error set by PyObject_Length */
  }
```

```
if (end_index_object == NULL) {
  /* by default use obj_length as end of slice */
  end_index = from_len;
}
adjust_slice(&start_index, &end_index, 0, from_len);

/* We still need to check that from_object is either a Python
   string or a bstreamobject.  If not, fail with an error. */
if (PyString_Check(from_object)) {
  bstDPRINT(("bst.write: congratulations, X is a string\n"));
  from_py_string = (PyStringObject *) from_object;
} else {
  if (is_bstreamobject(from_object)) {
    bstDPRINT(("bst.write: congratulations, X is a bstream\n"));
    from_bstream = (bstreamobject *) from_object;
  } else {
    PyErr_SetString(PyExc_TypeError, "Only string or bstream permitted");
    return NULL;
  }
}
/* check whether self needs to resize or shift to hold the data */
dummy = Check_bstream(self, (end_index - start_index));
if (!dummy) {
  /* could not make the bstream big enough... fail.  Assume error set. */
  return NULL;
}
/* Now locate the internal buffer to write the data from */
if (from_py_string) {
  from_string = PyString_AS_STRING( from_py_string );
} else {
  if (from_bstream) {
    from_string = from_bstream->data;
    from_start = from_bstream->valid_start;
    if (from_start>0) {
    from_len = from_bstream->valid_length;
    adjust_slice(&start_index, &end_index, from_start, from_len);
    }
  }
}
/* if there is no data to copy, don't do anything. */
if (start_index < end_index) {
  /* there is data to copy!  Copy it. */
  bstDPRINT(("bst.write: now copying...\n"));
  copyintobuffer(self->data, self->valid_length,
          from_string, start_index, end_index);
  /* adjust self->valid_length */
```

```
      self->valid_length = (self->valid_length) + (end_index - start_index);
   }
   bstDPRINT(("bst.write: Successful completion\n"));
   /* return None */
   Py_XINCREF(Py_None);
   return Py_None;
}
```

We will not detail the logic of this function. Instead, let a discussion of the subroutines called by `bstreamwrite` suffice.

The third argument to `bstreamwrite`, if it is provided, should be an integer indicating the end index of the data to write into the buffer. If the third argument is omitted, then the end index should default to the end of the `from_object`. In order to safely test whether the third argument was present, we allow `PyArg_ParseTuple` to parse the third argument as an arbitrary object, and then test later to see if it was an integer using the type test `PyInt_Check`. If the argument was present, and an integer, we extract the C long contained in the Python integer via `PyInt_AsLong`.

NOTE The type specific integer access operations are provided by the standard include file `Include/intobject.h`, which is only one of a number of include files that define standard ways that Python-encapsulated values can be accessed directly. Later the function uses the python type check `PyString_Check` and `PyString_AS_STRING`, which extracts the internal character buffer of a Python string—these string accesses are defined in the standard header file `Include/stringobject.h`. We will not cover all the standard access methods for each type in this book, please see the appropriate header files themselves for explanations of these operations.

NOTE It is often not necessary to access Python objects using type specific methods. For example, the `bstreamwrite` function determines the length of the `from_object` using `PyObject_Length`, which is one of Python's abstract object access functions. This length query works for any object that has a length query defined (including strings and bstreams, or even sequence class instances defined at the Python level).

WARNING When possible, it is preferable to use the abstract object interface defined in `Include/abstract.h` in place of direct object accesses. Using the abstract interface makes the extension module more robust and general than direct type specific accesses provide.

Three routines internal to bstreammodule.c (adjust_slice, Check_bstream, and copyintobuffer) are used by bstreamwrite but are omitted here, because they do not help explain the process of developing Python extensions. They are, however, beautiful examples of C functions, and we ask the interested reader to examine their implementation in the source file, available on the CD-Rom that accompanies this book.

Reading from a `bstream` Object

The bstreamread method implements the read method of bstream objects.

```
static PyObject * bstreamread(self, args)
    bstreamobject *self; PyObject *args;
{
  int length, calltest, start, last, maxdata, bufsize, newrealsize;
  char *buffer, *startpoint, *otherbuffer;
  PyObject *result;
  bstDPRINT(("bst.read(...)\n"));
  /* get information about self */
  start = self->valid_start;
  last = self->valid_length;
  buffer = self->data;
  bufsize = self->real_length;
  maxdata = last - start;
  /* check the calling sequence */
  length = maxdata;
  calltest = PyArg_ParseTuple(args, "|i", &length);
  if (!calltest) { return NULL; }
  if (length == maxdata) {
    bstDPRINT(("bst.read(): read entire buffer\n"));
  } else {
    bstDPRINT(("bst.read(%d): read up to length\n", length));
    if (length>maxdata) {
      bstDPRINT(("bst.read: truncating len to %d\n", maxdata));
      length = maxdata;
    }
    if (length<0) {
      length = 0;
    }
  }
  /* read from start point, length long, into a new Python string. */
  startpoint = buffer + start;
  result = PyString_FromStringAndSize(startpoint, length);
```

```
  if (!result) {
    bstDPRINT(("bst.read: String copy failed.\n"));
    return NULL;
  }
  /*  DO BOOKEEPING ON THE self OBJECT */
  self->valid_start = start + length;
  start = self->valid_start;
  maxdata = last - start;
  /* Check to see if the real data in buffer has shrunk enough to
     merit shrinking the buffer allocation. */
  if ( ((maxdata*BSTREAMSHRINK) < bufsize) &&
       (bufsize > BSTREAMMINSIZE) ) {
    otherbuffer = newbuffer(maxdata, &newrealsize);
    if (!otherbuffer) {
      /* JUDGEMENT CALL... We won't raise an error here ...  */
    } else {
      copyintobuffer(otherbuffer, 0, buffer, start, last);
      free(buffer); /* deallocate the too-big buffer */
      self->data = otherbuffer; /* use the new buffer, and do bookkeeping */
      self->valid_start = 0;
      self->valid_length = maxdata;
      self->real_length = newrealsize;
    }
  }
  return result;
}
```

Largely because it has a simpler calling sequence, the `read` operation is much simpler than the `write` operation. The only thing of interest in this function is the final segment where the internal buffer of the `bstreamobject` may be resized down to a smaller size. We chose not to signal an error on failure to resize down, reasoning that future deallocations might allow the resize at a later time, but this judgment may not have been advisable. The `PyString_FromStringAndSize` function creates a new Python string reference and copies the data from the buffer into the string. This is a type specific function defined in the standard `/Include/stringobject.h` header file.

The `bstream` Deallocator

If we create `bstreamobjects` for Python, we must allow Python to deallocate them as well. Every type object for a Python type must define a deallocator method. In the case of `bstreamtype`, we provide the following deallocation method:

```
static void
bstream_dealloc(op)
    bstreamobject *op;
{
  bstDPRINT(("del <Bstream %d> (bstream_dealloc)\n", op));
  free( op->data );
  free( op );
}
```

NOTE In this case, the `bstreamobject` contains no references to other external Python objects, so we can directly `free` all substructure. If the structure contained any references to Python objects, they would require `DECREF`s and should not be directly `freed` in the deallocation function, in case references to the objects are shared by other Python structures.

Implementing Sequence Accesses for `bstream` Objects

Just to be perverse, we didn't stop with implementing simple method accesses for `bstreamobjects`—we also define sequence accesses for `bstreamobjects` as well, allowing objects of this type to be indexed and sliced just like lists or tuples or strings.

Defining sequence accesses required providing a special structure `bstream_as_sequence` to the `bstreamtype` type object. The declaration for this structure follows:

```
static PySequenceMethods bstream_as_sequence = {
    (inquiry)bstream_len,           /*sq_length*/
    (binaryfunc)bstream_concat,     /*sq_concat*/
    (intargfunc)bstream_repeat,     /*sq_repeat*/
    (intargfunc)bstream_item,       /*sq_item*/
    (intintargfunc)bstream_slice,   /*sq_slice*/
    0,                              /*sq_ass_item*/
    0,                              /*sq_ass_slice*/
};
```

Note that we omitted the optional assignment operations, but defined the others. The length inquiry function is provided by a particularly simple implementation:

```
static int
bstream_len(ob)
    bstreamobject *ob;
{
  return (ob->valid_length - ob->valid_start);
}
```

We direct the interested reader to the source code for the other sequence methods, except for sequence concatenation, which is of particular interest because it demonstrates the use of the Python C-level abstract object interface.

Catenating `bstreams`

The following C implementation defines the catenation operation for bstreams:

```
static PyObject *
bstream_concat(ob, bb)
    bstreamobject *ob, *bb;
{
  bstreamobject *result;
  int resulttotal, success;
  PyObject *write_method, *dummy;
  /* both inputs must be bstreams */
  if ( (!is_bstreamobject(ob)) || (!is_bstreamobject(bb)) ) {
    PyErr_SetString(PyExc_TypeError,
                    "only bstreams concatenate with bstreams");
    return NULL;
  }
  result = NULL;
  write_method = NULL;
  success = 1;
  resulttotal =  bstream_len(ob) + bstream_len(bb);
  /* make a new bstream large enough to hold resulttotal bytes */
  result = empty_bstream(resulttotal);
  success = (result != NULL);
  /* from now on we use the success flag to determine if an error
     occurred */
  /* get the write method of result */
  if (success) {
    write_method = PyObject_GetAttrString((PyObject *) result, "write");
    success = (write_method != NULL);
```

```
  }
  if (success) {
    dummy = PyObject_CallFunction(write_method, "O", ob);
    success = (dummy != NULL);
    Py_XDECREF(dummy);
  }
  if (success) {
    dummy = PyObject_CallFunction(write_method, "O", bb);
    success = (dummy != NULL);
    Py_XDECREF(dummy);
  }
  Py_XDECREF(write_method);
  if (!success) {
    Py_XDECREF(result);
    return NULL;
  }
  return (PyObject *) result;
}
```

This is essentially an example of the transliteration of Python code to C, because this operation performs the equivalent of the Python:

```
def bcat(ob, bb):
    result = BStream( len(ob) + len(bb) )
    write_method = result.write
    write_method(ob)
    write_method(bb)
    return result
```

But since error checking must be handled explicitly at the C level, the C code is much longer, of course. The assignment

```
write_method = PyObject_GetAttrString((PyObject *) result, "write");
```

is the standard "abstract object" approach for extracting the `write` attribute from the object `result`. Furthermore, the call

```
dummy = PyObject_CallFunction(write_method, "O", bb);
```

calls the `write_method` with `bb` as the single argument, where `"O"` is a printf-like format string that allows `PyObject_CallFunction` to construct an argument list of arbitrary length. In both cases, the results returned are new references which must be DECREFed when `bstream_concat` is done with them.

The `bstream_concat` function uses the `is_bstreamobject` type test macro defined previously and uses a `success` flag to allow structured error handling.

At this point, we conclude the detailed discussion of the `bstreammodule.c` implementation, and conclude with some general commentary.

Interacting with "Opaque" Python Objects

Earlier in this discussion, we mentioned the abstract object interface in several places. The abstract object interface allows C-level Python modules to interact with Python objects in a uniform manner, almost as a Python program would interact with those objects. Thus, for example, the call

```
ob = PySequence_GetItem(seq, 4)   /* ob = seq[4] */
```

extracts the fourth item from `seq` whether `seq` is a string, a tuple, a list, or some other sequence object implemented in some other extension module (like the `bstream` module), or even an instance of a Python class with sequence interfaces. These C-level interfaces provide translations to most basic object accesses available to Python. Of course, the difference between using C with the abstract interface and programming in Python, is that the C code must still carefully check for error conditions and maintain reference counts.

We will not document the abstract object interface here, as it is carefully documented in `Include/abstract.h`. Get to know these functions and accesses, they make C programming a little more like programming in Python.

A Brief Tour of the Standard Header Files

The C-extension programmer must occasionally refer to the header files of the Python distribution, given in the `Include` directory in the standard distribution hierarchy. Of greatest interest are the abstract object interface `abstract.h`, which defines the abstract object interface, and `object.h`, which defines the generic structures used in the definition and manipulation of Python objects, such as

```
PyObject_HEAD PyNumberMethods PySequenceMethods PyMappingMethods
PyTypeObject Py_XINCREF Py_XDECREF PyObject
```

as well as various function prototypes used in extension modules.

Furthermore, for direct access to object internals per type, there are include files specific to many of the standard object implementations, such as

```
floatobject.h    mappingobject.h  stringobject.h   tupleobject.h
intobject.h      fileobject.h     listobject.h
```

Standard support functions for extension modules, such as `PyArg_ParseTuple`, are provided by `modsupport.h`. An important support function we have omitted from this discussion is `Py_BuildValue`, which works something like an inverse to `PyArg_ParseTuple`. Please see the standard extensions manual for more information on this function.

CHAPTER TWELVE

EMBEDDING PYTHON

This chapter describes how Python may be embedded as a component of another main program and includes a detailed discussion of how Python may be embedded under any Netscape HTTP Server product that supports the NSAPI server component API. This chapter does not intend to replace the documentation provided by the standard Python extensions manual of the distribution or by the various header files of the Python C API. Instead, this chapter intends to provide a detailed introduction to the topic of embedding Python with examples and motivation.

Embedding Python is only difficult in that the layers of abstraction that allow Python to talk to an arbitrary main program get a bit obscure—and this would be true for almost any embedding of any interpreted language in a separate main program. This chapter involves some subtlety, so do not be disturbed if it is confusing the first time through.

For simplicity, in this presentation much of the C code presented has been shortened, with error checking in particular excised. Please see the source code for the official versions available in the accompanying CD-ROM..

This chapter describes:

1. How the Netscape Server dynamically loads and initializes the Python interpreter and how Python registers a callback object for use by the Server interface module.
2. How the Netscape Server requests a service from the Python interpreter by invoking a method of the registered callback object.
3. How the Python interpreter request actions of the Netscape Server by calling Python built-in functions that make standard Server interfaces available to Python programs.

For the purposes of this presentation we will refer to an instance of a Netscape Server using this embedding simply as *the Server*.

Why Embed Python under the NSAPI?

The most obvious reason to want to embed Python under a Netscape Server Process would be to provide dynamic CGI-type server functionality without the overhead associated with running separate CGI processes for each request. For example, if we wish to provide a service that requires reading and parsing information from several large files for every HTTP request that uses the service, a CGI implementation could get computationally expensive and slow.

By contrast, using Python embedded under the NSAPI, the Python initialization process could read and parse the data files once at Server startup and then respond to subsequent HTTP requests without opening or parsing any additional files. By performing complex initialization before requests arrive and then using prepared data structures when the requests are handled, HTTP requests that may require multiple seconds and significant computational resources under a CGI implementation may take tenths of a second and little computational resources under an NSAPI embedding.

There are other possible applications for Python embedded under the NSAPI, such as custom authentication schemes, but we will not discuss them. A full discussion of how to use Python embedded under the NSAPI could easily fill a whole book.

Why Embed Python under Other Software Products, Generally Speaking?

Why does the Netscape Navigator embed Java and JavaScript? Why does the Oracle Server embed PL/SQL? Why does emacs embed elisp? Why do all these languages look a lot like Python (but not as flexible)?

Python embedded under another program can act as a scripting/extension language for that program. This allows easy implementation of complex initialization, special-purpose extensions, dynamic linking to other arbitrary Python modules, and all sorts of other uses that we haven't even thought of yet. Be creative! And when you come up with a really cool use for embedded Python, be sure to tell us about it, so we can be impressed.

A General Strategy for Embedding Python

There are many ways of embedding Python under another main program, all of which involve some sort of scheme where the main program calls Python via some sort of Python function call, and Python (optionally) calls back to the main program via special built-in methods designed for the purpose.

In this presentation, we will use an embedding strategy proposed by Mark Hammond (the premiere Python expert Down Under). In particular, we will associate the main program with a special Python module (`nsapimodule.c` in the particular case of the NSAPI embedding) that contains exactly one static reference to a Python class instance (`obCallBack` in the case of `nsapimodule.c`).

After everything has been initialized properly, the Python subsystem and the main program may then communicate as follows. When the main program desires a service of Python the program calls a method of the `obCallBack` object, as in:

```
/* C code from nsapimodule.c */
dummy = PyObject_CallMethod( obCallBack, "NSAPILog", "s", Statement);
```

To Python, this appears exactly as if a Python program had executed:

```
# Python Code from NSAPIHooks.py
dummy = obCallBack.NSAPILog(Statement);
```

The Python subprocess then performs the requested service by executing the method and returns a value to the main program as the result of the method call.

The interaction between Python and the Netscape Server may be more complex than this, because the Python subsystem may need to call back to the Server in order to request information or ask the Server to perform actions (such as logging an error message to the standard log files). In this case the method call from the Server to Python should provide built-in objects associated with methods that allow Python to call back for a Netscape Server function.

For example, when the server starts a Python service it may call

```
/* C code from nsapimodule.c */
resultobject =
  PyObject_CallMethod( obCallBack, "NSAPIcallback", "OOO",
                       (PyObject *)pbo, (PyObject *)sno, (PyObject *)rqo);
```

which to Python "feels" as if some Python program has called

```
# Python Code from NSAPIHooks.py (self test)
resultobject = obCallBack.NSAPIcallback(pbo, sno, rqo)
```

except that the arguments pbo, sno, and rqo are data structures provided by the Server, which may be accessed by Python like other Python built-in objects.

In particular, the Python module that implements the obCallBack.NSAPIcallback method may extract "user_agent" information from the request object rqo via:

```
useragent = rq.request_header("user-agent", sn)
```

where the rq.request_header method is a simple translation of one of the data access functions provided by the NSAPI interface, "wrapped" as a Python extension method.

The reason Mr. Hammond chose to use a class instance as the single point of entry for the main program to talk to Python is that this approach turns out to be completely general, and it allows different instances of the embedding to take advantage of Python's object-oriented features in order to provide different implementations for the services expected by the main program.

The NSAPI Embedding Outline

The following files are the primary files of the embedding of Python under the Netscape Server API described here:

- `nsapimodule.c`: This is the C language module that provides the entry points for the server to initialize and call Python and callback services that Python modules may use to obtain information from the Server, known to Python as the extension module `nsapi`.

- `NSAPIHooks.py`: This is the Python language module that initializes the callback object used by `nsapimodule.c` to request services of Python. It also may be configured to perform other initialization operations, such as imports of other Python modules and initialization of data structures at Server startup.

- `Py2NSAPI.py`: This is the Python language module that provides standard logic for providing Python services to the Server. In particular this module defines superclasses that encapsulate standard actions and error-handling strategies.

Furthermore, the Netscape Server configuration files `magnus.conf`, `mime.types`, and `obj.conf` all require editing in order to direct the Server to delegate certain functions to the internally embedded Python interpreter.

The general form of the embedding of Python under the NSAPI looks something like this, after the Server has initialized:

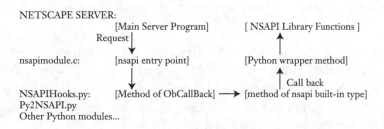

Thus, as the diagram indicates, when the main server program requests a service implemented in Python, it calls an entry point provided by the `nsapimodule.c` module source file. After initialization, any call to an `nsapimodule.c` entry point gets translated into a method of the `ObCallBack` object, which in turn is implemented in a Python module `NSAPIHooks.py`. Any parameters given to the `nsapi` entry point must be converted into Python objects before they are passed to the `ObCallBack` method.

The evaluation of the `ObCallBack` object method that implements the service requested may require interaction with the functions provided by the Server. Because Python code cannot directly call C functions, the API functions provided by the server are ``wrapped'' as built-in methods implemented by the `nsapimodule.c` interface layer.

More interestingly, the Python module `NSAPIHooks.py` may access any Python module or service in the process of handling a request initiated by the master Server process beyond simple interactions with the Server. Suddenly a world of flexibility and generality opens up to the Netscape Server. In fact, if you wanted the Netscape Server to talk to, say, a Sybase database in a simple and general manner, probably the easiest way to accomplish the connection would be to use Python to arbitrate between the Server and the database engine.

Now, let's examine how a Server embeds Python at initialization and how Python may then later perform a service for the Server.

Initialization

When the Netscape Server starts, it reads its initialization file `magnus.conf`, which includes the lines

```
Init fn=load-modules shlib=/big/arw/public_html/book/embed/nsapiPy.so \
    funcs=NSAPIPyInit,NSAPItoPython,NSAPIpyAtRestart
```

This directive instructs the Server to load the `nsapiPy.so` shared library, which contains the Python run-time library and the interface library defined in `nsapimodule.c`, registering the entry points `NSAPIPyInit`, `NSAPItoPython`, and `NSAPIAtRestart`. These entry points are the functions used by the Server to obtain services from Python.

After the Server has loaded the shared library and located the entry points, it reads the next configuration line and encounters the following configuration directive:

```
Init fn=NSAPIPyInit SRC="/big/arw/public_html/book/embed" \
    MDL="nsHOOKS" CALL="nsHOOKS.GO()"
```

This line instructs the server to call the function `NSAPIPyInit` providing the listed `SRC`, `MDL`, and `CALL` string parameters as part of the parameter block in the calling sequence. In response to this directive, the Server constructs a parameter block data structure `pb` containing the name/value parameter pairs listed in the directive and then calls

```
NSAPIPyInit(pb, NULL, NULL)
```

thus invoking the Python initialization function provided by `nsapimodule.c`.

The `NSAPIPyInit` function then performs the task of initializing Python and obtaining an `obCallBack` callback object to allow the server to make additional requests for Python services. This sets in motion a moderately elaborate chain of events, which we now outline.

With error checking and white space removed, here is an outline of the actions of `NSAPIPyInit`:

```
int
NSAPIPyInit(pb, sn, rq)
    pblock *pb;
    Session *sn; /* always NULL for init functions */
    Request *rq; /* always NULL for init functions */
{
  char PyStatement[1000];
  char *SRC, *MDL, *CALL;
  PyObject *dummy;
  SRC = pblock_findval("SRC", pb);
  MDL = pblock_findval("MDL", pb);
  CALL = pblock_findval("CALL", pb);
  Py_Initialize();
  PyRun_SimpleString("import nsapi\n");
  PyRun_SimpleString("import sys\n");
  sprintf(PyStatement, "sys.path.insert(0, '%s')\n", SRC);
  PyRun_SimpleString(PyStatement);
  sprintf(PyStatement, "import %s\n", MDL);
```

```
  PyRun_SimpleString(PyStatement);
  sprintf(PyStatement, "%s\n", CALL);
  PyRun_SimpleString(PyStatement);
  return REQ_PROCEED;
}
```

This function initializes the Python interpreter and then ``manually'' runs the equivalent of the following Python statements:

```
import nsapi
import sys
sys.path.insert(0, '<SRC>')
import <MDL>
<CALL>
```

as if they had been entered in the Python interpreter interactively. Here <SRC>, <MDL>,and <CALL> are the values associated with the parameters listed in the Init directive. In the case of the current configuration of magnus.conf, the commands executed translate to the following commands:

```
import nsapi
import sys
sys.path.insert(0, '/big/arw/public_html/book/embed')
import nsHOOKS
nsHOOKS.GO()
```

Essentially, this sequence instructs the Python interpreter to run the nsHOOKS.GO() method from the nsHOOKS module, but first it inserts the path /big/arw/public_html/book/embe) at the start of the Python path to make sure that the correct nsHOOKS module is found.

NOTE By using the parameters passed by the Server as Python statement fragments, the initialization process may be configured to use a different initialization module and initialization function without the need to rebuild any compiled components.

The nsHOOKS.GO() function then completes the initialization process by calling back to nsapi to register the obCallBack callback object, which the Server may later use to request Python services. The GO() function is actually imported from the generic Py2NSAPI.py module, where it is defined to perform the following actions:

```
# python code from Py2NSAPI.py
def GO():
    global obCallBack, nsapi
    obCallBack = nsCallBack()
    import nsapi
    nsapi.SetCallBack(obCallBack)
```

The `nsapi.SetCallBack` built-in function implemented in `nsapimodule.c` then records a static reference to the `obCallBack` object created by `GO()`, as follows:

```
/* C code from nsapimodule.c */
static PyObject *obCallBack = NULL; /* the call back object */

static PyObject * NSAPISetCallBack(self, args)
    PyObject *self; PyObject *args;
{
  int test;
  PyObject *theargument;
  test = PyArg_ParseTuple(args, "O", &theargument);
  if (!test) { return NULL; }
  /* dispose of the old call back object, if there was one */
  Py_XDECREF(obCallBack);
  obCallBack = theargument;  /* store the object, incref */
  Py_INCREF(theargument);
  Py_INCREF(Py_None);
  return Py_None;
}
```

With the `obCallBack` object initialized, the `nsapi` module is prepared to accept requests from the Server and translate them into method calls to the `obCallBack` object. At this point the embedded Python initialization process is complete; control returns to the Server, and the initialized Python interpreter lies dormant, awaiting requests from the Server to be delivered as method calls to `obCallBack`.

The `NSAPISetCallBack` function is the only function directly accessible to Python from the `nsapi` module, as we see from the following module initialization function:

```
/* nsapi MODULE METHODS STRUCTURE */
static struct PyMethodDef nsapi_module_methods[] = {
  {"SetCallBack",        (PyCFunction)NSAPISetCallBack,      1},
```

```
   {NULL, NULL} /* sentinel */
};

/* nsapi MODULE INITIALIZATION FUNCTION */
void
initnsapi()
{
   Py_InitModule("nsapi", nsapi_module_methods);
}
```

As we shall see, other services will be available to Python from the nsapi module, but only after a server has initialized a request.

Configuring the Server for Python

At this point we have described how the Server loads and initializes the Python interpreter, but we have not described how and when the Server might request a Python service. There are any number of ways to get the Server to ask for a Python service, but we will describe only one: When the Server receives an HTTP request that ends in ".pye" we will convince the Server that it must retrieve an object of type "magnus-internal/X-python-e" and therefore must hand the request to the function NSAPItoPython defined by nsapi-module.c. If the last sentence made any sense to you: congratulations—you are smarter than we are. These are all Netscape Server internals issues presented for completeness. If you have a Netscape Server, consult the Server documentation for more information; if you don't, don't worry about it.

We cajole the Server into calling NSAPItoPython for requests that end in ".pye" by adding the following line to the mime.types configuration file:

```
type=magnus-internal/X-python-e exts=pye
```

This line effectively makes a fake MIME type that the Server will associate with the extension ".pye" and understand as something that must be handled internally by the server process. To further associate the NSAPItoPython function with this fake MIME type, we add the line

```
Service fn="NSAPItoPython" method="(GET|HEAD|POST)" \
        type=magnus-internal/X-python-e
```

to the `obj.conf` Server configuration file. This line instructs the server to direct any request of the fake type `magnus-internal/X-python-e` to the server function `NSAPItoPython`.

What the Server Calls

Now let's examine the sequence of events that occur when the Server requests a Python service. When the Server receives an HTTP request from a client for a URL of form `/pye_ex1.pye` it interprets that request to be for an object of type `magnus-internal/X-python-e`. This type is then directed to the function `NSAPItoPython` thanks to the `Service` line in the `obj.conf` configuration file.

In the context of `nsapimodule.c`, the Server calls

```
NSAPItoPython(pb, sn, rq)
```

where `pb` provides parameters for the request, `sn` contains session information for the request, and `rq` provides ``request information.'' The precise meaning of these three parameters is beyond the scope of this discussion (and some of it is apparently beyond the intelligence of the authors, because various aspects of the NSAPI remain entirely mysterious to us); suffice it to say that in order to send a response back to the client the Python interpreter will need to use information within the `sn` structure to send the data, and similarly the other structures provide information sometimes needed by the Python interpreter to service certain types of requests.

This call to `NSAPItoPython` then must be translated into a method call of the callback object `obCallBack` to allow the Python interpreter to handle the request.

What `nsapimodule.c` Calls

The `NSAPItoPython` function in `nsapimodule.c` performs the following operations (again, with error checking and white space removed):

```
int NSAPItoPython(pb, sn, rq)
    pblock *pb; Session *sn; Request *rq;
{
  pblockobject *pbo;
  sessionobject *sno;
  requestobject *rqo;
  PyObject *resultobject;
  char *resultstring;
  int result;
  /* wrap inputs up in Python object packages */
  pbo = make_pblockobject(pb);
  sno = make_sessionobject(sn);
  rqo = make_requestobject(rq);
  resultobject =
    PyObject_CallMethod( obCallBack, "NSAPIcallback", "OOO",
                      (PyObject *)pbo, (PyObject *)sno, (PyObject *)rqo);

  /* Attempt to analyze the result as a string indicating which
     result to return */
  result = REQ_ABORTED;
  resultstring = PyString_AS_STRING( (PyStringObject *) result);
  if (strcmp(resultstring, "REQ_NOACTION")==0) { result = REQ_NOACTION; }
  if (strcmp(resultstring, "REQ_PROCEED")==0) { result = REQ_PROCEED; }
  if (strcmp(resultstring, "REQ_EXIT")==0) { result = REQ_EXIT; }
  /* dispose of object wrappers and method result */
  Py_XDECREF(pbo);
  Py_XDECREF(sno);
  Py_XDECREF(rqo);
  Py_XDECREF(resultobject);
  /* return the translated result (or default result) to the Server. */
  return result;
}
```

Thus `NSAPItoPython` uses the functions `make_sessionobject`, `make_requestobject`, and `make_pblockobject` to translate the parameters `pb`, `sn`, and `rq` into Python objects, and then it performs the equivalent of the Python method call:

```
# python translation:
resultobject = obCallBack.NSAPIcallback(pbo, sno, rqo)
```

The result of this method call, which is presumed to be a string (in the real implementation, of course, the type is checked), is translated into one of the NSAPI-specific return codes, and control is returned to the Server.

What Python Calls Back

During the sequence just described, the Python interpreter receives control of the handling of the request when `NSAPItoPython` calls the `NSAPIcallback` method of the `obCallBack` object. In order to do anything interesting (such as handle the request and return an HTTP/HTML response), the interpreter must interact with the Server data structures `sn`, `pb`, and `rq`.

For example, the following is a minimal implementation for a callback object class, which doesn't do anything interesting; it just exercises the embedding mechanism, using the minimum number of interactions required by the Server to generate a response to a request ending with "`.pye`" that will be interpreted by a client as an HTML response.

```python
MESSAGE = """
    <HTML>
    <TITLE>VERY SIMPLE HANDLER SAYS HI!</TITLE>
    <BODY>
    <h1>Hello.</h1>
    This was handled by a very simple nsapi call back object.<br>
    Here is some interesting data<br>
    <pre>
    %s \n%s \n%s
    </pre>
    </BODY>
    </HTML>
"""

class CallBack:
    def __init__(self):
        pass
    def NSAPIcallback(self, pb, sn, rq):
        import sys
        try:
            # must change the content-type to text/html:
            srvhdrs = rq.srvhdrs
            srvhdrs.pblock_remove("content-type")
            srvhdrs.nvinsert("content-type", "text/html")
            rq.protocol_status(sn, "PROTOCOL_OK")
            rq.start_response(sn)
            GREETING = MESSAGE % (pb.pblock2str(), srvhdrs.pblock2str(),
                            sn.client().pblock2str())
            sn.net_write(GREETING)
```

```
        return "REQ_PROCEED"
    except:
        print sys.exc_type, sys.exc_value

def NSAPILog(self, *args):
    pass

def NSAPIatrestart(self):
    pass
```

Note that the `srvhdrs` structure within the `rq` structure must have its content-type changed to `text-html`, the protocol status must be set, and the response must be started before the Server will correctly deliver an HTML response to the client. Furthermore, the response itself must be sent via the `net_write` function provided by the NSAPI interface. All of these operations require callbacks to the Server internal operations.

The `nsapimodule.c` module provides access to these operations by defining new Python types specific to the NSAPI embedding that wrap the external types `pblock`, `Session`, and `Request` inside `PyObject` representations.

For example, the following is an abbreviation of the implementation of the `pblockobject` Python type that provides native access to standard `pblock` methods to Python:

```
/* The object representation for the pblockobject structure */
typedef struct pblockobject {
  /* standard object header */
  PyObject_VAR_HEAD
  /* the pblock reference contained in the object */
  pblock *pb;
} pblockobject;

/* THE TYPE OBJECT FORWARD REFERENCE FOR PBLOCK OBJECTS */
staticforward PyTypeObject pblockobjecttype;

/* THE TYPE TEST MACRO */
#define is_pblockobject(op) ((op)->ob_type = &pblockobjecttype)

static pblockobject *
make_pblockobject(from_pb)
    pblock *from_pb;
{
  pblockobject *result;
  result = PyMem_NEW(pblockobject, 1);
```

```
    if (!result) { return (pblockobject *) PyErr_NoMemory(); }
    result->pb = from_pb;
    result->ob_type = &pblockobjecttype;
    _Py_NewReference(result);
    return result;
}
```

Here we see that a `pblockobject` is a simple container for a reference to a
`pblock`. Because the Server, not Python, owns all the `pblock`s, the deallocator
for `pblockobject`s deallocates the container but not the content.

```
static void
pblock_dealloc(op)
    pblockobject *op;
{
  free( op );
}
```

Now we define a number of access methods for `pblockobject`s that mirror
those documented by the NSAPI documentation and generally follow a boilerplate format, except for certain error-handling conditions.

```
/* pb.findval(string) */
static PyObject * Py_findval( pbo, args )
    pblockobject *pbo; PyObject *args;
{
  int test;
  char *string, *value;
  test = PyArg_ParseTuple(args, "s", &string);
  if (!test) { return NULL; }
  value = pblock_findval(string, pbo->pb);
  if (!value) {
    PyErr_SetString(PyExc_ValueError, "no such parameter");
    return NULL;
  }
  return PyString_FromString(value);
}

/* pb.nvinsert(namestring, valuestring) */
static PyObject *
Py_nvinsert( pbo, args )
    pblockobject *pbo;
    PyObject *args;
{
```

```
  int test;
  char *name, *value;
  test = PyArg_ParseTuple(args, "ss", &name, &value);
  if (!test) { return NULL; }
  (void)pblock_nvinsert(name, value, pbo->pb);
  Py_INCREF(Py_None);
  return Py_None;
}

/* pb.pblock2str() */
static PyObject * Py_pblock2str( pbo, args )
    pblockobject *pbo; PyObject *args;
{
  int test;
  char *tempresult;
  PyObject *result;
  test = PyArg_ParseTuple(args, "");
  if (!test) { return NULL; }
  tempresult = pblock_pblock2str(pbo->pb, NULL);
  result = PyString_FromString( tempresult );
  /* deallocate the tempresult (I assume this is okay, nsapi docs silent) */
  free(tempresult);
  return result;
}

/* pb.pblock_remove(name) */
static PyObject * Py_pblock_remove( pbo, args )
    pblockobject *pbo; PyObject *args;
{
  int test;
  char *name;
  pb_param *temp;
  test = PyArg_ParseTuple(args, "s", &name);
  if (!test) { return NULL; }
  /* imitated from nsapi/examples/session.c */
  temp = pblock_remove(name, pbo->pb);
  if (temp) { param_free( temp ); }
  Py_INCREF(Py_None);
  return Py_None;
}
```

With these methods defined, we may now define the `getattr` method and the `PyTypeObject` for all `pblocks`.

```
/* THE METHODS STRUCTURES FOR PBLOCKS */
static PyMethodDef Pypblockmethods[] = {
```

```
  { "pblock2str",      (PyCFunction)Py_pblock2str,     1},
  { "nvinsert",        (PyCFunction)Py_nvinsert,       1},
  { "findval",         (PyCFunction)Py_findval,        1},
  { "pblock_remove",   (PyCFunction)Py_pblock_remove,  1},
  { NULL, NULL } /* sentinel */
};

/* standard getattr for pblocks */
static PyObject * pblock_getattr(pbo, name)
    PyObject *pbo; char *name;
{
  return Py_FindMethod(Pypblockmethods, pbo, name);
}

/* THE TYPE OBJECT FOR ALL PYPBLOCK OBJECTS */
statichere PyTypeObject pblockobjecttype = {
  PyObject_HEAD_INIT(&PyType_Type)
  0,
  "nsapi_pblock",
  sizeof(pblockobject),
  0,
  (destructor)pblock_dealloc,      /*tp_dealloc*/
  0,                               /*tp_print*/
  (getattrfunc)pblock_getattr,     /*tp_getattr*/
  0,                               /*tp_setattr*/
  0,                               /*tp_compare*/
  0,                               /*tp_repr*/
  0,                               /*tp_as_number*/
  0,                               /*tp_as_sequence*/
  0,                               /*tp_as_mapping*/
  0,                               /*tp_hash*/
};
```

We proceed in a similar manner, wrapping the Session and Request structures within Python object containers and associating operations that seem appropriate. We omit the gory details from this presentation and refer the interested reader to the source file nsapimodule.c.

Compiling the Dynamic Library

At startup the Server loads a dynamic library nsapiPy.so containing the nsapimodule.c interface and the Python run time. Of course this library must be built via compilation and linking. Here is the particular `Makefile` we used to build the library:

```
CC=gcc -DSOLARIS -Wall

# Top of the build tree and source tree
blddir=                 /usr/local/lib/python/lib
srcdir=                 /usr/local/include/Py

# Netscape headers start here.
nsheaders=      /app1/netscape-server/nsapi/include
nsincludes=     -I$(nsheaders) -I$(nsheaders)/base -I$(nsheaders)/frame

# Compiler flags
OPT=            -g
INCLUDES=       -I$(srcdir) -I$(blddir) $(nsincludes)
DEFINES=        -DHAVE_CONFIG_H
CFLAGS=         $(OPT) $(DEFINES) $(INCLUDES)

# Libraries (must be in this order!)
MYLIBS=         $(blddir)/libModules.a \
                $(blddir)/libPython.a \
                $(blddir)/libObjects.a \
                $(blddir)/libParser.a

MODLIBS=        $(LOCALMODLIBS) $(BASEMODLIBS)
LIBS=           -lsocket -lnsl -ldl
SYSLIBS=        -lm
ALLLIBS=        $(MYLIBS) $(MODLIBS) $(LIBS) $(SYSLIBS)

all:            nsapiPy.so

nsapimodule.o:  nsapimodule.c
                $(CC) -c nsapimodule.c

nsapiPy.so:     nsapimodule.o config.o
                $(LD) -G nsapimodule.o config.o $(ALLLIBS) -o nsapiPy.so

# maybe -Kpic on cc line (recompile ALL)

# Build config.o, suppressing the main() function
config.o:       config.c
                $(CC) $(CFLAGS) -DNO_MAIN -c config.c
```

Most of this `Makefile` consists of standard constructs for building a Python interpreter by hand, except that we omit the standard Python main program and use the loader $(LD) to build a library for the standard target. Also, of course, the nsapimodule.c module required include files from the NSAPI distribution, so these additional include files appear as $(nsincludes).

As with a manual build of the interpreter, we created our own config.c configuration module by copying the standard Modules/config.c and adding references for the initialization function for the nsapi module.

```
/* config.c, hand edited... */
...
/* HAND ADDED */
extern void initnsapi();
...
struct {
      char *name;
      void (*initfunc)();
} inittab[] = {
...
/* ADDED BY HAND */
      {"nsapi", initnsapi},
...
};
```

In addition, we added dummy functions getprogramname and getpython-path at the end of the nsapimodule.c module, because these functions are required by the Python interpreter but are not part of the standard libraries.

Summary and Example

This chapter has described the techniques for an embedding of the Python interpreter under a Netscape HTTP Server that supports the NSAPI Server applications programmer interface. We have focused on the mechanics of initializing the interpreter and the calling mechanisms that allow the Python interpreter and the Server to interact. There is much more to be said about the use of this embedding, and we direct the reader to the source file Py2NSAPI.py for an example strategy providing embedded Python services within a Server. In this forum, we cannot describe the details of using this embedding further; that would involve a detailed description of the NSAPI, which is beyond the scope of this book.

But let's look at an example use of embedded Python under the NSAPI. The pye_ex1.py file provides a simple test program that formats information provided by the Server to Python into HTML tables, which are returned to the HTTP client as the HTML response to a request of the form /pye_ex1.py. The following discussion steps through the process that generates a response to a request using pye_ex1.py.

When the Server receives a request of form /pye_ex1.pye it recognizes it as a request that must be handled by the NSAPItoPython(pb, sn, rq) server function. The NSAPItoPython function implemented in nsapimodule.c directs the request to the nsCallBack.NSAPIcallback(obCallBack, pb, sn, rq) method implemented in Py2NSAPI.py, passing the parameters for the request to the method as Python objects.

The nsCallBack.NSAPIcallback method essentially interprets the requested object /pye_ex1.pye as a request to be handled by a Python module named pye_ex1, executing the equivalent of

```
handler = pye_ex1.NSAPIHandler(pb, sn, rq)
handler.GO()
```

In this case, the handler object has the following implementation, as listed in the source file pye_ex1.py:

```
from Py2NSAPI import *
from HTMLfmt import *
from string import *
from regsub import gsub

class NSAPIHandler(NSAPIHandlerProto):
   def get_text(self):
      try:
         info = misc_info(self.rq, self.sn, self.pb)
         return HTML("NSAPI Server Data", info)
      except:
         print sys.exc_type, sys.exc_value
         raise ValueError
```

In this case the NSAPIHandler.GO() function is inherited from the NSAPIHandlerProto class defined in Py2NSAPI, and the inherited implementation performs the boilerplate actions of preparing the session for a response and delivering the response generated by the NSAPIHandler.get_text() method listed earlier.

The misc_info function used by the NSAPIHandler.get_text Python function formats information extracted from the server parameters self.rq, self.sn, and self.pb as follows:

```python
def misc_info(rq, sn, pb):
    """Make a table representing miscellaneous data from pb, rq and sn"""
    pbt = pb_table( pb, "Parameter Block")
    SDict = {}
    SDict["Session DNS"] = sn.session_dns()
    SDict["Session Client"] = pb_table( sn.client(), "Client Data" )
    STable = HorizontalDictTable("Session Data", SDict)
    RDict = {}
    RDict["User Agent"] = rq.request_header("user-agent", sn)
    RDict["Parameters"] = pb_table( rq.reqpb, "Request Parameter Block" )
    RDict["Headers"] = pb_table( rq.srvhdrs, "Server Headers" )
    RDict["Variables"] = pb_table( rq.vars, "Request Variables" )
    RTable = VerticalDictTable("Request Data", RDict)
    return HR_Seq(pbt, STable, RTable)

def pb_table(pblock, name):
    pbstring = pblock.pblock2str()
    qsplit = string.split(pbstring, '"')
    qpairs = []
    try:
        while 1:
            qpairs.append( (qsplit[0], qsplit[1]) )
            del qsplit[0:2]
    except IndexError:
        pass
    return apply(VerySimpleTable, (name,) + tuple(qpairs))
```

The HTML response generated by get_text is then passed back to the Server via the sn.net_write function and thence to the client. If the client was Netscape Navigator, the client might present something like the screen shown in Figure 12.1.

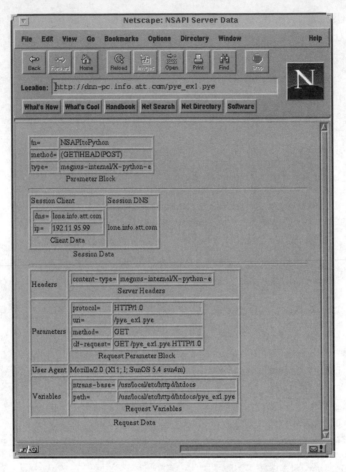

Figure 12.1 Table of Server information extracted by Python from the NSAPI interface and sent to the client as a formatted HTML response.

APPENDIX A

PYTHON VERSUS...

New Python programmers come in at least two varieties: those who jump in immediately and get hooked and those who want to know how Python relates to other languages they have heard of or used before they jump in and get hooked. It is with some fear and trepidation that we address the desire of the latter group to understand Python's relationship to other similar languages.

There are a number of quotes one should bear in mind when comparing Python to other programming languages:

> "I'll give you the twenty percent at the bottom and the twenty percent at the top. What I want is the sixty percent in the middle."—*Andrew Carnegie*

> "If you optimize everything, you will always be unhappy."
> —*Don Knuth*

Essentially, we believe that Python is an excellent general-purpose compromise for most applications, but each of the languages mentioned here may be better suited to specific domains. Python is well suited to "the sixty percent in the middle" or more.

> "Everything should be as simple as possible, but no simpler."
> —*Albert Einstein*

By citing this quote, we mean to suggest that Python provides an excellent compromise between simplicity and expressive power.

> "The best performance improvement is the transition from the nonworking state to the working state."—*John Ousterhout*

Python gets the job done, as we said earlier. We believe that for most computational tasks, programmers are more likely to come up with working, robust, and maintainable solutions using Python than by using the other languages mentioned, but this is not necessarily true for all computational tasks.

With these general comments in mind, we now launch into the unpleasant and thankless task of detailed language comparisons. In order to limit the scope of the discussion, we limit the set of languages discussed to those that are used in a manner similar to Python and those that are widely and freely available on many different hardware platforms.

Perl

Perl names two loosely related languages in wide use in the UNIX world: Perl 4 and Perl 5. The Perl family grew from the UNIX tradition, and in contrast to Python (a fairly minimalist language) the Perls are fairly maximalist languages—including many of the features of the C, sed, ksh, and awk programming languages as well as a number of features borrowed from elsewhere or simply invented on the fly. In spite of the large number of features in the Perls, we know of no Perl feature that cannot be emulated easily in Python. By contrast, we believe that Python's advanced exception handling features and many of the features of the Python object model cannot be emulated adequately using any version of Perl. One clear advantage that the Perls have over Python is that they include very powerful and fast regular expression matching facilities built into the language syntax. We believe that Python is a generally better language for most software engineering tasks due to its more uniform and simpler syntax and semantics. For more information, please see the Perl FAQ `http://www.perl.com/perl/faq/`.

Java

Like Python, Java is an interpreted programming language that compiles to portable byte code. Unlike Python, Java is statically typed, verbose, and relatively hard to use for most purposes. Java is partially object-oriented, although it lacks multiple inheritance and other common object-oriented features. Java includes various information-hiding features and other capabilities that may be useful in implementations of extremely large monolithic applications.

The Java interpreter main loop is faster than the current Python main loop implementation, but many programming concepts that are easily expressed in Python are extremely difficult to translate to Java, so speed comparisons are deceptive. In particular, by using Python's string facilities or the numerical Python extensions, it may be possible to implement Python programs that are much simpler, shorter, and faster than equivalent programs implemented in Java. One concrete advantage of Java over Python is that Java is delivered as part of the Netscape Navigator and Microsoft Explorer browsers. One concrete advantage of Python over Java is that Python is more flexible and easy to use.

Javascript

Javascript is an extremely limited language. One good thing about Javascript is that it is delivered as part of the Netscape Navigator browser. Javascript has no purely technical advantages over Python.

Tcl

Tcl is a very simple command interpreter. Tcl is the only language discussed here that may be embedded and extended as easily as Python, with the additional advantage that the Tcl language core is smaller than the Python core. The language model for Tcl is relatively limited compared to the Python model, as it lacks exceptions and true data types, among other things. In our view, Tcl is "too simple" for applications of any complexity. Please see `http://route.psg.com/tcl.html` for additional general information on Tcl.

Scheme

Scheme names a wide variety of implementations of various Lisp dialects with a common core functionality. The Scheme core is even simpler than Python, and probably strictly more powerful in a technical sense. Most programmers will find the model of computation underlying Scheme to be difficult to absorb at first, but we encourage the adventurous to give it a whirl. Many features that are built in to Python, such as name space modularity, exceptions, and object orientation, must be implemented in Scheme proper, and this has the disadvantage that different libraries implement these features in mutually contradictory ways. Programming language enthusiasts simply must explore the wild world of Scheme—starting at `http://www-swiss.ai.mit.edu/scheme-home.html`. A detailed discussion of all the features of all the implementations of Scheme would require another book, so we will stop here. We believe Python provides a greater degree of structure and syntactic convenience more appropriate for most programming tasks.

Legal Issues

There are essentially no restrictions on the use of Python in either source or compiled form. Tcl and some versions of Scheme also have little or no restrictions on their use. The legal status of Java is quite complex—in fact we don't really understand it, so we won't comment further. The Perls are governed alternatively by the GNU public license or the Perl Artistic License, which place a number of peculiar restrictions on how the languages may be used and distributed.

Embedding and Extending

Both Tcl and Python may be extended with additional functionality and embedded in other applications easily. The same is true for some Scheme implementations, each with its own API interface. Perl 5 and Java may be extended using various idiosyncratic methods involving code generation, which we cannot comment on in detail due to lack of experience. Perl 5 may also be embedded in other applications, but we cannot locate any good documentation on the procedures for doing so at this writing. Java cannot be embedded in another application unless the embedder purchases a source license from Sun—please contact Sun Microsystems for more information on embedding Java.

Summary

We believe that Python offers an excellent compromise of portability, power, and simplicity. We suspect readers will find Python to be as good as or better than the other languages mentioned here for implementing most programming tasks. Nevertheless, each language mentioned is exciting and interesting, and we recommend them all.

APPENDIX B

A BRIEF GUIDE TO THE STANDARD LIBRARIES

The canonical documentation for the Python libraries is provided in the Python Libraries reference, which constitutes one of the four standard Python reference manuals distributed with the language. The Tutorial, the Library Reference, the Language Reference, and the Extensions manual are available in HTML, PostScript, Windows `hlp` format, and LaTeX source form on the CD-ROM included with this book. The same information (which may be more up to date) is also available for download from `http://www.python.org`.

Nevertheless, to provide an accelerator to locate functionality quickly we provide the following summary of some libraries and extensions of special interest. We focus primarily on core libraries and libraries not discussed in other chapters.

Standard Core Features

We have described the standard intrinsic functions for the core built-in types and within the `__builtins__` module in some detail. The `sys` module contains some standard system functionality, including the standard input and standard output file objects and objects related to recent exceptions, such as tracebacks, the last exception object, and its associated value. The `sys.exit(n)` function exits the interpreter in a controlled manner (unless an `except SystemExit` is outstanding.

The `string` module, described earlier in this book, provides many indispensable operations for constructing and manipulating string objects. The `regex` and `regsub` modules provide even fancier methods for parsing and manipulating strings using a number of flavors of regular expression formats.

The `types` module provides names for the standard core type objects, and the `traceback` module provides functions for manipulating exception tracebacks. Fancy module import operations may be implemented with the help of operations available in the `imp` module.

The `math` module provides standard mathematical functions and constants. The `array` module provides compact representations for binary data (and should not be confused with the Numerical Python extension matrix and array modules). The `rand` and `whrandom` modules provide random number generators and related services. The `struct` module allows data to be packed into native structure formats and unpacked from native structures.

Archiving and Data Transmission Utilities

The `marshal` module provides primitive methods for converting certain basic Python types to and from string implementations very quickly, usually for storage in files or transfer across network connections. Marshalled representations are platform-independent, which means that an object may be marshalled on one machine and unmarshalled on another whether or not the two machines are binary.compatible. Also "fixed-size" structures (such as tuples containing three ints each) always marshal to fixed-size marshal strings, and therefore the marshalled representation can be "overwritten in place" in the middle of a file with a similar object. (Objects containing strings of differing lengths, on the other hand, may have marshalled representations of different lengths.) These features together make `marshal` very convenient for building file index structures.

WARNING For portability, all files that store binary data (such as `marshal` strings) should be read and written using the "binary open" or "binary write" (`open(name, "rb")` or `open(name, "wb")`, respectively). On platforms where the `b` flag makes no sense, it is ignored, but on those where is makes sense it is essential.

The `pickle` and `shelve` modules provide higher-level generic interfaces to the `marshal` functionality. They also generalize the `marshal` capability to include arbitrary Python objects (so long as those objects provide an appropriate interface—see the library documentation for these modules).

 WARNING Be careful when transferring `pickled` objects across network connections, because `pickle` sometimes executes code objects behind the scenes (at the time of this writing). In general, never unpickle an object that might have come from an untrusted source—use `marshal` directly instead.

The related module `copy` provides generic operations for creating deep and shallow copies of arbitrary Python objects in memory (again, if those objects provide an appropriate interface; see the documentation for the module).

Standard OS Interfaces

The `os` module provides standard interfaces and constants related to the current operating system. Portable programs should be careful to use the filenaming convention constants defined in this module. The submodule `os.path` provides file type tests and other operations related to manipulating file names and directories—operations documented for the module `posixpath`. For those environments that do not support complete Posix functionality (such as DOS or the Macintosh), the `os.path` generally emulates the `posixpath` features using non-Posix methods; elsewhere `os.path` is equivalent to `posixpath`.

The `time`, `getopt`, and `tempfile` modules, respectively, provide functionality for getting time information (including sleeping), parsing command-line arguments, and creating temporary files.

The `socket` module provides standard BSD-style socket interfaces. For Microsoft environments, certain BSD capabilities (such as the ability to convert a socket into a file object) are emulated using a Python wrapper layer, in order to enable portable networking programs. Similarly, on the Macintosh, `socket.py` wraps the radically nonstandard Mac notion of a network connection up in a BSD-like interface.

The `select` module allows polling of sockets (and on UNIX, other file-like objects) for available data or readiness to read.

The `thread` module, where available, allows a Python program to run many threads (lightweight processes) at once. Thread programming can be difficult, and it is not recommended for the novice.

On some systems that support signals, the `signal` module allows a process to be interrupted by external signals (such as timers) of various sorts.

There are also many OS-specific modules available for Microsoft, Macintosh, and the various UNIX environments, which we will not discuss here. In particular, readers who are primarily concerned with Microsoft environments (MFC and OLE) will be interested in the Python interfaces to the asynchronous sockets libraries.

Programming Tools

The `pdb` and `profile` modules provide a line-mode debugger and a execution profiler, respectively. The profiler is particularly useful for identifying bottlenecks in Python programs.

A number of other standard modules are available that we will not describe in detail here. We recommend a look through the Library reference for further information, and we note that a number of useful libraries are documented in their source implementations in the `Lib/`, `Tools/`, and `Demo/` directories of the standard distribution. Hearty programmers should look there also.

Contributed Stuff

There is an amazing collection of contributed libraries. Many libraries are either archived at `http://www.python.org` or referenced there. These include native interfaces to database engines such as `Sybase` and `Oracle`, the Numerical Python extensions, and data structure accelerators such as the `kjbuckets` Set and Graph utilities. Programmers should familiarize themselves with the `python.org` contribution collections.

Of particular interest to network programmers are the embedding of Python within the Apache HTTP server and the ILU/SYLU distributed object interfaces for Python. The Python Cryptography Toolkit provides extensive security tools that may be useful to intranet programmers as well. The `SOCKS` library allows network connection through firewall servers. Microsoft Windows programmers should also check out the `async` sockets library.

By the time this book is published, this list will be woefully out of date, so we stop here. The range of software available to the Python programmer can be overwhelming.

APPENDIX C

REGULAR EXPRESSIONS

Parsing strings is a basic operation in programming generally speaking, and it is particularly important in many networking applications, where data is often transmitted from one machine to another as formatted strings that must be parsed by the machine that receives them. Regular expression libraries provide convenient and general tools for identifying patterns in strings and extracting substrings that match the patterns.

Python provides standard regular expression libraries `regex` and `regsub`. In addition to this, a number of alternative regular expression libraries may be used. Regular expressions are a standard formalism used for parsing strings into substrings that match certain patterns. The patterns to match are specified by specially formatted "pattern strings."

```
import string, regex
lower_case_letter = "[abcdefghijklmnopqrstuvwxyz]"
lower_word = lower_case_letter + "+"
upper_case_letter = string.upper(lower_case_letter)
upper_word = string.upper(lower_word)
```

Here we use the default "gnu-style" regular expression syntax. The pattern `"[abcdefghijklmnopqrstuvwxyz]"` matches exactly one character, which must be one of the characters inside the brackets (the lowercase letters). The pattern `"[abcdefghijklmnopqrstuvwxyz]+"` matches one or more of the lowercase letters.

It is possible to use string patterns directly, but for efficiency reasons, among others, we recommend that regular expressions be compiled into regular expression objects before they are used.

```
lower_letter_prog = regex.compile(lower_case_letter)
lower_word_prog = regex.compile(lower_word)
```

Compiled regular expressions may be used to find substrings that match a pattern within a string.

```
>>> lower_word_prog.match("hello world")
5
>>> "hello world"[:5]
'hello'
>>> lower_word_prog.search("1 2 3 4 5 I caught a fish alive")
12
>>> "1 2 3 4 5 I caught a fish alive"[12:]
'caught a fish alive'
```

Here `lower_word_prog.match(str)` finds the end index of a match for `lower_word_prog`, where the match starts at the first character of `str`, and `lower_word_prog.search(str)` finds the start of the first match for `lower_word_prog`, searching from the first character.

A failed match or search returns -1:

```
>>> lower_word_prog.match("1 2 3 4 5 I caught a fish alive")
-1
```

Furthermore, both the `match` or the `search` methods allow an optional `start_index` argument, which specifies an index where the match or search should start:

```
>>> lower_word_prog.match("1 2 3 4 5 I caught a fish alive", 12)
6
>>> "1 2 3 4 5 I caught a fish alive" [12: 12+6]
'caught'
>>> lower_word_prog.search("1 2 3 4 5 I caught a fish alive", 18)
19
>>> lower_word_prog.match("1 2 3 4 5 I caught a fish alive", 19)
1
>>> "1 2 3 4 5 I caught a fish alive" [19:20]
'a'
```

While `lower_word_prog.search(str, offset)` returns an absolute index after the `offset` where the next match starts, `lower_word_prog.match(str, off-set)` returns the number of characters starting at the `offset` that match `lower_word_prog`.

Constructing Regular Expressions

Regular expression strings are normally interpreted as themselves, unless they include the characters $^. *+?[]\, which are special directives. For example, the string `"this"` interpreted as a regular expression matches only the substring `"this"` and no other pattern. Regular expressions that do not include special directives are not terribly interesting.

Repetition

Interesting regular expressions can be formed using directive constructs or concatenations of regular expressions that include directive constructs. For example, the expression `"a*"` matches any string of zero or more *a* characters:

```
>>> aregex = regex.compile("a*")
>>> aregex.match("123")
0
>>> aregex.match("aaa123")
3
```

Because `"a*"` matches zero or more occurrences of *a*, the match `aregex.match("123")` did not return –1. Instead it matched the empty string!

More generally, if `str` is a regular expression, then we may match zero or more consecutive matches for `str` using the regular expression `"\("+str+"\)*"`:

```
>>> str = "python"
>>> manypython = regex.compile("\(" + str + "\)*")
>>> manypython.match("pythonpython python")
12
```

In `manypython` we used both repetition `"*"` and grouping `"\(...\)"` because without grouping the expression, `"python*"` repeats only the final *n* instead of the entire word `python`.

```
>>> pythonnnn = regex.compile("python*")
>>> pythonnnn.match("pythonpython python")
6
>>> pythonnnn.match("pythosaurus")
5
>>> pythonnnn.match("pythonnnnnnnnn aroundddd myyy neckkkk!!!")
14
```

Here the compiled regular expression `pythonnnn` defined by the string `"python*"` matches a string beginning with `pytho` followed by zero or more *n*s.

Grouping

As shown earlier, in `manypython` a regular expression bracketed by escaped parentheses `"\( ... \)"` groups the regular expression inside the parens together as a single unit, which may then be repeated or applied to other operations, as we will see.

```
>>> babylove = regex.compile("\(baby \)*where did our love go\?")
>>> babylove.match("where did our love go? doncha love me no more?")
22
>>> "where did our love go? doncha love me no more?"[:22]
'where did our love go?'
>>> babylove.match(
    "baby baby baby where did our love go? doncha love me no more?")
37
>>> "baby baby baby where did our love go? doncha love me no more?"[:37]
'baby baby baby where did our love go?'
```

Here the `babylove` compiled regular expression matches zero or more repetitions of `"baby "` followed by `"where did our love go?"`. Note that in the string representation `"\(baby \)*where did our love go\?"` the backslash preceding the `"?"` prevents the question mark from having a special meaning as a regular expression directive. The regular expression `"\?"` just matches a single question mark, but the `"\(" + str + "\)?"` expression matches either at most or at least one occurrence.

Matching at Most One Occurrence

A question mark after a regular expression matches at most one occurrence of the expression. For example:

```
>>> smell_or_smells = regex.compile("smells?")
>>> smell_or_smells.match("smell a skunk?")
5
>>> smell_or_smells.match("smells nice")
6
>>> smell_or_smells.match("smellssss unpleasant")
6
```

Note that in the last match the extra *s*es are not included in the match.

Matching at Least One Occurrence

A plus following a regular expression matches any sequence of one or more occurrences of that expression:

```
>>> spider_scare= regex.compile ("Spiders!+")
>>> spider_scare.match("Spiders")
-1
>>> spider_scare.match("Spiders!")
8
>>> spider_scare.match("Spiders!!!!!!!!")
15
```

Note that the first match failed because the required "!" was absent.

Character Sets

A sequence of characters in square brackets "[" + chars + "]" defines a regular expression that matches one occurrence of any of the characters in question, even if the characters in the middle normally have a special interpretation outside of square brackets.

```
>>> numeric_caps = "[!@#$%^&*()_+|]"
>>> numeric_caps = regex.compile("[!@#$%^&*()_+|]" )
>>> for x in "abc&^%":
...     if numeric_caps.match(x)>-1:
...         print x, "is a numeric cap"
...     else:
```

```
...         print x, "ain't a numeric cap"
...
a ain't a numeric cap
b ain't a numeric cap
c ain't a numeric cap
& is a numeric cap
^ is a numeric cap
% is a numeric cap
```

If the close-square-bracket character is intended to be a member of a character set, it must be the first member listed, in order to avoid confusing it with the bracket that marks the end of the set, as in `bracket_char = regex.compile("[][(){]")`, which matches any single round, curly, or square bracket character.

Character sets are normally used in conjunction with one of the repetition constructs.

```
>>> num_prog = regex.compile("[0123456789]+")
>>> st = "12 dogs, 17 cats 34.568 cans of horse meat, 4 children"
>>> def print_matches(s, pat):
...     cursor = pat.search(s)
...     while cursor >= 0:
...         match = pat.match(s, cursor)
...         print repr( s[cursor:cursor+match] ),
...         cursor = pat.search(s, cursor+match)
...
>>> print_matches(st, num_prog)
'12' '17' '34' '568' '4'
```

Here the `num_prog` compiled regular expression matches any sequence of one or more numeric digits. A character set may be negated by placing a `"^"` as the first character of the set.

```
>>> not_num = regex.compile("[^0123456789]+")
>>> print_matches(st, not_num)
' dogs, ' ' cats ' '.' ' cans of horse meat, ' ' children'
```

A hyphen in the middle of a character set indicates an ASCII character range, but at the start or end of the set it just represents a hyphen.

```
>>> alpha = regex.compile( "[a-zA-Z]+" )
>>> print_matches(st, alpha)
```

```
'dogs' 'cats' 'cans' 'of' 'horse' 'meat' 'children'
>>> nonalpha = regex.compile( "[^a-zA-Z]+" )
>>> print_matches(st, nonalpha)
'12 ' ', 17 ' ' 34.568 ' ' ' ' ' ' ', 4 '
```

Alternatives

The "\|" mark is used to indicate alternatives.

```
>>> boowoo = regex.compile("bo*\|wo*")
>>> print_matches("He's the boogy woogy bugle boy from company b", boowoo)
'boo' 'woo' 'b' 'bo' 'b'
```

Here the pattern "bo*\|wo*" matches anything matched by either "bo*" or wo*". The \| operator has low priority, so it applies to the largest possible surrounding expressions. We could have written the boowoo pattern as "\(b\|w\)o*" using grouping or, better yet, as "[bw]o*" using a character set in place of the alternation notation.

Sequence

Any two regular expressions written one after the other "a*" + "b*" constitute a regular expression that matches a string whose first part matches the first regular expression "a*" immediately followed by a second part that matches the second regular expression "b*". We already used this, but did not introduce it until now.

```
>>> identifier = regex.compile("[a-zA-Z]+[a-zA-Z0-9]*")
>>> print_matches("max(x, 92, delta - 45 + lambda3);", identifier)
'max' 'x' 'delta' 'lambda3'
```

Here the identifier matches anything that begins with one or more alphabetics "[a-zA-Z]+" followed by zero or more alphanumerics "[a-zA-Z0-9]*".

Escaped Characters

As we have seen, the escape sequences "\|", "\(", and "\)" have special meanings. A backslash preceding other characters, such as "\[", prevents that character from having a special meaning. Thus, the regular expression `"\[."` matches a single open square bracket, but `"["` is an incomplete character set.

```
>>> test = regex.compile("[")
regex.error: Regular expression ends prematurely
>>> test = regex.compile("\[")
```

Note that in string literals, things get tricky because Python sometimes assigns special meaning to a backslash when the literal is parsed, before the `regex` module ever sees it. In particular, note that a double backslash in a string literal is interpreted as a single backslash by the parser.

```
>>> print "\\"
\
```

Now the regular expression that matches a single backslash character is a string containing two backslashes in sequence. But to construct such a sequence as a literal, the parser needs *four* backslashes!

```
>>> print "\\\\"
\\
```

Sorry about that!

There are a number of other special character conventions, which we describe here.

Pattern	Explanation
"." (period)	Matches any single character except a newline
"^"	Matches an empty string, only at the beginning of a line
"$"	Matches an empty string, only at the end of a line
"\b"	Matches an empty string at the beginning or end of a word
"\B"	Matches an empty string not at the beginning or end of a word
"\<"	Matches an empty string at the beginning of a word
"\>"	Matches an empty string at the end of a word
"\w"	Matches any alphabetic (word-constituent) character
"\W"	Matches any nonword-constituent character

Note that the regular expression that matches a period is "\.". It is possible to redefine what constitutes a word-constituent character; please see the documentation for the `regex` module.

WARNING

Many programmers who have attempted to make sense of someone else's awk or sed script can attest that long literal regular expression strings can be extremely difficult for humans to understand. The Python programmer should always try to construct regular expression patterns using symbolic names, in small pieces, to make programs more easily understood. For example, consider the following sequence of assignments, which constructs a number of patterns:

```
Python_Comment = "#.*\n" # from a pound to the first newline.

Digit = "[0-9]"
Alpha = "[a-zA-Z]"
AlphaNum = "[a-zA-Z0-9]"

# an identifier is an alphabetic followed by optional alphanumerics
Identifier = Alpha + AlphaNum + "*"

# an integer is a nonempty sequence of digits, with an optional sign
DigitSeq = Digit + "+"
IntegerPat = "[+-]?" + Digit + "+"

# a decimal can be an integer followed by a dot
# followed by an optional digit sequence
DecimalPat1 = IntegerPat + "\.\(" + DigitSeq + "\)?"

# or it can be a dot followed by a digit sequence, with optional
sign
DecimalPat2 = "[+-]?\." + DigitSeq

# either of those
DecimalPat = DecimalPat1 + "\|" + DecimalPat2
```

We submit that this sequence of declarations is easier to understand than simply declaring, for example:

```
DecimalPat = "[+-]?[0-9]+\.\([0-9]+\)?\|[+-]?\.[+-]?[0-9]+"
```

And keep in mind that this is a relatively simple regular expression! Furthermore, by constructing regular expressions incrementally, errors in a subexpression can be fixed in one place, automatically propagating to all expressions that use it.

Groups

If a search or match succeeds, the last string matching a compiled regular expression `pattern` is given by `pattern.group(0)`. For example, we can rephrase our `print_matches` function given earlier as:

```
def print_matches(s, pat):
    cursor = pat.search(s)
    while cursor >= 0:
        found = pat.group(0)
        print found
        cursor = pat.search(s, cursor+len(found))
```

Furthermore, for patterns that have groupings at the top level (not enclosed in other constructs), the subpatterns that match the groupings may be extracted as `pattern.group(n)` for n larger than one.

```
>>> num = "[0-9]+"
>>> area_code = "(" + num + ")"
>>> phonenumpat = "\(%s\)\(%s\)-\(%s\)" % (area_code, num, num)
>>> print phonenumpat
\(([0-9]+)\)\([0-9]+\)-\([0-9]+\)
>>> phonenum = regex.compile(phonenumpat)
>>> phonenum.match("(908)555-1212")
13
>>> phonenum.group(0), phonenum.group(1), phonenum.group(2), phonenum.group(3)
('(908)555-1212', '(908)', '555', '1212')
```

Here `phonenum.group(0)` returns the match for the whole pattern, but the other calls returned the matches for the subexpressions grouped within `\( ... \)`.

If the last match failed, the `group` method will fail, raising a `regex.error`.

```
>>> phonenum.match("wally")
-1
>>> phonenum.group(0)
regex.error: group() only valid after successful match/search
```

It is quite easy to get regular expression strings wrong. We recommend that all regular expression strings be tested extensively using the interactive interpreter before they are used in programs.

It is possible to globally alter the behavior of the regex module, for example, to force it to recognize alternate regular expression notations. It may occasionally be convenient to do this in order to support regular expressions extracted from legacy programs, but we advise against using these features unless it's absolutely necessary; use the default instead. The global syntax flags and the group method are not safe for multithreaded programs.

The regsub Module

The regsub module extends the regex functionality to allow aggregate operations along the lines of string.joinfields and string.split-fields. These extensions are straightforward, so we direct the reader to the standard documentation for regsub.

Also of interest may be the t_parse module, which provides some slightly higher-level parsing conveniences above the regex model.

```
>>> import t_parse
>>> T = t_parse.Template("MMDDYY X:X",
...          wild_card_marker="X", single_char_marker="MDY")
>>> T.PARSE("122961 Birthday: Jamey Pedersen")
(['12', '29', '61', 'Birthday', ' Jamey Pedersen'], 31)
```

Please see the documentation string of this module for more information on the use of the t_parse.Template class.

APPENDIX D

HOW TO
GET PYTHON

This appendix is short, because we primarily direct the reader to other sources of information.

This book includes a CD-ROM containing the latest version of the Python distribution at the time of this printing, including many binaries for various platforms. Please see the README file in the CD-ROM main directory for detailed information on the contents of the CD-ROM and how to install Python for your platform.

Another great source of information is the Python Software Activity homepage, `http://www.python.org`. Currently, this site is mirrored on the following machines:

```
http://www.cwi.nl/www.python.org/ in Europe
http://www.dstc.edu.au/www.python.org/ in Australia
http://eiffel.rosnet.ru/python/www.python.org/ in Russia
http://w3.lab.kdd.co.jp/www.python.org in Japan
```

See any of these sites for current information on downloading Python in either source or binary form.

INDEX

Using The CD-ROM

Please consult the files with the "txt" extension in the root directory of the CD-ROM for instructions on how to use the contents of the disk.